BEYOND
the
FAIRWAYS

David and Patricia Davies wish to pay tribute to
the invaluable assistance given unstintingly by the
entire Solheim family, in particular by Karsten,
Louise and John, and also by everyone at PING,
in the compilation and production of this book.
Without their support and encouragement
it could never have happened.

BEYOND
the
FAIRWAYS

THE PAST, PRESENT AND FUTURE
OF WORLD GOLF

DAVID & PATRICIA DAVIES

Illustrations by Harold Riley

Foreword by Severiano Ballesteros
and Jose Maria Olazabal

First published in 1999 by CollinsWillow
an imprint of HarperCollins*Publishers*
London

© David and Patricia Davies

1 3 5 7 9 8 6 4 2

The HarperCollins website address is:
www.**fire**and**water**.com

A CIP catalogue record for this book is
available from the British Library

ISBN 0 00 218725 6

Design: GDAdesign

Printed and bound in Great Britain
by Clays Ltd, St. Ives plc

Picture acknowledgements

Allsport: picture no. 4; Simon Bruty (Allsport):
13; David Cannon (Allsport): 2, 3, 10, 12, 15
Steve Dunn (Allsport): 16; Matthew Harris, Golf Picture Library: 9
Lawrence Levy Collection: 1, 5, 7, 8, 14; Stephen Munday (Allsport): 6
Harold Riley: endpapers, 18-33; Pascal Rondeau (Allsport): 11, 17

ACKNOWLEDGEMENTS

There are so many people to thank that it becomes a worrying process, a bit like drawing up a guest-list for a wedding. Where to stop if things are not to get out of hand? How to ensure that there are no sins of omission? A blanket acknowledgement, covering our friends, colleagues and family is one answer but there are some names that need to be named, if only because they've been so closely involved with this project since the beginning or gone out of their way to help.

Here they are alphabetically: Mike Blair, Bob Cantin, Jeremy Chapman, Joanna Chisholm, Peter Dobereiner, a friend and inspiration who is much missed, Maureen Garrett, Bridget Jackson, Maureen Madill, Shirley Mason, John Pawsey, Harold Riley, who has been immense, Karsten and Louise Solheim and family, Bob Sommers, Donald Steel, Chris Stone, Jerry Tarde, and Ian Wood.

Our families deserve special thanks and will be relieved to know that they can, at last, mention the book.

The publishers would like to give special thanks to Harold Riley for the provision of all the sketches in the book.

Statistics on page 11 are provided courtesy of Tony Greer at International Management Group.

CONTENTS

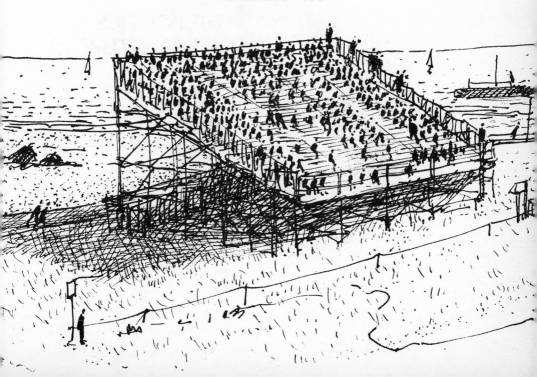

FOREWORD

As soon as I found out that Dai and Patricia were writing a book I was thrilled. Coming from them it just has to be good. They have always been extremely accurate with their facts, exposition and analysis, and so they are now. For me personally it is a very special moment and a true joy to read the poetry and contents of Dai's columns in *The Guardian* on the occasions I have the chance to do it. I have known Dai since my amateur days, which seems like ages now. But being with him for an interview, having dinner or simply reading him has always been an enriching experience.

Jose Maria Olazabal

Introducing David 'Dai' Davies is pointless. All through my golfing career I have been a reader of his columns and anyone connected with the game of golf knows him well enough already. I have always enjoyed his writing, not just for its style or content but even for his criticisms – well, most of the time anyway! He is, worldwide, of the few who tries to be positive and constructive whenever he approaches a controversial subject, and I know you will enjoy this book.

Severiano Ballesteros

INTRODUCTION

A GAME IN CRISIS?

As golf moves into a new millennium it is about to change, at professional tournament level, totally and completely and for ever. In fact the process has already begun and is, already, irreversible. The World Tour, so stoutly resisted by so many people for so long, already exists in fledgling form, and then, because it is essentially a very good idea, it will flourish.

It will enable the world's best players to compete against each other on a far more regular basis than the four major championships that have formed golf's core all these years. That in turn will enable a genuine world ranking system to come into being and everyone will know, at last, who's really best.

But what it will also do is shake up those four majors as they realize that, while they may have tradition on their side, they may well not be as strong in terms of depth of field as the newcomers.

In fact, you can hear the sneers already. In 20 years' time the young bloods in the locker-rooms will be saying, 'Okay, so Jack Nicklaus won 18 majors. Well half of them were against old men and amateurs.' They would be referring to the Masters, and they would be passing lightly, as is the way with young bloods, over a few facts. Nicklaus won only a third of his majors at Augusta and there were plenty of good players in the field.

Of course, there is a tinge of truth in that predicted sneer. There were, and are, a lot of old men in the Masters field, for anyone who wins a green jacket can compete there until he can no longer walk. There were, and are, some amateurs, because, when the event started, Bobby Jones felt that this should be so. Both are lovely old traditions, and neither may mean a thing to the cashmere-clads of the future.

The World Tour will concentrate a few minds among the players, the sponsors and the authorities. If there are four majors recognized as such, plus, say, six or seven events carrying World Tour ranking points, and if the prize money is such that it would be financial suicide not to play in them, where does that leave the remaining tournaments and their host tours? The short answer is with not many appearances of their biggest stars in their home events. That in turn will force a radical re-thinking of schedules, so that existing big tournaments do not clash with the mega-events.

All the professional tours in the world now recognize a world rankings system for the players, and that same system also produces a ranking for championships and tournaments. (See figures below.) It has been in operation throughout the 1990s and shows very clearly which of them has the strongest field in any given year. In recent years it has been dominated by the USPGA championship – whose enlightened policy of inviting a contingent of the best overseas players has consistently produced the strongest field of the year – based on the number of competitors in the top 100 of the world rankings.

The Masters, however, has consistently produced the worst field of the majors, and, not only that, it has also been overtaken by the Players championship – the US Tour's flagship event – usually held two weeks before at Ponte Vedra, near Jacksonville, in Florida. No fewer than four editions of the Players event have had stronger fields than the best Masters field of the 1990s and a table comprising the strongest fields of the major championships, plus the Players, through the nineties, looks like this:

US PGA: 1, 2, 6, 7, 8, 9, 10, 14, 25.
The Open: 3, 5, 11, 12, 13, 17, 18, 19, 22.
Players: 4, 15, 16, 23, 28, 37, 43, 45, 48.
US Open: 20, 21, 30, 31, 32, 33, 36, 40, 42.
Masters: 24, 26, 27, 29, 35, 38, 39, 41, 44.

(Three non-championship events, the Nestle Invitational in 1995, the Memorial Tournament of the same year and the 1998 Bay Hill Invitational would figure in that list in terms of strength of field.)

The figures for the championships of the nineties reveal that all 10 of the fields for the US PGA have been in the top 25 for the decade, and if you total those figures they come to 82. A table thus reads:

US PGA:	82
The Open:	120
Players:	259
US Open:	285
Masters:	303

There should only ever be four major championships; to have more would invalidate history and make measuring the achievements of men like Jack Nicklaus impossible. But there are no tablets of stone decreeing that the majors must consist of the same events and in the early 1990s Hord Hardin, then chairman of Augusta National, worrying about the rising levels of prize money and the ability or otherwise of the Masters to keep pace, said that the membership would kill off the tournament rather than have to accept sponsorship and call it, say, the Pizza Hut Masters.

But as the millennium approached, with Hardin succeeded first by Jackson Stephens and now by Hootie Johnson, the club modified their attitude. As the above table shows, they had already fallen drastically behind the other majors and for the 1999 event they decided, after a long resistance, to allow the top 50 players in the world rankings into the Masters automatically.

There were other changes, too, to reflect the way in which the rest of the world had caught up golf in the United States. Perhaps the most significant was that from the year 2000 the winning of a US Tour event, a qualification first implemented in 1972, would no longer guarantee a place.

This redefining of the Masters came only just in time. With its demonstrably weak field for the last 20 years or more of the century it had been in danger of becoming simply a quaint old relic of gentler times gone by.

But those are problems for the professionals, who represent the tiniest tip of a very large iceberg. Golf, in a recognizable form, has already been played on this planet for over 400 years. It has prospered wherever it has gone, adopting, adapting, improving itself in a constant process of renewal. Initially the gospel was spread very largely by dour, Calvinistic Scots who, having escaped the confines and strictures of their own society, re-imposed them in the form of a game that demands, if it is to be played at all, rigorous honesty and an adherence to a code that almost amounts to self-flagellation.

Such is the game's intrinsic merit that it has not just survived but also flourished in such unlikely places as the deserts of Arabia, the mountain ranges of the Himalayas and the literally deadly heat of Death Valley, where the course, aptly, is called Furnace Creek.

But in all its long history, golf as it should be – the game we know and love – has never been under greater threat than it is now. It is under attack from the forces of indolence and ignorance, of apathy and greed, as the game that it has been for centuries is subverted for commercial gain.

Golf, proper golf, has a simple formula. Anything up to four people gather together on the first tee, agree on a format for the game, make their bets, hit their shots and walk off after them. And the key word in all that is 'walk'. What is happening through much of America and, unfortunately, many copy-cat countries throughout the world, is that people ride off that first tee, ride to the general area where their ball lies, hit it and ride off again. Concrete paths wind their way, like tapeworm, round the very guts of the game, serving the carts, which are themselves the condoms of golf, preventing full enjoyment of the act. Mark Twain may have considered golf to be a good walk spoiled but at least it was always a good walk. There are very many places in America where carts are mandatory. At least one course in Myrtle Beach, South Carolina, demands the hire of a cart for non-golfers too.

There should only ever be four major championships; to have more would invalidate history and make measuring the achievements of men like Jack Nicklaus impossible.

The line peddled as an excuse for this unprincipled money-grabbing greed is the wholly spurious one that carts speed up play. This is a bare-faced lie. Four golfers who know how to play, are aware of the etiquette of the game, are aware of when it is their turn to play and where to leave their bags/trollies when putting out, will always be faster than four players who are cart-bound, over 18 holes.

At The Greenbrier, that magnificent resort in White Sulphur Springs, West Virginia, my wife and I secured the first tee-time on three successive days. We walked and, simply by being aware of what had to be done next, completed each round in under three hours. On the one occasion when the next group was also a twoball but using a cart, they were three holes behind when we finished. We had not hurried and to do so in that glorious tree-lined valley, with its river running through, would have been a denial of what golf should be about – a chance to celebrate beautiful surroundings together with the challenge of the course itself.

The fourball version of the game, played in carts, is an abhorrence on several fronts. It is the slowest form of the game known to man, even when carts are allowed to drive up to the ball. When they are restricted to the cart-paths it becomes not a game but an endurance test – and a frustrating one at that. The club you need is invariably still in the bag, which is on the cart now 200 yards away.

Another thing about carts. If you turn up as a two and get allocated another two with whom to play, they are likely to disappear to their cart, travel and chat together and you may never speak more than half-a-

The dutiful caddy, a far more pleasurable alternative to the cart.

dozen words to them in the whole miserable five hours. That aspect alone deprives us of the essence of golf, the companionship, the camaraderie and the occasional joy of meeting a like mind. Those who walk together, talk together.

Then there is the physical aspect. Golf is a walking game. It was devised to give exercise and provide a diversion along the way and while it is acceptable that the diversion has overtaken the exercise, it is not acceptable that the exercise has been deleted. It is wonderful to play well, to come in with a good score and to talk it up afterwards. But it is wonderful, too, to know that the body has been properly – albeit not rigorously – put through its paces. The feeling of slight fatigue at the end of it makes the martini or the beer an allowable, guilt-free delight: you have made your moment of relaxation the old-fashioned way, you've earned it.

The reason for carts is profit, profit, profit. One sales director in England said, 'I can assure the club professional that they will make money, just like a kiddies' rocking chair outside a superstore makes money.' Another was just as frank: 'The boom in golf carts began in the States when people realized just how much profit could be achieved. That's when most of the traditional objections went out of the window.'

The exceedingly sad thing about all this is that there is now a reliable variant on carts that enables the golfer to walk without having to carry his clubs: the battery-driven trolley. Its greatest virtue is that it restores the game to the walker, it gives back the use of the legs to a sportsman who ought never to have lost it – the golfer.

There have been campaigns against carts, none of which has succeeded. The USGA have tried and in the latter half of 1997 the R&A delivered themselves of the following: 'In his much acclaimed book, *The Principles Behind the Rules of Golf*, Richard Tufts, a former president of the USGA, wrote that "there is only need for three rules of golf: 1. Play the ball as it lies, 2. Play the course as you find it, 3. If you cannot do either, do what is fair. In this day and age," continued the R&A, "a fourth reminder is necessary: golf is meant to be a walking game. It surely defeats the object to ride around in buggies when taking healthy exercise, except of course for the genuinely handicapped. The increasing use of buggies is also a significant cause of wear and tear damage to the golf course, and they tend to slow play down."'

There is nothing more pleasurable than to be able to walk on to the course, to be able to play from the first tee without delay and to be able to walk briskly around 18 holes without having to wait for those in front.

Increasingly that is rare and as the game soars in popularity, it is getting worse. In an American clubhouse, I heard an indignant member complaining to a friend that he had been accused of playing too slowly by the people he had held up. In a righteous whine, he said, 'Hell we were round in five hours, you know, not fast but not slow …' There are courses in Scotland where you would run the danger of getting thrown off if you did not play two rounds in that time.

Historically, a day's golf has meant 36 holes. At many clubs in Great Britain and Ireland a green fee encompasses as much golf as you can play that day and most people still interpret that as being 36 holes. But increasingly that is not so elsewhere and the malign influence of televized golf is largely to blame. It is not possible to play quickly if the methods and mannerisms of the professional are employed by the less gifted and yet such is all too often the case.

We have all cursed those inconsiderate, selfish so-and-so's, The People in Front, but none so vividly as Bernard Darwin, one of golf's great essayists, who once wrote to that very title. 'The People in Front,' said Darwin, 'waggle for hours; they stroll rather than walk; they dive into their monstrous bags in search of the right club and then it is the wrong number, but they are not sorry that we have been troubled; their putting is a kind of funereal ping-pong … They will insist on waiting for the people in front of them when it must be palpable even to their intellects that the best shot they ever hit in their lives would be 50 yards short.'

What infuriated Darwin beyond measure was when they stood in the middle of the green to 'write down their horrid little score', at which point he suggested yelling 'Fore!' and watching them dive for cover. 'They may think us ill-mannered, but what does that matter? The worst they can do is write an article about the people behind.'

Golf is fortunate in that where we have been is fairly well documented but no one knows for sure where we are going, and it would be no fun if we did. Nevertheless, on 26 March, 1997, a series of 'Vision Statements' for the year 2047 were buried in a time capsule in the grounds of the World Golf Village near Jacksonville in Florida. Twenty-one organizations contributed their view of what the game might be like 50 years hence, some of them radical, some of them frankly disappointing.

Pleasantly, one of the most encouraging came from exactly the right quarter – the American Junior Golf Association – which by 2047 expected to have become the World Junior Golf Association. They said, among other things, that 'golf will have the strongest youth programmes of any sport in 2047, as society continues to realize that the values inherent in the game can significantly benefit the personal development of young people everywhere.' They went on, 'Golf will continue to do what it has always done from its very inception – mystify all who play the game and remain the most unconquerable challenge in all of sport.'

The American Society of Golf Course Architects envisioned 'new sturdy grasses that require little water to allow courses to be built in desert areas' plus many more floodlit courses to cater for increased demand. The greenkeepers, the Golf Course Superintendents' Association of America, addressed the problem of pollution with the words, 'Plant protectants of the day will show zero non-target toxicity', while the PGA Tour in Australia completed a tournament threatened by darkness 'by the glow of a phosphorescent grass developed for just such an occasion.'

What will they be playing for in 50 years' time? The Professional Golf Tournaments' Association predicted that 'only tournaments with purses in excess of US$10 million' will remain in America. And what will they be playing with? Much the same as now if the R&A were correct. They said, 'We believe that improvements in the golf ball and golf clubs have just about reached their limit.' And who will be winning all this money with these clubs with their 50-year-old technology? The R&A said, 'We believe that countries such as China and Russia will very possibly have provided winners of the Open championship.'

And how will anyone know who has done what? The Golf Writers' Association of America predicted wide-scale computerization 'with just a handful of newspapers remaining.' They added, 'Golf writing as we know it will not exist in the year 2047.'

Well, at least that means I won't be missing anything.

CHAPTER 1

GOLF:
THE MARVELLOUS MANIA

THE LURE OF THE LORE
JERRY TARDE

THE LURE OF GOLF OVER THE LAST HUNDRED YEARS can be distilled down to these essential truths:–

• It is a game of luck, despite the fact that throughout time man has worked to eliminate chance from the outcome.

• We search and search, pay huge sums of money, invest the brain power of nuclear physics and the metallurgy of outer space, all to find the right equipment when we know, as Lee Trevino says, 'It's the Indian, not the arrow.'

• Golf is dominated by people of monumental ego, but none has ever considered himself above the game.

• It costs too much and takes too long to play. The march upward in time and expense has, oddly, only served to make the game even more appealing.

These are the paradoxes of golf – a game full of nonsense and contradiction. As Toots Shor, the late New York restaurateur, said, 'In what other sport do you have to hit down to make the ball go up, swing left to make the ball go right, take it back slow to come down fast – and when it's over, the winner buys the drinks?'

The incongruity of golf is emphasized by pondering the unlikelihood of 'Golf the Game' being invented today. Say you were to go into a patent office. 'I have a new game I want to register,' you'd say.

'Go ahead,' a clerk would reply, without looking up. 'How do you play?'

'It requires 150 acres of prime real estate. It would cost about US$10 million minimum to get ready. There'd be years of delay with all sorts of zoning and environmental problems. When the thing is built, if you want to play, you have to call in at least a week in advance to make a reservation, or sleep in your car the night before in the car-park. It will cost a couple of thousand dollars to buy a bag of equipment plus about US$100 a round to play. And it will take most of a day to do it.'

'What is it that you're expected to do?' the clerk might ask.

'The object is to swing a hunk of metal at the end of a stick around your body on an arc 40 feet in circumference but the only part that matters is the thousandths of an inch during which the hunk of metal contacts a 1.68-inch ball. If you are just two degrees off, you will miss the target by more than 30 yards.'

'That sounds hard,' he might say.

'You will never be any good at it. Your bad shots will outnumber your good 10 to one. No matter how long you play, you will never have a day that couldn't have been better. And the better you get, the more frustrating it becomes.'

'Get out of here,' the clerk will eventually say.

And yet here it is, the best and – among civilized men and women – the most popular game in the world.

A GAME OF CHANCE

Luck is the only thing that keeps golf from turning into chess but there has been a conspiracy throughout the twentieth century to discredit 'rub of the green'. The plot started in America's élite country clubs, seeped on to the pro tours and then through television is spreading around the world.

All greens are manicured to the same speed; all fairways cut to the same width; all rough blown and dried to the same height. Bunker sand is not only graded to the same depth but players also practically demand that each particle be weighed and ground to the same specifications.

Courses are overwatered to eliminate the bad bounce, so a more predictable air attack has replaced the old guerrilla warfare. Courses are designed to have all the natural beauty of a terrarium with potted plants and plastic rocks. Not only have blind holes disappeared but you also have to be able to see the bottom of the flagstick and there's a whiffle ball attached to tell you if the flagstick's in the front, middle or back of the green.

In tournaments, players are given charts and maps; some even use electronic binoculars with satellite technology so they don't even have to calculate their own distances. Veteran pros have come to rely on this cartography so much that Raymond Floyd and Tom Kite once sat down on their bags and refused to play at Merion in the US Open because a mistake had been made on the hole-location sheet they were given at the first tee.

The Rules of Golf have bowed to the conspiracy as the stymie has been rendered extinct. There used to be clubs called the 'track iron' and 'rut iron', designed ingeniously to extricate the ball from unplayable lies; now if the ground is merely discoloured, you call over the rules official and get a 'free drop' – modern golf's equivalent of welfare. As recently as 1959, you weren't allowed to lift and clean your ball on the putting green; now if there's even a forecast for cloudy skies, pros have the ball in their hand. 'Lift, clean and cheat,' one USGA man called it.

In the constant striving for perfection and uniformity and that most insidious goal of all-fairness, we are losing what is at the heart of golf. Without luck, golf is a duller game.

Our forefathers have always appreciated this. 'Golf was just what the Scottish character had been seeking for centuries,' wrote Alistair Cooke. 'Namely a method of self-torture, disguised as a game, which would entrap irreligious youths into principles of what was to become known first as Calvinism and then as golf. The main tenets of this faith are that life is grim and uncomfortable and that human vanity cannot prevail ...

The missed putt.

The golfer's credo is that men should expect very little here below and strive to gain it.' Bad luck should be a test of character.

THE INDIAN, NOT THE ARROW

It has been proven time and again that three immutable laws govern golf equipment and none of them is written by the R&A or the USGA.

Law No.1: The Hawthorne effect. This phenomenon was based on testing done in 1924 at the Hawthorne plant of the Western Electric Co. in Chicago. Engineers there wanted to see if workers would improve their productivity with better lighting. In one study, illumination was increased dramatically for some workers and kept the same for others. In another study, illumination was decreased to the level of 'dim moonlight'. Completely confounding the researchers, productivity improved the same in every case. That's the way golf is. Any perceived change will bring improvement, at least temporarily. That's one reason why you should never get rid of an old putter. Someday, when it is new again to you, it will work.

Law No.2: The 100-day theory. This one is based on the testing of thousands of golfers who bought a new driver to give them 10 or 20 extra yards. (There is also a little-known fact that distance comes only in 10-yard increments – nobody hits the ball six yards farther.) These golfers found that their distance gradually dissipated, until after a three-month period (or 100 days, to be exact) they were driving the ball precisely the same distance as they had before switching clubs. A contest in which drives are actually measured may also cause a golfer's distance to revert to a former shortness.

Law No.3: The invisible hand. This theory is actually endorsed by the USGA and the R&A, although they live in fear that it might be wrong. It is that for every advantage a piece of equipment offers you, there's an equal and opposite disadvantage: more length comes at the cost of more crookedness, accuracy comes at the cost of distance and so on.

The ill-fated Polara ball was a classic example of the invisible hand. Polara's gyroscopic dimple design caused it to self-correct and fly straighter than any previous ball but it flew so pitifully short that no golfer would use it. The USGA spent millions in court costs trying to declare the ball illegal, when the marketplace would have eliminated it for free.

MONUMENTAL EGOS

The statement that golf is dominated by people of monumental ego is as time-honoured as the game being played with a club and a ball. The evidence goes way beyond Nicklaus and Palmer – or even Ken Schofield, Tim Finchem and Deane Beman (not to be confused with id, ego and superego).

My favourite character who typifies the nature of golf's psyche was John Arthur Brown, who ruled the Pine Valley course in New Jersey for half a century and died, aged 92, while still president. He may have been the prototype for all golf dictators and their aspirants. Nothing was ever put to a vote and the longest meeting he chaired lasted four minutes.

One Sunday afternoon, when women were allowed to play the all-male enclave, Brown had his wife out for a round. Jerry O'Neil, the chairman of the giant corporation General Tyre Co. and three of his guests were playing in front of the Browns. The foursome of rubber barons plodded on, looking for balls and hitting mulligans and did not invite Mr and Mrs Brown to play through.

At the 10th green, Brown sent his caddie ahead with the instructions, 'Tell those boys to take their bags in. They're through.' Sorely embarrassed, O'Neil had to go home with a six-month suspension from membership privileges.

In a letter of apology, O'Neil wrote, 'It takes a son-of-a-bitch like you to run a club like this.' Brown, in a rare moment of weakness, commuted the sentence to 30 days.

TOO MUCH ... AND TOO LONG

While the game originated with shepherds, over the last hundred years or so golf has been claimed by bankers and lawyers. Still it survives, although the cost and length of time involved has risen significantly.

A round of 18 holes at Pebble Beach costs US$275, which is okay in my book because it is the life experience. The problem is that courses billing themselves as the Pebble Beach of the East, the Pebble Beach of New Jersey, the Pebble Beach of Myrtle Beach and even the Pebble Beach of West 42nd Street now charge US$150 for a round. Some people pay it but the beauty of golf continues to be that it's also available for a pittance and everything in between.

There is a golf course as good as any other in the world called Pinon Hills, open to the public, in remote Farmington, New Mexico. It costs US$11 during the week to play and US$13 on weekends and holidays.

Those Scottish shepherds got around faster than today's golfer, too. The fault here should be shared by the professionals, who play the game at a glacier-like pace; television, which has propagated the pace and rules officials, who have failed to do anything about it.

We would all be better off if our heroes moved along a little quicker. Years ago, in a US Open, Joe Dey of the USGA approached Ben Hogan and told him to pick up his pace. 'If you're thinking of giving me a two-stroke penalty, then give it to me now so I know where I stand,' said Hogan, who should have been played by Humphrey Bogart, not Glenn Ford, in the film of his life.

Dey never gave him a two-stroke penalty. Hogan never really picked up the pace and was never penalized for slow play. In later years Jack Nicklaus played slower. Nick Faldo and Greg Norman played slower still. It's too early to clock Tiger Woods but his golf in the US Amateur had to be recorded by time-lapse photography.

Dr Cary Middlecoff, the golfing dentist and notoriously slow player of the 1950s, once explained the rationale. 'I couldn't take it back until it felt just right,' he said. The pundit Herb Graffis replied, 'That's a fine attitude for a dentist but it's hell for a golfer.'

There is, for some, an upside to slow play. President Bill Clinton has said the most appealing thing about golf is that it does take so long to play. It transports you away from everything, from all your troubles, which is nice for a president.

* Jerry Tarde is the hugely respected editor of Golf Digest. His monthly column, personal and provocative, is required reading and at least one of them has been pinned up in a Ryder Cup locker-room, where it had the unlooked-for effect of inspiring the 1995 European team to an unexpected victory.

THE ORIGINS OF GOLF

Golf, in its earliest days, was played very quickly indeed and given that it was being played mostly in Scotland, this made sense. There are some months in Scotland when the weather makes it a pure pleasure to play; there are many more when you would be better off hitting shots in a refrigerated wind tunnel.

There was once a day in the 1987 Open Championship at Muirfield when a stygian gloom descended upon the course, the wind howled and icicles masquerading as rain cut people to pieces. It was loathsome in East Lothian, and it was July, the height of summer. In the middle of all this the third round of the championship was played and at the height of it all Sandy Lyle got round in 71, still regarded by many people who were present on that day, as one of the finest rounds of golf ever played.

But it begged the question of how golf ever caught on in a country capable of such conditions and the probable answer is that it was an ideal form of exercise to work off the excesses of the gargantuan appetites of the rich of that time. The early records show that drinks were measured by the bottle, servings of meat by the joint and the length of a meal by the time available. What better after such over-indulgence than to get out into God's good air and walk briskly for a couple of hours, stopping only occasionally to whack a ball with a stick? And if you could whack it fewer times than McCorquindale, then jolly good show and hand over the money.

If the match were not a single and, say, four people wanted to play, then the game became too slow and so the foursomes game was invented. This was, in the early days, very nearly singles in that two of the protagonists went to the teeing area at the first and made their preparations. While they were so doing the other two players walked forward a couple of hundred yards and waited for their partners to hit. As soon as this was accomplished, those who had gone forward went to the ball and, before their partners had arrived, hit the ball again. This leapfrogging form of the game meant that everyone was moving continuously, the 18 holes were completed in around two hours – and no one froze to death.

Nowadays, of course, foursomes is rarely played properly and in the Ryder Cup it is played completely improperly, with the result that the danger is death by boredom. All the players congregate on the first tee, drives are driven and they all walk to where the balls are. There is then a committee meeting at each ball between the two players on the same side and their caddies to discuss the lie of the ball, the lie of the land, the distance to go, the strength of the wind, the condition of the green, the placing of the pin and, like as not, the wicked price of sausages these days. Only after the entire agenda has been completed and the minutes of the last meeting agreed, does a player hit a shot, after which all four persons concerned go into a de-briefing process before gathering themselves for the next consultations. It is an interminable process, completely contrary to the traditions of the game and playable only by men possessed either of a high degree of patience or an extremely low boredom threshold.

But in the days when the game was young, such pseudo-sophistication had not yet been invented. Golf was fun and it was fashionable, particularly among Army officers, on whose hands time hung heavy during the years of peace. There is only so much time, after all, in any given day that you can spend on the parade ground bawling at the lower orders.

In those days Great Britain ruled much of the world. Its empire was one 'on which the sun does not set' so extensive was it, and the conquering Army took the game with them wheresoe'er they went. Thus the first golf club outside Scotland was actually in India: the Dum Dum club in Calcutta, later to be Royal Calcutta, which was established in 1829. In December 1830 *The Oriental Sporting Magazine* published the names of 30 members of the 'Dum Dum golfing club', congratulating them 'on the prospect of seeing that noble and gentleman-like game established in Bengal.'

By 1876 there were 70 members and such was the progression of the game that a second club, the Tollygunge, was established in 1895. Three years before that the first Amateur Golf Championship of India was played over 54 holes of stroke-play, an event which, despite its title, was competed for only by Europeans. It was won by one J.F. MacNair and it was not until 1949 that an Indian, Mohinder Bal, won the title. Dum Dum became Royal Calcutta in 1911, when the prefix was bestowed by King George V and nowadays there are over 100 clubs on the sub-continent.

The first recognised club in England came 35 years after Dum Dum and featured another unlikely name, Westward Ho!. This has transmogrified into Royal North Devon and largely because it is so far from anywhere, it remains one of those wonderful museum pieces, along with the likes of Royal West Norfolk, also known as Brancaster.

The first club on the Continent was another result of military adventurism. Pau is a lovely spa town, famous now for its food and for the fact that it is one of the few places where you can, quite genuinely, go skiing in the morning and play golf in the afternoon. It nestles below the Pyrenees and the golf course entwines itself around the river, Gave de Pau; it is a thoroughly pleasant place to play. It came into existence in 1856 when officers from a Scottish regiment were sent there to convalesce after the Peninsula War against Napoleon and it is quite extraordinary how the British influence lingers on. The honours boards for the early competitions feature mainly British names, of course, and the clubhouse is a throw-back to the style of the twenties and thirties. But perhaps the oddest facet of all is a bookcase, one of those waist-high revolving bookcases, which is crammed with books – all of them written in English, all of them exceedingly old and musty and all of them obviously unread in years, if not decades.

Royal Adelaide was the first course in Australia, opened in 1871 and host, first in 1910 and latterly in 1998, to the Australian Open. It moved around in its very early days, finally settling in Seaton which had the advantage of being very easy to get to – the railway line ran through the course. A halt was built for the members to get off – right by the clubhouse naturally – and this still exists. Disappointingly it was closed for the latest manifestation of the Australian Open, although with the need to cross the line, on foot, to get to the first tee, perhaps it was sensible so to do.

Royal Melbourne, although conceding that Adelaide is older, claims to be the oldest golf club in Australia 'with a continuous existence under the same name' while in Tasmania there is the nine-hole Bothwell club, which, according to the Australian golf writer, Tom Ramsey, was founded in 1830 by the Scot, Alexander Reid. Unfortunately, written records of the early days have been lost.

The present Royal Montreal course is relatively young, being built in 1958. But the club itself goes back to 1873 and was the first in Canada and has some claims to be the oldest in North America. Strangely, when they wanted a professional they did not summon someone from Scotland, they sent for W. F. Davis, from Hoylake. They paid his passage and his wages were £1 per week. Back in 1898 they conceived the idea of playing an inter-club match against The Country Club of Brookline, the course in Boston that hosted the Ryder Cup in 1999. Despite the distances involved – and in the late 1890s they must have seemed formidable – the matches have been played ever since and are thought to be the oldest continuous series of international golf matches anywhere in the world.

Royal Cape Town is the oldest club in South Africa, founded in 1885, and again the Army was the big influence. General Torrens was commanding the British troops in South Africa and decreed a course be built. When that was done he decreed a competition be played and, one suspects, the remaining competitors decreed that it would be wise if the general won. He did, with a score of 94.

Golf was, by 1885, well-established around the globe although not – oddly enough – in the country that was to refine and define it in later years, America. There are a number of claimants to the title of Oldest in America and there are a number of qualifications attached to the claims. It is likely that the first place in which golf was perpetrated in the US was a large, sloping field in White Sulphur Springs in West Virginia, called Oakhurst Links. But when the originators moved away, the club faded and has only recently been revived. Charleston, an Army base, has some claims but, with the qualification that it is 'the oldest permanent golf club' in the States, most people argue that the St Andrews Club in Ardsley-on-Hudson, New York, was where it all started, in 1888.

Robert Lockhart and John Reid, guid Scottish names, imported several sets of clubs and a large number of balls from Scotland and, with some friends, set about playing. First they devised a course of three holes, then one of six and then yet another of six, this time in an orchard which led to this small band of golfers being called the 'Apple Tree Gang.' Next came a nine hole course and finally, in 1897, they moved to their present 18-hole premises. Although named after the home of golf, it resembles nothing so much as a typical American country club, proud of its origins but no longer related to them.

With golf now covering the globe there was only one place left for it to go – upwards, to the Moon. It hardly seems over a quarter of a century ago that Alan Shepard, in 1971, smuggled a six iron on to his spaceship and, on landing on the Moon, hit a shot with it, to take the first, unsteady, space-suited steps towards inter-planetary golf.

Golf being the game of infinite variety that it is, it can only be expected that it will dive off into some unexpected highways and byways from time to time. There are some totally unexpected names, for instance, that present themselves in the long and diverse history of the game; names that are completely unfamiliar to most, and yet who had quite a profound influence on the game.

Not many golfers will know of Ernie Sabayrac, for instance, but no one today ventures on to the course without using something he popularized and it is more than likely that they will be wearing something else that he promoted. Sabayrac, who died in 1997 aged 82, was an American who began his career in golf as a caddie in Houston. But it was he who took golf out of the hob-nailed shoe era and into shoes purpose-built for spikes. And it was he, too, who created what has become a multi-million pound business that has spread into every nook and cranny of the game. Sabayrac was the first man to think of logo'd clothing.

The late Henry Longhurst was once approached by a clothing company and asked if he thought a special tie for a hole-in-one would be profitable for them. Longhurst dismissed the idea out of hand, saying that golfers were not braggarts and would want nothing to do with a tie that spoke loudly of an exploit such as that. The company went ahead anyway and proved Longhurst hugely wrong. Sabayrac also realized that golfers would welcome some form of visible 'been there, done that' on their clothing, and that logos could become momentos. His first logo was that of a West coast resort embroidered on a cap and he was also responsible for introducing the Lacoste alligator featured on Izod shirts in the US.

When Sabayrac died the chief executive officer of the US PGA, Jim Awtrey, said: 'Ernie was one of the best friends a PGA professional could have. He was a man of foresight who changed the way our industry conducted its business.'

Ernie really ought to have met Beryl Brown: they both might have been considerably better off financially if he had. Miss Brown was a member of the Formby Ladies golf club and a frequent Lancashire ladies' champion. She reached the semi-final of the British Ladies' three times and in 1923 lost to Doris Chambers, the eventual champion, by 3&2. *The Times*, ever gallant, recorded that Miss Brown 'patters her way round the course with remarkable steadiness.'

But it was Miss Brown who is first recorded as using head-covers, which she took to the English Ladies' championship at Ganton. A local paper recorded: 'A new fashion note was struck when Miss Beryl Brown caused a stir by appearing for her match with Miss Phyllis Lobbett, the Somerset county player, with the heads of her golf clubs capped in little Tam O'Shanters made of wool and each, according to true Scottish taste, bearing a tassle. Each "hat" was of a different shade from its neighbours and altogether a pretty colour scheme was afforded by the crimson cover of the driver, the sky blue of the brassie, and other shades.' Ernie could have done wonders marketing that little lot.

Gene Andrews is another whose influence on the game is massive. There are some who would say it has not been wholly good, for there is little doubt that his invention slows play, but who among us has not taken advantage of it from time to time? For Gene Andrews developed the yardage guide, printed books that specified accurate distances from point to point on a golf course.

Jack Nicklaus was the first great golfer to become dedicated to the idea of playing by yardages. Peter Thomson, on the other hand, despises them but there is no doubt that for the average player, on a strange course, they are invaluable. Nicklaus picked up the idea of a yardage book from Deane Beman, for years the US Tour commissioner but before that a friend and fellow-competitor.

And Beman, so the USGA's magazine *Golf Journal*, tells us, got the idea from Andrews. The two men were both still amateurs, both in insurance, when they played each other in the US Amateur of 1958 at the Olympic Club in San Francisco. Andrews said: 'I had been playing by yardage for years. All people ever talked about in those days was feel. Feel, feel, feel – all my life I've done whatever I could to get away from it. Feel takes so much damn time and effort to develop and then you lay off for a couple of weeks and you've lost it.

'So I played by yardage and my friends were always asking me for notes and guides on any course they were going to play a tournament on. So there was I with my little book at the Olympic, and Beman spies it and he asked me "What is that?"' When Andrews told him, Beman was immediately sold on the idea.

Eventually, Andrews had the idea of formalizing his yardage books and selling them to the various clubs. He wrote first to the USGA asking if they might be counted as 'artificial devices' and so contravene the rules but they were cleared. Nowadays, of course, they are standard issue at most courses and the idea of using yardages has spread to the extent that most courses have 150 yard markers, use sprinkler heads to spell out the distance to the green and, recently, there has been a big market for binocular-like devices that use satellite technology to give the precise distance from where you are to where you need to go. Andrews cannot be blamed for them, though – they are illegal in actual play.

Of all the unsuspected names in golf, perhaps the former Poet Laureate, the late John Betjeman, is one of the most unexpected. Golf somehow seems too hearty for a poet. But Betjeman not only loved the game, he played it at one of the game's lovely places, and he wrote a wonderful poem about it too. Its subject is the 13th hole at St Enodoc and it expresses much about the game that so many hackers feel, but fail to put into words. It is called Seaside Golf.

How straight it flew, how long it flew,
It cleared the rutty track
And soaring, disappeared from view
Beyond the bunkers back –
A glorious, sailing, bounding drive
That made me glad I was alive.

And down the fairway, far along
It glowed a lonely white;
I played an iron sure and strong
And clipped it out of sight,
And spite of grassy banks between
I knew I'd find it on the green.

And so I did. It lay content
Two paces from the pin;
A steady putt and then it went
Oh, most securely in.
The very turf rejoiced to see
That quite unprecedented three.
Ah! seaweed smells from sandy caves
And thyme and mist in whiffs,
In-coming tide, Atlantic waves
Slapping the sunny cliffs,
Lark song and sea sounds in the air
And splendour, splendour everywhere.

The club celebrated their centenary with a dinner on April 14, 1990, at which Sir Robin Butler spoke. It would have been worth a great many unprecedented threes to be there to hear him deliver this riposte to Betjeman's work.

How low it flew, how left it flew,
It hit the dry stone wall
And plunging, disappeared from view
A shining brand new ball –
I'd hit the damned thing on the head
It made me wish that I were dead.

And up the fairway, steep and long,
I mourned my gloomy plight;
I played an iron sure and strong,
A fraction to the right
I knew that when I reached my ball
I'd find it underneath the wall.

And so I did. I chipped it low
And thinned it past the pin
And to and fro, and to and fro
I tried to get it in;
Until, intoning oaths obscene
I holed it out in seventeen.

Ah! seaweed smells from sandy caves
They really get me down;
In-coming tides, Atlantic waves
I wish that I could drown
And Sloane Street voices in the air
And black retrievers everywhere.

IMPLEMENTS AND BALLS

The game of golf has gone from carrying an armful of clubs to mechanical cart contrivances; from wearing tight-fitting jacket, tie and cuff-links to cashmere intarsia'd sweaters; from hitting featheries, gutties and Haskells to dodecahydron-patterned balls (DDHs) and from spade-mashies and niblicks to titanium inserts and perimeter weighting. The game has become user-friendly. These days, with modern equipment, any duffer can get the ball airborne and propel it forwards. In the days of hickory shafts rather than graphite, it took a process of elimination before finding a club that 'worked' and even then it took real skill to make it work well and consistently.

If you think that is an exaggeration, take yourself off to West Virginia, to the remarkable Oakhurst Links, which has a good claim to be the oldest golf course still in existence in the United States. There Louis Keller, a man who has been known to take money off both Sam Snead and Ben Hogan – but not often – has for your old-fashioned delectation and delight a truly old-time golf course.

Keller bought the property as a horse farm but when he found a map that showed that a golf course had been laid out in the ground in 1888, he yearned to restore the course. It was re-opened officially – by Snead – in 1994 and all who play there must use hickory-shafted clubs and gutty balls. Replicas, not originals, are available for hire.

The first free-standing golf bag, 1893.

It is a fascinating exercise and gives a valuable insight into the game as it was and is an object lesson in the skills needed to make the equipment work. The eighth, for example, is a long hole; at 318 yards it would be a drive and a wedge with modern clubs and balls but at Oakhurst it's a genuine par five. It puts into perspective the scores of the early golfers and confirms that a champion then would be a champion now.

It was a champion who discovered the successor to the gutty and so found a ball that made the game more fun because it didn't disintegrate too easily and flew a great deal farther. The Haskell ball was invented by Coburn Haskell, an American who, while searching for something to replace the gutty, chanced upon some rubber strips while visiting a friend at the Goodrich Rubber Co. in Akron, Ohio. He realized the possibility, made a ball and found that, while it was an improvement, it was not dramatically so.

Golf, of course, is the ultimate ground guidance system, but it was not until 1956 that Solheim became interested in the sport. Like Saunders before him, he thought of a better way.

Then James Foulis, the man who won the second US Open in 1896, was experimenting with some gutty balls by placing a dimpled casing on them and, by accident, covered a Haskell in like manner. Not knowing what he had done, he noticed one ball of the batch flew miles farther than the others and, on cutting it open to find out why, discovered it was a Haskell. The combination of rubber core and dimpled exterior was perfect.

From that point the gutty was doomed in America and when Sandy Herd used a Haskell to beat Harry Vardon to win the 1902 Open at Hoylake, the gutty was finished everywhere.

The game with the new ball was suddenly more pleasurable and there have been a great many developments of that kind over the years, some of them unexpected. Who would have thought, for example, that a man called Sidney Alphonse Saunders, from England's industrial Midlands, working as a mill manager in a steel factory, would be indirectly responsible for saving the game completely?

What Saunders did, in 1912, was take up golf. As he was working for Accles and Pollock he decided that rather than buy hickory-shafted clubs he would make some of his own, from the straight tapered tubing produced by his mill. He found that they were immeasurably better than the clubs used by his friends, so he patented the idea in 1913. The specification reads, in part, 'This invention has reference to golf clubs and consists in improved clubs in which the shafts are made from taper steel or other metallic tubing ...'

The R&A, of course, immediately banned the idea, until in 1929 the Prince of Wales played a round with them and suddenly the ban was lifted. It was only just in time. The world's supply of hickory was running out and in any case would never have sustained the booms in the game that were to come.

Over the course of the twentieth century many things have developed apace. The steel shaft, while still the most widely used, is gradually being supplanted by graphite, and other aspects continue to improve. There are, for example, better and quicker mowers, to cut better and more resilient grasses, while the ball itself has been developed to the point where people like Jack Nicklaus want it controlled. He, and many others, believe that our classic courses are being overpowered by a ball that goes too far.

The authorities, perhaps because of the fearful battle that would ensue with the manufacturers over 'restraint of trade', have been reluctant to decree a totally standard ball, maintaining that while there has been a small measurable increase of around 10 yards in how far the ball goes in recent years, much of this can be put down to people getting bigger and training harder for their sport. The latter is certainly true of professionals, who now have fitness vans following them to every tournament, with a mobile gym for them to work out in and a physiotherapist to ease away the aches and strains – all very different to the turn of the twentieth century.

If Sid Saunders was responsible for one of the great breakthroughs of the early part of the century, then another figure – at first sight just as unlikely – is responsible for one of the biggest in the latter half.

Karsten Solheim was born in Bergen in Norway in 1911 and was taken to America as a very young child. He grew up during the Depression, which meant that the money ran out before he had completed his university education but it could not deny his innate genius. During the Second World War he became a flight research engineer working on the Fireball jet and later was a project engineer on the Atlas missile's ground guidance system. Golf, of course, is the ultimate ground guidance system but it was not until 1956 that Solheim became interested in the sport. Like Saunders before him, he thought of a better way.

Solheim, an excellent player through the green, felt that matters could be improved on the putting surface and started tinkering in the garage. Realizing that even with a putter the 'sweet spot' is not always delivered perfectly to the ball, he set about enlarging it, bringing heel-and-toe weighting to golf for the first time.

This gave the *Redwood City Tribune*, and their sports editor of the time, Ed Jacoubowsky, a world-class scoop, although they knew it not at the time. In an article dated 1 April, 1959 Jacoubowsky wrote, 'While many men have set their sights on inventing a better mouse trap and a five cent cigar, Redwood City's Karsten Solheim apparently has found success in his search for a better putter. And what a putter it is. Not only does it aid the golfer in finding the hole, but it has a resounding "ping" to it when it strikes the ball.'

The article quoted the opinion of Al Maus, head pro at the Los Altos Golf and Country Club, who said, with great prescience, 'Solheim's putter isn't just a quirk thing, it's scientifically and mechanically sound. It's good, and it's going to reach the level of national popular demand.'

That first effort was an ugly-looking thing. Julius Boros, the winner of two US Opens and a US PGA and the first man to win a tournament with one (the 1967 Phoenix Open), said, 'It looked like a bunch of nuts and bolts welded together. But, the ball goes in the hole.'

It is a commentary on all of us and our preference, at least initially, for style over substance, that Solheim had the greatest difficulty in selling this thing that made 'the ball go in the hole'. He would travel to tournaments and haunt the practice putting green, often ignored and occasionally laughed at. George Archer summed up the feeling of those times when he said their reaction to the presence of Solheim was, 'Oh Christ, here comes that old man with the goofy putters.'

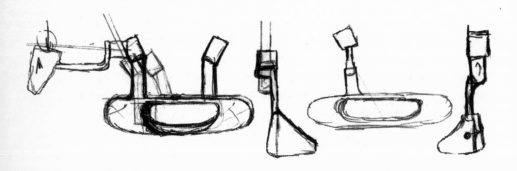

Solheim's sketches provide the 'answer' to many golfers' putting problem.

But eventually, sheer persistence paid off. If only to get him to go away, people began to try his invention, and found that it worked. It is the longest-lasting and most sincere tribute that could possibly be paid to the genius of Karsten Solheim that those 'goofy putters' have found their way, at some time or other, into the bag of almost every professional golfer and a large percentage of the amateurs, too.

The putter has been developed since the first model, and in 1966 Solheim, doodling on the dust cover of a record, roughed out the design for what was to become the best-selling, most successful, single golf club ever created. It was called the Ping Anser and for a reason. Solheim, who became known for his ferocious quality control, had just returned from the Los Angeles Open, where he felt his success was being threatened by other putters. 'I've got to find the answer,' he said to his wife, Louise. Then came the doodlings and the need to find a name. 'Why not "Answer"?' suggested Louise, given that that was what it was. 'It's too long,' said Solheim, 'it won't fit on the club.' But 'Anser' did and has been solving putting problems ever since.

Sir Winston Churchill once remarked, 'Golf is a curious sport whose object is to put a very small ball in a very small hole with implements ill-designed for the purpose.'

Putters occupy a special place, both spiritually and physically, at Karsten Manufacturing, now known as Ping, in Phoenix. Every time a professional wins a tournament on a major tour with a Ping putter – and by late 1999 there had been over 1,900 – two gold-plated replicas are made. One goes to the player, the other is put into a vault at the factory. The player with the most (45) is Severiano Ballesteros. Nick Faldo has 26.

Sir Winston Churchill once remarked, 'Golf is a curious sport whose object is to put a very small ball in a very small hole with implements ill-designed for the purpose.' Solheim consigned such implements to the past and hundreds of thousands of players, from hackers to professors of the game, beat a path to his door. He set standards that were copied throughout the industry, inspiring other inventors and giants of entrepreneurship. Truly a tale of America's times.

THE GOOD, THE BAD
AND T'HOUTMOSIS

PETER DOBEREINER

So what, in these 90 and some years, have been the best bits, and the bad bits? This, the last article Peter Dobereiner wrote before he died in 1996, addressed that very question, with the vision and wit that were his hallmarks.

We all recognize that it was a good thing for golf when, for example, the indestructible ball came along or fabrics which actually kept out water were introduced. In both those cases the game's benefactors were teams of industrial chemists and, on behalf of golf, in my role as one of the game's inky-fingered recording angels, I make deep obeisance in their general direction. Thank you chaps, whoever you are.

In drawing up a balance sheet of innovations which shaped the game of golf we can in many cases identify the innovator. And on the credit side of the ledger my first nominee as a GOOD THING must be Jack Nicklaus. He is the founding father of the modern era of golf, the role model who set the standards of personal deportment, sportsmanship and playing ability against which all who followed him are measured.

Some may argue that Harry Vardon was the founder of the modern game, or Bobby Jones, or Ben Hogan or, above all, Arnold Palmer. I see them as the ultimate expression of the era which began with the gutta ball and hickory shafts although, of course, all of them had a strong influence on the young Nicklaus. His philosophy of golf being as cerebral a pursuit as chess, and his belief that the physical side of the game should be a triumph of artistry over brute strength, influenced the thinking of two generations of golf course architects. Nicklaus permeates golf, in where we play, how we try to play, what we wear, the equipment we use and the way we think.

My second entry on the GOOD THING side of the ledger is the Pharaoh T'Houtmosis III (1490–1436 BC). The earliest known record of someone hitting balls with a club refers to T'Houtmosis and the pastime in which he indulged was uncannily similar to our present-day practice of whacking a bucket of balls on the range. His club was carved from olive wood and the balls were remarkably similar to golf's featheries, stitched leather cases stuffed with wool and clay. Priests teed the ball up for him and slaves retrieved them from the desert. It seems there was a spiritual element in this exercise just as there is for modern pilgrims to St Andrews as they stand on the first tee of the Old Course in the footsteps of Allan Robertson and Young Tom Morris.

In no sense can we say that T'Houtmosis played golf; at best it was foreplay without consummation and it did not catch on. But it was a ritualized expression of man's primitive instinct to whack away at any inviting object in his path once he had taken a club into his hands. And that instinct is the real genesis of the game of golf.

We have no idea who invented golf, if indeed there was one individual who was responsible for the original idea. More likely the game simply evolved, absorbing

Peter Dobereiner

elements of different ball games which men had played since the earliest days of the Chinese civilization. Some Scottish historians have based their claims that golf was invented in Scotland on the fact that only in 'goff', or 'gowfe', or 'gouf' or, possibly, 'goof', is the explosive assault on the ball combined with the delicate touch of holing out. That argument collapses under the obvious fact that there was no delicacy of touch in early Scottish golf. We know from the earliest surviving code of rules that the ball had to be teed within a club-length of the previous hole and that the golfer made his tee by scooping a handful of sand from that hole. It does not take any great stretch of the imagination to realize that the condition of the hole and its immediate surrounds precluded any suggestion of a delicate touch. Holing out must have been more like chipping into a bucket.

Putting as we know it was impossible until the rules designated separate areas for teeing grounds and putting greens and equipment was available to keep those grounds in trim. Hence a major asset on the credit side of golf's balance sheet must be Edwin Budding of Stroud, England, who invented the lawnmower and patented it in 1830. Real golf was possible from that day forward.

The Rev. Dr R. Paterson has an honoured place in the history of golf as the inventor of the gutta ball. The story is as endearing as it is enduring. The Rev. Paterson received a statue of the Hindu god Vishnu from his half brother, a missionary in India. The piece had been packed for protection in chips of gutta percha, a substance akin to latex derived from tree resin. Some of the stone-like gutta percha chips fell into the grate during the unpacking and softened in the heat of the fire. The Rev. Paterson retrieved some of this molten material and idly rolled it into a ball which set hard as it cooled. 'I wonder, I wonder ...' mused the venerable gentleman as he hurried to the links with his clubs slung across his shoulders.

His first shots were disappointing as the ball stubbornly refused to become airborne but he persevered until the ball became nicked and dented from his mis-hits and then it flew like a bird. Eureka! He had invented the gutta ball. A variation of this yarn has the Rev. Paterson moulding incredibly durable soles for his son's shoes from this magical oriental substance.

Alas for romance, the story is almost certainly a myth since the only R. Paterson to be found in the record of births was 16 years old when the gutta was invented. A clockmaker named W. Smith of Musselburgh has also been credited with introducing the gutta but the evidence is scanty. But somebody invented the gutta and whoever he was he was more than a GOOD THING, he was the BEST THING that ever happened to golf. At that period, in the middle of the nineteenth century, golf was dying, kept alive by only a handful of enthusiasts who were wealthy enough to afford the prohibitively expensive featherie balls and the extravagant dining and carousing which were the essential elements of their golf.

The cheap gutta, which could be boiled up and remoulded when it became chipped or split, made the game available to all and golf enjoyed an unprecedented period of global and domestic expansion. We may couple this unknown benefactor with the name of Coburn Haskell, the Chicago dentist who invented a method of winding latex thread under tension around a central core and thus became a GOOD THING as the pioneer of the rubber-cored ball which greatly enhanced the pleasure and scope of golf.

The Earl of Eglington must be classified as a GOOD THING for golf. He was on the committee of Prestwick Golf Club and he proposed that it might be a jolly wheeze if the Club were to add an embellishment to its annual open amateur championship. At the end of play why not let the caddies have their own private championship? It might be amusing and even instructive, for some of them were known to be extremely skilled practitioners of the golfing arts. Of course they could not all play, because most of them were drunkards and ruffians, but we could invite a hand-picked selection of the more respectable ones, such as our own keeper of the green, Morris. There would probably be enough daylight for them to play three circuits of the green, 36 holes in all, and we could put up a prize, say a red Morocco belt with silver plates attached to it like the ones they give the champion prize-fighters.

The committee was persuaded and the inaugural tournament in 1860 was a great success in every respect but one. That name had to go. The following year the committee abandoned 'A General Golf Tournament for Scotland', threw open the championship to the entire world and called it the Open championship.

International golf was an obvious development waiting to happen but it was a long time coming. The American sisters Harriet and Margaret Curtis played in an unofficial match against the British ladies in 1905 and by unanimous acclaim the encounter was deemed to have been jolly super and they should jolly well do it again. For year after year the Curtis girls badgered the authorities and canvassed support for a formal Anglo-American match on a regular basis. In 1932 it came to fruition as the Curtis Cup match. By then George Walker and Sam Ryder had given their names to men's matches, amateur and professional. Down the years those founders have increasingly been recognized as GOOD THINGS for golf.

It was, or so I believe, at the spring meeting of the Royal & Ancient Golf Club of St Andrews in 1949 that the assembled company was astonished to observe Lord Brabazon of Tara bearing down on the first tee with his clubs strapped to a two-wheeled contraption. He called it a caddie car. These days we call it a trolley and it has proved to be one of the greatest boons to golf the game has known. Definitely a GOOD THING.

The time has now come to unscrew the top of the red ink bottle and address the debit side of the ledger, to identify – how can we put it? – those who would have rendered a profound service to golf had they only devoted all their energies and talents to the game of cricket. And greatly to my distress the first nominee as a BAD THING for golf has to be the same candidate who opened the bowling for the GOOD THING team, namely Jack Nicklaus.

He couldn't help it, goodness knows, because he became so tightly focused on the job in hand that he was unaware of everything else, including the passage of time. Thus, when faced with a 12-foot putt to clinch a major championship he surveyed the problem carefully from every point of the compass until he was satisfied that he had charted every undulation down to the last micro-millimetre. Then the texture of the projected line of approach had to be examined in minutest detail, including a census of the number of blades of poa annua grass. Having programmed his mental computer with the physical data he now had to rehearse the 10,000 or so nervous responses needed to take the putter head back five inches and reverse its direction through the ball. The only outward sign of this process was of Jack poised immobile over his putt for so long that his supporters feared that he might have been struck by paralysis or, like poor old Lot's wife, had been turned into a pillar of salt.

Eventually, after what seemed like a quarter of an hour holding this statuesque pose, the putter head moved very, very slowly away from the ball. Then, still in slow motion, the putter head returned and met the ball. The curious thing about this ponderous ritual was that the ball ran straight and true into the dead centre of the hole every bloody time.

The only outward sign of this process was of Jack poised immobile over his putt for so long that his supporters feared that he might have been struck by paralysis or, like poor old Lot's wife, had been turned into a pillar of salt.

It worked. Young golfers just setting out on their careers took note of every element in the Nicklaus routine and copied them slavishly. They started wearing sweaters adorned with the emblem of a bear. On the course they spent a lot of time standing by the ball and staring myopically into the distance. Kids who had routinely completed 18 holes in an hour and three-quarters now needed four hours and a bit. The tempo of golf was reduced to a turgid ponderoso.

Just as the speed of a convoy has perforce to be the speed of the slowest ship, so everyone in golf had to throttle back to a crawl because the pace of play was dictated by Nicklaus clones. And the curious thing about this phenomenon, which endured for a quarter of a century until a brash young Spaniard who had never even heard of Nicklaus burst among us and stood the game on its ear, was that those who aped the Nicklaus putting method never once, not in 25 years, holed out from 12 feet. The teachings of George Duncan had never penetrated the remotest region of Spain but young Seve acquired the 'Miss 'em quick' philosophy by himself. Golf had a new role model and another GOOD THING.

Tom Kidd experimented with ribbed clubs and the ones with which he won the first St Andrews Open championship in 1873 were reputedly suitable for grating nutmeg and parmesan cheese. What those wicked club faces did to the ball beggars the imagination but we can be sure of one thing – they imparted plenty of backspin. Kidd's clubs started a sorry saga which was to bedevil golf right up to the present day.

It would be unjust to label him a BAD THING simply because he pioneered a method of exploiting the ballistic possibilities of the golf ball to the full and in doing so gave himself a winning edge over his rivals. To a certain degree he was a GOOD THING. But his clubs set such a problem for the ruling bodies, who were totally unsuited to the task of legislating in this highly technical area, that the grooves issue festered for decades.

Eventually, back in the 1920s, the USGA called in an engineer named Anderson to devise a formula for the regulation of club-face grooves. He came up with the notorious formula (V-shaped grooves no wider than 0.035 inch, spaced at three times the width of the groove) which incorporated what I believe to have been a wicked hoax on the ruling bodies. The salient point about the Anderson formula, which he surely must have realized and, indeed, planned, was that clubs with these new grooves imparted an identical amount of backspin as clubs with perfectly smooth faces. In other words the formula lumbered golf with legislation involving useless technical gobbledegook for the sake of technical gobbledegook. He would have done the game a huge service if he had recommended that club-face markings be limited to decorative sand-blasting only. The playing characteristics would have been the same; the rule would have been easily understood and monitored; and golf would have been saved the ugliest episode in its history.

Anderson's formula introduced a climate of technical exploitation. Everyone knows what a golf club is, under the old definition of 'traditional form and make'. That was all the ruling bodies needed to control the introduction of undesirable features and if the prospective manufacturer challenged the authorities to justify their decision all they had to reply was, 'Your proposed club does not conform with the Rules of Golf because we say so.' The introduction of a technical specification opened the door to a search for loopholes.

The Anderson formula endured until Ping introduced clubs with square section grooves, for which legislation had made provision and which were perfectly legal. But not for long. The USGA brought in a new groove specification known as the 30-degree rule, resulting in a surge of messy litigation – which always must be designated a BAD THING. The rumpus caused the ruling bodies to become inhibited by the threat of litigation, hence the spate of such abominations as woods made of metal and 60-inch putters which are not even recognizable as golf clubs, let alone as being of traditional form and make.

Charles 'Steam Shovel' Banks is perhaps a slightly surprising candidate for inclusion in golf's Hall of Infamy because those who belong to clubs owning courses designed and built by Banks revere his memory as a genius. But in my book old Steam Shovel has a lot to answer for because, as his nickname implies, he loved to move earth, excavating hazards deeper than anyone ever before and elevating greens higher than anyone before.

What the world really wants is a good cheap golf course — and plenty of them so that everybody who would like to play golf can do so.

Previously the great architects such as Willie Park, Harry Colt, Donald Ross and A.W. Tillinghast were constrained by the limitations of a pair of shire horses and a scraping board. They couldn't move quantities of earth, even if they wanted to, and they had to let the landscape tell them how the holes should run. It was this ability to identify a golf hole or, more often, the natural site for a green, that marked their genius. Their courses are in perfect harmony with nature because for the most part they were shaped by nature.

The development of the steam shovel gave Banks an opportunity to improve, as he saw it, on nature. He could command mountains to rise and lakes to appear and he rather overdid it. When he was engaged to redesign Donald Ross' Whippoorwill club in New York State he was excavating a particularly deep lake on a site where nature had never intended a lake to be and the steam shovel sank slowly into the mush. The members believe it is still there under the fifth fairway, possibly continuing to sink ever deeper into the ecosystem.

As with some of the other pioneering figures on the debit side of golf's ledger, Banks was not himself a particularly BAD THING. He built courses which look decidedly odd and out of proportion but which are not without a certain charm. It was the people Banks influenced who condemned him retrospectively. Banks' zeal for the steam shovel spawned a school of golf course architects who saw themselves as landscape sculptors. They regarded a site as no more than a block of raw marble, to be hacked and chiselled into a creation of the designer's imagination. We might call them designers who knew better than God.

They vie with each other to produce ever more spectacular extravaganzas and see nothing incongruous in importing designer boulders made of cement on a wire frame because they look more realistic than the real boulders on the site. Ye gods!, they use them to create cascades and grottoes in the desert.

The cost of all this vulgarity is phenomenal, of course, and only millionaires can contemplate joining such clubs. It makes you feel that when the revolution comes the starving proletariat will start by storming the ornamental portals of these temples of bad taste. Worse, it makes you feel like joining the restive proletariat.

W.C. Fields was wrong when he said that what the world wanted was a good cheap cigar. What the world really wants is a good cheap golf course – and plenty of them so that everybody who would like to play golf can do so. Now wouldn't that be an item worth entering in the credit side of the ledger?

* Peter Dobereiner was the most civilised and erudite man ever to sit in a golfing press room. He was the warmest and wittiest too and as a writer was so good as to be the despair of his contemporaries. He completed this piece only days before he died, to length, with not a word needing to be altered.

CHAPTER 2

ARCHITECTURE

MOULDING THE LAND

DONALD STEEL

G OLF COURSE ARCHITECTURE IS LIKE WINE OR ART: everyone knows what they like but one of the problems – or joys – has always been the lack of agreement on what is good or bad, right or wrong.

In the beginning, courses evolved. What nature created, man adopted. Slowly, attempts were made to lay out courses by means of haphazard arrangements, although some arrangements were so haphazard as to be almost unfathomable. Nowhere was this truer than Old Prestwick on whose 12-hole course the first dozen Open championships were contested. As the cradle of championship golf, Prestwick's place in history is unique. It is a key part of the game's folklore but, in design terms, it became more an example of what not to do.

One look at the original plan reveals how easy it must have been to be sucked in to the crossfire of hooks and slices. In the days before statistics, the size of the crowds cheering Old and Young Tom was not revealed and it is not known how the spectators fared. Maybe they were more help than hindrance in signifying to the players when it was safe to hit but Old Prestwick's 12 holes could never have lasted long as a championship venue if the game were to expand – and expand it did.

Consciously or not, a degree of regularization in course layout became acknowledged as essential. It also became essential for strategic thought to be an ingredient of design, a quality more likely to be found in those who knew and studied the game. At first, the professionals – Old Tom Morris, Willie Fernie, Tom Dunn and Willie Park jnr – were regarded as the men with that knowledge, although the founders of clubs such as Royal St George's felt that they had the skill and the right to try their hand.

The more modest gave the credit to a higher power. General Moncrieffe's comment that Westward Ho! was a spot 'designed by Providence for a golf links' became a slogan oft repeated and another common remark was that 'anyone could lay out a good course on that piece of land'. It was first said of the old course at Sunningdale but before it was built the consensus was that only madmen could hope to grow grass on such barren wastes. Maybe, after all, golf course architecture is not as easy as it may appear.

Certainly, a fine site gives a head start and begs the question, how much does the picture owe to its frame? How would the holes of Pebble Beach sit if recreated in the setting of the Sahara? Would Gleneagles lose some of its gloss if reproduced on Hackney Marsh? An equally intriguing fantasy applies to the architects themselves. Would Harry Colt have made a better fist of Cypress Point than Alister MacKenzie? Could Pete Dye have improved on Pine Valley? What would Robert Trent Jones have made of Augusta? Would Donald Ross, given the benefits of modern machinery, have flouted his traditional principles?

The earliest golfers accepted what they found. They could do little else. The first form of the game was played across country with only agreed starting and finishing points, although some extra incentive was introduced on occasion by proceeding from 'pub to pub'. The next step was to confine the arena to the abundance of sandy wilderness around the coastline without which golf might never have taken off. The land known as links, furnished by sandhills and sparse vegetation, was ready made for a pursuit which demanded freedom of space. Its lack of fertility and unsuitability for agriculture, apart from grazing, meant that it had no more profitable use than golf, fuelling the argument that golf courses, properly managed, remain one of the best mediums for encouraging conservation.

When man did chance his arm at design, the results were disappointing. The blessings of nature were held to ransom. Courses looked stiffly unattractive, with tees like artificial gun platforms, mounds unshaped and greens geometric. In mitigation, there were no machines to work wonders but those early architects showed scant appreciation of the lessons of the links – although one penny to drop was that heavier soils are not as easy to mould and rake as sand and are a limiting factor in the quest for perfection.

Sand has always been the ideal foundation for golf but the biggest single influence in the game's development came with the realization that good courses could be built away from the coast and had to be to meet the demand fostered by the prosperity of the Victorian era in Britain. To the traditionalists, links golf remains the ultimate and it is inconceivable that the Open championship will ever contemplate a move inland. Its roots are still firmly entrenched in the fescues and other wild, wiry grasses that adorn the sand dunes. However, the diversion of courses away from the sea led to golf's emergence in other countries, notably America, and undoubtedly heralded the need for courses to be well designed, well built and well maintained. Golf course architecture as a career took off.

Greenkeeper

It's impossible to put an exact date on its birth but the 1890s saw the first surge in golf course building and the United States Golf Association was established in 1894. In 1898, Donald Ross arrived in Boston from Dornoch to embark upon the building of more than 500 courses over the next 50 years and Charles Blair Macdonald had already made something of a reputation for himself on the basis of what he had learned as a student at St Andrews University.

Familiarity with the Old Course at St Andrews was virtually a prerequisite for qualification as a golf course architect. Everybody worshipped at its shrine and was quick to preach its gospel. Macdonald's dedication to St Andrews and North Berwick even extended to producing replicas of some of their holes in his design of the National Golf Links on Long Island, which remains a monument to him. Duplication is no more innovative than copying paintings but likeness is harder to appreciate when surroundings are different. Many attempts have been made to reproduce the Road Hole at St Andrews but they are doomed to failure since nobody can repeat the famous background of the town. Nevertheless, knowledge of as many courses as possible is an essential part of any architect's education.

In the early days, there were fewer models with which to compare. St Andrews, Prestwick, North Berwick and Westward Ho! set the precedents but the first architects were men of invention as well as followers of the faith. They determined that golfers should display imagination, invention and improvization as well as skill if they were to be successful. They also encouraged

Familiarity with the Old Course at St Andrews was virtually a prerequisite for qualification as a golf course architect.

the need for tactical awareness and placed importance on the devising of a well considered strategy. Players had to explore the options and choose the right one to suit situation, mood, ability and the shot in hand.

Golf became a battle of wits, a test of manoeuvrability and an exercise in course management. Refinements were made by a more sophisticated approach to the design of greens – tilting, angling, bunkering them stoutly and contouring them to give advantage to those hitting second shots or pitches from the correct part of the fairway. Positional play was hailed as a virtue. Daring brought its rewards and its penalties.

Two schools of thought emerged. One favoured the penal code, which dictated the line of play and punished a player who strayed from it out of all proportion to the degree of error. The other school preferred the strategic approach, which offered options of varying difficulty and, while hampering the poor shot in subsequent play, rewarded the good one. It acknowledged, for instance, that running the gauntlet of a string of bunkers involved a risk but it launched two distinct attitudes: the greater the risk the greater the reward and let the punishment fit the crime. Spectacular, all-or-nothing holes did find their way into more conventional layouts but more as the exception than the rule. Variety and balance are vital considerations in any concept.

Slowly, some golf course architects became as well known as some of the players, although, in common with artists and composers, most became better known in retirement or after their death. Golf courses are every bit as enduring as paintings and symphonies and capable of giving just as much lasting pleasure. Certain architects had their trademarks but, with so much wonderful land to exploit, a general conformity of style began to be forged and reflected products of the highest quality. It also explained the prolific efforts of the pioneers – Colt, MacKenzie, Simpson, Fowler, Braid, Ross, Tillinghast, Mackenzie Ross and Alison. A number of the greatest courses were built as virtually single creations by Jack Neville, George Crump, the Fownes family and Hugh Wilson. Pebble Beach, Pine Valley, Oakmont and Merion are their masterpieces, examples of courses built by men with an eye for the main chance who then resisted the temptation to make a habit of designing, no doubt in the belief that perfection is hard to better.

Golf's popularity spread like a bush fire in the period between the First and Second World Wars very largely because the work of the architects proved so mouth-watering. They were fine ambassadors with a thorough understanding of the game. In a technical sense, too, they developed their knowledge, studying the species of grasses most suited to the climate and volume of play, learning the fundamental value of good drainage for greens and fairways, avoiding blind holes where possible and appreciating that courses were most likely to be popular if they were honest, straightforward and fair.

Golf course architecture became an alchemy of skills allied to acute powers of observation. Specialist, scientific advizers became an accepted part of a team on the basis of 'I don't know but I know a man who does.' However, greatness in an architect depends rather more upon subjects you cannot teach – intuition, imagination and an eye for land.

Tractor used in golf course construction, circa 1920.

Bobby Jones, who witnessed so much development, particularly in America, was more aware of this than any. 'No man learns how to design a golf course simply by playing golf, no matter how well,' he said, words that are frequently forgotten today, as more leading players put their names to multi-million pound ventures. Knowledge of playing courses, preferably under competitive conditions, is invaluable but Jones knew his place when he and Alister MacKenzie were creating Augusta. 'I think MacKenzie and I managed to work as a completely sympathetic team,' he wrote. 'Of course, there was never any question that he was the architect and I his advisor and consultant.'

Although Augusta and St Andrews have about as much in common as St Petersburg and Chalfont St Peter, there is no denying that the love that MacKenzie and Jones had for the Old Course shines through the more fertile acres of Augusta, which had been a nursery prior to becoming a golf course. It became a watershed in golf course architecture, highlighting wide, rolling fairways with plenty of uneven lies and stances, little or no rough, sparing use of bunkers, each exerting maximum impact. It

Golf's popularity spread like a bush fire in the period between the First and Second World Wars very largely because the work of the architects proved so mouth-watering.

also featured large, heavily rolling greens and strategic water features at intervals on the second nine, a stretch that has decided the fate of many a Masters tournament. In every way Augusta was a fashion setter and, in the thought behind its creation, Jones was ahead of his time.

It has taken colour television and a worldwide audience of the Masters every April to convey the message that beauty can be a desirable diversion if the climate allows – a big if – but it underlined the division that split architecture into two camps. The traditional 'leave-well-alone' approach versus the belief that you can – and should – use heavy machinery to transform the land and bring about improvement to nature. Augusta is a bit of both and for some this involved an apparent betrayal of the principles established by Ross and MacKenzie, whose names still prompt a high degree of forelock touching among modern architects in America and elsewhere.

Ross was referring to golf in his homeland of Scotland when he expressed the feeling that 'we can learn...by making our [American] courses less artificial, for the fascination of the most famous hazards in the world lies in the fact that they were not, and could not, have been constructed.' Perry Maxwell, an American architect of Scottish descent, put it this way, 'Nature must precede the architect in laying out the course. The site of a golf course must be there, not be brought there. In this way, it will have its own character, distinct from any other in the world. The less of man's handiwork, the better the course. Leave the earth where you find it and the tee where it lies.'

Those sentiments are the antithesis of those who proclaim that reshaping the land is the only way. There are architects who, given the Garden of Eden, would rip it apart and piece it together again in some totally unrecognizable form. Begging their pardon, it isn't always necessary but, like it or not, by the 1960s courses away from Europe became products of the bulldozer, irrigation systems and bottomless purses. In *Golf Architecture*, published in 1920, MacKenzie's first words were, 'Economy in course construction consists in obtaining the best results at the minimum of cost.' That is rarely the first thought nowadays and therein lies the fundamental difference between golf in America and golf in the British Isles: money.

British – and Irish – golf has always been accessible to the local pocket because there are so many simple courses working entirely with the existing land form. Many enjoy wild settings and are not manicured wall to wall but are built along sound, sensibly priced lines representing value for money. Clubhouses are comfortable and modest compared to the marble palaces that other golfing nationalities seek and take for granted. Overseas, golf is on an altogether more luxurious scale, a far cry from its humble beginnings.

Until fairly recently, only a handful of courses in Britain cost more than £1 million and even in the late 1990s good courses could still be built for far less than that. On some sites, heavy earth moving is the only means by which poor land can be transformed into something special and, in hot countries, it is a case of no irrigation, no golf course. That is fair enough. Advances in plant breeding have allowed miracles to be performed in refining grass

There are architects who, given the Garden of Eden, would rip it apart and piece it together again in some totally unrecognizable form.

when not so long ago coarse-bladed varieties of grass gave much poorer playing surfaces. Improved engineering techniques have led to mountains being moved, mangrove swamps drained, seas reclaimed and domestic refuse tips reinstated – all in the interests of golf.

Ignoring MacKenzie's entreaty, some architects seem to think only of how much they spend and by relying solely on the bulldozer, they have changed the face of golf. It is a case of applying a formula, excavating vast lakes and using the spoil to reconstruct the land and build hills and large bunkers, producing a sort of identikit picture with lavish accoutrements, expensive to build and to maintain. What is paid out has to be recouped. Heavy capital outlay, inflated by the bills for the chemicals and fertilizers essential in looking after such courses, has to be passed on to the customer. One of the reasons for building more courses is surely to allow more people to take up the game but courses costing millions take it out of the reach of the vast majority.

Other characteristics of expensive creations are total reliance on irrigation of fairways, tees and greens, leading to a clear lack of playing options and a resulting insistence that golf should be played through the air and never, except when putting, along the ground. That is absurd. Many modern golfers expect a computerized approach, fair, predictable, free of quirks, with no place for uneven lies or stances. Their dictionary has no entry under 'rub of the green.'

Much of this philosophy has been generated by advances in the manufacture of clubs and balls, which have gathered pace alarmingly in the last 25 years, although every generation of architect has faced the same threat. As long ago as 1905, John Low complained, 'The game has been waging a battle against the inventor. The one aim of the inventor is to minimize the skill required for the game.' It is certain that a brake must be applied sooner or later. Most clubs can no longer go on adding 20 or 30 yards to every hole to preserve the status quo.

Many years ago, Gerald Micklem, the wisest of golfing administrators, considered that the lawmakers had made a mistake in the 1930s in not limiting the width of the sole of iron clubs. No curb was invoked and the wedges and sand wedges have become so laid back that the best players perform miracles with them and getting down in two from everywhere is now a fact of golfing life. This talent has severely exercised the minds of those trying to combat it. With tight bunkering to give challenging pin positions on receptive greens, more emphasis has been placed on the aerial route to seek out small optimum landing areas. Complementing this trend has been a fashion for longer carries to greens, often over water.

A craving to make every new course of championship standard has saturated a market patronized largely by those who cannot handle even modest demands. The starting grid of Formula One isn't littered with learner drivers or the highest mountain with inexperienced climbers but near beginners at golf – happily attempting mission impossible – are rarely turned away from new courses. To compound the stupidity, they have been known to play from the championship tees. Losing a host of balls in lakes is not much fun and fuels the game's biggest problem of slow play but the plain truth is that, when championships are not being staged, which is 51 or even 52 weeks of the year, since there are not enough championships to go round, the so-called championship courses depend for their revenue on the handicap golfer.

However, all is not lost. Some architects in America have, with notable success, built new courses costing a tiny fraction of the monsters, although the puzzling economic question remains why developers feel happy paying vastly more than they need for a great course. Many modern players, too, express their approval when tournaments are played on more traditional courses, which give greater freedom and require more imagination in shot making. As with chefs indulging in cordon bleu cooking, some architects have been guilty of giving golfers what they think they ought to have rather than what they want and like.

Commercial interests, projects designed to sell real estate and the spread of the game to encourage tourism have helped to contribute to the modern style of architecture in which the bump and run shot is as rare as the foursome but sane voices are increasingly being raised in favour of what is tried, tested and enjoyed. Nick Price is one who is in favour of courses that offer options to players and enjoyed a round on a new course that afforded the liberty of skipping and running the ball on to the green. 'A lot of architects forget that the majority of people don't carry the ball through the air like professionals,' he said. 'You have to give them an opportunity to run the ball through to the greens. I've never felt you should penalize somebody for hitting a straight shot even if it is along the ground. If the golfer has hit the fairway, that's what the fairway is for.'

In days gone by, British courses with water features were very few and far between. Nowadays, they are the rule rather than the exception on modern courses. In the right place and not overdone, lakes can be attractive visual and playing features as well as habitats for wildlife but they are not a natural part of some landscapes. Ideally, they should never double as water storage, although practical reservoirs can be built specially for the purpose. Many modern courses, manufactured entirely artificially, make preposterous promotional claims that they are the work of nature.

Natural courses, blending with the surroundings, are much more likely to please the environmentalists – an increasingly important consideration – and architectural styles may have to change in the new millennium, with reverberations through the whole golfing world. Fears over pollution levels could see a ban on the use of fungicides and severe limits imposed on the application of fertilizers. Coupled with that could be stringent rationing of water supply, confining what is available to greens and tees. In certain areas, fairway irrigation would be out of the question. Revisions in course management and design will be inevitable. There will be a return to old-fashioned methods of maintenance, with firm, dry and running conditions obtaining once more.

Modern greenkeeping equipment has revolutionized the art of course maintenance.

Construction and design methods will have to keep in step in order to keep courses playable during dry periods. Courses that rely heavily on water to make greens receptive to high shots may become impossible. Also, heavily watered greens are more susceptible to disease and, without fungicides, cures could prove impossible. In construction, high percolation rates may have to be compromised in favour of increased water retention. This could mean a move away from the more sterile soils, which demand nutrients, being 'force-fed', which in turn leads to more chemicals and fungicides being used to thwart disease. The architectural upshot of that could be a return to firmer approaches and wider entrances to greens – the traditional style, no less.

The dramatic improvement in scoring over the last 30 years has been a consequence of several factors: a higher standard of teaching; much greater fitness; equipment which allows the ball to be hit so much farther; and improved levels of greenkeeping, which give players no excuse for poor performance. Better scoring is reflected among professionals, good amateurs and club golfers. Qualifying scores in professional tournaments nowadays would have been good enough to lead the field not so long ago. Generally speaking, golf course architects are happy if their secrets are unlocked by the leading players playing at their best – provided that there are penalties to pay if they are not. Preventative architecture is nothing to be admired, although it must be said that architects are very much in the hands of those responsible for presenting a course for a major event. Too much rough, rock hard and lightning quick greens surrounded by thick collars and often absurd pin positions are the weapons with which committee men can – and do – fuel the fury and frustration of competitors and architects alike.

Having witnessed how Tiger Woods demolished Augusta National and a distinguished field so comprehensively in the 1997 Masters, the compelling and pertinent question is where will it all end? Can we allow courses to become 8500 yards long and will it be necessary if advances in the manufacture of equipment remain unchecked? If that is the case, what about all those established courses, which long ago were stretched to their last inch? We can't say we weren't warned. In Martin Sutton's *Book of the Links*, published in 1911, there was a cartoon lamenting 'the steadily increasing length achieved from the continued improvements in the modern golf ball.' It was amusing, exaggerated – and proved eerily prophetic. It showed two golfers in imitation buggies viewing a hole of one mile 293 yards through a telescope, with one saying to the other, 'Did you hit yours well, old chap?' 'Not very,' came the reply, 'but I think I'm on the green.'

If there are similar advances over the next 80 to 100 years, will they be good for the game and how can they be accommodated? Those are the challenges for the golf course architects of the 21st century.

*Donald Steel, now an international golf course architect was, for almost 30 years, the golf correspondent of the *Sunday Telegraph*. He has also been president and chairman of the British Institute of Golf Course Architects and has designed and built more than 50 courses in more than a dozen countries.

THE GREENING OF A DESERT

At first sight, golf and the desert seem an unlikely mix, if not a contradiction in terms – after all golf courses need grass, which needs water, which is not a desert speciality. However the greening of the desert continues apace particularly in literal hotbeds of the game such as

Arizona and the Palm Springs area, with courses springing up as fast as the grass can grow. In the desert, paradoxically, that's pretty fast. Providing there's enough water, the growing conditions are ideal: plenty of heat and good sandy soil.

Tom Weiskopf, who's an acknowledged whiz at building courses in the desert, said that it was a 'pretty simple place' and listed some of the rules.

• You cannot have a lake or lakes any bigger than 2.5 acres of surface area. So that means the golf course for the most part is void of water.

• You cannot drain into the desert. You must drain into the natural washes – that's to preserve the desert plants, they cannot accept too much water.

• You always start construction in the fall, for grassing in the spring- and summer-time. You use, in the higher elevations, over 2000 feet, bent grass greens. Probably better off under 2000 feet with Bermuda grass greens because of the heat ...

• You're required to try to save as many plants as possible when you clear and then relocate 'em.

Weiskopf, who has lived in the Phoenix area since 1977, has several highly regarded courses to his credit, notably Troon North, which is in the foothills of the high desert north of Scottsdale, Arizona. Weiskopf's philosophy is 'traditional golf', albeit in an untraditional place, something he achieves by what he calls 'strategy'. He and his fellow desert designers in the upper reaches are blessed with terrain that is anything but flat and boring. The landscape is all rolling hills and mountains and one of the most distinctive features is the magical saguaro cactus, a potent symbol of the rugged southwest and Arizona's state flower. It is the mighty oak of the desert and can be up to 50 feet tall and 200 years old. It is protected now but in the past was likely to be ripped up and replaced by a palm tree.

There are plenty of flat, Floridian-style, lake-and-palm courses in Phoenix, many of them perfectly playable and highly lucrative. They were built in the days when greens were for putting on, urban sprawl belonged back east and the only definition of a desert golf course was a course in the desert. Desert golf is now very different, a unique experience dictated by environmental concerns. It is target golf, with players hitting from one piece of grass to another, among the rocks and plants.

Things started to change in the late 1970s and early 1980s, when the Arizona Department of Water Resources came into being, essentially to look into ways of saving water or, at least, of using it more wisely. Paul

McGinnis was president of the Golf Course Superintendents Association of America in 1997–8 and is a native of Arizona. He has spent his whole career working in the desert and was on the first Department of Water Resources committee. It was an eye-opener for everyone.

'I'll never forget the first day,' McGinnis recalled. 'Their answer to golf courses was going to be to flood-irrigate. Two days a week you'd open big valves on the course and put a foot of water all over it, so it would be unplayable for a couple of days, way too wet for another couple, good for a couple of days, then you'd irrigate it again … We had to educate them about what the turf needed and the golfer expected. We had to tell them they'd put golf right outa business.' Instead, golf has flourished and is one of the mainstays of the economy in the Valley of the Sun.

McGinnis conceded that there was a lot of education both ways. 'We really fought against any restriction because we didn't think we could do it at first,' he said, 'but in some ways the law really helped us in that it made us more conscious of where we were putting the water down and how much.' They commissioned research to find out just how much water a grass plant needed to survive and discovered that it was a lot less than they thought – at McGinnis' course at the time he cut the water by 30 per cent and the turf didn't suffer. Courses are now restricted to 90 acres of turf and many use a lot less because there are also strict

Desert Highlands

limitations on the amount of water a course can use per year.

All in all, the need for restrictions, initially resented, proved beneficial because they made people think. The Phoenix area averages seven inches of rainfall a year and the foot-hills area of Scottsdale, where a lot of the newer courses are, averages 10–11 inches. Research, development and experience have produced highly sophisticated irrigation and watering systems at the newer courses (which all adds to the cost of each course – US$1 million would be a fair estimate). Space satellites monitor the weather during the day and tell the computer system, to the precisest decimal point, how much water it will need that night. The grass itself has come under the minutest scrutiny – bent, Bermuda and rye no longer remotely exhaust the possibilities – and resilient, warm-season varieties are being developed.

Desert golf is now very different, a unique experience dictated by environmental concerns. It is target golf, with players hitting from one piece of grass to another, among the rocks and plants.

Water and the sharing thereof tend to be emotive issues in the desert, and there are those who see golf courses as playgrounds for the wealthy, undeserving of any consideration when it comes to doling out a precious resource. It's a potentially fraught situation but at least the golfing fraternity recognized the need to curb its greater excesses and has gone to great lengths – with the encouragement of legislation – to adapt to its surroundings. There are still courses that are 'a waste of a perfectly good desert' – the immortal words of a visiting Scot, frustrated beyond measure by his inability to land his ball on the odd patch of grass available – but there are plenty of others that provide a fair challenge in a unique and beautiful setting.

One man who has developed more desert than most is Lyle Anderson, the property developer who persuaded Jack Nicklaus to build courses in the desert. Desert Highlands was their first project together and their flagship is Desert Mountain, which features five courses in spectacular, saguaro-studded country and hosts the Tradition, one of the major championships on the Senior PGA Tour.

'We were innovative,' Anderson said, 'and we were very, very water-conservative in our designs. We were the first ones to develop what is now known here as desert golf and we helped pioneer the guidelines that everyone now has to adhere to, like moving plants and limitations on water usage.

'At Desert Highlands, we used anywhere from a half to a third of the amount of water of any other golf course in the state. We created a better design and used water much more efficiently. We limited the amount of acreage we put into turf and designed irrigation systems that make sure the areas to be watered were areas of turf. We kept our water on our fairways, drained our sides and didn't water the desert. The philosophy was to create an oasis in the desert and it's very crisply delineated, very focused and very sharp. You have this contrasting landscape architecture, which I think looks very beautiful.

'The bottom line is that we have probably been as responsible for the conservation of water as any company in Arizona. We're very proud of that. Originally our water came from underground wells and then we converted over to treated sewage effluent. We got a 20-mile line that cost US$14 million built up here and it solved a problem the City of Scottsdale had with what to do with their treated water. We found a very good place for it – the golf courses – and we gave the city our well water for domestic purposes. Everybody wins, including the environmental concerns.'

However, if you're using up to one million gallons of water a day on your golf course, which is the case at the height of summer, it doesn't matter that golf uses a tiny fraction of the water consumed by agriculture, it is still a sensitive issue. Golf contributes a lot of money to the economy, directly and indirectly, but despite the fact that more than 300,000 spectators swarm to watch the Phoenix Open each year, there are still plenty of people in Arizona who don't play golf,

It is prime territory for wildlife and since the early 1990s the USGA has been committed to environmental research.

don't appreciate it and have no desire to see more courses with the inevitable attendant housing.

Golf has its élitist image – in Arizona, play in general is not cheap and courses are expensive to build – but all over the world the realization is growing that golf can, indeed should, enhance the environment. As Anderson pointed out, the desert is a pretty arduous place and probably only a few hikers saw much of it before the courses were built. Now people go for the golf and leave with a much better appreciation of the desert. Another bonus is that the wildlife is healthier and more prolific than ever – because of the availability of water. Coyote, javelina (wild pig), wild boar, jackrabbits, deer, the odd mountain lion, even black bear are thriving and, of course, the rattlesnakes. If they are found on the course, they are scooped up – using a long pole with a noose at the end of it – and returned to the desert, where they keep the rodent population in check.

Such considerations will not pacify those who believe that golf has no place in the Sonoran desert but as environmentalists learn more about golf – and vice versa – they realize that it is not necessarily the monster they once thought. In the early 1990s, Robert Trent Jones jnr, a golf course architect from a family of golf course architects, wrote about his concern that the so-called 'Environmental Movement' had targeted golf for capital punishment. 'They can make a golf course sound like a toxic waste dump … We need to shout loudly that golf is the absolute preservation of open space, an animal habitat, a bird sanctuary and a permanent green belt area.'

There are around 15,000 golf courses in the United States, occupying roughly 1.5 million acres of habitat and on a typical course about 70 per cent of the land is rough or non-fairway. It is prime territory for wildlife and since the early 1990s the USGA have been committed to environmental research, funding studies into improving grass conditions, the use of non-chemicals to control pests, the effects of pesticides and fertilizers and many more. They have taken a lead in encouraging courses to nurture their natural resources, establishing programmes with bodies like the Audubon Society (birds) and the National Fish and Wildlife Foundation.

'We had to educate them about the turf needed and the golfer expected. We had to tell them they'd put golf right outa business.' Instead, golf has flourished and is one of the mainstays of the economy in the Valley of the Sun.

A few years ago Friends of the Earth and the USGA would have been an unlikely if not unimaginable combination but they and other groups came together in January 1995, at the first Golf and the Environment Conference at Pebble Beach. Few new projects are undertaken without an ecologist on the team, even if the site is less than sensitive and lacks a potential cause célèbre such as the natterjack toad, lizard orchid, turtle or red-cockaded woodpecker.

The R&A have become more environmentally aware and have tried to encourage improvements to the condition of courses in Britain and Ireland after a tendency to over-water and over-fertilize caused problems and raised costs. The Augusta factor has undoubtedly played a part, with people lusting after similarly vibrant green fairways and immaculate greens at home. They forget that millions of dollars are poured into the maintenance of Augusta National and the course is closed from May to

October. Even in Arizona, they have learned that turf and golf are both better a little on the dry side and are thinking of allowing courses to brown out a bit, of cutting back on the watering at certain times of year and allowing nature to take its course. For most courses in the UK, especially during the summer, shades of brown and yellow should be regarded as the norm and not an aberration caused by the greenkeeper's incompetence.

Such measures require members with a sound understanding of the principles involved – and that is a stumbling block, since course maintenance is a combination of science and art imperfectly understood by most golfers. The job encompasses a lot more than just cutting the grass and raking the bunkers but the inclination is to

Golf has its élitist image – in Arizona, play in general is not cheap and courses are expensive to build – but all over the world the realization is growing that golf can, indeed should, enhance the environment.

interfere – any farmer or gardener thinks he knows all there is to know about looking after land. Far too often the greenkeeper is not even on the greens committee, when he should head it or, ideally, be the committee of one.

Changing old ingrained habits is never easy but initiatives like the 'Committed to Green' campaign launched at the 1997 Ryder Cup at Valderrama hope to dig away at the intransigent and the indifferent. There are more than 5,000 golf courses in Europe and the campaign, which was developed by the ecology unit of the European Golf Association, with support from the R&A, the PGA European Tour and the European Commission, is aimed at persuading them all to improve their environmental performance with a little thought, effort and good management.

Simon Barnes, the golf-loathing sports columnist of *The Times*, described golf courses as 'the airport lounges of landcape architecture', but by their very nature courses should be models of good environmental practice. Admittedly, there will be clashes, as P.G. Wodehouse pointed out perceptively in *Ordeal by Golf*. 'If golf has a defect,' he wrote, 'it is that it prevents a man being a whole-hearted lover of nature. Where the layman sees waving grass and romantic tangles of undergrowth, your golfer beholds nothing but a nasty patch of rough from which he must divert his ball. The cry of the birds, wheeling against the sky, is to the golfer merely something that may put him off his putt.'

CHAPTER 3

THE
POLITICS
AND THE FUTURE

G OLF – OR AT LEAST THE AMATEURS who make up 99.9 per cent recurring of the game – is ruled for the most part by a few professional administrators and a polyglot collection of amateurs who give willingly of enormous amounts of their time to help cover the game's myriad aspects. The United States Golf Association (USGA) and the Royal and Ancient Golf Club of St Andrews (R&A) between them cover the globe, with the USGA responsible for America and Mexico, and the R&A the rest.

In general terms they do a good job, although not as good as they think they do and certainly not as good as needs to be done. There are crevices appearing in the game that are widening into cracks and could become canyons unless dealt with and both sets of authority are being stretched to the limit.

What was once a recreation, ruled by benevolent consent, is now a huge business, subject to the same conditions and constraints as the multi-national companies. Where once the R&A or USGA writ ran automatically, it is now being challenged by companies with shareholders to satisfy who see any restriction on their activities as being unfair or unjust or both. There is much talk of legal challenges and of who has the deepest pockets to sustain those challenges.

And while all this may be regrettable, it was inevitable once the game began to boom as it has done since the end of the Second World War. Millions of players have been attracted to golf by the fact of television bringing it into their living rooms, by the presence of charismatic characters like Arnold Palmer and Severiano Ballesteros, by the emergence of the most successful golfer of all time, Jack Nicklaus, and by developments in club technology that have made the game more manageable for the average player.

THE EQUIPMENT REVOLUTION

Golf is now a distinctly more pleasurable activity for the majority than it was even thirty years ago and particularly for the club hacker. This is because of technological developments in golf balls and clubs, which have made the former longer-lasting and the latter easier to use.

Anyone who played golf in the fifties and sixties will remember how easy it was to destroy a ball. One topped shot meant a deep cut in the cover and a ball that was immediately useless. Often even a slightly thinned shot was enough to dent the cover and anything less than a perfectly executed bunker shot left the ball grazed. Now most balls will survive the harshest of treatment and remain playable. Once, at the Open at Royal Birkdale in 1991, Sandy Lyle's caddie, Dave Musgrove, showed a group of reporters the ball with which his boss had just completed a round in the championship and it was indistinguishable from one freshly out of its sleeve.

Similarly, golf clubs have become so much more sophisticated that it is now possible to hit a ball off the toe or the heel of the club and see it fly as if struck properly. It will not go as far, of course, but it will go nearly as far and it will at least look like a golf shot. At such moments golfers should breathe a silent prayer of thanks to Karsten Solheim, the man who created the Ping empire and developed perimeter weighting, which is the reason those suspect shots look genuine.

If technology stopped at that point – helping club golfers look better than they are – then there would be no cause for the concerns that have frightened the authorities to death during the last years of the millennium. But the fact is that the golfing world is changing at the same rapid pace as the real world, with high-tech developments affecting every nook and cranny of the game.

The major area of concern is, naturally, the equipment and the greatest fear is that space-age clubs are sending supersonic balls so far that golf courses are being overpowered and rendered redundant. That these are substantial fears can be seen by the fact that golf clubs as steeped in tradition as St Andrews and Augusta National have both, in the years 1995 and 1998 respectively, lengthened their courses in an attempt to cope with some of the huge hitting now on show.

Good young players like Tiger Woods and the Spanish phenomenon Sergio Garcia hardly know what it is like to be less than 300 yards from the tee if hitting a full driver shot and in favourable conditions drives of 330-350 yards are not uncommon. When Woods left the amateur ranks, his first act as a professional was to smash his opening tee shot 336 yards – an impressive statement of intent.

But while the USGA and the R&A can just about stomach developments so far, they are clearly, and rightly, worried about what may be around the corner. If there is a material out there for the shaft of the club, or the head, or for the core of the ball, which will enable players to hit the ball 10-20 per cent further without any extra effort, then a lot of golf courses are going to be ruined, in no good cause.

Bunkers meant to penalize a drive will be flown, holes that are meant to be played with a long iron second will need only a nine or so and the size, shape and contours of the greens themselves will be all wrong. In short, nothing other than a complete re-vamping of thousands of courses, at unimaginable expense, would do.

What, in essence, the authorities are worrying about is that there may be a successor to a metal like titanium, which they have okayed and which is one of the incredible success stories of recent years. Titanium is a metal which is present in the sun, the moon, in meteorites and in the stars. It is, in its original, a lustrous silver-

What titanium has done is enable clubheads to be made bigger without being heavier and, as a result, a larger sweetspot has been created.

white metal with a very high tensile strength which makes it suitable as a substance for aircraft, space craft, guided missiles and as armour plate for tanks.

None of that suggests a re-incarnation as a metal for golf clubs, but when its suitability was realized, it took off – like a rocket. A company called Coastcast decided to make titanium golf club heads and the first was cast in August 1995 from the only furnace capable of the work. A second furnace was on stream by December; by March 1996 there were three more and by the end of the year there were eight in total. Such was the demand that by early 1997 Coastcast were melting and pouring 7,000,000 pounds of titanium, enough for 2.5 million clubheads per year.

What titanium has done is enable clubheads to be made bigger without being heavier and, as a result, a larger sweetspot has been created. That in turn reduces the need to hit the ball as expertly and as exactly as previously to get the same, or even better, results, and the authorities fear that if there is another development of the same proportions, then the game will be changed radically.

The R&A and the USGA feel that the game as we know it needs to be protected and that dramatic improvements in the standard of an individual golfer should be through practice and perseverance and not the ability to go to the pro and be able to afford the latest technology, i.e. to be able to 'buy' shots in the shop.

Perhaps the biggest concern of the authorities at the moment is what is called 'the trampoline effect.' This is a reference to what happens at the moment of impact with the huge metal-headed drivers and fairway clubs now available, which, the manufacturers claim, give the player added distance. This is a complex, scientific subject and is best explained, in layman's terms – well, comparatively – by Frank Thomas, the technical director of the USGA. This is what he wrote in the inaugural edition of *Golf Science International*, in April 1999.

'When a golf club hits a golf ball, the face of a wooden clubhead does not deform very much. Most of the deformation is in the ball which squeezes down to about two thirds of its free standing diameter. This deformation in the ball and its recovery back to the original diameter when it leaves the clubface is not a perfect bounce, sometimes referred to as "not perfectly elastic." This means there is some loss of energy during impact.

'To explain what "perfectly elastic" is we need to introduce the term "Coefficient of Restitution" (COR). This is a measure of the resilience of the collision between two objects. If for example a ball is thrown at a huge steel block at 100mph and it bounces back at 100mph then the efficiency of this collision is perfect and has a COR of 1.0.

'This does not happen in real life. The bounce back speed is always somewhat less than the incoming speed. For a golf ball the COR is approximately 0.75, which means that a ball fired into that steel block at 100 mph would bounce back at about 75mph.

'When a wooden club travelling at 110mph hits a ball the speed at which the ball leaves the club is about 160.5mph. The clubhead slows down during impact and is travelling at about 76mph after impact. The ball and clubhead remain in contact for only a fraction of a second (in fact only 1/200th of the time it takes to blink your eyes). The speed of the ball is faster than the initial clubhead speed because it was squashed against the face of the club and bounces off the club which is still moving forward during and after impact.

'Now, when we examine some of the latest large titanium heads with relatively thin faces, we find that on impact the face flexes and recovers at the same time the ball is recovering. This is known as the trampoline, or spring-like effect. The ball leaves the large titanium clubhead faster than it would off a wooden club, even though the two clubheads are the same weight and travelling at the same speed.

'The collision between the titanium clubhead and the ball has a COR of 0.82. This is more efficient than the collision between the wooden clubhead and the ball and as a result the ball speed is faster, about 165mph. The speed of the titanium clubhead after impact is about 74.8mph, which is lower than that of the wooden head. This means that there is more energy transferred to the ball. In distance terms there is an increase of around ten yards or more.'

By their various utterances during 1998 and 1999, the USGA seem able to accept this latest development but reiterate constantly that there must be safeguards laid down and enforceable to prevent some future metal providing another 10 yards, or 20 or 30.

For instance, while both the USGA and the R&A were still deliberating on what form their regulations would take, a company called Liquidmetal came to the market with some hugely expensive golf clubs. They proposed to charge over £3,000 for a set of eight irons, a driver and two putters, all of them made with Liquidmetal. The company claimed that this was the first new metal to be found in a generation and that 'it moves golf technology forward by a quantum leap.'

The metal, discovered in 1991 and hitherto used for aerospace purposes, is made up of nickel, zirconium, titanium, copper and beryllium and, say the company, 'is twice as strong as either titanium or stainless steel.' And what does it do? 'Due to its unique atomic structure,' they say, 'Liquidmetal absorbs less energy on the clubhead surface but transfers more energy to the ball. This...propels the ball straighter and further.'

It has been ever thus. Golf balls have been propelled straighter and further since golf clubs began to propel them and while, for the most part, the straightness and the distance have just been gleams in the eye of the advertizer, now there seems to be some scientific justification for the claims.

Not surprisingly the manufacturers, for whom making better clubs/balls is their whole raison d'etre, are reluctant either to be restrained from so doing, or even to be reined in. The point was made, with eloquence, at the World Scientific Congress of Golf at St Andrews in 1998 – 'approved and grant-aided by the R&A' – by Wally Uihlein, known in the trade as Mr Titleist. Uihlein is the chief executive officer and president of Acushnet, owners of Titleist (balls), Cobra (clubs) and Footjoy (shoes and clothing) and he made a powerful speech, interlarded with compelling figures.

Earlier in 1998 Buzz Taylor, the president of the USGA, had said that he and his fellows felt that 'the skill of today's players, in concert with high-tech, custom-fitted equipment would combine to threaten obsolescence of many of the game's historic venues.' Taylor was also the man who said that the USGA's franchise was 'to preserve and protect the game's ancient and honourable traditions' adding that 'there is no lawyer in the world who is going to stand in the way of our doing that.' The manufacturers pricked up their ears when they heard the word 'lawyer' and said that surely he meant lawyers, plural.

From what many of the leading manufacturers have said on the subject, (people like Ely Callaway, John Solheim and Uihlein) they would certainly be prepared to go to court if they felt that their right to research and develop, and then trade, was being in any way restricted.

Uihlein perhaps summed up their feelings at St Andrews. He first of all took the statistics from the 1998 US Open and then poured scorn on Taylor's assertion that venues could become obsolete. He said: 'The Olympic club in San Francisco certainly qualifies as one of the game's historic venues. In the three previous times the club has hosted the US Open the winning scores were a seven-over par 287 in 1955, two-under par 278 in 1966 and three-under par 277 in 1987. The winning score in 1998 was Lee Janzen's 280, level par.'

He went on: 'The average driving distance for the week at Olympic 1998 was just over 262 yards, compared to the 247 yards in 1987. While this six per cent increase over 11 years certainly seems to support the notion that today's players hit the ball further, a gain of slightly more than one yard per year hardly seems like end-of-the-world stuff.'

Uihlein looked at the overall scoring, too, and produced figures which demonstrated that there had been a slight decline, if anything, in standard. 'In other words,' he went on, 'when you take the greatest players in the world and arm them with the latest and greatest products from Satan's den of development, the week's results hardly support the idea of imminent apocalypse.'

Uihlein could, and did, mention other factors. Men are literally bigger and certainly better trained than they were even 20 years ago. They are hitting to better-mown and better drained fairways, too; was it any wonder, he seemed to be saying, that the ball was going further?

Golf balls have been propelled straighter and further since golf clubs began to propel them and while, for the most part, the straightness and the distance have just been gleams in the eye of the advertizer, now there seems to be some scientific justification for the claims.

So what of the figures arrived at by Frank Thomas, which seemed to prove that the ball was going significantly further when struck by titanium rather than wood? Surely that merits further investigation? Uihlein would have none of it. 'The USGA,' he said, 'have yet to identify any harm to the game of golf caused by technology....they are moving away from what happens on the golf course to what happens in the testing laboratories, which does not correlate to the game as it is played.'

Of course, he would say that. And the authorities would refute it, saying that you can't argue with proven scientific facts. Which leads to the questions, are metal woods desirable in the first place and can you put a cap on progress? Should the game be freeze-framed as it stands or is there room for more research and development? And what happens if some future 'moon metal' club appears which drives the ball 400 yards dead straight every time, even when wielded by an elderly spinster?

The first thing to be said is that the club golfer has voted overwhelmingly with his/her pocket. They have gritted their teeth, nicked the holiday money and paid outrageous sums for the metal drivers on offer. The evidence can be heard at courses all round the world, where the harsher clang of titanium on ball has replaced the satisfying clunk of persimmon.

In fact the new drivers are so popular that they have attracted the attention of those who run the sweat-shops in Taiwan and make huge profits by producing counterfeit clubs that look like, and are labelled like, top quality clubs, but are in fact seriously deficient. Because Callaway have been so successful recently they have been the company most targeted by the pirates, and they have retaliated by pursuing the matter through the police. In February 1999 a US Customs 'sting', codenamed 'Project Teed Off' resulted in the arrest of 12 people and two months later three raids on separate factories were carried out in Taiwan itself.

Over 1,000 counterfeit 'Callaway Golf' golf club components were seized by officials of the Investigation Bureau of the Ministry of Justice, the department responsible for the enforcement of intellectual property laws in Taiwan. A month after that a major golf club counterfeiter was located and raided, producing over 500 metal woods fully assembled, with a further 800 ready for assembly. With counterfeit shafts, bags, gloves, headcovers and grips, the total value of the goods seized came to over US$4 million.

Paramor believes change should be introduced slowly, inch by inch, and to do that 'You have to limit how fast the ball comes off the clubface.'

But such popularity does not necessarily make it right. Should the latest technology be a case of so far and no further? The manufacturers point out in their advocacy of unfettered progress that in measurable terms sports men and women are running faster, jumping higher, leaping longer, all of which is undoubtedly true. If you cap progress, they say, the game stagnates and a stagnating game is quickly a dead one.

But there are some practical problems involved here, as well. No matter how fast they are run, the 100 metres or the 10,000 metres, remain the same distance. There is no need for physical expansion of the stadium. But if club and ball development really does continue at the present rate, can our golf courses accommodate the results of new technology? What if, in the next breakthrough, Liquidmetal is made to look like plasticine? That would totally change the game we know and love and would it still be worth playing?

John Paramor, the European Tour's chief referee, has been involved in administering the game and invoking its rules for nearly 25 seasons and has seen the game's incredible expansion, both numerically and technically. He is for 'progress' but against 'change.'

He says: 'I don't think anybody wants to stop golf dead in its tracks and say "Right, this is the most you're ever going to have" because that is not progress. But I think that everybody who really feels for the game doesn't want it to change. Yes, let golf progress and let equipment changes progress but not change. The sort of progress made over the past 10 years is almost change and that is what I don't think anyone wants to see who loves the game.

'Golf balls are being hit further, there's no question about it. I think drivers have become more forgiving, they hit the ball straighter. We all remember the old persimmon wood and the mishits that went nowhere. Now a mishit with these big titanium-headed drivers is still going 230 yards.'

Paramor believes change should be introduced slowly, inch by inch, and to do that 'You have to limit how fast the ball comes off the clubface.' However, that would not be popular with the manufacturers. He adds: 'It's not in the best interests of the manufacturers to destroy the game. But their business is selling golf clubs, making golf clubs which we are going to go down to our pro's shop and buy. I just say that I would like Mr Callaway, together with Mr Ping, Mr Titleist, Mr MacGregor, Mr TaylorMade, Mr Wilson and Mr Mizuno to continue to make their golf clubs and improve them bit by bit but not suddenly come out with some material that's been found on the moon – which hits a ball five to six per cent further – because that unfortunately will change the game.'

For Jack Nicklaus, the distance the ball goes is the key to all the game's evils. He has long held the belief that the answer to the problems of course obsolescence in professional golf is simply to make a tournament ball, one used exclusively by professionals, which goes between five to eight per cent shorter than the current balls. He uses as ammunition the fact that for the first 10 years of the tournament he created, the Memorial, held annually at Muirfield Village, no one broke 280. That was between 1976 and 1985. Since then, every winner has been below that mark and in 1994 Tom Lehman was 20-under par, 268, while the following year Greg Norman won with 19-under.

Scores like that offend the course designer in Nicklaus, particularly when done on a course he has designed. He was not much enamoured of things when John Huston knocked it round in 61 to create a new course record and he could hardly believe some of the strokes played by the European Ryder Cup team – and in particular Sandy Lyle – when they went there and won in 1987.

Nicklaus had specifically designed the par fives at Muirfield Village to be unreachable in two. At the 11th Lyle was able to get up with an iron for his second, ditto the 15th. Nicklaus was aghast, and said so. He believes a shorter ball is necessary not just to save the golf courses but also to ensure that tournaments are not won by players hitting driver/wedge to all the par fours and even some of the par fives. 'The farther the ball goes,' he says, 'the harder it becomes to separate the best from the rest. All players need do now is develop their driving, pitching and putting, which is not golf as we know it.'

THE BROOMHANDLE

The fusty threat of the courtroom hangs over another issue facing the R&A and the USGA. During the latter's unavailing fight with Ping over the allegedly illegal grooves issue there arose the long putter issue which, because the authorities were consumed with the grooves problem, was passed over.

But there can be no doubt that the long putter does not conform to the authorities' own definition of what is a golf club, a definition contained in the Rules of Golf (4-1a). This states that the club 'shall not be substantially different from the traditional and customary form and make...' The long putter very obviously does not fall within that definition and furthermore it offends against another Rule (14-1) which says that the ball 'shall be fairly struck at with the head of the club and must not be pushed, scraped or spooned.'

The long putter is customarily anchored around the chest or the

Sam Torrance was one of the first exponents of the broomhandle technique.

chin with one hand and hangs down in a straight line to the ball. It is then drawn back with the other hand, the clubface returns to the ball, which is despatched in the general direction of the hole.

But the argument is that this club, totally unlike any other which is deemed legal, is capable of a pendulum effect; that once it is aligned with the hole then it is only necessary to draw it back and the clubface will return to the ball of its own accord. Clearly there is skill involved in determining the right line and how hard the ball needs to be hit, but in no sense does the long putter require a 'stroke' as determined by the Rules.

There are now belated moves being made to get rid of this cuckoo in the nest but because it has been allowed for so long, and because the careers of some professional golfers and the enjoyment of the game of some amateurs, depend on their being able to use it, there is an absolute certainty of lawyers becoming involved if the long putter is unilaterally, and immediately, banned.

The probable solution will be an extended 'grandfathering' of the club. This is a period when its use will continue to be legal and after which it will become illegal. It will need to be extensive, though, because seniors golf now offers the prospect of a much longer career for all classes of golfer.

THE 'PROFESSIONAL' AMATEUR

Then there is the question of amateur status. How much longer can golf continue with separate sections, run by differing bodies? Once the amateur game was all-important. Now it is seen, at competitive level, as a training ground for professionalism. The major amateur events, the Amateur championship, the Brabazon, Berkshire and Lytham Trophies, in Great Britain; the NCAA and the weekly college events in the USA, have fields which consist of full-time amateurs who, if they work at all, do so in jobs like stacking supermarket shelves during the winter to earn enough money to play golf for the rest of the year.

Most of these players will turn professional and, by the nature of things, most will fail. The US PGA Tour can cope with around 250 professionals in any one year, similarly the PGA European Tour, but literally thousands of hopefuls attempt to get their card every year. Having failed, they go into a kind of limbo where they are unable to play for the big prizes and cannot continue to play for the glory either.

Some, a very few, will make it onto the big tour through the medium of, in America, the Nike Tour and in Europe the Challenge Tour but the success rate is minuscule. It may be that a new category of golfer will need to be created for all those who wish to play golf full-time, encompassing all those who do not hold a card for the major tours around the world, whether technically amateur or professional.

Such a category would solve the problem that college golf in America creates for amateurism as it is at the moment. The existence of college golf is a ludicrous loophole in the amateur regulations, for it creates thousands of players, technically amateur, who do nothing but play golf all day while being paid to do so by the 'golf scholarships' they have been awarded.

This is a wonderful device for training golfers to become professionals but it has absolutely nothing at all to do with education. Some of the brighter players may enjoy classes as a relaxation from the practice ground: most just beat balls.

Perhaps the only certainty is that there must still be ruling bodies and they must not only be divorced from manufacturing interests, they must also be the only ones who make the rules. They can make them with input from the manufacturers, with contributions from the professional tours but ultimately it must be they who make them. It would help if they could acquire the wisdom of Solomon in the meantime.

THE WOMEN'S GAME

Over the years this wisdom has been in short supply, particularly as far as women are concerned, although the USGA has a better record than the R&A, who are positively antediluvian when it comes to the fairer sex. The USGA has had, for instance, a woman president in Judy Bell, who was appointed to the executive committee in 1987. She was the first woman to act as a rules official at the Masters, paving the way for this to become a common occurrence. She became the USGA's treasurer, secretary and vice-president but even then hardened cynics didn't think that Bell, out-going, hard-working and competitive would be given the top job. They were wrong. In 1996 she was made president and in 1997 she was re-elected.

The R&A do not even have women members. In fact they discriminate positively against them, the best illustration of which involved Ms Bell. Every previous president of the USGA, if not already a member of the R&A, has promptly been invited to become one.

In the case of Ms Bell this never happened. It would be impossible to think of anyone better fitted to become the first woman member of the R&A and in fact there was a meeting of the former captains on the subject, which is the way the R&A sorts out particularly prickly problems. At times it became heated as those who did not think that women were a menace to society as we know it fought to convince those who thought that the clubhouse might collapse if anyone of the female gender were accorded membership. The curmudgeonly mysoginists won and to the great disappointment of many, both men and women, Ms Bell failed to make a fuss about it. Now Carol Semple Thompson, the second woman on the Executive Committee, must have a sporting chance of becoming the first daughter to follow her father, Harton S. Semple, who held the office in 1974 and 1975, as president.

In 1893, there was Horace Hutchinson's famous response when he was asked about the proposal to form a Ladies' Golf Union. 'Don't,' he wrote.

Although the standing of women in the game has improved, certainly at executive level, there is still a lot of work to do in the fight to change attitudes at the game's grass roots. It often seems to come as a surprise to the average male club golfer that women like to play golf too. They are traditionally referred to as ladies or, in polite Antipodean circles, associates; the impolite follow the NFS – No F***ing Sheilas – principle. You'd think they'd have got used to the idea by now – after all Mary Queen of Scots played and the fishwives in Musselburgh played in competition in 1810 – but far too many of them still see women on the fairways as an irritation, women in the rough as unmentionable and women in the clubhouse as unspeakable. The old prejudices stubbornly persist – although places that have taken to golf relatively recently, such as continental Europe, do untraditional things like running the club championship as a mixed event, which means women can play on a Saturday morning and have the run of the clubhouse. The sky has yet to fall in over France, Germany and Sweden but in Britain, Johnny Briggs, an actor starring in a long-running soap *Coronation Street*, still felt that he could refer to women golfers as 'cockroaches'. It was not intended as a compliment.

Such irritable comments are nothing new. In 1893, there was Horace Hutchinson's famous response when he was asked about the proposal to form a Ladies' Golf Union. '*Don't,*' he wrote. His reasons all centred on the inability of women to organize anything and he pontificated that, 'Constitutionally and physically women are unfitted for golf ... the first ladies' championship will be the last.' He reckoned without Issette Pearson, the LGU's redoubtable founder and the LGU celebrated their centenary in 1993. Based in St Andrews, they run several championships annually but they are no longer seen as a pioneering body, fighting for emancipation and running a gauntlet of ridicule and prejudice. They co-exist happily with the R&A, who have been helpful with grants over the years, although there aren't too many invitations to tea in the clubhouse. At least one woman was apopletic when the captain of the R&A was invited to the centenary dinner. Perhaps she was remembering the old story about the time some women sheltering from a storm in the lee of the clubhouse were approached by a retainer and asked to move because they were blocking the view. Or was that Muirfield? Or Troon?

It is a myth that golf is a man's game but it is no myth that women have too often been treated as inferior beings and that many clubs, such as the R&A (which sometimes finds itself in an invidious position, being also one of the game's ruling bodies), Muirfield, Royal St George's, Merion, Pine Valley and Augusta National, are for men only. Women need not apply. However, it is possible for women to play their courses, which are consistently ranked among the finest in the world and that is infinitely more important than being able to join their clubs.

Admittedly, it can be a bit chilly hanging about outside waiting for your male partner to appear, as Joyce Wethered recalled vividly. A golfing legend, held in the highest regard by none other than Bobby Jones, she was not automatically treated exceptionally or well. She recalled, 'There were all too many clubs where you had the feeling that you were not wanted. In fact, women mattered

Joyce Wethered

so little that they didn't have to pay green fees. Often they wouldn't be allowed in the clubhouse and I well remember an occasion, while waiting for my partners to emerge from the locker-rooms at Sandwich, I kept my hands warm on the radiator of someone's Rolls-Royce.'

If that was the treatment meted out to one of the world's top players, imagine how lesser mortals were treated. If they were allowed to enter the clubhouse at all, it was by a side door and if they were allowed to play at weekends, it would be after three o'clock in the afternoon, which was not much good in the winter. Such strictures still exist in too many places even in the 1990s, as women continue to struggle to be regarded as *persona gratae*.

The oldest strokeplay tournament in Scotland is held at the Glasgow Golf Club, which was founded in 1787, two years before the French Revolution and has maintained attitudes to match. Not so long ago, the only journalist present was a woman. As such, she was banned from the clubhouse, where the scores were posted, making reporting the event well-nigh impossible. She created such a fuss – her boss was a member – that she was eventually allowed in to look at the scoreboard, under the strictest surveillance.

As idiotic was the treatment of Sara Baddiel, a well-known dealer in golf books and artefacts, who visited a club in the course of some research. She had to stand outside while someone described two paintings hanging on the wall of the main lounge. 'The room was completely empty,' she recalled, 'as was the clubhouse, but I was not allowed in.'

Many of the best – or worst – tales emanate from Scotland and not all of them are apocryphal. Peter Irvine's guide *Scotland the Best!* noted that women were welcome at one course in Edinburgh and added 'and that ain't true everywhere round here.'

Royal Troon and Muirfield have particularly bad reputations, although they have both hosted women's events. In 1952, when the latter staged the Curtis Cup, the clubhouse was out of bounds to the teams during the match but they were graciously invited in for tea beforehand. The thrill of being permitted to cross the threshold was tempered by a notice from the club committee regretting 'the inconvenience to members caused by admitting women to the building.'

Now, whisper it quietly, Muirfield has players lining up to compete in an annual match against the women professionals. This unexpected and informal occasion has just grown, like Topsy, and encompasses everything that's good about the game – friendship, sociability and a strong dollop of competitiveness. It was also at Muirfield, in 1992, that women golf writers were first given access to the men's locker-room at the Open championship, although news of this obviously did not reach Troon, for in 1997, women, on legitimate business, were thrown out by an outraged official.

The old exclusionary customs die hard but some women faced a harder battle than others. For years blacks were quite acceptable in golf – as caddies. Playing was another matter. In 1956, Ann Gregory became the first black woman to compete in one of the USGA's national championships when she played in the US Women's Amateur at the Meridian Hills Country Club in Indianapolis. She was narrowly beaten by Carolyn Cudone but showed she could play and in 1971 was just pipped for the US Women's Senior Amateur title when Cudone, again, beat her by a shot. 'Ann was a lady and a fine competitor,' Cudone said. 'She played the game as you wanted to see it played.'

Gregory spent her life fighting prejudice with dignity and determination, a battle movingly catalogued by Rhonda Glenn in *The Illustrated History of Women's Golf*. In 1959, the US Women's Amateur was at Congressional and the club let it be known that Gregory was not welcome at the pre-championship dinner it hosted. Joe Dey, of the USGA, relayed the news to Gregory, who was unfazed and, as everyone else seemed to, accepted this as normal behaviour. She had a hamburger and went to bed. Everyone else went to the dinner. Gregory won two matches before being beaten in the third round – her caddie had been sacked by the club for turning a somersault when she won her second round match at the 18th. The club president had the gall to tell her how wonderful she was and that she was welcome to play there any time she was in the area. 'I thought, "He's got to be crazy",' Gregory recalled.

In the early 1960s, she got fed up with being restricted to an untesting nine holes at Gleason Park, a public course in her home town of Gary, Indiana, where only whites were allowed on the 18-hole course. She put her money down and headed for the first tee with the words, 'My tax dollars are taking care of the big course and there's no way you can bar me from it. Just send the police out to get me.' They never came and soon blacks were playing the big course whenever they wanted. 'Racism works best when you let it affect your mind,' Gregory said. 'It was better for me to remember that the flaw was in the racist, not in myself. For all the ugliness, I've gotten nice things three times over. I can't think ugly of anybody.'

As Glenn wrote, 'Ann Gregory teed it up during a difficult era against odds that few of us can ever know. She endured painful slights with warmth, humour, courage and good sense. More than most of us, she cherished the game.' And the game should cherish her memory.

The other pioneers of that time were the women professionals, predominantly white, who threw themselves into their own golfing roadshow, barnstorming across

Laura Baugh, seven months pregnant with her seventh child, played in the 1997 Oldsmobile Classic and shot 67, bolstered by cries of 'You the Mom.'

America in the wake of the flamboyant Babe Zaharias and the pint-sized showwoman Patty Berg, playing tournaments, giving exhibitions and revelling in the competition. Players such as Louise Suggs and Marilyn Smith, founder members of the LPGA, have golf in their veins. Smith used to play baseball with the boys but on the day she flung down her glove and swore, her mother washed out her daughter's mouth with soap and her father decreed that golf was a more ladylike sport.

Kathy Whitworth, who won 88 tournaments over three decades (1960s–1980s), is still in awe of those pioneers and players like Peggy Kirk Bell, Betsy Rawls and Mickey Wright, who taught her her trade. 'For them ever to get to the point where they felt like they ever had a chance to form an association was pretty spectacular,' Whitworth said. 'In that day and age it wasn't the sort of thing that women did. They had a lot of help from the sporting goods companies Wilson, Spalding and MacGregor and the guts and the idealism to stick with it.'

Whitworth never felt discriminated against, or at any real disadvantage, even though the life was not all that secure. As she said, 'There was nothing else in town and we thought we were doing just great. The men weren't doing much better than we were. In fact, when you look back in comparison, which everybody loves to do, it wasn't until television and Arnold Palmer came on the scene that they just absolutely zoomed away from us.'

Women are playing in greater numbers than ever, at all ages and in all countries – Sweden has a stream of would-be stars anxious to emulate Liselotte Neumann, Annika Sorenstam and Helen Alfredsson. They are persevering in all conditions. Laura Baugh, seven months pregnant with her seventh child, played in the 1997 Oldsmobile Classic and shot 67, bolstered by cries of 'You the Mom.' Fiona Macdonald became the first woman to play for Cambridge and win her blue – she had to be designated an honorary man to socialize with her team-mates and opponents at some clubs. Vivien Saunders, professional, teacher, lawyer, and campaigner, got so fed up with being overlooked that she celebrated her 40th birthday by buying herself her own golf club, Abbotsley in Cambridgeshire.

Some redoubts hold out, however. The R&A is in many ways an enlightened body not averse to women. Many of its members even claim them as friends and playing partners and a grant from the Open-rich men amateurs helped the Women's European Tour survive in the early 1990s. Even so, the men should have taken the chance to make Judy Bell a member. Gender apart, she'd have been the ideal member, funny and steeped in the ways of golf. She'd have made a great captain – imagine the heart attacks at all those red-coated dinners around the country when they realized who the guest speaker was. Bell, the mistress of the bon mot, summed up the game's universal appeal, 'Golf is a personal kind of experience that's much more art than science. Golf is elusive. Like chasing a butterfly, you never quite catch it.'

How on earth did men ever think they'd be able to keep it to themselves?

SPONSORSHIP AND APPEARANCE MONEY

The two principal tours, the US PGA and PGA European, face plenty of problems as they enter the 21st century, including most of the issues that exercise the governing bodies. The tours are also dealing with large amounts of money and as the love of money is the root of all evil, there are necessarily some difficult decisions to be taken.

One of the longest running problems has been that of 'appearance money', the system by which leading players are paid often obscene amounts of money just to turn up for the tournament. Indeed, if there are a number of imported stars in an event, the total amount they are paid can exceed the total prize money, which leads to severe dissatisfaction among the lesser players, who naturally consider that if all that money is available, it should be in the prize fund and available to all.

But of course sponsorship does not work like that. Sponsorship exists to get the name of a product exposed on the television screen, the air waves and in the public prints, and if the managing director considers the best way of doing that is to pay a particular player to be in his event,

Janny Sunesson, the first female caddy on Tour, and one of the most respected

he will do it, regardless of the wishes of either the tour itself, or the remaining players.

Appearance money is, nevertheless, an evil. It leads immediately to an uneven playing field, allowing those who receive it to play without the pressure of having to make money that week, and denying the lesser mortals the chance to make as much as they might have done. It can even shorten careers. Severiano Ballesteros is a case in point, for he was paid to play in every European event in which he appeared for almost the whole of his golfing life.

Seve was always too proud to take the money and then be content to finish in the pack; he always gave everything. No one has ever tried harder to make a cut when struggling with his game and ultimately the pressure he put himself under to satisfy those who paid the fees led to a more rapid burn-out than many of his contemporaries.

Recently there has been a development at the other end of the scale, with tour journeymen in both Europe and America demanding that they get paid whether they make the cut or not. This, in the most rampantly capitalistic sport ever invented, is an astonishing demand, revealing that the vast majority of the players have little understanding of why the professional golf tours exist.

One of the leading supporters of the journeymen and certainly not someone who would need the benefits such a scheme would bestow, is Tom Lehman, the Open champion of 1996. He said, 'In my opinion when the BellSouth Classic markets the BellSouth Classic, they're marketing 156 players who tee it up on Thursday. And since you're part of the show, you're part of what's going on. Why should you go home without getting paid?'

Now Lehman is a Christian and one of the game's nicer blokes but he reveals a fearful misunderstanding of what the promotion of a golf tournament is all about. It is not, and never has been, about providing a living for 156 players, or any other number. It is about increasing the sales of the product that is financing the tournament and when BellSouth, or any other tournament, markets its event, they are not marketing 156 players, they are marketing at the most half a dozen. They will be interested in getting a strong field, of course, but that will consist of, say, 30-40 players, with the rest making up the numbers.

But Lehman, who is supported by Mark O'Meara in this matter, wants to turn sponsorship values completely base over apex. He wants appearance money to be paid to those who, that week, have nothing to offer; those who are not good enough, that week, to make the cut; those who, most weeks, would not attract a single spectator through the gate.

This, of course, is ridiculous. There are exceedingly few golfers in the world who would put a single bum on a seat and as all tournaments are watched by the largest number of spectators at the weekend and as, by definition, those who missed the cut would not be there to be watched, to pay them is a nonsense.

Lehman and O'Meara appear to believe honestly that anyone who enters a tournament should be paid US$5,000 a go, which, when extrapolated, means that if a golfer played in, and missed the cut in, 20 tournaments in a year, he would 'earn' US$100,000 (£62,500). This is a handsome income for being hopeless at your job, a job that furthermore will only occupy 20 weeks of your year. As evidence that many of the top golfers now earn so much money that they have totally lost touch with reality, this is a great example.

In fact, the pity of it is that so far the commissioner of the US PGA Tour, Tim Finchem, has shown not the slightest sign of adopting the proposal. For if the US Tour were to be featherbedded in this way it would mean that the Ryder Cup would be won, in perpetuity, by Europe.

O'Meara is at the centre of another controversy, involving both money and the Ryder Cup, for he believes that the players should be paid for agreeing to take part in it. Again there is a

Appearance money is, nevertheless, an evil. It leads immediately to an uneven playing field, allowing those who receive it to play without the pressure of having to make money that week.

breath-taking ignorance of what the Ryder Cup is about and why it has become one of, perhaps the, most compelling dramas in world sport.

The reason why it occupies that position is precisely because the players are *not* paid. Everyone knows that for one week every two years the game's superstars get together and they fight it out for the glory, not the groceries. The fact that these superstars are normally extremely highly paid is the catalyst for all the excitement: because they are getting nothing they are doing it for you and for me, not for themselves. It is that feeling which is wonderful. It is what sustained the Ryder Cup when, for many years, it lost money.

O'Meara has also said that if paying the players is not to be allowed, then they should be allocated a sum of money which they can pass on to a charity of their choice – at first sight a worthy thought. But again it does not work. What kind of mind is it that wants his charitable contributions paid for him? And what kind of sum would be suitable? The size of first prize in a tournament? Say US$400,000. That comes, when multiplied by the participating players (24), to US$9,600,000 or £6 million.

That, in turn, would use up every penny generated by the event, leaving none for the development of the game, which is where the PGAs of the respective countries spend the profits at the moment. In any case the players already make good money out of simply being Ryder Cup golfers. If there is one that has a contract, or contracts, that does not allow for guaranteed increases for making the team, he should get a new agent.

TOO MANY TOURNAMENTS?

The Ryder Cup is now a huge commercial success and it has led to the creation of the Presidents Cup by the US Tour for a match, America versus an International side, which essentially is the Rest of the World, bar Europe. This too has been successful, even when the Americans won the first two playings of the event.

But since December 1998 it seems set to become very big indeed. The Americans had to leave their own country for the first time and they had to travel the huge distance down to Melbourne, at the end of a long, hard season. Furthermore they had a captain in Jack Nicklaus who has proved, time and again, that he has no idea of what being a team captain means. Because he never needed any motivation, he seems to feel that neither does anyone else and he treated the whole trip as if he were an ambassador for American golf, not the captain of a team whose sole intent was to beat the living daylights out of the opposition.

As a result, they didn't. They in fact were beaten to a pulp and with just the final singles series of 12 matches to be played, the International team led by 14 ½ points to 5 ½. That meant the Internationals had only got to win two of the 12 matches and yet with a logic that defied comprehension, Nicklaus, who obviously needed every early point he could get and had at his disposal the world ranked numbers 1, 2, 3 and 4 players, placed them at...1, 2, 3 and 4? Well no, actually. Tiger Woods went in at no. 11, so ensuring that the world's best player was highly unlikely to have any impact on the proceedings; Mark O'Meara was put out 12th and last; David Duval was second and Davis Love III was ninth.

The Internationals promptly won the first two singles and with them the entire match.

From the moment that he appointed his son, Jackie, as vice captain, Nicklaus showed that he was approaching the match in the wrong spirit but at least that resounding result should ensure that nothing like that will ever happen again. The Americans, as they have shown in the Ryder Cup, do not appreciate a thing until it is no longer theirs and when the next Presidents Cup is played, in America, the Internationals can expect a ferocious attack.

Soon the schedules would be filled with more events than could possibly be good for it: no one would know what was worthwhile and what was just another beanfeast.

This proliferation of events is, so far, a good thing. The Presidents Cup gives an involvement to players like Greg Norman and Ernie Els who, without it, would have no team stage on which to strut. Similarly the Solheim Cup has given the women professionals of the US and Europe their chance to compete at the very highest levels.

But there is a danger, nevertheless, that matters could get out of hand. There is talk of a Seniors Ryder Cup, a Junior Ryder Cup and if they come into being why not a Seniors Presidents Cup.... Soon the schedules would be filled with more events than could possibly be good for it: no one would know what was worthwhile and what was just another beanfeast. And worse, the properly established events would be in danger of being swamped and dying from overkill.

HORSES FOR COURSES

For the most part the conditioning of the courses on which tournaments are played these days is quite remarkable. There is the occasional exception, when the greenkeeper gets it wrong, or the weather does not allow him to get it right, but generally the professionals of today play in conditions that only 30 years ago would have seemed like the unlikeliest dream.

This applies to the entire course but in particular to the greens, which have reached a level of speed and true roll that would quite literally have been impossible only a few years ago. Not only have fertilizers improved, watering procedures are hugely sophisticated and computerized to the nth degree, while the mowers themselves are capable of taking as much, or as little, off the putting surface as is needed.

You might have guessed, though, that even these Elysian Fields are not good enough for some folk. Paul Azinger has written several letters to the US PGA Tour complaining that the greens these days are too hard and too fast. He has said in one of those letters that 'greens are meant to receive the ball, not reject it' and adds that if the greens had always been prepared the way they are now 'we would never have heard of Arnold Palmer.'

What he means by all this is that Palmer, as Azinger does now, always hit the ball low and if he were playing now he would find it impossible to hold a ball on the over-firm surfaces. But this is self-serving rubbish. Azinger has been brought up on the well-watered greens that are prevalent in American golf and now, when something different is in vogue, is upset.

In golf that would mean pudding greens one week, granite the next: one week the low ball hitters, the next the high–ballers come out to play. It hardly bears thinking about.

But the policy that is being applied at the moment is one that has been formulated by the tour players themselves. Each week a different 20 players are asked what they thought of the ground conditions for the tournament they have just completed and, says Davis Love III, one of the most frequently mentioned things was to get the greens firmer and faster.

This was not, of course, to spite the Azingers of this world; simply a bid to reward the skill of being able to stop a ball on a hard green by hitting it with sufficient spin. It is reassuring that the majority of American players think in such terms, rather than looking for the easy option.

For if Azinger had his way presumably golf would go the way of horse-racing, where horses are only entered for races if the going suits them. In golf that would mean pudding greens one week, granite the next: one week the low ball hitters, the next the high-ballers come out to play. It hardly bears thinking about.

GOLF IS A WALKING GAME

Neither does the predicament in which Casey Martin, the young American golfer, found himself prior to the 1998 US Open at the Olympic Club. Martin, a gifted player, has a serious leg condition which, while not preventing him hitting shots, makes it extremely painful for him to walk. But he is good enough to have won an event on the Nike tour and in 1998 was good enough to qualify for the US Open.

But once again golf found itself in the courtroom, for Martin wanted to use a cart in the championship and none of the authorities was eager for this to happen. No one disputed that Martin was seriously handicapped, both in a strict physical sense and also in the golfing sense of having to expend a great deal more energy to achieve the same result when, for instance, walking up a hill.

The reason why the authorities, and many of the players, were wary about allowing even such a deserving case as Martin to use a cart in a championship was summed up by Jack Nicklaus in a press conference prior to the event itself. Martin had won his case at law and Nicklaus said, 'I don't like it (the ruling) as it relates to the game of golf. But I understand it and from Casey's standpoint I'm delighted for him as an individual.

'But I worry about what its ramifications are for the game. I mean, is there somebody else who is injured this week who would like to ride a cart? I am sure Casey is at a disadvantage, but I am just questioning what is the ultimate? I promise you, someone is going to qualify for the Open and then come in and say "I sprained my ankle. I need to have something." You are going to have a mess. It is going to happen.'

Nicklaus represented the worried majority, those who believed that walking and the fatigue generated over the likely six-day period of a championship, was all a part of it. He seemed to think that the benefits of a cart over that length of time would outweigh the disadvantage of his illness.

Nicklaus represented the worried majority, those who believed that walking and the fatigue generated over the likely six-day period of a championship, was all a part of it. He seemed to think that the benefits of a cart over that length of time would outweigh the disadvantage of his illness.

There were some who did not. Payne Stewart, the 1999 champion and a close second at the Olympic Club, was all for allowing Martin to ride, although the one man who could put himself even vaguely into Martin's shoes, on a literal basis, sided with the majority. Jose Maria Olazabal was out of the game for 18 months because of a back condition that led to him being unable to walk at all.

For a large part of that time he was able to hit shots and did so on a daily basis but when the offer was made for him to compete in a pairs event, for unofficial money, using a buggy, he declined. He, too, spoke about the Martin problem at the Open, and said, 'I think that walking is part of the game. Obviously we all feel sympathy for Casey and I don't think that anybody would like to see himself in a situation like this. But golf is for walking.'

If Martin was upset by all the constant references to him, it did not show in his play. He rode his cart, he was cheered to the echo by the spectators, he produced rounds of 74, 71, 74, 72, for 291, finished tied for 23rd, a shot behind Tiger Woods and won US$4,043.

He has not played as significantly well since but Casey Martin made golf take a good look at itself. There will be those who think that the game did not try hard enough to help a young man in obvious difficulties and that his request to use a cart should never have gone to court.

Equally the traditionalists would insist that Nicklaus and Olazabal are right and perhaps this is a case where time really will tell. If there are more requests for the use of a cart for medical reasons, it should not be beyond the wit of man to draw up a set of rigorous conditions that have to be fulfilled, for the last thing an honourable game like golf needs is to be seen to be, or thought to be, inhuman.

CHAPTER 4

THE OTHER
SIDE OF GOLF

THE CHEAT: A GOLFING PARIAH

CHEATING IN GOLF IS A LOATHSOME THING, AN ABOMINATION. It is so because it destroys the whole point of the game, which is the only sport of them all which puts you on your honour not to cheat.

In no game is it easier to cheat. The vast majority of the time the golfer is on the course he is unsupervized and for large parts of the time no one can see what he is doing. The opportunities for cheating are abundant, which is why, if you take only one of them, ever, and are found out, you become an instant pariah, despised by all your fellow players. To be a cheat at golf is to be an outcast.

There are many sports in which cheating is expected of the player. In soccer it is understood that the professional foul is preferable to the probable alternative – a goal being scored – and in rugby the idea is to get away with as much as possible without being penalized. It's called playing the referee. In cricket, bowlers have used all sorts of substances, from vaseline to suncream, to make the ball behave oddly, not to mention the simpler tactic of picking at the seam. And the wicketkeeper who has not appealed for a catch off a ball he knows has struck nothing has probably not yet been born.

But in golf you must be honest. You must, unless the rules allow you to do otherwise, play the ball as it lies, and it can lie in some horrible places. Cheating comes in many forms, from the blatant to the obscure, from stealing a quarter of an inch to moving a ball yards. If you are in the woods and moving your ball, say, three feet takes a tree out of your line and gives you a shot where none was available before and no one's looking, then why not? Because eventually you will be found out and you will be damned in a golfing hell, that's why not.

Years ago, in the Cannes Open, a French player was seen to be marking his ball improperly on the greens and his partners refused afterwards to sign his card. He was first furious and then in a distinctively Gallic way, puzzled. 'Two centimetres in 20 metres,' he said, 'what can it matter?' Ah, but it does, and it must have mattered to him, otherwise why do it?

Then there was the extraordinary case of David Robertson, from Dunbar, who was a good player, but inclined to take the odd liberty on the green. He had been in trouble before he got to the Open championship qualifier where he effectively disappeared from golf. He devised a procedure on the greens that enabled him, so he thought, to steal yards, for when he bent down to mark his ball, he did not put down a marker. So, when it came to replace his ball, he could put it back where he liked. His caddie noticed what was going on after a while, was appalled, dumped the bag and called in the R&A. Robertson was banned for 25 years. Any hope he had of a career as a tournament-playing professional was sacrificed at that moment.

Some players simply cannot count. This is more prevalent at club level and with some of the poorer players understandable in that they may only have lost count. But most club members have been faced with the problem of a fellow golfer who, when asked how many he has taken calls out airily 'five.' Now, you may not know how many he has taken but you know it isn't five, so what do you do? Risk implying he is a cheat by asking him to count again? Maybe not, but if you say 'I'm not sure it wasn't a six' at least he will probably have a re-think.

There was once a European Tour player who could count – only too well – and when it came to too many at a Qualifying School, and it meant that he would not get his card, he decided that the only thing to do was to alter his score. It was, of course, spotted and the Tour, faced with their first case of forging and realizing that they had to produce a watertight case, called in Scotland Yard. They were able to produce proof of an erasure and determine that the new figure had been written in a different hand from that of the original marker. The player was banned.

THE 'SANDBAGGER'

But of course the easiest, most effective and profitable way for an amateur to cheat is to do it *before* going on the golf course. If you can arrange a handicap for yourself that is several strokes higher than your real one, then there is no need for crude cheating on the course itself – you already have the edge, the advantage.

Nowadays, of course, most clubs possess computers and in theory it should be difficult to 'arrange' a handicap. But *Golf Digest*, in 1995, ran a lovely story from an allegedly reformed 'sandbagger', a man who doctored his handicap to play in and win, local events. He described how it was possible to belong to a resort course and take his handicap from there.

The anonymous golfer in question told Guy Yocum, 'There's a resort course in Dallas that has maybe 350 names in the handicap computer. It reads like a most-wanted list of handicap hustlers. Why? Lack of internal policing. Resort courses are a transient, factory environment where hardly anybody knows one another. There are few circles of friends to police each other and the handicap chairman and head pro are helpless because they don't know anybody, either.

'At a lot of resort courses shady characters stand in line to load the most preposterous scores you can imagine into the computer. My handicap was basically anything I wanted it to be. The scope of the resort course sandbagging problem is enormous...the bottom line is when you ask someone where they play and they say "I'm not a member anywhere but my handicap is at such and such a resort" – keep your wallet in your pocket.'

The reason most people who are prepared to 'farm' their handicap actually do so is not to win matches at their club but to win prizes either in local competitions, or in pro-ams. In fact, pro-ams around the world are won these days with absurdly low scores, with nothing over the mid-50s likely to get a look-in in a format featuring four amateurs and a professional.

At one US Tour event in 1999, the winning score in this format was 52, which was done early in the day, twice in the middle of the day and again late in the day, in fact by the last team out. To do that on a par 72 course meant someone birdieing every hole, with two eagles thrown in and the tournament can only be congratulated on having in their pro-am 16 amateurs who all managed, on the same day, to be at the very peak of their form, playing the golf of their lives.

But handicap manipulation is not just an American problem. Any organizer of the multitudinous pro-ams that take place in Spain and Portugal every European winter knows that, no matter the precautions, he is going to have players in his field whose ability bears no relation to their handicaps. There is only so much checking that can be done, only so much telephoning to the club of the person concerned and even that is likely to be pointless because the computer will probably bear out the alleged handicap. It's reality that doesn't.

Perhaps the most notorious pro-am sandbagger of all time was the Japanese golfer, Masashi Yamada. His was the most blatant cheat in the history of handicap cheating. Yamada played in the 1995 AT&T Pebble Beach Pro-Am, perhaps the most prestigious pro-am in world golf and one which has a huge waiting list. The format is one amateur, with one pro, for four rounds and Yamada's professional was the journeyman Bruce Vaughan. The Japanese declared his handicap to be 15 and produced a certificate to that effect. It soon became clear, however, who was carrying whom in this relationship for Vaughan scored 71, 75, 79 to miss the professional 54-hole cut by 10 shots.

Yamada posted scores of 63, 65, 64, which meant that he had improved on his professional by 33 strokes in three rounds. Because of the format, Vaughan played on for the fourth round and this time their team score was 59, with Yamada improving on his professional no fewer than 12 times, or 45 times in total in the four rounds.

People talked. In fact they yelped. Even in the cynical world of sandbagging, this was too much and an investigation began. The organizers went first to the club from which Yamada had entered, Mangijo Country Club in Chiba, Tokyo and found that he had indeed got a handicap of 15. Except that the certificate had been forged by the owner of the club – Yamada himself.

So they went to the Japanese Golf Association, whose handicap records showed that Yamada's actual handicap at Mangijo was six and that he had handicaps of six and four at other clubs. Mortified, the Association not only banned Yamada from all future Japan GA events, but the entire Mangijo club, until they agreed to a system of handicap monitoring. Next to be in on the act was Dean Knuth, the handicapping expert from the United States Golf Association, who said, 'Such prolific scoring in four successive rounds is statistically impossible. There was a zero per cent chance that Mr Yamada was a 15 handicapper.'

So what to do about him? The tournament organizers had a meeting, chaired by Clint Eastwood no less, and they decided to make their own day by removing the title from Yamada and asking for the trophy back. Yamada, of course, refused.

Almost exactly a year later Yamada showed that his business scruples matched his golfing ethics. In 1990 he bought the Welcombe Hotel in Stratford-upon-Avon, with a golf course with 407 members attached. Suddenly, in February 1996 he informed the club that all the members would be evicted, that they would not be able to renew their subscriptions due at the end of the month. No reason was given. At the time Yamada was president of the golf club. The then club chairman, Tom Wood, decided that maybe Yamada was not the ideal person for the post and said that he would be removed at the

> **Such prolific scoring in four successive rounds is statistically impossible. There was a zero per cent chance that Mr Yamada was a 15 handicapper.**

AGM. Wood was asked whether it was because he had thrown the club off its course or because of the events at Pebble Beach. Wood, commendably, replied, 'The second reason.'

Bill Gates, the Microsoft man who has more money than he or a whole Army could spend, has also been in a sandbagging situation when he played in a charity golf tournament near Seattle. Gates, an irregular golfer, played off a handicap of 30 and came in with a gross 87, to win the low net prize, as well he might. The USGA's Knuth once again proffered an opinion. 'A 30 handicap,' he said, 'cannot shoot an 87. He cannot.'

Knuth has worked out the odds of a player beating his handicap and it might be interesting to remember that when perusing some of the scores in any pro-am. He says that it's 200-1 that you'll beat your handicap by three shots; 570-1 that you'll beat it by five strokes and 82,000-1 that you'll beat it by 10. For Gates to beat his handicap by 15 shots the odds, says Knuth, are 1,000,000-1.

And what did the man with the billions of dollars get for his day's golf? Among other things, a box of balls and – some computer software!

CHEATING ON TOUR

Because cheating is such an obnoxious thing active touring professionals are rarely accused of it. And because, often, it is one man's word against another, it is even rarer that anything is done to the accused. After all, if one man says cheating occurred and the other says it didn't, and there is no corroborative evidence, what can be done?

The perfect example of this occurred at the 1995 World Series in Akron, Ohio, during the course of which Greg Norman accused his playing partner, Mark McCumber, of removing a spike mark from his line. He called an official, complained and at the end of the round refused to sign McCumber's card. The American steadfastly refused to admit that he had done anything untoward and eventually officials, as they are entitled to do, signed the card for him.

Norman threatened there and then to withdraw from the tournament, but was persuaded to remain – which was as well, because he went on to win it. But a week later, at the Canon European Masters in Switzerland, he was still seething over the incident. He described what had, in his eyes, happened.

'I could not believe what I saw on the seventh green' he said. 'I believe strongly what I saw. He repaired a spike mark. He did not tap it down. I refused to sign his card because I felt so strongly about what I had seen. I've never done that before. It was blatant. I have never seen anything so blatant in my life.

'He said first of all that he was removing a fly, then a bug and by Saturday it was a locust. That was the sequence. The next day, going to the tournament, I have never been so nervous because I didn't know what the reaction would be. But there was not one negative reaction from anybody and a lot congratulated me on having the strength in doing it. It made me feel good.

'You have to be very protective and I was being very protective because I do not want the game to slip. It has been built up by Jones and Palmer and Nicklaus. I was in a state of shock. I could not believe that a fellow professional would do something like that. I will talk about it until the day I die.'

After the tournament, Norman wrote a letter to Tim Finchem, commissioner of the US Tour, and to all the members of the Players Policy Board. In it, he said, 'I don't want to see this matter dismissed, I don't want it to be pushed into history. The more players are aware that they might do something inadvertently and have to call a penalty on themselves, the better. Nobody is above the rules of the game of golf, professional or amateur.'

McCumber, of course, denies the whole charge. He insists that he was removing a loose impediment, which is perfectly legal, from his line. He says that he bent down, picked up a small black insect with a hard shell with his forefinger and thumb and threw it away. And it is, of course, impossible to prove otherwise.

However, despite these protestations McCumber has acquired a reputation among some of his fellow professionals and on four separate occasions before the Norman incident, since McCumber began on the Tour in 1978, rules officials have been called in by his partners. The men concerned were Bill Kratzert, Hubert Green, Mark Lye and Davis Love III and if any confirmation were needed as to how seriously cheating is regarded in golf, the American magazine *Sports Illustrated*, devoted four pages to examining these and the Norman incidents.

The most telling evidence was that from Lye who said that in 1983, in the Anheuser-Busch Classic, McCumber chipped a ball that finished in a small depression. 'By the time he finished marking it,' said Lye, 'it was no longer in that depression.' A rules official was called and the ball replaced.

More recently there was the spat between Mark O'Meara, the American who, in 1998 won the Masters and the Open, and Jarmo Sandelin, three times a winner on the European Tour. Tom Watson, notoriously, once said that there were cheats on the US Tour, and that the players knew who they were – but then refused to name them. Had he done so, it is certain that the name of O'Meara would not have been one under suspicion: his reputation was impeccable.

Nevertheless, his actions on the 69th green at St Nom la Breteche in the 1997 Lancome Trophy undoubtedly amounted to cheating: it is on video and indisputable. And yet O'Meara's good name remains and, if anything, that of his accuser has been denigrated.

What O'Meara did, while he was on his way to winning the tournament, is miss a par putt, the ball finishing some two feet from the hole. The video then shows that he slid his marker in under the ball, as many players do, picked it up very briefly and almost immediately replaced it – but maybe half an inch forward of his marker. O'Meara has said that 'my intentions were to mark the ball, clean it, and replace it in the same place.'

And intentions are what have been judged important in this case. Sandelin was alerted to the existence of the video and when he saw it was incensed. Not only that, he felt robbed, for he finished second in that tournament, one stroke behind O'Meara. After seeing the video, which only came to light several months after the tournament was over, Sandelin was immediately quoted as saying that while he did not want any money out of it, he felt that O'Meara should return the trophy.

O'Meara was fully exonerated by the European Tour, whose rules officials have seen the incident and the R&A. John Paramor, chief referee on the European Tour, said, 'I have spoken to Mark about this at length and our view is that he was extremely careless in that particular situation. He wasn't as careful as he should have been on that particular procedure in marking and lifting his ball. He did put his ball back a little bit nearer the hole and it is very clear on TV. But the other players in the three-ball didn't see it and Mark didn't realize he'd done it.'

But Sandelin remains adamant 'All professional golfers I know,' he says, 'always mark their ball the same way. If you do that, how can you make such a mistake without noticing?'

But if this whole messy business highlights one thing, it is the implications for a golfer of even being suspected of being even a little careless with the rules, never mind being labelled a cheat.

THE SUB-60 ROUND

No one would, of course, label Kim Jong Il a cheat. To do so might result in all sorts of unpleasantries, such as being locked up in a dungeon for ever more or, as the *Mikado* once lovingly speculated, 'something with boiling oil in it.' For Kim Jong Il is the Dear Leader of North Korea, a man capable, so they all say, of bringing about record rice crops simply by going and standing in the paddy fields. So is it any wonder that when he turned his attention to golf, it was simply unable to withstand his incredible, all-consuming powers?

In October of 1994, with a round of golf that seems to have gone strangely unaccredited elsewhere, he completed 18 holes in only 34 strokes. During it he had five holes-in-one, perhaps inspired by the fact that (allegedly) he holed his second shot at the 400 yard first at Pyongyang Golf Club. As there is no record of fore-caddies being present on the course, it seems we must accept the word of the pro at Pyongyang, who has no doubt that the man in charge of his country went round in a score that utterly scrambles any previous record. Park Young Nam said: 'Dear Leader, comrade general Kim Jong Il, whom I respect from the bottom of my heart, is an excellent golfer.' But then, he would say that, wouldn't he?

Duval is a laid–back individual who rarely shows emotion and even when he holed an eight–footer for his 59 the best he could do was pump his arm a couple of times.

In the real world many professional golfers have problems in getting round in something more mundane, like 59, although that score was done rather a lot on various American tours in 1998 and 1999. Notah Begay and David Dunakey both had 59s on the Nike Tour in 1998 and then, at the start of 1999 David Duval, who had been threatening something of the sort for a long time, had one in the Bob Hope Classic, played over the Palmer course at PGA West in Palm Springs, California. Furthermore, he

In October of 1994, with a round of golf that seems to have gone strangely unaccredited elsewhere, he completed 18 holes in only 34 strokes.

had it in the final round, he achieved it by eagling the final hole and it gave him victory over the unfortunate Steve Pate by one shot.

Duval is a laid-back individual who rarely shows emotion and even when he holed an eight-footer for his 59 the best he could do was pump his arm a couple of times. When asked whether he was nervous over that putt, he said that he was, but 'You just kinda do your best to do what you would normally do.' That laconic description of one of the great putts says a great deal about Duval.

He can be withdrawn to the point of brusqueness with the media and in public is rarely seen without the wrap-around sunglasses that afford him the anonymity he seems to seek. His golf, though, is always going to ensure that he will not be left alone entirely and when he can be induced to offer a comment or answer a question, he reveals an astute grasp of affairs – while all the time indicating that he'd far rather be somewhere else. Part of the reason for his unease in the early part of his career was the fact that he had a poor record in the major championships and this was invariably brought up at press conferences. There is, of course, no sensible – or polite – answer to the question 'Why haven't you won a major yet?' and it is irritating when asked constantly. Duval, understandably, avoided press conferences whenever he could.

A sub-60 score has a fascination to it that frequently destroys those who might achieve it. No sooner the thought of it, than the collapse. But David Llewellyn, a Welsh World Cup player who was on the winning side, with Ian Woosnam, in 1987, once almost had one without knowing it.

Llewellyn, playing in a European Tour event in Biarritz in the southwest of France, was heavily into Zen at the time. He was concentrating so hard on the 'here and now' that while he knew that he was playing well, he was not aware of just how well. When he came to the 18th and hit his shot onto the green he saw a number of his fellow professionals come out of the clubhouse and stand by the green – and vaguely wondered why. He then missed with his first putt, missed with the next as well and it was not until he saw the shock and sadness on the faces of his friends that the dreadful dawning came. 'That was for a 59?' he said. 'Oh dear. Oh dear, oh dear, oh dear.'

THE GLOBAL ANTI-GOLF MOVEMENT

At that moment Llewellyn might have willingly joined GAGM, the Global Anti-Golf Movement, an organization that basically wants to wipe golf from the face of the planet. It might be thought that there are other more urgent and all-encompassing evils that deserve attention but not for Gen Morita, a Japanese who founded the movement, as well as World No-Golf Day. All he sees is exploitation – of the land and the people who work on it.

Morita, who seems to be living in some sort of time warp, believes that golf is responsible, on a daily basis for a multiplicity of sins, including death and genetic harm from deadly chemicals used indiscriminately. He claims to represent the dispossessed and alleges that golf, and those who create it and play it, are responsible for the destruction of virgin land, the poisoning of groundwater, the ruin of indigenous peoples for the benefit of the rich multi-nationals and for the corruption of local officials.

Now there is no doubt that some of those things, maybe even all of them, have occurred in the last 30 years; certainly in Japan, and in a few other countries as well. During the great golf boom in Japan during the seventies and eighties, when that country went berserk about the sport, there simply were not enough golf courses to feed the appetite of the nation.

To build one and charge hyper-prices for membership for playing privileges was a certain way to become a multi-millionaire and hundreds of courses were built, some in places where they should not have been. There is no doubt that villagers were displaced, and not sufficiently compensated, and there is no doubt that there was a high level of corruption among local officials. There is evidence, too, that developers were careless with chemicals they knew little about, other than their primary function which was to make the place look nice.

But that was then and this is now. Thanks to all the various shades of Green movements there is an awareness of the environment in which it could be said that golf leads and deserves praise, rather than castigation. Now, whenever a golf course development is mooted, the first people to be consulted, lest there should be a colony of natterjack toads on the

The St Andrews invasion. The crowds, the corporate hospitality and the general hiatus surrounding a modern Open championship are a far cry from its humble origins among a group of Scottish caddies in 1860.

Royal Dornoch is the northernmost first-class course in the world and in the opinion of many, including Tom Watson, it is without equal. 'I have played none finer,' said Watson 'a natural masterpiece.'

The 17th at Ballybunion. One of the greatest holes on one of the greatest golf courses

Pine Valley. The sublime
setting of this course –
among the backwoods of
New Jersey – is undeniable,
but the degree of difficulty
of many of the holes
present insurmountable
problems for the average
golfer. It is one of the
'worst' of the 'Best Courses
in the World.'

Augusta in bloom. A round of
golf at Augusta National must
count as one of the highlights
of any golfing career. Sadly,
the club's exclusivity means it
is a pleasure few can enjoy.

Christy O'Connor Jnr usually needs no help from on high, but when he gets it, he is always grateful.

Right: Seve Ballesteros produces another miraculous recovery. During a distinguished career, Seve's propensity to save par and make outrageous birdies from the most unlikely of places has been remarkable.

The Masters is no joke. Bernard Langer and Jack Nicklaus see the funny side of Nicklaus' sensational victory at Augusta in 1986. His storming last round 65 saw him take the title for a record sixth time.

Golf is played in some of the strangest places. The inaugural World Ice Golf Championships held in Greenland in 1999, attracted a field of 21 arctic adventurers.

An artificial hazard on an artificial golf course. A pond full of crocodiles lies in front of the 13th green at Sun City. Any golfer on this tee will be concerned by much more than the usual swing thoughts!

A Japanese addiction. For many Japanese, beating balls on a driving range is as close as they get to real golf. Joining a club is prohibitively expensive for all but companies and the wealthiest individuals.

Trish Johnson leads the celebrations of the greatest moment in European women's golf and, unfortunately, a false dawn. The United States, comprehensive winners of the first Solheim Cup at Lake Nona in 1990, were beaten by the amazing margin of 11½ to 6½ at Dalmahoy, Edinburgh, in 1992. Europe has not come remotely close in the three matche

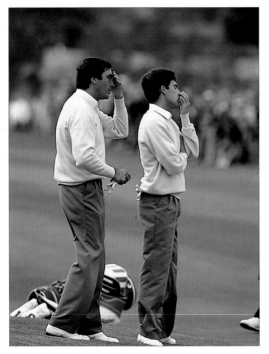

A moment of anguish for Ballesteros and Olazabal in the 1993 Ryder Cup, but there were not too many incidents like this during the compilation of the most stunning statistic in Ryder Cup history – P 15, W 11, H 2, L 2.

The intense pressure of Ryder Cup golf was too much for Mark Calcavecchia at Kiawah Island in 1991. His capitulatio against Colin Montgomerie in the final day's singles almost cost his side the cup

The sun goes down on Europe's hopes. The 1993 Ryder Cup was lost at the Belfry, when the home team's tail, theoretically comprising its strongest players, were comprehensively beaten.

The wondrous setting of Pebble Beach golf course and the distant Carmel Beach is one of the many beautiful places in world golf which induce the golfer to stop all the 'flailing about' and simply sit and enjoy the view.

The end of another day at the links.

proposed property or a wild orchid that blooms only on Tuesdays every seven years, are the local environmentalist group.

In the nature of things, because the average environmentalist regards the average golfer as a rich, fat, elderly moron with nothing better to do, there will be objections to any proposal. But increasingly, as the course architect is brought into play, the level of objection declines, simply because almost every imaginable environmental factor can be catered for, and because nowadays it is undeniable that a modern golf course creates a wildlife habitat that will be superior to anything that existed before.

Gen Morita and his GAGM followers come across as an enthusiastic and dedicated group, convinced of their cause but then so many single-subject protesters are that. It is just that in this case, Morita is at least 20 years too late. Morita, expert though he is, probably does not realize the depth of the problem he faces in trying to exterminate golf, or appreciate the number of places it has penetrated. Golf is everywhere around us, from the inner city to the wilderness, from rain forest to desert, from mountain top to beneath the sea – or, to be strictly accurate, below sea-level. Even on the sea, as we shall see later.

GOLF IN THE STRANGEST PLACES

You can even play golf as a prisoner, that is if you should be sent to Elmley jail, in Kent. There they have a 13-hole pitch-and-putt course, complete with bunkers, which was built by the inmates. The discovery of this course sent one of Britain's tabloid newspapers into a tizzy and the fact that they devoted three pages to what they described as a 'prison golfing scandal' shows that they had the misguided impression that golf is a toff's game and therefore insupportable.

The Express hired a helicopter to fly over the prison and take pictures of the course and then roundly condemned its existence, even though the holes were either side of a football pitch. It was evidently all right to mount a moral high horse over the playing of golf in prison, while completely condoning the playing of football. *The Express*, without a blink, quoted a Prison Service spokesman as saying, 'Convicted prisoners are required to work, do training and undertake education. But Elmley has a significant proportion of unconvicted prisoners not obliged to work. The pitch-and-putt course also provides exercise for older, less fit prisoners.'

Perhaps the ultimate in prison golf was played during World War II,

Of all the places golf has alighted, none is stranger than ice golf in the Arctic.

at Stalag Luft III, a wonderful account of which is contained in the book *Not Only Golf,* written by one of my predecessors on *The Guardian,* the late Pat Ward-Thomas. Having been shot down early in the war, Ward-Thomas and his fellow prisoners tried to keep themselves occupied and a little fitter than they might otherwise have been by playing their preferred sport.

Ward-Thomas, much to his obvious delight, became the first Stalag Open champion on an improvized course that necessarily brought into play many features of the camp not intended to be so. One hole was played over a tiny allotment and Ward-Thomas recalls the anguish of a 'horticulturist' when a golf ball 'decapitated a cherished tomato plant.' He goes on, 'On one occasion a German Unteroffizier's morning constitutional was disturbed by the crash of glass all around him. Someone had shanked.'

Golf is played wherever it can be and in some places where it obviously cannot. Into that latter category comes Uummannaq golf club, which is a moveable feast, situated as it is on the ice floes of Greenland. Because icebergs move about a bit, the course is different each year and it came to fame in 1999 when the Drambuie World Ice Golf Championship was staged there.

It was won by a British golf writer, Peter Masters, who risked his extremities, he says, to get both the story and the glory. 'The temperatures,' he reported in the UK magazine *Golf World,* 'were around minus 21 Celsius and the organizers were quite serious when they suggested that massaging one's extremities was a good practice to get into. If you think that your nose is getting a bit cold, then give it a good rub. Also, keep a close eye on your opponent, not to prevent them from cheating but to make sure they do not have any little white spots that are the first sign of the skin freezing.' Masters went on, 'Uummannaq's golf course had a faint whiff of links about it. No sand and no bunkers perhaps but in place of dunes you had icebergs and while a links is by the sea, ice golf goes one better – it's on the sea.'

Whereas that tournament was played 150 kilometres into the Arctic Circle, Bjorkliden Golf Club is around 240 kilometres inside the circle and is, furthermore, a regular golf club with 6,000 members. This is because anyone who books a flight with SAS can become a 'VIP member' of the club, a membership that entitles you to a 'Polar Certificate' which proclaims that you have entered the 'Arctic Circle into the land of the midnight sun.' The sun rises in the middle of May and does not set again until the end of July and during that time Bjorkliden holds 'Midnight Sun' tournaments. They are usually shotgun starts, at around 2230 hours, finishing at around 0330 hours, at which time there will be the prize presentation. Some people then go to bed: others do not.

At Augusta, Western Australia they have serious flies. The plague of Australia in general, these have been known to carry off small sheep.

Furnace Creek, in California's Death Valley, could hardly offer a greater contrast. Death Valley is aptly named, for to attempt to cross it on foot, as the early settlers had to, in summer, was to invite almost certain demise. Things have obviously changed since those covered wagon days and Death Valley, while still threatening to the careless or unwary, now has an 18-hole course open all the year round. It is, furthermore, 218 feet below sea-level, which, it has to be reported, does not help one way or the other.

Anyone can play there and anyone can play Augusta, too. Not, unfortunately, the Georgian version, but the Augusta Golf Club that is situated on the tip of Western Australia, in a town where the Southern and Indian Oceans meet. It is only a tiny town and the golf course is just outside, on top of a hill, and the silence when you get out of the car is profound – until the first fly delves deep into your ear, the first slap is slapped and the first cry of 'F**k off' rings out.

Here they have serious flies. The plague of Australia in general, these have been known to carry off small sheep; well, maybe not, but it certainly feels that way at times. The locals have decided that the only way to cope with these pestilential nuisances is to wear the kind of fine-mesh nets over their heads, down to their shoulders, that beekeepers wear. This has the unlooked-for side-effect of telling the golfer, forcibly, not so much whether his head is moving, as by how much. As such it might be labelled an artificial aid by the R&A, but one visit and they would change their minds in an instant.

It's a pity, because the course is in a lovely place, with big panoramas stretching down to the oceans, plus the Blackwood river. It's the last course before the South Pole, some 5,439 kilometres (3,400 miles) away and it features, unfortunately, browns rather than greens. They play a Masters tournament here, of course, with the winner getting a green jacket, but it not quite as rigorous as that affair in America. It is played with the far friendlier Stableford system and in 1994 was won with scores of 44 and 42 points, which would be remarkable when compiled by anyone. When compiled by Ray Buller, who was 82 at the time and who won from a field of 150, it is astonishing.

PULLING A STROKE

GAMBLING IN GOLF

JEREMY CHAPMAN

*'In betting, there are two elements that are never lacking: hope
as hope and an incomplete recollection of the past.'*

E.V. LUCAS, OF THE *NEW YORK TIMES*

Since its earliest days golf has had a special attraction for gamblers.
Great hustlers like the legendary Titanic Thompson operated in
America in the 1930s, and there have also been the great 'money'
professionals like Englishmen Lionel Platts and Hedley Muscroft and, in
America, Raymond Floyd and Lee Trevino. Their definition of pressure
was playing a challenge match for US$100 when all you have in the
world is US$50.

Then there are the punters like the notorious Hole-in-One Gang who
terrorized the little one-shop bookmakers up and down the United
Kingdom, exploiting the ignorance of non-golfers in a £500,000 scam.
There was also the young computer buff from Oxford who took the Big
Three bookies in the UK – Ladbrokes, William Hill and Corals – to the
cleaners for a world-record profit of £814,000.

Gamblers have wagered their life on the outcome of a game of golf
and since time immemorial the lure of lucre has encouraged cheating
and handicap banditry. There are plenty of stories of people winning
pro-ams in Spain off a handicap of 17 when they are seven at home. Yet
for the most part it has been a game of honour for the best of gentlemen.

The Honourable Company of Edinburgh Golfers at Muirfield, for
example, have their Bett Book which records all wagers struck over club
dinners. They would play for flagons of wine and gallons of whisky but
always with the object of having a fair, close match with no obvious
advantage to either side. All the volumes of the Bett Book from 1776 to
the present day are still extant, though there is much secrecy as to the
names and contents. Members lived in fear of being ridiculed if they did
not turn up to play out a wager, for the defaulter's name would be
entered for posterity. For example, in 1880, the match 'C v M' was 'not
played, C funked.'

Muirfield historian Archie Baird said that the whole club still revolved round the Bett Book and the camaraderie of the dinners every seven weeks and all the bet striking, not only at Muirfield but also at neighbouring courses like Gullane and Luffness. 'The bets themselves are very small beer,' said Baird. 'At Gullane the maximum bet is £4. At Muirfield it's a bit more but £100 bets are unheard of. It's the tradition that makes all the fun, not the size of the wagers.'

Thompson's greatest hustle was when he trained a man to play golf from a wheelchair. For three months the game thrived as the 'cripple' worked his scores down to 78 and Thompson worked the bets up to $200,000.

Money, of course, is not everything. In the R&A minutes of 1870 Sir David Moncreiffe 'backed his life against the life of John Whyte-Melville of Strathkinnes for a new silver club as a present to the St Andrews Golf Club, the price of the club to be paid for by the survivor, and the present bet to be inscribed on it.'

Archie Compston, professional at Coombe Hill, was a gambler and not a man to stake your life against. He once offered to play the best ball of Henry Longhurst and two of his Cambridge undergraduates. Longhurst, good enough to have won the German Amateur championship, thought they were on a good wicket and bet accordingly, but the big-hitting Compston played his trump card: the match, in the winter, was off the back tees. From there, there were six holes that only he could reach in regulation. 'It was learning a lesson the hard way,' recalled Longhurst, who had to sell his car to pay his percentage of the wager.

In the States, the Depression bred some hard men and some hustlers and

Lee Trevino. learned his trade working as a hustler in the early days.

the greatest of them all was Titanic Thompson, a man who once, it was said, took US$500 off Al Capone and lived to tell the tale.

Thompson's real name was Alvin Clarence Thomas and he would take on almost anybody for almost anything, so long as he thought he had an edge. Often, in fact, he knew he had an edge, because he had arranged matters that way. For instance, when living near Joplin, Missouri, he noticed some workmen putting in new road signs reading 'Joplin 20 miles.'

He dug it up, replaced it five miles nearer the city and then, after a fishing trip with two friends, remarked as they passed the sign that it could not possibly be right. The friends insisted that it must be, two bets of US$500 were struck and Thompson, unabashed, took the money. The friends, as Thompson tells it, later used the same sign to get their money back, and more.

He was an expert card shark and pool player and he could play golf with almost equal facility either right- or left-handed. In fact, some of his golfing exploits beggar belief – and have undoubtedly grown in the telling. It was said, for instance, that he once scored 29 on the back nine of a course in Texas and took Byron Nelson and his backers for US$3,000.

As that was said to be in 1934, it was a huge sum of money but 60 years later Nelson had little recollection of it. 'We played a match,' he said when asked about Thompson, 'and he was backing himself. I wasn't a gambler so the members said they'd take care of that side of things. I had to give him three shots and he had a 71, I had a 69. I don't have any idea about the money.'

Thompson's greatest hustle was when he trained a man to play golf from a wheelchair and then took him to Miami to proposition wealthy vacationers. Titanic told the action-minded businessmen that his friend had been in an accident but was still good enough to get round Miami Country Club in 98 or less. The victims saw the two plaster casts and were hooked. Little did they know that the casts were taken off each night so that the 'cripple' could get his blood circulating properly for the next day's sting. For three months the game thrived as the 'cripple' worked his scores down to 78 and Thompson worked the bets up to US$200,000.

It was Thompson in another role, as backer, who was behind the famous matches between Raymond Floyd, hot-shot professional and the then unknown Lee Trevino, at Horizon Hills in El Paso in 1965. Thompson had been at El Paso playing some blackjack and poker, plus some right- and left-handed golf, and had won so much money that the members asked him to leave.

But by then he had noticed the talented Trevino and when he later met up with Floyd, in Dallas, he realized there was a match to be made. Floyd remembers that he was asked by Thompson if he'd ever heard of Trevino. 'I said no, he asked me if I'd play him and I said "Certainly, I'll play anybody I've never heard of." He then asked me if I'd play him on his course and I said "I'll play anybody anywhere that I've never heard of." '

Trevino remembers the first time he saw Ti, as he calls him in his book, *Super Mex*. 'I'll never forget that morning when Ti stepped out of his taxi in front of the clubhouse. As he squinted his eyes in the desert sun he looked like an ageing Clint Eastwood. Clint made a movie once called A *Fistful of Dollars*. That pretty well fit Ti's line of work too. I'm sure he had heard about the cotton farmers at Horizon Hills who loved to bet big money. He'd come to check them out.'

Betting is not encouraged, officially, by the R&A, and there is still no book-making presence at the Open Championship.

The result of that checking out was the series of matches against Floyd. Trevino again. 'I'd never met Raymond so when he drove up I got a cart and went out to pick up his golf bag. I carried his clubs into the locker-room, put them in a locker, brushed his shoes, cleaned them and polished them. Raymond asked me: "Who am I supposed to play?" and I said "Me." He looked at me and said "You? What do you do?" So I told him "I'm a combination everything. I'm the cart man, the shoe man, clubhouse man and pro." '

The combination man won the first match they played, with a 65 to a 67 and Floyd wanted to play another nine. But Trevino couldn't – he had to put the carts away and clean the clubs. They played again the next day and Trevino, with another 65, beat Floyd's 66. The third match, though, saw Floyd get at least some of his money back. 'On the last hole,' said Trevino, 'I had an eight foot eagle putt and Raymond a six foot birdie putt and if I made my eagle and he missed his birdie I would win. But I missed and Raymond won the round. That's when he got his clubs, shook my hand, and said "I can find mu-u-u-ch easier games than this," and left.' Trevino, of course, went on to win six majors, Floyd four.

Thompson was probably not good enough to win at the top level but there is a consensus among those who saw him play that he could have competed on what passed for a tour at that time. He didn't because he could make more money hustling on the golf course. Paul Runyan, a Ryder Cup player and twice US PGA champion always said that Thompson was the best left-hander in the world until Bob Charles came along and Tommy Bolt, who won the US Open in 1958, was another admirer. 'He had a gambler's swing,' he said. 'A good solid compact swing, not one that you had to practise every day to keep. He could have been the greatest.'

Thompson eschewed alcohol, the better to keep his hand-eye co-ordination as perfect as possible, but drink has frequently featured in golf betting. For instance, the *Golfer's Handbook* records that 'a match was arranged in the South of England for a considerable bet between a scratch player and a long handicap man, playing level, the scratch man to drink a whisky and soda on each tee. On the 16th tee the scratch man, who had a one-hole lead, collapsed and was not very well for some time afterwards.'

Both in Britain and America the Calcutta, or golf auction, was a very popular form of gambling, particularly between the wars. The idea was to bid for the amateur who would be in the winning team in a pro-am and the man who bid the most got him. Some amateurs who fancied their chances used to buy themselves and in one such case in the States the total

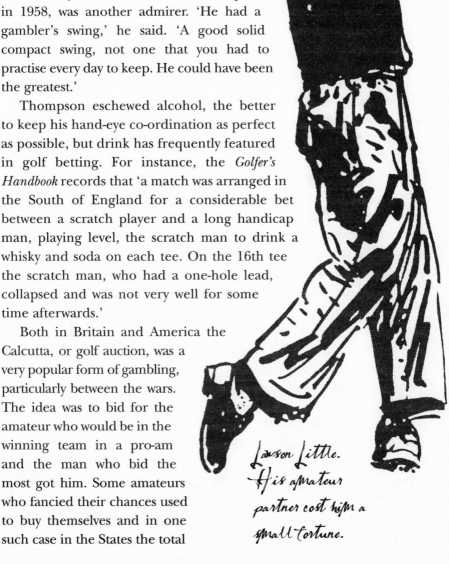

Lawson Little.
His amateur partner cost him a small fortune.

Calcutta pool ran to US$100,000. Eventually, the amateur who had bought himself and his professional, Lawson Little, stood to win US$40,000, a huge sum for the period. They came to the last hole needing a five to win, it was all on the amateur, who hit the green in two and putted up to within a foot. But his tap-in putt stopped within an inch of the hole and the amateur, who was used to having such putts conceded, reached out with his putter to rake the ball back. Little screamed at him not to touch it but it was too late. A two-shot penalty for hitting a moving ball meant goodbye to a fortune.

Betting is not encouraged, officially, by the R&A and there is still no bookmaking presence at the Open Championship. But the European Tour has had two bookmaking sponsors – Corals in the early eighties and, in the late nineties, Victor Chandler. It has been a long journey since the day in 1898 when the first bookmaker appeared at a tournament in Carnoustie. In 1927, a Glasgow bookie and two assistants took their chance at sacred St Andrews, causing quite a stir, and again at Max Faulkner's Open at Royal Portrush in 1951, put up his odds on a board in the qualifying rounds, drumming up plenty of business.

It all came to a head in 1971 when Ladbrokes were asked by the sponsor, John Player, to provide a betting facility at their Classic tournament at Turnberry. It was widely rumoured that Ryder Cup Scot, Harry Bannerman, got a price of 50-1 to finish ahead of Brian Huggett, after Huggett had taken 69 in the first round and Bannerman, in dreadful conditions, had taken 80. The bet came up and although there was not the slightest suggestion of any impropriety or collusion between the players, the R&A perceived a potential danger to the good name of the game. Shortly afterwards, in a joint statement with the PGA, they banned bookmakers from all tournaments.

As a golf watcher for more than a quarter of a century I have seen only one incident which could possibly be blamed on a punter. It came at the 1983 World Matchplay championship at Wentworth when Nick Faldo, the home hero, was playing Graham Marsh. Faldo's shot to the 16th was bounding through the green when it mysteriously went into reverse and came to a stop 25 feet from the hole. Whether that was a punter at work or someone who had over-indulged in the hospitality tents is not known.

Ladbrokes have particularly unpleasant memories of the 1979 World Matchplay. Bovis, who had built some luxury holiday homes, were offering one to any of the 12 players who aced the short second. Bovis asked for the odds against a hole-in-one there during the four days, were quoted a generous 40-1 and invested £1,000. Lo and behold, with almost the first shot struck, Isao Aoki holed out at the short second at around 8.40am and the deed was done. Ron Pollard, the former Ladbrokes director, recalled, 'The event was being televized and it was my misfortune to turn the set on in my office just as Aoki played his shot. I just couldn't believe it. I went up to see Peter George, managing director of the racing division. "Good morning", he said brightly. "Not really," I replied, "We've already lost 40 grand." '

Without a shadow of a doubt the biggest official haul from a day's punting on golf came in the early spring of 1995 when Graham Hill, a 26-year-old computer wizard from Eynsham, near Oxford, relieved Ladbrokes, William Hill and Coral of a cool £814,257.

Odds in golf are generally heavily stacked against the punter but in the 1990s there were two outstanding occasions when 'the little man' put one across 'the big bad bookies': the Hole-in-One plot in 1991 and the Florida Sting four years later.

The former was perhaps the most audacious of all. It was cooked up by two boys from Essex, Paul Simons and John Carter, known as the Hole-in-One Gang by quivering, wrecked and broken bookmakers throughout the land. These young men knew exactly what the chances were of a hole-in-one occurring in professional tournaments. The aces were all listed in the European Tour's media guide, so there was no big secret about it. If there were 36 tournaments in a year and 18 holes-in-one, the odds were even-money, perhaps a little more since some of the aces had been achieved at the same tournament.

Simons and Carter knew that the major bookmaking chains were very well aware of the correct odds but decided, quite correctly, that there were many one-man businesses that didn't follow the golfing scene and thought a hole-in-one was a rare bird sighted about as often as a dodo or Halley's Comet. Armed with telephone directories for the length and breadth of England, a great line in bluff and Cockney charm and unlimited patience, they drove thousands of miles, taking all prices from 3–1 to 100–1 on holes-in-one being recorded at five televized tournaments – the US Open, the Open, the Benson & Hedges, the Volvo PGA and the European Open. They all came up.

The biggest howler and the biggest howl came from Arthur

Whittaker of Derby, whose shop manager had laid three £50 bets at 100–1 on the Benson & Hedges and the two majors. When they all copped, Whittaker took the case to the *Sporting Life*'s Green Seal service, which arbitrates on betting disputes, confident that it would rule in his favour on the basis of 'human error' i.e. that his staff man had laid the wrong price. However, to general glee, Green Seal ruled in favour of Simons and Carter. They said, 'There is a world of difference between a palpable error and an error of judgement. If a bookmaker, or member of his staff, accepts a bet at mutually agreed odds and neither the bet nor the laying procedures contravenes the bookmaker's rules, there is no way in which the bet can be retrospectively voided or amended.'

In fairness, most bookmakers stumped up without a murmur but sadly Simons and Carter never did see all of that half million. Whittakers paid up under extreme duress but other firms went bust rather than cough up, the worst offender being Spectrum Racing, who sold up rather than fork out £43,000. In total the boys had to forego £80,000 but still had enough for a Mercedes, a holiday home in Florida and trips to Las Vegas, South Africa and Australia.

Without a shadow of a doubt the biggest official haul from a day's punting on golf came in the early spring of 1995 when Graham Hill, a 26-year-old computer wizard from Eynsham, near Oxford, relieved Ladbrokes, William Hill and Coral of a cool £814,257 for the relatively minor outlay of £109, including betting tax.

Hill was going to spend the money on a soccer bet but was worried that the foul weather would lead to many cancellations. So he switched targets to the Doral Ryder Open in sunny Florida for a series of accumulator bets that left the bookmakers dazed. William Hill were hit for £274,903, Ladbrokes £271,630 and Coral £267,724. The plan, when he struck the bet, was to relieve them each of £500,000, their payout limit on sports bets. But the £1.5 million coup foundered when Billy Mayfair failed to be the clear winner of his first-day, three-ball match. All the other nine picks obliged but party-pooper Mayfair was only joint-winner of his game, thereby halving the stakes going on to the other nine outright winners. Hill, who four years earlier had won £39,000 on a soccer bet, was heard to murmur, 'If only Mayfair had done his stuff ...'

* Jeremy Chapman is probably the foremost expert on golf betting in the world. His appearance at the Open championship media centre is eagerly awaited by hundreds of press punters, all of whom have forgotten that their selections failed to deliver the previous year.

CHAPTER 5

THE
MAJORS

THE OPEN CHAMPIONSHIP

THE OPEN IS NOW, in the opinion of most of those outside America, the world's premier championship: a genuine World Open. This championship has more great players from around the globe than any other and furthermore it sets out to encourage just such participation, for it is the Open. Not the British Open, for why should it be? When it started in the 1860s, it did not have to be distinguished from any other event, so there was no need to call it anything other than the Open.

Even when Young Tom won three times in a row and therefore was awarded the championship belt outright, causing a one-year hiatus in 1871, there was never the least doubt that it would be back. The organizers, originally the Prestwick Club, then the R&A, knew they had created an event worth preserving and preserve it they have.

It now distinguishes itself by its presentation. It is run by a small group of dedicated professionals and a larger group of besotted amateurs and the mix has kept the Open from being too big or too small, too ancient or too modern. It has become a festival of golf, an annual celebration of most of the facets and aspects of the game, contained off-course in a huge tented village and on-course by players whose dearest wish is to win this, the oldest title of them all.

The Open has hit on the perfect formula for its playing. The R&A have identified eight courses, all links, which they believe worthy of hosting a championship and which, importantly, have the infrastructure to support the large enterprise the Open has become. The R&A are constantly on the look-out for more places to play but the current big eight are: St Andrews, Royal Birkdale, Carnoustie (which returned to the rota in 1999 after a 24-year absence) Royal St George's, Royal Lytham & St Annes, Muirfield, Turnberry and Royal Troon. Given the inherent problems of some of those venues – Carnoustie's tiny-town roads; Turnberry's lack of access and nearby accommodation – it is not impossible to see a day when, with ordinary goodwill, the Open could go to, say, Saunton, that magnificent test tucked away in Devon. It should certainly be played at both Royal Portrush and Portmarnock but political goodwill is rather more difficult to achieve.

Old Tom Morris.

Considerable benefits accrue from having a championship that rotates around a limited number of courses. They can be permanently cabled for television and radio and for the various food outlets that sustain the huge crowds that flock to an Open. It also helps that a club acquires knowledge of presenting a championship, which is passed on when the Open comes round again.

Just as the current rota has evolved, so has the method of determining a champion in the event of a tie. For many years it was a 36-hole play-off the following day and when that became too much it was reduced to 18. Then, with a display of admirable pragmatism and almost certainly ignoring the instincts of the majority of their older members, the R&A dispensed even with that. They decided that the Open champion should become known on the final day of the championship and to this end they installed what is undoubtedly the best compromise of any of the major championships.

The Masters and the US PGA favour a sudden-death play-off, which can be desperately unfair and the US Open retains an 18-hole decider, which is desperately slow and anticlimactic. The Open has a four-hole aggregate play-off, which is excruciatingly exciting and serves the twin purposes of fairness and immediacy. No one who saw Mark Calcavecchia take advantage of Greg Norman's rush of blood at the 18th at Royal Troon, or watched John Daly pile so much pressure on Costantino Rocca that the Italian self-destructed in the Road Hole bunker at St Andrews, could doubt the efficacy of this method.

The Open is, perhaps, the greatest attraction in world sport that anyone can go and watch. It is not an all-ticket affair and will not be for as long as the R&A have their way. They have set their faces firmly against the idea of limiting tickets, not just because of the inevitable black market but also because they genuinely wish as many people as possible to attend. There are those who think that they are close to the limit – that at the weekend they are over a limit that enables people not just to attend but also to see some golf. The R&A do not agree and in 1997, in an attempt to further the game's following, allowed people under 18, accompanied by an adult, to get in free – an admirable exercise in keeping the Open tradition alive.

Most of golf's truly great names are inscribed on the championship trophy – the Claret Jug – although, as the Prayer Book has it, 'all kinds and conditions of men' have succeeded. There were those early caddies and clubmakers; gentlemen amateurs; club professionals; those who won almost by accident and those who dedicated their entire lives in pursuit of the Jug. All were subjected to the pressures and many suffered the problems that afflict the modern game.

It has become a festival of golf, an annual celebration of most of the facets and aspects of the game, contained off-course in a huge tented village and on-course by players whose dearest wish is to win this, the oldest title of them all.

In 1866, the *Scotsman* reported that some wealthy men of Mussel-burgh and Edinburgh clubbed together to send three players across the country to Prestwick for the Open 'to keep up the honour of the 'honest toun'. It was worth it. Willie Park won and his brother David was second and they were both Musselburgh men.

John Ball jnr was the first amateur to win, in 1890, and he was runner-up to his clubmate Harold Hilton in 1892. Hilton won again in 1897 but had his troubles during the defence of his title in 1893. He opened with a round of 88 and, according to *The Field,* came to grief 'at the back of a wall and, missing the globe twice, so awkwardly did it lie, he took 10 strokes to hole out.'

The 1921 Open was held at St Andrews and won by a player – Jock Hutchison – from the United States, although he was in fact born in St Andrews and was only a 'naturalized' American. While it may now seem surprising that no American had won the championship before then, the First World War and the difficulties of transatlantic travel undoubtedly contributed.

One American-born competitor that year did not complete the championship. Bobby Jones, then 19, had a tough time in the third round and popular legend has it that he tore up his card at the 11th. Jones insisted that while he did not return a score the card was not torn up, just kept in his pocket.

Be that as it may, in 1922 there was no doubt about the nationality of the winner. It was the quintessentially American Walter Hagen, who never left anyone in any doubt about anything. Two years earlier, at Deal, his golf made no headlines but his style did. Hagen arrived in a limousine, strode into the locker-room and described what happened next. 'While we were changing our shoes a little man in a white coat came hurriedly in our direction. "Are you Mr High-gen?" he asked brusquely. "I am," I said, "and this is Mr Jim Barnes." "Gentlemen," he said importantly, "you're in the wrong place." "This *is* Deal?" I asked. "Oh yes indeed," he assured me, "but you gentlemen are professionals. You'll be using Mr Hunter's golf shop for dressing".' One look at Mr Hunter's facilities and Hagen decided to change in the limo.

At Royal St George's in 1922, Hagen set an early target of 300 with a final round of 72. Almost last out was George Duncan, a man of unpredictable brilliance, who was having one of his days and came to the 18th needing a par four to tie. He hit a second shot that appeared to be good but it trickled off into a hollow on the left of the green, just as Sandy Lyle's would 63 years later. By then it was called Duncan's Hollow, for it cost him the championship. He failed to get the ball all the way up the slope to the pin, took five and Hagen was home by a shot.

The first champion of the 1930s was Bobby Jones, who was, appropriately, the last amateur winner. At Hoylake, he won by two shots from Macdonald Smith and Leo Diegel. The decade was also notable for

Henry Cotton's ending of the streak of American victories, at Royal St George's in 1934 and the drama it entailed.

Cotton opened with rounds of 67,65, golf of surpassing brilliance surely in any age. The Dunlop 65, the leading ball in Europe for almost 40 years, was named after that second round. Cotton had 11 birdies and the longest putt he holed for any of them was nine feet, an indication of iron play of the highest quality. After a third-round 72 he was 10 ahead of the field and surely had only to turn up to win.

One look at Mr Hunter's facilities and Hagen decided to change in the limo.

Cotton, however, was a finely-tuned character who lived on his nerves. He could be erudite and forceful, stubborn and generous and he had a stock of near-the-knuckle stories that could keep any company entertained, but there were times when he withdrew into himself. When he got to the course for the final round and found that his tee time had been put back 15 minutes, he spent the time morosely in the starter's tent, communicating only with himself. He emerged pale and afflicted with stomach cramps and had obviously been thinking about the consequences of becoming the first 'home' player to win the Open since 1923. The first drive was hooked into the hay, he went out in 40 and began the homeward half with three fives. A collapse of almost unprecedented proportions – and a career-destroying one at that – seemed a possibility but he holed a long birdie putt at the 13th and the clouds lifted. Cotton won by five and there were some delirious scenes at the presentation and an emotional one after it.

The new champion went to the Guildford Hotel, now defunct, on the sea-front, to visit Harry Vardon who had been watching the championship but was taken ill on the last day. In *Thanks for the Game*, Cotton recalled, 'I went to Harry's room and gave him the Cup to hold again. He had won it six times and, with the trophy in his arms, tears began to run down his face. I sobbed unashamedly too!'

Cotton was the product of a public school, a 'toff' of the times, a player whose whole life was dedicated to the winning of tournaments and championships around the world. He had a club job because that was demanded of him but it was only a base for his competitive play. Alf Perry, who succeeded Cotton as champion, was a club pro first and foremost. He played in the Open because in those days the members expected it of their professional, if he could play at all.

Perry, who beat Alf Padgham by four shots at Muirfield, provides perhaps the most vivid contrast imaginable between the Open competitor of then and now. He was a short stocky man, invariably dressed in a large flat cap and enormously inelegant, baggy trousers. He played as he looked, with a grip that showed all four knuckles under the shaft of the club, a stance far wider than his shoulders and a flailing swing that depended for everything on timing. The Open finished on a Friday in those days precisely so that Perry and his like could be back in the shop for the weekend. The extent of his recognition from the members might be, 'Well done, Perry, see you won that Open thing.'

As little as possible was being left to chance and by the time the championship arrived there was not a Scot who was not convinced that Hogan, the 'Wee Ice Mon', would win. He did and each round was lower than the one before. He never played in another Open.

As for contracts and making a fortune, *Golf Illustrated*, the weekly magazine of the time, only ever showed one advertizement featuring the winner of the 1935 Open. 'Mr Perry was strengthened in his task,' it proclaimed, by eating a well-known brand of bread. Years later, in 1970, when the R&A hit on the happy idea of inviting all the living Open champions to a dinner, almost all of them accepted. Perry, perhaps typically, declined.

After the Second World War, Bobby Locke, the South African known as 'Old Muffin Face', became the dominant force and won the Open three times between 1949 and 1952. He was interrupted in 1951 by Max Faulkner, the colourful Englishman who was so confident that with two rounds to play at Portrush he was signing autographs 'Max Faulkner, Open champion, 1951.' It made brave men cringe but as Henry Longhurst wryly remarked, 'The fates spared him.'

In 1953 at Carnoustie, Ben Hogan won although it was a somewhat joyless victory. He had no real desire to play in the championship, which at this period was not what it had been or would become again and Hogan detested the pain and inconvenience of long-distance travelling. He only came because friends like Gene Sarazen and the great American amateur, Chick Evans, insisted that he could never be called a truly great golfer until he had won the oldest championship of them all. He had also already won the Masters and the US Open and there was the thought that to win three successive major championships might be considered an achievement – but it was with a sense of duty rather than desire that he made the trip to Carnoustie.

He arrived two weeks early to adjust to the time change, the conditions and the smaller ball. He based himself in Dundee, where there was an American company who fed him familiar foods and he practised in solitary fashion, with only his caddie for company. Hogan was the greatest golfer in the world at that time and he gave a new definition to the word dedication.

One of the pivotal holes at Carnoustie is the long sixth, which has a bunker in the middle of the fairway at about the spot where a good drive will pitch. It forces most mortals to take a safe line to the right although this means a more difficult second shot. The other option is to go left, down a narrow path between the bunker and the out of bounds, a route so dangerous that it is only taken by accident in most cases. However, it offers a much safer chance of going for the green in two, and during this Open it became known as Hogan's Alley as the American unerringly directed his drives down it. It gave him something like a two-iron for his second and the story has it that during practice he sent his caddie up to the green, hit three shots – one left, one right and one centre – and demanded to know how they had bounced on landing.

As little as possible was being left to chance and by the time the championship arrived there was not a Scot who was not convinced that Hogan, the 'Wee Ice Mon', would win. He did and each round was lower than the one before. He never played in another Open.

Almost no one could be less like the single-minded Hogan than the man who was to win for the next three years. The Australian Peter Thomson was and is a cultured man of many interests, including wine and politics. He has a good cellar and stood for the national parliament. Spurned at the polls himself, he has derived satisfaction from the success of his son, Andrew, who became Australia's Minister for Sport and Tourism in 1996.

Intellect can be a dangerous thing on a golf course but Thomson had a simple repeating swing and his major asset was a mind that enabled him to use that swing under the greatest pressure. Perhaps the greatest compliment from one golfer to another was that paid to Thomson by the British Ryder Cup player George Will, who had a notoriously fickle temperament. 'Peter is the only player I have ever been on a course with whose swing got slower as the situation got tighter.' Thomson's reward was five Opens in 12 years.

The last was in 1965, five years after Arnold Palmer had set about the task of revitalizing the Open. In the 1940s and 1950s some of the fields were not of the requisite standard, largely because the Americans chose not to compete. There was little reason to. The prize money was poor, the food dull and the hotels awful. In addition, the title itself had fallen into disrepute. It was arguable that not since the early 1930s (1953 apart) had it been won by a golfer who was indisputably the world's best player.

The 1960 championship, at St Andrews, was deemed to be the Centenary Open and the authorities, aware of the criticisms, went after – and got – Arnold Palmer. They could have done no more, for Palmer at that time was demonstrably the world's best and when he arrived at St Andrews he had already won the Masters and the US Open. It seemed, if not a certainty, then at least a strong likelihood that he would equal Hogan's feat of winning three majors in a year and have a chance at the Grand Slam. In the event, Palmer finished second – he never led – and the Centenary champion was Kel Nagle, of Australia, one of the most popular men in the game.

There was a theory abroad that Palmer had struggled to come to terms with the small British-size ball (1.62 inches to the 1.68 of the American ball). It travelled farther in the wind and was infinitely livelier, which made it more difficult to control around the greens. The bigger ball demanded more accurate striking in all departments of the game and when this was ultimately recognized, the rest of the world joined the Americans in using it.

Palmer had overcome the problems by 1961. At Birkdale, he won his first Open and got his revenge on Nagle the following year when he successfully defended the title. The Australian was six shots behind Palmer but seven ahead of Brian Huggett and Phil Rodgers, in third place. Pat Ward-Thomas of *The Guardian* hailed Palmer's victory as 'the greatest exhibition of golfing supremacy that Britain has seen in modern times. It was a rout without parallel.'

The occasionally irascible Ward-Thomas then launched himself on the authorities and their organization – or lack of it – and 'the disgusting exhibition of a huge stampeding crowd' at the end. He concluded, 'The whole conception of stewarding must be reviewed. It was pathetically inadequate for crowds which behave in this manner.' Even with better controls, the last-hole stampede remains a problem to this day.

It was not that, though, that persuaded Palmer to boycott the Open at St Andrews in 1964. It was a calculated snub because everyone had to undergo 36 holes of qualifying for the championship proper. The outdated practice deterred many Americans, who felt it was demeaning –

and too time-consuming – although such antediluvian attitudes persisted within the USGA, in regard to their own Open and European participation in it, into the 1990s. In 1964, Palmer was the Masters champion and he was fed up with being treated like any old club pro on his annual trip to Britain. The British public, who could not get enough of him, wanted to know where he was and the resultant outcry ensured that the rule was changed.

At Hoylake in 1967, the champion was Roberto de Vicenzo, arguably the most popular man to emerge from Argentina. A wonderful golfer and a huge man in every way, he was 44, the oldest winner since Vardon in 1914. De Vicenzo, who could have bogeyed one of the two final holes and still won, hit huge drives at both, needing no more than a nine-iron for the second shots. At the last the crowd surged irresistibly on to the fairway behind him. There were thousands of us jammed tightly together and the man behind me, almost frantic in his excitement, began shouting, 'Hurrah, hurrah, hooray for Roberto,' over and over again. It was some time before I could safely turn and see who it was. It turned out to be Henry Cotton.

There was similar emotion at Lytham in 1969 when Tony Jacklin, dressed appropriately in purple, became Emperor of European golf with the first British win since 1951. In fact, it was rather better than that, for Jacklin beat a strong international field, really the first Briton to do that since Cotton in 1937. Jacklin went on to win the 1970 US Open and for that all-too-brief period was probably the best player in the world.

In 1969, it seemed as if Jacklin was the saviour that all of British golf wanted. He had a superb all-round game and a highly competitive attitude and he was a great favourite with the fans and the press, who were delighted for him, particularly because he had won so well. He played

Arnold Palmer at the 1960 Open.

the closing five holes with a succession of superb drives and, when he struck a superb seven-iron on to the 18th green, the spectators went barmy, in the nicest possible fashion. Jacklin stood, looking slightly stunned, trying to absorb his victory. He celebrated with champagne and, when the bottle was lifted up for the photographers, Jacklin's manager, Mark McCormack, was on hand to ensure that the maker's name was facing the cameras. The commercial era had truly arrived.

If 1969 was big for Britain, the finish of the 1970 Open at St Andrews sent golfing chills around the world. The championship was won by Jack Nicklaus and lost by Doug Sanders and no one who has ever struck a short putt that meant anything at all, and missed it, will fail to sympathize

Rocca's delight was shortlived. He holed a monstrous putt on the 18th green to tie, but lost the play-off to John Daly.

with the latter. One of the great clichés in sport is that no one remembers who came second but when it comes to the 1970 Open they do, and Jean Van de Velde will always be renowned for his heart-breaking eight at the 72nd hole at Carnoustie in 1999.

At St Andrews, Sanders had a putt of at most three feet, slightly downhill, left to right, to win the championship. He took an age surveying it, stood to it, then bent down to remove something only he saw on his line. 'Oh dear,' breathed Henry Longhurst, on television, as so often putting into words the thoughts of millions. Henry, like the rest of us, suspected there was nothing to remove and that Sanders simply could not bring himself to hit the putt.

> **Sanders took an age surveying it, stood to it, then bent down to remove something only he saw on his line. 'Oh dear,' breathed Henry Longhurst, on television, as so often putting into words the thoughts of millions.**

When he did, he knew instantly that he had failed. The ball had travelled barely half its intended length when Sanders stretched out his putter, in the classic gesture of the weekender who knows his putt has missed and wants to rake it back to try it again. Although Sanders got a second chance of sorts – an 18-hole play-off next day – there was an inevitability about Nicklaus' win. Great champions may doze but if you wake them they win.

That was a wonderfully dramatic Open – much, much later Sanders was to say that he sometimes went a whole five minutes without thinking about it – but the championship that may be the greatest of them all so far was in 1977. It was at Turnberry, on the west coast of Scotland, one of the most scenic of our great championship courses. There are those who denigrate Turnberry on the grounds that it is not a proper links, which is true, and that it has a weak start and a less-than-glorious finish, which is not always true. Turnberry is heavily dependent on a wind, from the south or northwest it matters not, and then it is a challenge for the best. It may also be the most photogenic of all the world's championship courses, with the possible exception of Pebble Beach.

The 1977 Open featured Jack Nicklaus and Tom Watson, the two greatest players of that time, indeed two of the greatest of all time, in head-to-head combat over 36 holes, playing at the absolute peak of their powers. At the end of it the man who said, 'You've seen my best and you've beaten it,' was Nicklaus. He was walking off the 18th green, his arm draped round Watson's shoulder, both utterly exhausted by the intensity of their battle. This had been a 36-hole match in which each had given everything: it was almost primitive; in nature it would have been a fight to the death. Watson, the young lion, had deposed the long-time leader of the pride.

For once the scores tell a large part of the story. Both men started with rounds of 68 and 70 and were paired together for the third round. They both took 65 and no one else was to feature on the last day. Ward-Thomas wrote, 'One never thought to see the day when the champion would have to play the final 36 holes in 130 strokes and finish with a birdie for a total of 268 to win by a single shot; nor that the Open's record aggregate would be beaten by eight'. Hubert Green was third, 11 strokes behind Watson.

The Open is much given to epics and the 1979 version at Lytham was one such, ushering in the epic career of Severiano Ballesteros. If ever a man illustrated that Opens can be won by will-power, by sheer bloody-minded aggression and, of course, by the best pair of hands European golf has ever known, Ballesteros did so that year. It is an incredible statistic that during the course of the championship he hit only nine fairways with his driver but the Spaniard was a genius out of the rough – if ever they had played golf tournaments without fairways at all, Ballesteros would have won the lot.

There was a lot of talk about the 16th hole, the 70th in the championship, where Seve hit his drive into a temporary car park, got a free drop and birdied. However, the hole that illustrated perfectly the reason he won was the 13th, only 340 yards long and almost reachable for some. Seve went for it with every fibre of his being from the tee, almost made it but found the very bunker he had been trying to avoid. He played a poorish bunker shot to some 30 feet and it seemed that he had been rash – a birdie was almost commonplace for players taking an iron off the tee and some sort of wedge for their second.

Ballesteros, internally angry with himself, lined up the putt with extreme care and when he eventually hit it made sure it would reach the hole. Almost from the moment it left the putter it looked good and with about 15 feet to go, Seve extended his right arm, pointed the putter at the hole and, in effect, commanded the putt to drop. It seemed it had no alternative. It went in at a rate of knots and Ballesteros had his birdie. There were to be a lot like that in the years to come.

Long before Sandy Lyle won the 1985 Open, Ballesteros had been telling all who would listen that the Shropshire Lad was a great ball-striker and would be a champion. Most people knew the first part and doubted the second, for Lyle was a laid-back young man who gave little apparent thought for the morrow. However, he confided that he thought that if he was to win an Open, it might well be at Sandwich. He felt it suited his strengths – the ability to hit it long off the tee and hit penetrating long irons into the wind. There has been no better one-iron player in modern times than Lyle and that ability came to his rescue at the long 14th in the final round. He hooked horribly into waist-high rough and could only chop the ball out short of the canal, which runs across the fairway and gives the hole its name. It needed a superlative shot just to get the ball on the green and Lyle crashed a two-iron on to

Royal St George's. 1993. The hustle and bustle of a modern championship.

the putting surface, 40 feet from the hole. Perhaps it was the stimulus of that great shot but he holed the putt, turning a probable bogey six into a birdie four – the kind of break that all champions need.

As the championship moved into the 1990s and the Europeans – a modern dimension – challenged what had been almost an American monopoly in the first three decades after the Second World War, golf was becoming hugely popular and the Open was in the vanguard. Attendances were breaking all records and the official world rankings, which rated the strength of championship fields by the number of top players competing, showed that the Open and the US PGA were by far the strongest.

One of the best fields of all assembled at Royal St George's in 1993 and the leader-board at the start of the final day was a recital of the best players in the game, with 11 men covered by five strokes. It read: 202: Corey Pavin, Nick Faldo. 203: Greg Norman, Bernhard Langer. 205: Nick Price, Peter Senior. 206: Ernie Els, Wayne Grady, Fred Couples. 207: John Daly, Fuzzy Zoeller. Ten of the 11 were, or were to become, major champions. Pavin faded in the final round but Faldo went round in a five under par 67 and still lost by two to Norman.

Any Open at St Andrews is special but the 1995 Open there was more memorable than most. John Daly, the eventual champion and Costantino Rocca were the main protagonists at the end of the week but, early on, everyone was upstaged by a 66-year-old American. Arnold Palmer was playing in the Open for the last time. The man who, 35 years earlier, had started the process which led to the Open becoming once more the championship it should always have been, had first threatened to retire at Muirfield in 1980. Now he sensed that the time had come. Oakmont the year before had been his last US Open; where better than St Andrews to say farewell to the Open? Palmer took 83 in the first round but achieved respectability in the second with a 75. He was accustomed to acclamation but there was an especial warmth in the cheers that greeted every step he took in that farewell round and the huge crowds around the 18th made his final walk up that fairway an emotional thing. 'I kept thinking about 1960,' he said, 'and what that led to. It's been a lot of great years – a happy and warming time.'

Nick Faldo was one of the players who had waited to shake the great man's hand. He knew what Palmer had done for the Open. 'If it hadn't been for Arnie,' he said, 'who knows where we'd be. Probably in a shed on the beach.'

THE MASTERS

Golf can be profoundly thankful that, for the last 60 or more years, the Masters Tournament has been present and very correct, setting the standards for the sport both on and off the course. Every field of endeavour needs excellence to aim at and the Augusta National Golf Club, in their presentation of the Masters, have time and again surpassed themselves. No golf course on earth is better conditioned than the

The Augusta National Clubhouse.

National; no championship more free of hassle to play in than the Masters. For many of the world's top players it is their dream event.

It is the first, chronologically, of the four major championships each year and is played in a beautiful place during a lovely season. Even though tournament golf nowadays is well under way by the time the Masters comes around, it still signals for many the real start of the new season.

The Masters was first played in 1934 and quickly became a significant force in the game. Right from the start a Masters invitation was a treasured object because the man doing the inviting was none other than Bobby Jones. It amounted to a royal command although Jones himself would have been horrified at the thought. He objected to the event being called the Masters because he thought it too presumptuous but the Masters it became because, modesty or not, it was the perfect description of what the event then was: a meeting of all the best players in the world – the masters of golf. It remained just that for something like 40 years, with the best Americans being supplemented by the occasional foreigner deemed worthy of an invitation.

Recently, however, the Masters has not been a place where the best meet the best. Every year there have been significant omissions from the field and the event has been demonstrably the weakest of the majors.

Recently, however, the Masters has not been a place where the best meet the best. Every year there have been significant omissions from the field and the event has been demonstrably the weakest of the majors. It has required radical change and whenever that is proposed the club always turns within itself to ask the question, 'Would Bobby have wanted it?' No one can really know the answer to that but it is certain that he would never have wanted to be associated with anything second-rate and in admitting the recognized top 50 players in the world – as decided by the world rankings – the event has been upgraded at a time when it definitely needed to be.

There was a time, a glorious time, when the Masters did not have to worry about any of this. Any tournament that was associated with the name Bobby Jones was bound to succeed and the attention of the sports media, who would stop off at Augusta every year on their way back from baseball spring training in Florida, ensured that it did. Jones was still the biggest name in golf.

He had retired after his Grand Slam in 1930 but played in those early events purely because he felt obligated, as host, so to do. He never threatened to win but it was still Jones who was written about, to the exasperation of Clifford Roberts, the man who essentially ran Augusta. The imperious Roberts eventually became so annoyed that he summoned Alan Gould, of Associated Press, whose reports went around the world. Why, Roberts demanded, could not Gould devote himself more to the good golf of others rather than the indifferent or just plain bad golf of Jones? Gould, unintimidated, told Roberts that it was his job to run the tournament and AP's to write about it, adding, 'There is more news value in a putt missed by Jones than brassie shots holed out by any other player in the field.'

That was an exaggeration, of course. In 1935, Gene Sarazen had holed not a brassie but a four-wood at the long 15th for an albatross, or double eagle. It became 'the shot heard around the world' and it made the Masters. It also enabled Sarazen to come from three behind Craig Wood with four to play and force a play-off, which he won.

In *Thirty Years of Championship Golf*, Sarazen recalled his moment. The ball was not lying well and he needed to hit a four-wood rather than the three-wood the distance – 220 yards – required. He asked his caddie, known only as Stovepipe, what he needed to win. 'You need four threes, Mister Gene, 3,3,3,3,' he said, with a groan. Sarazen calculated, 'I could possibly get a birdie four on the 15th, maybe a birdie two on the 16th and then maybe a birdie three on either the 17th or 18th which would give me the tie.'

While he was working it all out, Walter Hagen, his playing partner, shouted across the fairway, 'Hurry it up, willya? I've got a date tonight.' Sarazen barely heard him and said, 'I took my stance with the four-wood and rode into the shot with every ounce of strength and timing I could muster. The split second I hit the ball I knew it would carry the pond. It tore for the flag on a very low trajectory, no more than 30 feet in the air. Running forward to watch its flight I saw the ball land in the green, still dead on line. I saw it hop straight for the cup and then, while I was straining to see how close it had finished, the small gallery behind the green let out a terrific shout and began to jump wildly in the air. I knew then that the ball had gone into the hole.' The play-off on Monday was an anti-climax. 'It was raining and the newspaper guys had all gone home on Sunday thinking Craig Wood had won,' Sarazen said.

The altogether less flamboyant Ben Hogan was to win only twice, in 1951 and 1953, rather less of a return than might be expected given his accuracy and the fact that his natural shape of shot – a draw – was perfectly suited to Augusta. In 1951, his final round of 68 was adjudged almost perfect and the official account of it recorded, 'Not one of those strokes could be called a missed shot or a mistake in judgement.' The approach to the 18th finished short of the green but Hogan had already twice failed to win by three-putting from above the hole on this treacherously sloping green and he deliberately underclubbed. He chipped close and holed for his par, to win by two shots from Skee Riegel.

The following year Hogan had a final round of 79 of which he was 'thoroughly ashamed' but before the tournament started he made a suggestion which led to the formation of one of the great traditions in golf, the Masters Club. Hogan's idea was that it should be open only to those who had won the event, plus Jones and Clifford Roberts. It was also Hogan's idea that the reigning champion should host the dinner and that led to one of his rare recorded jokes. 'I discovered the tab for the dinner came to more than the winner's share of the purse,' he said, 'so I finished second four times.'

Joking apart, Hogan won again in 1953, his *annus mirabilis*, with scores of 70,69,66,69 – 'the best four rounds of tournament golf I've ever had' — and his total of 274 beat the previous record aggregate by five shots. Roberts thought that 'it was the best 72-hole stretch of golf ever played by anyone anywhere' and wondered if the score would stand, 'if not permanently, then for a long, long time.' It turned out to be only 12 years, until 1965, when Jack Nicklaus recorded 271, a mark equalled by Raymond Floyd in 1976. Then, in 1997, Tiger Woods scored 270 and what, one wonders, would Roberts have made of that?

One of the most dramatic moments in Masters, or for that matter any major championship, history occurred in 1968 and robbed Roberto de Vicenzo of possible victory in the tournament. Coming off the final green Bob Goalby signed for a final round of 66 and de Vicenzo a 65, then the lowest final round ever played at Augusta. This meant that they were tied and had to play off, but before long a rumpus started. Cary Middlecoff, who was working for CBS at the time, approached Goalby with the words, 'There's a problem here, Bob. I think you may have won this.' It transpired that de Vicenzo was going to have to accept a 66, not a 65. His marker, Tommy Aaron, had put down a four at the 17th where de Vicenzo had in fact had a birdie three – a birdie seen by thousands of spectators and millions of television viewers.

The Argentinian, however, a genial giant of a man, was always casual in the extreme about checking his card. At Hoylake the year before, when he won the Open, he signed his card while standing in among the crowds congratulating him, barely giving it any attention whatever. This time that trait was to cost him a chance of a second major championship. He signed the card and was whisked off to the press tent to talk about his record round. Aaron, who had been checking his own card very carefully, noticed de Vicenzo's card lying on the table with the figure 66 on it. In panic he jumped up shouting, 'Where's Roberto? Get Roberto,' but it was too late.

There was pandemonium. Everyone knew that de Vicenzo, 45 that Easter Sunday, had made a three, scored 65 and should be in a play-off but the rules were clear – and unbending. Goalby was the champion. He said, 'Everyone looked so glum it was hard for me to feel elated although I had just played the best golf of my career. But of course you had to feel sorry for Roberto.' The one person who didn't was de Vicenzo himself, who said it was his own fault and summed it all up with one of golf's classic lines, 'What a stupid I am.'

The 1975 Masters has good credentials for being regarded as one of the finest major championships of all time, if not the finest. If tournaments do not start until the final nine on Sunday afternoon, then the drama attached to the homeward half that year was of a higher pitch than any previous Masters. It featured the three finest players in the world at that time – Jack Nicklaus, Tom Weiskopf and Johnny Miller – who were all capable of sustained bursts of brilliance and produced them that week.

After 36 holes Nicklaus, the *primus inter pares*, led by five shots with rounds of 68 and 67 and there was a feeling that the championship had been decided already. In the third round Nicklaus, who is partially colour blind, looked up at a scoreboard and

Ben Hogan.

saw that Miller, suddenly, was on it. 'Are those red or green figures?' Nicklaus asked his caddie, meaning did they denote birdies (red) or bogeys (green). They were red and Miller was racing out in 30. He finished with a 65 but Weiskopf had a 66 and led by one from Nicklaus and by four from Miller.

The changes of leadership over the final round were bewildering and in the end it was a Nicklaus putt that decided everything. It was at the 16th, where he had left himself some 60 feet from the hole. It was diabolically difficult, a bogey rather than a birdie opportunity, but Nicklaus weighed it very carefully while Tom Watson, his playing partner, was hitting two balls into the water. Weiskopf, who was one ahead of Nicklaus, and Miller – who was one behind – had to wait on the 16th tee. What they saw was Nicklaus holing the putt, thrusting his putter aloft and performing what even he described as a war dance. It won him a championship that he called 'the most thrilling shoot-out I have ever been involved in.'

Ben Crenshaw, the 1999 US Ryder Cup team captain, has a long game he frequently characterizes as 'ridiculous'. At times it is simply absent without leave but in 1984 it was all present and correct and, allied to an always immaculate putting stroke, helped him to a popular win. Years before Crenshaw had said that he did not think he could carry on living if he had not won a major championship before he retired and he was beginning to have his doubts. He had finished second twice at Augusta;

Crenshaw said that he felt Penick's presence throughout the tournament and when he holed the winning putt on the 18th he broke down and cried. 'I could feel Harvey with me,' he said. 'I had a fifteenth club in my bag.'

hit a ball in the water on the 71st hole of the US Open; lost the US PGA in a play-off; and double-bogeyed the 71st hole at the Open. When Severiano Ballesteros draped the green jacket around his shoulders, Crenshaw said, 'This is a sweet, sweet moment. More than anything, it's a feeling of relief.'

In that Masters he had thought it might be his day when he holed a putt of some 60 feet at the 10th but the really spooky thing happened at the par five 13th. Crenshaw was surveying his second, trying to decide whether or not to go for a shot over Rae's Creek, when he spotted Billy Joe Patton in the crowd. Crenshaw immediately thought of 1954 when Patton, a gung-ho amateur, was leading and elected to go for the carry from a similar position. He ended in the creek, took seven and finished third, a shot behind Snead and Hogan. Crenshaw put his wood away and laid up. Patton, who was told the story later, was mystified. He had not been at the 13th that day; he had not been at Augusta all week.

In 1995, Crenshaw won his second green jacket and it was an emotional occasion that also seemed pre-ordained. Harvey Penick, one of golf's great teachers, mentor to both Crenshaw and Tom Kite, had died and the day before the Masters started both players had been in Texas to act as pall-bearers at their friend's funeral. Crenshaw said that he felt Penick's presence throughout the tournament and when he holed the winning putt on the 18th he broke down and cried. 'I could feel Harvey with me,' he said. 'I had a fifteenth club in my bag.'

In 1985, Curtis Strange could, and maybe should, have won. He was leading by four strokes going into the last nine holes of the championship – quite remarkably, for he had started with an 80 and booked a flight out of Augusta for the Friday night. It was the 13th that proved pivotal. Still leading by three shots, Strange had 208 yards to the green – 'not a hard shot,' he insisted – and he went for it. He finished up in the water, took six and another splashdown at the 15th and another six meant that, suddenly, it was Bernhard Langer who was winning his first Masters.

The fine line between being hailed as champion or consoled as unlucky was highlighted by what had happened to Langer at the 13th in the third round. Off a side-hill lie he hit a three-wood which pitched in front of the creek – and hopped over. 'Seven times out of 10,' said the German, ever precise, 'that shot goes in the water.' It was an extraordinary win in many ways for Langer. He of the 'yips' had only three-putted once in four rounds on the lightning-fast, bent grass greens. Afterwards he was asked what the German word for 'yips' was. 'There isn't one,' he smiled. 'Germans don't get the yips ...'

The tournament of 1986 marked the 50th playing of the Masters, there having been no competiton during the war years of 1943–5, but there was no celebration. Hord Hardin, the chairman of the club, explained that Jones had always thought that each and every Masters tournament deserved equal celebration and so nothing special was done. But something special happened on the golf course: Jack Nicklaus won his 18th professional major championship, astounding the entire golfing world – again – at the age of 46.

Nicklaus, playing well after three rounds, was on 214 and lying ninth, a respectable position for a man of his age but nothing to get too excited about. After all, in front of him were, among others, Greg Norman, Nick Price, Langer, Ballesteros, Kite and Watson. On the Sunday morning Nicklaus' son Steve rang him. 'Hiya Pops,' he said, 'whaddya think it'll take today to win this thing?' Pops' best guess was a 66 for a play-off and a 65 to win. 'Yeah, 65,' said Steve, 'that's the number I had in mind. Go do it.' Which is what he did.

He went to the turn in 35 and holed 20-foot birdie putts at the 10th and 11th but that still didn't amount to a charge. When he took four at the par-three 12th, the round looked like spluttering to a halt but paradoxically, that bogey got him going. Realizing he needed to be aggressive, this most conservative of golfers bent a three-wood shot right to left round the corner of the 13th. It almost went into the creek but was in the perfect place and set up a birdie. 'Shots like that are a little too much for my 24-year-old heart, Dad,' said Jackie, another son, who was caddying.

At the long 15th, Nicklaus was 202 yards from the green. 'Do you think a three on this hole would go very far?' he asked Jackie. 'Let's see it.' Dad then hit a four-iron to 12 feet and had a flashback to the Sunday of 1975 when he had the same putt. 'I didn't hit it hard enough and it broke off,' he said. 'This time I hit it straight.' Eagle. Mayhem. 'The noise was deafening,' said Nicklaus. 'I couldn't hear anything, I mean nothing.'

The blood was up and when Nicklaus hit a five-iron to three feet at the 16th, the amphitheatre there exploded. Standing on the 15th fairway the leader, Ballesteros, heard the incredible racket and knew what was happening. Not that it mattered too much. He had a two-stroke lead and faced only a four-iron shot into the green. Seconds later, in a moment that haunts him still, he had hit the shot fat, the ball splashed into the lake and Ballesteros stood there stunned. Norman threatened the fairytale with birdies at the 14th, 15th, 16th and 17th but he bogeyed the 18th. There was only one comet on the course that day and Nicklaus, home in 30 for a 65, called it his greatest victory. He should undoubtedly have retired there and then, indisputably at the top. It would have been a fantastic end to a fantastic career and it would have left everyone with memories of a man at his peak.

Nicklaus played with Sandy Lyle that year and two years later it was the turn of the Scot to cause a sensation of his own. When single great shots at Augusta are recalled, it is probable that Sarazen's may be accorded premier place because of its timing, but Larry Mize's chip in 1987 to beat Greg Norman and the Lyle bunker shot in 1988 had a similar resonance – great shots hit at moments of great pressure.

In April 1988, Lyle was probably the best golfer in the world. In the run up to the Masters he had won the Phoenix Open and the Greater Greensboro Open; he was top of the US money list, a position he was to occupy for 133 days that season; he was putting well, an Augusta essential; and he was confidence personified. After three rounds he was leading by two strokes and, remarkably, had used only 81 putts. Crenshaw, that master of the art, was lying second and needed 92.

Lyle led by three after nine holes of the final round but after 12 holes he was only level with Mark Calcavecchia. He had three-putted the 11th and then gone in the water at the 12th. 'That's it,' Lyle said, 'I've blown it.' Dave Musgrove, his caddie, was more pragmatic. 'Just be sure to make a five here. Let someone else lead for a while, we've been doing it for long enough.'

Nicklaus had a flashback to the Sunday of 1975 when he had the same putt. 'I didn't hit it hard enough and it broke off,' he said. 'This time I hit it straight.' Eagle. Mayhem.

At the 16th, Lyle sank a 20-footer from above the hole. Not a demonstrative man, he punched the air five times, a Lyle and British all-comers' record. On the 18th, again level with Calcavecchia, Lyle hit a one-iron, which had been taken for safety, into the first of the fairway bunkers. 'I've really done it now,' he said. Luckily, he found that his ball had pitched in the middle of the bunker and run half way up the fairly gentle face of the sand, offering him very little lip to clear and an uphill stance and lie. He knew he could get the ball up very quickly and fly it all the way to the green but it would require absolutely perfect contact. He took a seven-iron and, putting every ounce of his strength into it, picked the ball almost completely clean off the sand and sent it towering into the sky. The next most people saw of it was when it came to earth again, some 150 yards away, slap bang in the middle of the green. There was an enormous roar, then a crescendo as the ball began to move back towards the pin. It stopped no more than 10 feet from the hole. Herb Warren Wind, the historian, said it was the greatest bunker shot in the history of golf and he was probably right — because Lyle holed the putt, to become the first British winner of a green jacket.

'It'll go down in history that finish,' agreed Musgrove but his thoughts at the time were more prosaic. 'There I am,' he said, 'slogging up that hill, me back's hurting and I'm thinking there's going to be a bleedin' play-off when all I want to do is get off and have a beer. I knew he couldn't hole the putt – that sort of thing only happens in fairy stories.' And at Augusta.

Lyle, it seemed, was destined to win and Nick Faldo was similarly irresistible in 1989 and 1990. No player likes to be called a scrambler but there are times when even the most imperial striker has to attend to the mundane duties of pitching and putting. To say that Faldo putted his way to victory in 1989 is merely to emphasize a temperament that refused to buckle even when the shots were not being struck truly.

On the Saturday of the miserably rain-affected event, Faldo had holed what is probably the longest putt in the championship's history – 100 feet – at the second, yet at the end of that third round, completed early on Sunday morning, that putter was itself history, discarded after Faldo had run up a 77. He strode angrily from the 18th green to the locker-room, grabbed five putters and marched to the practice green, refusing to say anything to journalists, most of whom were on deadline and in need of his summing up.

Eventually, he finished putting and on the lovely lawns outside the clubhouse, in full public hearing, he spoke. The air was filled with asterisks. 'You're always asking me ******* questions,' he said, 'why don't you ******* watch the golf? It's all up there on the ******* leader-board.' He strode off but later apologized to the recipient of most of the abuse, who managed to salvage something from the wreckage. His paper employed a sports psychologist to say that Faldo's rant had probably had a calming effect on him, which in turn led to the remarkable headline, 'How I won the Masters for Nick Faldo.'

Faldo's putter was responsible for some of the most remarkable work ever recorded on Augusta's greens. On the first hole of the final round, Faldo faced a 54-foot birdie putt with at least two distinct breaks and in it went. 'When you hole things like that you get a sense of destiny,' he said. He hardly stopped holing sizeable birdie putts after that, including vital ones at the 16th and 17th.

Faldo's 65 tied him with Scott Hoch, who then had a two-foot putt to win at the 10th, the first extra hole. He missed and at the 11th, a reprieved Faldo hit a 209-yard three-iron perfectly to 25 feet. Like almost everything else that day it went in and Faldo raised his arms aloft.

The following year he successfully defended his title – the first man to do so since Nicklaus in 1966 – and one of the reasons was Fanny Sunesson, who became the first woman to caddie for the winner of a major championship. It was her first time at Augusta and her presence forced Faldo to prepare in a different way. In practice he'd tell her how he was going to play the course, where he was going to hit the ball and why.

'It was like a refresher course for myself,' he said, 'like thinking aloud.'

In the final round Faldo, three behind the leader Raymond Floyd, was paired with Nicklaus and thought it was a great omen. 'It's like being out in front of the class, showing him and everyone else that you can play,' he said. Faldo played well enough to get into another play-off, with Floyd. The turning point was the 12th, where Faldo's tee shot plugged in the back bunker. 'I could play a career bunker shot here and it will still go into Rae's Creek,' he thought, for all he could see from the sand was water. Somehow he conjured the ball to 15 feet and holed the putt for his par. A three, when a five or even a six had been lurking in the inner recesses, is a wonderful thing. 'That did it for me,' he admitted.

Eventually, Faldo finished putting and on the lovely lawns outside the clubhouse, in full public hearing, he spoke. The air was filled with asterisks.

In the end he won at the 11th again, when Floyd put his second shot in the lake to the left of the green. 'Gosh,' said Faldo to himself, 'what has he gone and done now?' He had lost the Masters and Faldo had won his third major championship.

Ian Woosnam and Fred Couples, two men whose talent ought to have taken them to the heights more often than it has, won the next two Masters. Woosnam, memorably, holed a six-foot putt on the last green in 1991, following the ball into the hole with a huge uppercut that has since become his trademark. The fiery little Welshman had to cope with some ill-disciplined crowds during his last round, including a lout at the 14th tee, who shouted, 'Hey Woosnam, you're not on no links course here.'

The people disturbing the peace were fortunate that Jones himself was no longer alive. He would have been horrifed at the behaviour, which was repeated the following year when there was a danger that Craig Parry, an Australian, might beat Couples. In 1967, Jones wrote the following words, which appear every year in the spectator guide. 'In golf, customs of etiquette and decorum are just as important as rules governing play. It is appropriate for spectators to applaud successful strokes in proportion to difficulty but excessive demonstrations by a player or his partisans are not proper because of the possible effect upon other competitors. Most distressing to those who love the game of golf is the applauding or cheering of misplays or misfortunes of a player. Such occurrences have been rare at the Masters but we must eliminate them

The sixth green. The lake was removed in 1931.

entirely if our patrons are to continue to merit their reputation as the most knowledgeable and considerate in the world.'

The words were ignored and Woosnam was incensed but Tom Watson, his playing partner, urged him to take no notice and told an unprintably funny story about what Don January used to do with hecklers. Woosnam laughed, the tension dissolved and he went on to win.

Later in the year, Woosnam started worrying about what to give his peers at the champion's dinner and had a practice run at the Wynstay Hotel in Oswestry. Several menus were tried out and in the end he decided on a Welsh speciality, lamb in hay. The lamb would be best Welsh and the hay, which is wrapped around the joint, would come from the rough at Llanymynech, the club which had fostered him as a junior. It was a great idea but officialdom got in the way. They demanded export licences for the meat and implied that the hay, if let into the country, would spread death and destruction along the entire eastern seaboard. Woosnam had to use American ingredients.

Jose Maria Olazabal, who might have won in 1991 but for taking seven at the short sixth, was by 1994 one of those players too good not to have won a major championship and yet by no means a favourite to win at Augusta. He had an immaculate short game but his driving sometimes gave the best part of his game – his irons to the green – little or no chance. There was also the question of his temper. The Spaniard was hugely hard on himself and on those around him and, given the built-in frustrations of Augusta, he was not guaranteed to get round without fusing. Furthermore, until two months before the Masters, he had been in a two-year slump, which led to a prolonged sulk. Everyone knew that Olazabal's technical problem was a reverse pivot but he refused to listen. Sergio Gomez, his manager, said, 'For him, going to the golf is like going to the slaughterhouse.'

Then, in February 1994, two things happened. At a tournament in Tenerife, Olazabal played yet another poor shot, lost his temper yet again and used language more suited to the fishermen of his native Fuenterrabia, near San Sebastian. Watching this unedifying display was Maite Gomez, wife of Sergio and a friend of Olazabal's for almost all his life. She was appalled and said so. 'You are learning nothing,' she told him. 'You are wasting everybody's time. You are a disgrace and you will be over as a golfer in a short time unless you grow up. If you carry on like this, I shall come to no more tournaments.' Olazabal was shocked. Many people had berated him over one thing or another over the years but never such a close friend. He resolved to change.

The problem of the bad shots was solved by a complete fluke two weeks later. Gomez literally bumped into John Jacobs, a former European Ryder Cup captain who had been Olazabal's only teacher but had not seen him for over two years and Jacobs agreed to have a look. He recognized what was wrong within seconds but said, 'It was finding the right form of words to tell Jose what the problem was.' Nevertheless, he found them and the cure was instant. Olazabal finished second that week, won the tournament the following week and five weeks after that was the new Masters champion. He had gone from Mr Irascible in February to Master Olazabal in April.

On the Sunday, the day he would achieve his lifetime's ambition, he had in his pocket a piece of paper on which had been scribbled a note.

It was from Ballesteros and was addressed to 'Fuenterrabia', one of his nicknames for Olazabal. It read, *'Tienes lo que hay que tener para ganar. Eres el mejor del mundo. Mucha suerte, Seve.'* 'You have all that it takes to win. You are the best in the world. Much luck, Seve.' Given the man who sent it, that message sent shivers down Olazabal's spine and he went out and became the second Spaniard to wear the green jacket. Like so many before him, he fulfilled his destiny.

Surely no one has ever had to dig deeper into his reserves of physical and mental determination than did Olazabal when, in 1999, he won his second Masters, and his second major.

But, just as surely, there have been few occasions in the history of golf when a player has been so stubbornly set to win, so unyielding and so defiant of the odds against him. For Olazabal was a man who had come back from the golfing dead: a man who, due to a terrible misdiagnosis, had spent 18 months out of the game and only came back into it through a fluke, a totally unforeseen twist of chance.

He had spent most of those 18 months thinking that he would never play again, that he would more than likely spend the rest of his life in a wheelchair when the happiest of accidents brought him into contact with a controversial, and unconventional doctor, who cured him. And by Sunday April 11, 1999, he was not only back on the golf course, he was in a position to win a major championship. Not Greg Norman, his main rival, nor all the forces of fate, could have stopped him.

That is not to say that Olazabal could not have stopped himself. But every time there was a crisis, he drew on some inner reserve, the kind of strength that had sustained him during the dark days, and recovered. There was the time, at the long 13th, when Norman holed a 40-foot eagle putt, to take the outright lead. Olazabal immediately holed from 20 feet for a birdie,

Double-masters champion,
Jose Maria Olazabal.

to re-join the lead, and Norman pointed his finger at Ollie and Ollie pointed his finger at Norman and the two men acknowledged, in the most sporting fashion, a pivotal moment in the championship.

There was another at the 17th. Olazabal's drive crashed into Eisenhower's Tree and suddenly a five, even a double bogey six, seemed a possibility. But the Spaniard smashed a long iron low under the branches and when it finished on the green and when he then two-putted for his four, he was, effectively, clothed again in green.

But the fact of that astonishing win was no more amazing than the fact that he was there at all. For several months in 1996, the Adidas company, knowing of Olazabal's plight – which a clinic in America had diagnosed as rheumatoid arthritis in his feet – had been trying to get him to their factory in Germany so that they could build him a special pair of shoes, simply to improve the quality of his life.

But, stubborn Spaniard that he is, Olazabal would not go until eventually his manager, Sergio Gomez, said to him, with some asperity: 'You have been here at home for one year without moving. Why don't you go, just to get out?' Olazabal, walking bowed and bent like an old man, hunched up against the pain, flew to Munich, where, to his surprise, the Adidas representative who met him, Ulrich Schulte, was an old acquaintance from amateur golf days.

They chatted, and at one point Schulte asked if he had heard of the wonder doctor who lived in Munich? Even before he had finished the sentence and anticipating what would come next, Olazabal turned to Gomez and said, firmly, 'No.' Schulte carried on, though. He said the man, Hans-Wilhelm Müller-Wohlfahrt, treated the German Olympic team, the Bayern Munich soccer team, he had treated Luciano Pavarotti and the pianist Alfred Brendel.

As he went on, Olazabal turned again to Gomez and, pointing one finger to his temple, indicated in the classic gesture that he thought Schulte was mad. When the German continued, Olazabal exploded. 'No!' he said again, 'no way. I'm not going to another doctor who will tell me I am done for life.' And that seemed to be that. At around 1.30pm they went for lunch, during which Olazabal had a change of heart and uttered the words that certainly saved his career, possibly his life. 'Okay,' he said, 'I will go and see this doctor but only because you want me to.' Gomez was to say, much later, 'Going to see another doctor, any doctor, was the last thing he wanted.'

That afternoon they went to see Müller-Wohlfahrt, who made

Olazabal undress and walk up and down. He saw the feet, emaciated, with no padding on the sole, with one toe pointing straight up in the air, another out of its socket. He realized why, when at home, Olazabal crawled rather than walked. Then he made him lie down and, closing his eyes, he felt the entire length of the spinal cord. Half an hour after entering the doctor's surgery, Müller-Wohlfahrt, whose English is limited, said to Olazabal: 'I do not think you have what you have been told you have.'

Olazabal had intended to spend three days in Munich being fitted for a special pair of shoes. In the event, he never even saw the shoemaker. Instead he spent three weeks with Müller-Wohlfahrt and others, and went back to Spain as a man able to hope again. There was still a long way to go, rigorous exercises to be done, long and painful treatments to be undertaken and Müller-Wohlfahrt asked Gomez if Olazabal was sufficiently disciplined to undertake it all. His answer was simple. 'If you ask him to jump out of a fourth-floor window twice a day, if it will cure him, he will do it.' They didn't know it at the time, but Greg Norman and Davis Love III and the other contenders for the 1999 US Masters never had a chance.

US OPEN CHAMPIONSHIP
Robert Sommers

The rise of the US Open was relatively quick. It began in 1894, when the St Andrews Golf Club in Yonkers, a suburb of New York City, conducted both an Amateur and an Open tournament. On a bright clear afternoon in October, Willie Dunn beat Willie Campbell by two holes and won the first, although unrecognized, US Open championship. A few weeks later, the USGA was created and took over the US Open, which over the next 100 years or more produced many of the game's greatest champions.

The growing realization that Americans could indeed play the game became a burgeoning belief when Francis Ouimet – a young local amateur – defeated the English gods of the game, the storied professionals Harry Vardon and J.H. Taylor at The Country Club at Brookline, Massachusetts, in 1913. Then, led by home-bred players such as Walter Hagen, Bobby Jones and Gene Sarazen, along with naturalized citizens such as Jim Barnes and Tommy Armour, Americans not only established themselves as the best players in the world but also elevated the US Open to the game's premier championship, a status that lasted nearly 60 years until the late 1970s, when European golfers began to assert themselves and the Open flourished again.

The US Open role of honour has also included Willie Anderson, Chick Evans, Ralph Guldahl, Byron Nelson, Ben Hogan, Cary Middlecoff, Arnold Palmer, Jack Nicklaus, Lee Trevino and Tom Watson — men who mastered the country's best courses set up to play at their most demanding. Nowadays, the US Open is consistently the year's most severe test of golf, with fairways bordered by deep dense rough and greens so fast it's like putting on a frozen pond. Furthermore, places in the field are not easily won. More than 7000 men entered in 1997 and, excluding the 65 players totally exempt from qualifying because of their records, competed for the remaining 91 places in the final field of 156. In other words, only one in 77 entrants made it to the championship proper.

It wasn't always that difficult. In 1894, only four men played and just 11 showed up in 1895. That was the year that Theodore Havemeyer, the president of the USGA, handed prize money to a Canadian amateur – who handed it back. In those days British-born professionals were the best players and they won the first 16 Opens but in 1911 their grip was broken by John McDermott, a 19-year-old from New Jersey. He beat 78 others at the Chicago Golf Club and remains the youngest US Open champion.

The Americans were learning but they were beating mainly the second rank of British golfers because the top men usually didn't bother to play in the US Open. The sea voyage was long, expensive and uncomfortable, the prize money wasn't much and, frankly, the championship itself was of little consequence. Vardon came over three times but only because his expenses were paid and he made a lot of money on exhibition tours. He won in 1900, lost in a famous play-off in 1913 and was second in 1920, one stroke behind his fellow countryman Ted Ray. Vardon was 50 by then and Ray 43. They had reached the end of the line, and Britain had no one to follow them, not least because a generation of golfers had been butchered in the war.

Nowadays, the US Open is consistently the year's most severe test of golf, with fairways bordered by deep dense rough and greens so fast it's like putting on a frozen pond.

It was now the Americans who dominated. Sarazen, just 20, won the 1922 US Open and Jones, also 20, was runner-up. He won in 1923 and made the title his personal property, winning three more times and finishing second three times in the next seven years. The championship was growing in stature – and in size. By 1920 the entry was 265 and by 1930 it had reached 1177 and sectional qualifying was well established.

Prize money was also growing, from US$150 in 1895 to US$5000 in 1931, the year of the longest major championship in history. Billy Burke and George Von Elm both played Inverness in 292, to set up a 36-hole play-off. They tied again and had to play another 36 holes and by the end of their 144-hole marathon, Burke had beaten Von Elm by one stroke. They weren't paid double for their trouble.

That was also the year that a new bigger ball was used as standard. No less than 1.68 inches in diameter, it weighed 1.55 ounces and was known as the 'balloon ball' because it was too light to hold its line on the green and too easily blown off course. It lasted only one year. In 1931 the USGA adopted a ball with the same diameter but heavier – 1.62 ounces – and by 1990 it had become the standard ball throughout the world.

The 1930s were Sarazen's time. In 1932, he won the Open at Prince's with a new record of 285, then sailed home for the US Open at Fresh Meadow Golf Club on Long Island, New York, where he had been club professional a few years earlier. Playing conservative golf, Sarazen had fallen seven strokes off the lead after 44 holes but, seeing the championship slipping away, he attacked. He birdied the short ninth, played the next nine holes in 32 and in the afternoon had a 66 for a total of 286, to beat Bobby Cruickshank and the Englishman Phil Perkins by three strokes. He had played the last 28 holes in 100 strokes.

In 1938, the authorities imposed another limitation: on the number of clubs a player could use. Vardon usually carried only six clubs, while Evans won the US Open with only seven; players relied on their ingenuity to create shots like the run-up, the high pitch and the half-shot. Over the year, however, others carried more clubs – and more: at one stage, Lawson Little had 31. The USGA and the R&A called a halt, believing their championships should be won by the players with the best swings not the most implements and set a limit of 14. Little, for one, coped and won the US Open in 1941.

In 1939, Byron Nelson, a tall mild-mannered Texan, who could claim to be the finest player of irons who ever lived, won his only US Open. Sam Snead, who should have won that year, was to win none. Standing on the 18th tee of the Philadelphia Country Club's Spring Mill Course, he needed only a par five to win or a bogey six to tie Nelson, Craig Wood and Denny Shute – he took eight. One other footnote: in his third US Open, Ben Hogan made the cut for the first time and finished 78,80 to tie for 62nd place, 24 strokes behind Nelson and company.

The Second World War over, the US Open resumed in 1946 and Nelson lost a play-off to Lloyd Mangrum at Canterbury, in Cleveland. The following year Snead lost to Lew Worsham in St Louis, in another play-off and in 1948 Hogan took over, at Riviera, in Los Angeles. Playing flawlessly, he shot 276 and broke the scoring record by five strokes. Eight months later his car was in a head-on collision with a bus and Hogan's career was apparently over.

He didn't think so, however, and won again at Merion in 1950, beating Mangrum and George Fazio in a play-off. In the fourth round, Hogan nearly fell when his legs locked as he drove at the 12th and he wasn't sure he could finish but he fought on and played the shots he had to when they mattered most. He won again in 1951, at the diabolically prepared Oakland Hills; in 1952, he was third, behind Julius Boros and he won his fourth – and last – US Open at Oakmont in 1953.

At the Olympic Club in San Francisco, in 1955, it seemed that Hogan would be champion for the fifth time in eight years after posting a total of 287 but Jack Fleck, professional at a municipal course in Iowa, tied him late in the day and won the play-off. Hogan wasn't quite finished – he tied for second behind Cary Middlecoff in 1956 and was in contention at Cherry Hills, in Denver, in 1960. There were still 36 holes on the final day and Hogan had hit 34 consecutive greens when, assuming he needed a birdie to win, he played an attacking shot to the island green at the 17th. His ball fell a yard short, ended in the water and that was that.

It was the championship that ushered in a new era. Arnold Palmer came from seven behind to win and Jack Nicklaus, still an amateur, was second. Palmer blistered to the turn in 30 on his way to a 65 in the final round and his total of 280 was two shots clear. It was his only US Open, although he kept coming close, losing in three play-offs: to Nicklaus in 1962, Boros in 1963 and Billy Casper in 1966 at Olympic, a

Somehow Jacklin conjured a 71, led for all four rounds and won by seven strokes from Dave Hill, who insisted that the architect Robert Trent Jones had ruined a good farm when he built Hazeltine.

crushing loss. This time, it was Palmer who was leading by seven shots — with only nine holes to play. Casper, worrying about holding on to second place, instead came home in 32 and Palmer struggled back in 39, holing a scary six-footer at the last to do that. He was second again in 1967 to Nicklaus.

However, the most melodramatic championship of the period was in 1964, when Ken Venturi won at Congressional, near Washington DC. On a miserably hot and humid day he fought off heat-stroke – there were doubts he'd even be able to start the final round – to shoot 278 and beat Tommy Jacobs by four shots. It was a wrenching – and heart-warming – experience and a major surprise. Venturi had been out of form for years but for one season he played wonderful golf.

The following year at Bellerive, Gary Player, of South Africa, became the first foreigner to win the US Open since Ray in 1920. Then in 1970, at Hazeltine on the broad Minnesota prairie, Tony Jacklin became the first Englishman to be champion since Ray. Conditions were dreadful and with nothing but a couple of fence posts between the clubhouse and the North Pole the wind roared in from the northwest. At its weakest it was 35 miles an hour and it gusted over 40, ripping tents to shreds and nearly uprooting a huge scoreboard anchored by six-foot square pilings driven four feet into the ground. Distances were absurd – downwind, nearly everyone drove 300 yards and many players hit it more than 340 – and the scores were just as crazy. Out in 43, Nicklaus shot 81, Dave Marr had 82, Player 80 and Palmer 79. They all made the cut. Somehow Jacklin conjured a 71, led for all four rounds and won by seven strokes from Dave Hill, who insisted that the architect Robert Trent Jones had ruined a good farm when he built Hazeltine.

Three years previously, at Baltusrol, Nicklaus had won his second US Open with a total of 275, breaking Hogan's record. The following year, Lee Trevino won at Oak Hill and established himself as a

A young and free-flowing Jack Nicklaus, won his first US Open at Oakmont in 1962.

serious challenger to Nicklaus' supremacy. As dark and swarthy as Nicklaus was blond and Teutonic, Trevino won again, at Merion in 1971, beating Nicklaus in a play-off. Nicklaus won again in 1972 at Pebble Beach. It was his third US Open but it was eight years before he won his fourth, to match Jones, Hogan and Willie Anderson – a mysterious figure from early in the century who won four US Opens between 1901 and 1905. He might also have won in 1897, aged 17 but at the 468-yard last hole of the Chicago Golf Club, Joe Lloyd ripped a brassie eight feet from the cup, made three and beat Anderson by a stroke.

Nicklaus threatened only once more, at Pebble Beach in 1982, and was thwarted by Tom Watson's miracle pitch at the 17th in the final round. It was Watson's only US Open victory, although he came close the following year. However, Larry Nelson, striking his irons superbly, played the last 36 holes in 132 strokes – and the last 27 in 99 – a scoring burst that broke the record set by Sarazen in 1932 and beat Watson by a stroke.

The year before, there had been a little indication of golf's growing global appeal. David Graham, an Australian, albeit one who lived in the US, won the championship and three years later, at Winged Foot, Greg Norman, who had sharpened his game on the European Tour, made an impact. He holed a 20-foot putt for a par four on the last hole to tie Fuzzy Zoeller, who won the next day by eight shots. Undoubtedly, however, American domination of the US Open was no longer a foregone conclusion. Britain's Nick Faldo tied Curtis Strange at The Country Club at Brookline, in 1988 but Faldo made a series of mistakes in the play-off, including a chip that rolled from one side of the 15th green to the other and lost by four strokes.

Strange also won at Oak Hill the following year, the first to win consecutive US Opens since Hogan in 1951, and

Tony Jacklin tamed Hazeltine in 1970.

143

demonstrated that par could still be a measure of excellence. He started the last round in third place, three strokes behind Tom Kite but after 15 consecutive pars Strange had overtaken those ahead of him and opened up a lead of two when he birdied the 16th. He finished with a 70, level par, for a total of 278, to win by a stroke over Chip Beck, Mark McCumber and Ian Woosnam.

Strange then had the chance to become the first man since Anderson to win three consecutive US Open titles but, at Medinah in 1990, the hype and the hoopla proved too much. Strangely uninspired, he finished 21st, 16 strokes behind Hale Irwin, the unlikely champion, who had received a special exemption. He had won the title in 1974 and 1979 and became only the fifth man to win three or more times when he beat Mike Donald in an extended play-off. Some four strokes behind Donald with 18 holes to play, Irwin raced home in 31 and holed a monstrous putt of 45 feet on the home hole to tie. The normally stoic Irwin went demented, running round the green, exchanging high-fives with everyone. He still had enough energy to play the 19 holes it took him to win the next day.

Lee Janzen won in 1993, a surprise at the time but soon to be shown as the first flowering of a major talent. He goes about his business in an outwardly unflustered manner but has a near-insatiable appetite for the game, and when he won the championship again in 1998, at the Olympic club in San Francisco, it confirmed his position of one of the leading players of his era.

Ernie Els, the languid South African, was another double winner of the championship, in 1994 and 1997, and by the time of his first win so much had changed in 100 years – equipment, courses, players, the game itself – that it is unlikely that Willie Dunn, the first champion, unrecognized himself, would have recognized the US Open as it is now.

Good players, players who are not yet great by golf's own definition, are fond of saying that they have won X tournaments, Y Orders of Merit, a trillion dollars and have looked after their families and their families' families for the next thousand years. They are, they insist, satisfied with their careers thus far. They would not, they insist, trade that for a major championship.

Some of them, and Tom Kite was fond of saying all the foregoing, then go and win a major – and boy, is the relief obvious. They can finally confess all. Yes, it hurt not to have won a major and yes, it was almost unbearable to be tagged 'The Best Not To Have Won A Major.' The monkey, more likely the orang-utang, is off their backs. But the paradox is obvious. To get as far as 'The Best Not...' have got they must have a consuming ambition, to be driven to be the best and yet, because golf defines the best as those who have won majors, they have not, again by definition, become the best. So how can they be satisfied?

The question hangs in the air, almost unanswerable and if and when Colin Montgomerie wins his, the reaction from this sensitive and intelligent man will be worth listening to. Montgomerie is one of the most extraordinary golfers of the century. He appears to have it all in a golfing sense. He is longer than he needs to be, he is straighter off the tee than almost

Irwin raced home in 30 and holed a monstrous putt of 45 feet on the home hole to tie. The normally stoic Irwin went demented, running round the green, exchanging high-fives with everyone.

anyone, he has the finest of short games and, when on form, a putting touch to die for. He has won countless tournaments in Europe, he had won, at the start of 1999, the last six Orders of Merit, some in exceptionally tight circumstances and he has, many times, proved to be the rock on which America has foundered in the Ryder Cup.

Not only that, he was once congratulated, by Jack Nicklaus no less, 'on becoming our national champion.' Nicklaus was convinced that Montgomerie's score, on a foul day at Pebble Beach in 1992, would win him the US Open. It didn't. That was the day that Kite chose to discard 'The Best Not...' tag. Twice Montgomerie has reached play-offs for majors, at Oakmont in 1994 when he lost to Ernie Els and at Riviera in 1995 when Steve Elkington, with a 25-foot putt, beat him at the first extra hole.

This, then, is a considerable player. So why has he, going into 2000, played 34 majors without winning one? Again there are no easy answers. It is too facile to say that he allows himself to get distracted too easily on the course (although he does) because he has coped with such things in moments of the highest tension in the Ryder Cup. It would be trite to say that he ought to spend more time in America, where three of the majors are played, because that is not necessarily an ingredient of success – witness Jose Maria Olazabal.

But it may be true that Montgomerie, who sees the US Open – with its narrow fairways and tall rough – as playing to his strengths puts too much emphasis on winning that particular event. And in so doing subconsciously downgrades the other three. It is difficult for any player, no matter how good, to nominate a tournament and say that he is going to win it and it is surely impossible to do that with a major – not even Nicklaus in his pomp could do that. Montgomerie should win a major: he is far too good not to. Surely all it needs is the right bounce of the ball at the right time and one of the great talents will be rewarded – and lose that nastiest tag of all, 'The Best Not...'

Payne Stewart was to get rid of that particular tag when he won the 1989 US PGA Championship, albeit assisted by a collapse by Mike Reid, who had a six-stroke lead over him going into the final round. Five majors later Stewart won the 1991 US Open and the world looked wide open for the man whose game clashed so colourfully with his garb. Stewart was, and is, the possessor of one of the smoothest, most admirable, repeating swings in the business and yet he chooses to go about that business dressed, for the most part, like a man aping his elders and looking like a complete buffoon.

His garishly coloured plus fours, together with matching shirt, give the appearance of a clown having strayed from a nearby circus, albeit one with a swing good enough not to have to wear the ludicrous clothes he has adopted. After winning the 1991 US Open, Stewart went into something of a decline. He felt he had to play like a US Open champion and when he didn't, he began to look for reasons other than the natural one – you can't play your best all the time. He played in the 1993 Ryder Cup team, but not in the 1995 or 1997 teams and it took his win in the 1999 US Open (his third success) to get him into the team for that year.

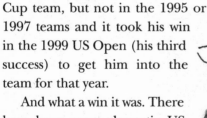

Ernie Els. Two time US Open champion.

And what a win it was. There have been many dramatic US Opens but this was one to match the best. Stewart had been battling with Phil Mickelson for the whole of the final round and when

they arrived at the 16th was one behind his rival. It seemed set to stay that way with Stewart 20 feet away, Mickelson only seven, in three shots. But Stewart holed, Mickelson missed and the men were level. The pin at the short 17th was tucked away in a completely inaccessible corner but, risking all, Stewart hit the most daring tee shot possible, found the right square inch of green and saw the ball settle 3 ½ feet from the hole. Mickelson did not flinch. He took the same route, and when the ball stopped, it was six feet from the pin. The clamouring crowd were delirious.

Mickelson, of course, is the man famed throughout golf for his putting stroke but as he stood over this putt he must have known that Stewart was all but certain to hole his – that he had this putt to stay level. He missed. And Stewart holed. The man who plays, as the Americans have it, in knickers, was one ahead going to the last. But after his drive it looked odds-on a play-off. His tee shot settled into heavy rough, he hacked out and after Mickelson had found the green, he hit a shot from 77 yards out to around 20 feet. It was Mickelson's putt first, he missed, but made certain of a par four and now Stewart had his putt for the championship. All around the green the words 'play-off' were being whispered: in the press tent people were on the phone desperately trying to make new hotel and flight arrangements.

Then Stewart holed the putt and the world went potty. The man himself vented some primaeval screams, punched the air viciously, allowed his caddie to leap into his arms and, in the fullness of time, went over and shook the hand of his vanquished opponent. It was an extraordinary moment and it atoned for the anguish that Stewart must have felt when he went into the final round of the 1998 US Open with a four-stroke lead, only to lose to Lee Janzen.

At the end Stewart, on a Pinehurst No. 2 course that was beautifully presented and hugely difficult, was the only man under par – and only one-under par at that. The father-of-two had beaten the father-to-be, for Mickelson played the whole championship with a beeper in his bag, in case his pregnant wife Amy, in Arizona, went into labour with their first child. 'If she does,' said Mickelson before the championship started, 'she'll call me on the beeper, punch in a secret code and I'll go to her whatever the position. Even if I'm three ahead on the last nine holes. I'll

Montgomerie should win a major: he is far too good not to. Surely all it needs is the right bounce of the ball at the right time and one of the great talents will be rewarded – and lose that nastiest tag of all, 'The Best Not...'

just leave.' But the baby knew better than that. With Stewart's putt having saved the play-off, Mickelson flew home, arriving at about midnight. Twelve hours later, at precisely the time an 18-hole play-off would have been finishing, Amy went into labour and later that day Mickelson was father to a 7lb 4oz daughter, Amanda Brynn, and both men had what they wanted most dearly out of the 1999 US Open championship.

* Robert Sommers, a former editor of *Golf Journal*, the magazine of the United States Golf Association, has written the definitive book on the US Open. It is sub-titled 'Golf's Ultimate Challenge' and ranges eruditely along the highways and byways of one of the four major championships.

THE US PGA CHAMPIONSHIP

For much of its life, the US PGA Championship was perceived as the major with the minimum impact but by 1999 it had been revitalized. The last major of the millennium, at Medinah, just outside Chicago, was a vibrant testament to youth and when Tiger Woods, a canny veteran of 23, held off the exuberant challenge of Sergio Garcia, a 19-year-old rookie with Ballesteros-like self-belief, to win his second major title, the old championship soared to new heights.

Created in 1916, to mark the foundation of the Professional Golfers' Association of America, it used to be overshadowed by the other three great championships and there were valid reasons for this. It was and is played last of the four, so most of the season's passions were spent; it was and is always held in August, in weather that varies only from awful to even worse; it seemed always to be held on a crummy course somewhere on the patch of that year's PGA boss; it was, commercially, too late for the winner to capitalize; there was a long run of (in the greater context) insignificant winners in the 1950s and 1960s; the administration was dodgy; and it always had the weakest field because of the inclusion of 40 club professionals. Yet another problem in the past had been that the organizers, the PGA of America, seemed to feel that they had a valid event, so if anyone wanted to come and see it, or report it, all that was needed was to tell them the dates and wait for them to roll up. It was an attitude firmly fixed in the days when there was no competition for the people's leisure-dollar or for the attention of the media and it did not work. Player polls always showed that a substantial number of them, after first saying that they did not mind which major they won so long as they won one, would go on to rate all three of the US PGA's rivals ahead of it.

Had there ever been a press poll it would have been even more vehemently in favour of the others, in whatever order. Through the 1950s, 1960s and the early 1970s there were some excitements – most championships have some – but there was little to thrill to in venues like Blue Hill Golf and Country Club, Llanerch Country Club, Pecan Valley Country Club or Kemper Lakes. And with more than a quarter of the field being club professionals, quality was seriously diminished, too. In fact, the press poll would have been from a fairly small sample, for not many bothered to travel if it were far to go.

It was a formidable list of faults and it is hugely to the credit of those associated with the US PGA that they recognized the problem and decided to put things right. For example, midway through the 1970s someone realized that the venues were not what a championship needed and from 1975 there has been scarcely a weak course on the US PGA roster – although liking Kemper Lakes or PGA National is a matter of personal preference. You cannot help liking venues such as Pebble Beach, Oakmont, Oak Hill, Southern Hills or Crooked Stick.

Having addressed the venues, they then had to improve the field. Having reduced the number of club professionals, there was room for more top rank tour professionals and the PGA, to their enormous credit, realized that quite of lot of these were from outside America. They expanded their international section, with the result that by 1996 the US PGA championship had achieved the two strongest entries of any event in recorded history.

Having got players worth watching on courses worth watching them on, attention switched to the media. After all, it is pointless having a golf tournament if there is no one there to tell the world what is going on. The US PGA began by giving everyone a nice bag. Now, that sounds pathetic and if they had hoped magically to cure the media problem simply by handing out a freebie, it would have been pathetic. But inside that bag there was as much information as anyone could reasonably expect about every aspect of the US PGA championship, saving every journalist hours of research.

The city hosting the championship was also roped in, on the grounds that it would be of benefit to show the visiting journalists the local attractions. The result was at least a couple of parties per week. The PGA also organized media hotels, efficient media shuttles to take the assorted journalists to and from the golf course and provided facilities inside the press tent that were all a bunch of professional writers at or near the top of their profession would hope for. In short, they eliminated much of the hassle that inevitably attends a big event.

All these things would, of themselves, have been relatively unimportant. What was important was the change in attitude from 'come if you feel like it' to 'why don't you come and experience a really great week?' As a result, in a short space of time the US PGA overtook, completely, the US Open and the Masters in terms of media organization as well as strength of field. Not only was it no longer the runt of the litter, it was a big bruiser shouldering rivals aside.

By the close of the century the championship had become a vibrant, pulsating event consistently producing the strongest field of any tournament or championship in any given year and the magical happenings at Medinah during the 81st championship confirmed its place in the first rank.

Of course, it helped that the 1991 US PGA championship at Crooked Stick, Indiana, produced one of the major sports stories of the century. John Daly began life that week as a pudgy blond in Arkansas with a comic-strip haircut, the ninth reserve for the championship. He was eventually summoned to play on Wednesday evening, drove for 7½ hours to get there and, without a practice round, opened up with a 69. Not many had seen him play but those who did were astonished. He regularly ripped drives over 300 yards, with a backswing that seemed never-ending and was in certain danger of clipping his left ankle. David Feherty, the voluble Ryder Cup player, said at the start of the week that the Crooked Stick course, at 7295 yards, demanded that the curvature of the earth be taken into account when weighing up shots; after seeing Daly play, he amended that to say that it was the American who needed to take account of that sort of geography when deciding on his next club.

Both course and Daly were ridiculously long but that week the latter was also straight and, if ever there was a shock winner, he was it. No one knew the problems behind a seemingly uncomplicated, 'grip-it-and-rip-it' life. The boom 'n gloom of fame, alcoholism, marriages, divorces, rehabilitation, winning the Open, another decline and so on up and down all lay ahead. At Crooked Stick, Daly was a great sports story and his name and that of the US PGA championship reverberated around the world.

It was a far cry from the first contest for the Rodman Wanamaker Trophy, named after the department store magnate with an eye for marketing, who was instrumental in the formation of the PGA of America.

In 1916 the big news was that most of the world was at war and a final (the championship was matchplay until 1957) between a Cornishman, Jim Barnes and a Scot, Jock Hutchison, was not guaranteed to raise the American pulse. Barnes won but the war intervened and the next championship was not until 1919. Barnes won again.

In 1920, there was an uncanny precursor to the Daly tale when Hutchison failed to qualify but got in after two withdrawals and went on to win. Things began to pick up in the 1920s, largely because of the inimitable Walter Hagen. He won five times, including four in a row and the first was in 1921. The last was in 1927 and in the semi-final Hagen showed that he understood perfectly the psychology of matchplay – more crudely called gamesmanship. He was playing Al Espinosa over 36 holes and for 35 of them, whenever his opponent got within three feet, Hagen, acting the sportsman simply said, 'Pick it up, Al.' Al was always glad to do so, for three footers are never a certainty, even for the best putters on the best greens and he was one up playing the last. Hagen was through the back of the green, chipped back to 12 inches and was given the par putt. Espinosa, 25 feet away in two, then putted up to the kind of range he had become accustomed to – three feet. There was the sound of silence. Espinosa looked at Hagen, who smiled at him and quite deliberately turned away to chat with the gallery. Espinosa missed the putt, three-putted the 37th and lost.

Incentives come in many forms and before the 1933 US PGA, Gene Sarazen, only 31, read that Tommy Armour believed he was 'all washed up as a championship contender'. Sarazen won in spectacular style, his hardest match being a 4&3 victory.

In 1948 Ben Hogan won, beating Mike Turnesa 7&6, but despite the ease of that victory, Hogan had played 213 holes in all – he was 35 under par – and was so exhausted he doubted he would ever play in the US PGA again. He did not have the chance to in 1949, because of his horrific car accident, and he did not play in the championship again while it was still matchplay.

Hogan's absence might have been one of the reasons for the change to strokeplay in 1958 and certainly by this time the event was inured to mediocrity. Nothing much changed. The last matchplay winners were Chick Harbert, Doug Ford, Jackie Burke jnr and Lionel Hebert; the first strokeplay winners were Dow Finsterwald, Bob Rosburg, Jay Hebert and Jerry Barber, all much of a muchness, good players but not great.

It was a bit of a relief all round when Jack Nicklaus won in 1963 and again in 1971 and on both occasions Deane Beman had an influence on the result. In 1963, Nicklaus revealed that he was using yardage charts in the championship, at Dallas Athletic Club, so that he knew exactly which club to use for every distance. It was Beman who first thought of this aid and told Nicklaus and in 1971, it was Beman who spotted a fault in the Bear's putting style when they practised together. That night the Nicklauses entertained the Bemans in their new home and lost at bridge to them but Deane made amends by mentioning that Jack had not been completing the backswing on his putting stroke. Nicklaus immediately retired to his practice putting area and went on to win, leading from start to finish at PGA National.

He won three more US PGA titles, the last in 1980 at Oak Hill, where he won by seven shots, then the largest winning margin since the championship became stroke-play. He had not been expected to win and neither was Lee Trevino four years later at Shoal Creek. Trevino was 44 and his biggest challenger was Gary Player, aged 48. It was to Trevino's advantage that his wife put a stop to all the ageism nonsense by pointing out, 'Your clubs don't know how old you are.'

Greg Norman is heartily fed up of being told that he should have won more championships, probably because there is so much truth in the remark. He should, for example, have won the 1986 US PGA at Inverness. He failed not because Bob Tway holed a bunker shot at the 18th but because he himself was in the process of taking 76 in the final round. That was the year Norman created history when, after three rounds, he led the field. It meant he had led on the Saturday night of every major championship that season – but he won only one: the Open at Turnberry.

Norman created more unfortunate history when the US PGA returned to Inverness in 1993. He had a putt of around 15 feet to win and when it was a foot away it looked in. Somehow it shaved the hole and stayed out. That meant a play-off with Paul Azinger and at the first extra hole, the 18th, Norman again appeared to have the title won – but his putt hit the hole and horseshoed out. They played the 10th next and, with Azinger certain of a four, Norman had a nasty four-footer, downhill, to stay alive. He missed it and in so doing gained golf's most unfortunate Grand Slam: he had lost a play-off for all four of the major championships.

The championship continued to be fortunate with its winners. In 1997, Davis Love III won a hugely popular and sentimental victory at

Winged Foot and he was followed by the extraordinary Fijian, Vijay Singh, long due a major. That perhaps the hardest worker in the game should triumph in one of the hardest of all championships to win was entirely appropriate.

However, there has probably been no more fitting winner of the USPGA title than Love III. His father and teacher, Davis Love junior, as he called himself, had been a member of the PGA all his professional life. He was a considerable player in his own right, contending for the Masters in 1964 and the Open in 1969 and a renowned teacher but in 1988, tragically, he was killed in a 'plane crash. Love III was just 18.

A talented amateur who played in the Walker Cup, he emerged on tour as a loose, lithe, huge-hitting young professional. He was, in fact, too long and it was not until he learned to rein himself in that he began to have the career that had been predicted for him.

By 1997, Love had his game under control and at Winged Foot he played magnificently. Jack Nicklaus, asked to rate the difficulty of the course, said, 'On a scale of one to ten, it's about a 12.' Love, hitherto an under-achiever in major championships, had rounds of 66, 71, 66 and 66 and won by five shots from Justin Leonard, the Open champion, who had won his own first major at Royal Troon that year. A huge rainbow arched over the course as Love holed out at the last, with scarcely a dry eye anywhere. He was asked how often he thought of his father, a man who taught him everything and replied with the words that became the title of his book, 'Every shot I take.'

Emotions of a different kind were unleashed at Medinah, where Woods, expected to win everything when he took Augusta by storm in 1997, had to withstand an inspired charge from Garcia. The young Spaniard, such a forlorn figure after rounds of 89 and 83 at the Open at

John Daly came from ninth reserve to champion in 1991 at Crooked Stick.

Carnoustie, electrified the crowd with his youthful enthusiasm and produced one of the shots of the century in the final round.

At the 16th, a right to left dogleg of 450 yards, Garcia, who was two shots behind Woods, drove into the roots of a substantial oak tree. The only option was a wedge out sideways, surely? Garcia bit his lower lip as he surveyed the shot. He had just bogeyed the 15th, another bogey would mean the end of his title challenge and it became apparent that he intended trying to reach the green. He was 189 yards from the pin and a broken wrist was a distinct possibility if he attacked the ball. 'Don't watch, children,' cautioned TV commentator Gary McCord.

Garcia took a six-iron, opened the face of the club, took a full swing, closed his eyes and blasted away with all his might. Then he sprinted after the ball, leaping high with delight when he saw where it had finished. It was on the green and there was pandemonium. 'That's one of the most beautiful things I've ever seen on a golf course,' said Ben Crenshaw, the US Ryder Cup captain and twice Masters champion. 'When Sergio hit that shot, he captured America's imagination.'

He already had Woods' attention – after a birdie two at the 13th, Garcia had looked back at the American on the tee, letting him know that there was work to do if he wanted to win the championship. Woods had a double bogey five there and dropped a shot at the 16th, to be only one shot ahead when not so long before he had been five. It was a nail-biting time but Woods showed a champion's nerve at the 17th, where he holed an eight-footer to save his par and a professional's nous at the 18th, where he got a cast-iron par four, to win.

He was drained but happy and Garcia, who had already hugged Butch Harmon, Tiger's coach and kissed Kultida Woods, Tiger's Mum, on both cheeks, was waiting for the man himself. They embraced and the Spaniard, the youngest runner-up in the championship's history, said, 'I've never had so much fun on a golf course. I want to be a rival – but always being friends with Tiger.'

It was, in the end, exactly the right result. Woods fully deserved to win the last major championship of the millennium and Garcia fully deserved the acclamation that came his way for finishing second. 'That is the future of golf,' said Crenshaw. 'How poignant it was to see players of that magnitude playing out the last championship of this one hundred years.'

And how exciting to think that their exploits – and the telling thereof – should light up the next one hundred years.

CHAPTER 6

GREAT CUPS

RYDER CUP

In the last quarter of the twentieth century the Ryder Cup established itself as the world's greatest sporting contest. Not the world's greatest event in 'sport', although many golfers would argue for that too, but the greatest contest to which the word sporting, in its old-fashioned and best sense, can be applied. There is, I believe, no other contest at this level to which such glory is attached, which is played by professional athletes who would, without hesitation, penalize themselves for an infraction no one else had seen. In other sports cheating is endemic, even coached and demanded of the players. In golf, where the opportunities in every round are countless, it is almost unheard of. Those who cheat, and are found out, become outcasts.

There is another fact about the Ryder Cup which, because it is unique to the contest, is in many

Professionals on both sides of the Atlantic go to extraordinary lengths to get themselves into the team so that they can undergo a week of the fiercest pressure they will ever endure.

ways more remarkable. The match is played beween the 12 best European golfers and the 12 best Americans, professionals all, who for the most part would not, under normal circumstances, budge from their living room unless there was a good chance of making money. Yet, recent haggling notwithstanding, that attitude alters dramatically when the Ryder Cup comes around. Professionals on both sides of the Atlantic go to extraordinary lengths to get themselves into the team so that they can undergo a week of the fiercest pressure they will ever endure; so that they can expose their game to possible ridicule and humiliation or, alternatively, experience the pure jubilation of winning a team event at the highest level.

Take, for example, two of the most famous matches ever played, both of them in the 1991 Ryder Cup at Kiawah Island, South Carolina. In the first, between Mark Calcavecchia and Colin Montgomerie, the latter came back from four down with four to play, to halve his match. In the second Bernhard Langer missed a five-foot putt on the last green which, had he holed it, would have meant that Europe retained the trophy. Naturally Montgomerie was elated about his own match, although asked about it two years later he said, 'People don't understand the pressures of the Ryder Cup. I didn't until I played. The major championships are easy by comparison. Why do we try to get into the team? Surely people would think again after the sort of thing I went through at Kiawah and Bernhard went through later that afternoon. I mean, I'm incredibly proud to be in the team – but can you enjoy it? Can you actually enjoy the playing? I don't think so. I can be proud and I'm certainly honoured but the enjoyment only comes later. I mean, those figures over the last four holes against Mark were amazing. I played them in three over par, and won them all. Par was 4,5,3,4 and he went 7,6,6,5 – I think that tells you what the Ryder Cup is all about. Sometimes I sit down and I watch a video of that match and now I can enjoy it.'

For Calcavecchia to watch that video would be a waking nightmare. In his distraught state after the match he had convinced himself that if his team lost, he would be the sole cause of it. It got so bad that Payne Stewart, who had lost to David Feherty, had to take him away to hide the embarrassment and the tears that were flowing down his face. They went to the nearby beach. 'When we got there, I wanted to throw myself in,' said Calcavecchia. 'It's a good job that Payne didn't give me the chance because I was hyperventilating. I would certainly have drowned.' This from a man who had won an Open, in 1989 at Royal Troon, in the most nerve-wracking of conditions, a play-off with Greg Norman and Wayne Grady.

Meanwhile Langer was missing his putt, but stoic that he is he was just about coping with the bitter disappointment. This, after all, was the man who would go on to win the German Open the following week. Then

Severiano Ballesteros decided that he wanted to console Langer. 'He put his arm around my shoulder,' said Langer, 'and then he started to cry. Maybe if he hadn't started, I wouldn't have. Maybe, I don't know ...'

'As hard-bitten as we all get,' says Feherty, 'the Ryder Cup is still the measure of intestinal fortitude. People sit in the locker-room pretending not to be nervous on the principle of auto-suggestion, if you say it often enough you'll believe it. But inside you know – you might be the guy, you might be in the last match when it's all on you ... The responsibility can seem enormous. You know that tens of millions of people want you to win. It's not just Britain, it's the Continent as well ... But you have to want it, and that seems crazy.'

Feherty is himself sufficiently crazy, in the nicest possible way, to know why he wanted to be in the team. 'At Kiawah the Europeans were all crammed together in the ladies' locker-room, which was so small you had to go outside to change your mind. But inside it was great because there were players you'd admired all your career and essentially they were hanging on your every movement. Normally players are secretly delighted when someone drops a shot but here you are genuinely wanting someone else to do fantastically well. Golf is definitely not a team game – you're in charge of your own head – but the Ryder Cup offers a different dimension and inside that team-room things happen that don't at any other time. The players, even the stars, are willing for once to let their vulnerability show. You can say "Anyone else feel awful?" and there'll be "Yeahs" from all round the room.'

It was inside the team-room, in quite remarkable fashion, that the European renaissance began. The record over the years had been little short of appalling, with the Americans winning so often they had ceased to regard the Ryder Cup as a contest. The British and Irish had tried every conceivable selection formula and every conceivable mix of matches and nothing worked. It had become a walk-over, which was perhaps not all that surprising given that Great Britain and Ireland would fit comfortably into Texas and twice into California.

Samuel Ryder.

Mark Calcavecchia hits into the water at the par-three nth. He could only tie with Colin Montgomerie at Kiawah after having been four up with four to play.

Jack Nicklaus recognized that one of the game's great traditions had become so meaningless that it should be changed or discontinued altogether. He said so quite bluntly at Royal Lytham & St Annes in 1977 and by 1979 GB&I had become Europe.

For the next two decades the contest was to lead the explosion of golf throughout Europe and the world. It worked itself up to a fever-pitch – within the constraints of the game, of course – and, at least on the course, became the epitome of all that was good and great about golf.

Much good the change did, though, initially. America produced what was probably their strongest-ever team in 1981 at Walton Heath and dismissed the supposedly strengthened European team by 18½ to 9½. Tom Kite was one of the few in the American team who, at that time, had not won a major championship and he caught Sandy Lyle at his very best. Lyle was eight under par after 16 holes and yet lost to Kite who was 10 under. Eventually every member of that US side bar Bruce Lietzke was to win a major – and Lietzke almost certainly could have had he bothered to play in enough of them. The cast, in order of appearance was: Lee Trevino, Larry Nelson, Bill Rogers, Lietzke, Hale Irwin, Ray Floyd, Tom Watson, Jack Nicklaus, Kite, Johnny Miller, Ben Crenshaw and Jerry Pate.

It looked then as if making the team European was not sufficient; that maybe the rest of the world might have to be brought in if interest was to be stimulated once again. Two years later that theory was demolished. In 1983, Europe went to the headquarters of the PGA of America, played superbly and gave America such a fright that Nicklaus, captain for the occasion, kissed the divot made by Lanny Wadkins in his execution of the shot that won the match.

It was during that match that Ballesteros hit what some people regard as one of the finest, perhaps the finest, shot ever struck. The Spaniard, bunkered in two at the 18th, still had 242 yards to go and, needing to reach the green, hit a three-wood off a lie close to the lip that settled on the fringe of the green. No one who was there could believe it; anyone who was not there would be unable to comprehend the magnitude of what the Spaniard had done. Seve halved his single with Fuzzy Zoeller but the Americans squeaked the series. Europe had only just lost but they had lost.

Nick Faldo remembered what happened next. 'We were all in the team-room feeling down and dejected. Half of us felt we should have won and the other half were not sure but we all knew we had got mega-close. I mean, we'd lost by half a point or whatever. Anyway at that point, in marches Seve. He had his fist clenched and his teeth were bared, just like he is when he's excited, and he kept marching around the room saying to everyone, "This is a great victory, a great victory." Then he said, "We must celebrate," and he turned the whole mood of the team around. That was the spark, Seve in 1983. By 1985 we knew we could do it.'

The venue for that year was The Belfry and the score was 16½–11½ to Europe. It had been 28 years since the Americans had lost and it was the first time a team called Europe had ever won. The reasons were two-fold: one was the influx of players from Europe – Ballesteros, Langer, Jose Maria Canizares, Manuel Pinero and Jose Rivero; the second was Tony Jacklin, the captain. He had been in charge in Florida and now he had a stronger team and was at home. Jacklin had three great gifts: a magnificent golf game when wholly interested in the project at hand, a superb talent for captaincy and an unerring instinct for getting up people's noses. He is beyond doubt the best captain the Ryder Cup series has seen. He talked Ballesteros out of a sulk and into playing Ryder Cup golf after a spat with the European Tour, then imbued the Spaniard with the spirit of the thing.

'Anyway at that point, in marches Seve. He had his fist clenched and his teeth were bared. That was the spark, Seve in 1983. By 1985 we knew we could do it.'

In 1983, Ballesteros, partnered with Paul Way, aged 20, complained that he felt like the boy's father. Jacklin, unmoved, said, 'That's how you're supposed to feel.' The pair won 2½ points.

In 1985, Jacklin created his own Spanish Armada and on the second afternoon it sailed forth and routed the opposition. Canizares and Rivero destroyed Tom Kite and Calvin Peete 7&5 and Ballesteros and Pinero beat Craig Stadler and Hal Sutton 5&4. At the end, Concorde dipped its wings over The Belfry and Jacklin introduced his team to the crowd with a fairground barker's relish, including, 'The best player in the world – Seve Ballesteros.' The crowd loved it. The Americans did not.

In an extraordinary illustration of the cyclical nature of sport, in 1987, only six years after the hammering at Walton Heath, the Europeans produced what Ballesteros is convinced was the strongest European (or GB&I) side ever. It is impossible to disagree. It featured the Famous Five, the men all born within 12 months of each other from April 1957 to March 1958: Ballesteros, Langer, Lyle, Faldo and Woosnam. They were all at, or close to, their peak and had to go to Muirfield Village, the lair of the Bear, the course designed, built and nurtured by Nicklaus, to play a team captained by Nicklaus, the man all of golfing America regarded as a god.

The score was USA 13–15 Europe after some of the finest golf ever witnessed and such drama that it stretched credulity. The opening series of foursomes set the standard. Europe, it seemed, had frozen: after nine holes the USA were three up in the first and second matches, four up in the third and two up in the fourth; by lunch it was two–all. In the fourballs that afternoon, it was four–nil to Europe and Nicklaus knew he was in trouble. He praised the Europeans, then lamented the lack of vocal support from the home fans, 'Why don't they get some flags, for Chrissake, and wave them?' In truth, there had been little for them to cheer but 20,000 little Stars and Stripes were handed out the next day.

They had little effect. Europe won the

Bernhard Langer. a stalwart of Europe's Ryder Cup resurgence.

foursomes 2½–1½ and in the fourballs the Americans produced some remarkable golf. Tom Kite and Curtis Strange went round one of the world's most difficult golf courses – all 7104 yards of it – in five under par. Larry Nelson and Lanny Wadkins were an incredible eight under. Both pairs lost. Kite and Strange were playing Faldo and Woosnam, who started with five birdies and were five up after five. When the match finished, on the 14th, they were 10 under par. Wadkins and Nelson at least got to the last green, playing desperation golf because their opponents, Lyle and Langer, had been three up with three to play.

The 18th hole of this match summed up the general brilliance of that Ryder Cup. All four players hit good drives. Nelson played first and was on the green; Lyle was next and hit an eight-iron three feet from the hole; Wadkins nearly holed his shot, the ball pitching inches from the pin and rolling 10 feet away; then it was Langer. Lyle had said to him, after hitting his own shot, 'Get inside that and we'll be all right' and Langer hit a shot he may never better. It flew straight at the flag, pitched a few feet short of the pin, screwed to a halt and finished inches from the hole. There was pandemonium. The Americans picked the ball up and Wadkins summed up: 'Larry hit a good shot; I hit a very good shot; Sandy hit a very, very good shot and Bernhard hit something special.'

Europe needed 3½ points from 12 singles to retain the Ryder Cup and eight of the matches reached the 18th hole – and, astonishingly, the Americans did not win one. Eamonn Darcy was Europe's unlikely hero. The Irishman was in his fourth Ryder Cup and had yet to win a match. He had been three up against Ben Crenshaw, who was putting with a one-iron after breaking his putter in anger early on but by the 18th they were all-square. In the end, Darcy faced a four-foot, lightning-fast, downhill putt – not only for his first-ever win but also to make his side all but safe. He holed it and turned towards his team-mates with an expression of the purest possible delight. It was the moment of a lifetime.

As the celebrations came to a close, late into the night, Woosnam stood on a chair and called for order. Pointing at Jacklin, he said, 'This man here, for what he's done, he needs a knighthood.'

Sir Tony – in reality, he's still waiting – had one more match as captain, at The Belfry in 1989. Raymond Floyd, his opposite number, stated, 'We're going over there to kick butt. We'll find out who're the best golfers in the world.' Jacklin said, simply, 'The cup is going nowhere.' Nor did it. The match was drawn but only after the by now customary pyrotechnics on the final day, encapsulated in the match between Christy O'Connor jnr and

Fred Couples. O'Connor's selection had been criticized by the golf correspondent of *The Guardian* (guilty as charged), who said the Irishman was not good enough for Ryder Cup golf and never had been. So. All-square at the 18th, O'Connor hit the greatest shot of his life, a two-iron to three or four feet; Couples, with a nine-iron, missed the green; O'Connor won the match; *The Guardian* eats its words.

As the celebrations came to a close, late into the night, Woosnam stood on a chair and called for order. Pointing at Jacklin, he said, 'This man here, for what he's done, he needs a knighthood.'

At Kiawah Island in 1991, the Americans won by a single point, in a match labelled, ludicrously, the 'War by the Shore'. The concept upset a lot of people, given that operation Desert Storm was being waged against Iraq and it left a bad taste. More happily, it was also the match that saw the full flowering of one of the game's great talents. Couples had been haunted by his finish against O'Connor but US captain Dave Stockton paired him with Floyd and the two gelled formidably. Almost better than the points they won was the visible confidence and enjoyment the phlegmatic Couples got from it all. Only seven months later he won the Masters.

In 1993, back at The Belfry in a less belligerent but no less tense atmosphere, the Americans again won by a point but in 1995, at Oak Hill, it was the US captain Lanny Wadkins who came under fire before a ball was hit. One of his two selections was Curtis Strange and it baffled most pundits, because Strange had not won in America since his US Open victory in 1989 – at Oak Hill, admittedly. At the end, much, if not all, depended on him and it proved too much. One up with three to play against Nick Faldo, Strange bogeyed all three holes, to lose. At the 18th, Faldo hit the stroke of the year, a wedge from 98 yards to four feet and when Philip Walton, yet another Irishman, held on to beat Jay Haas, Europe had won. For America, the singles had been a shambles and Strange was inconsolable.

So, almost, was Wadkins. He had never countenanced failure and had taken such immense pains over captaincy that it never occurred to him that he could lose. When the time came to hand over the cup, he lost the words. The silence was broken by the European captain Bernard Gallacher, who quickly stepped forward and saved the ceremony by saying, 'Here, let me help you out.' The man who had lost the two previous cups with immense dignity explained, 'After all, I'm used to it.'

At Valderrama in 1997, Tom Kite was another painstaking US captain and he went to great lengths to ensure that nothing that could be done to win the match remained undone. He also dedicated himself to the idea that the Ryder Cup was, above all else, a great sporting occasion that was there to be enjoyed. As a man who had played in seven of them, he was in a position to know.

Kite's misfortune was to be up against 13 European captains. No one told him that he would be up against a man capable of cloning himself, able to beam himself down, Star Trek-style, simultaneously at each of the 12 singles matches, while at the same time being back at headquarters directing the action – or so it seemed. Severiano Ballesteros was omnipresent. He was not so much a hands-on captain, as a hands-on-the-club, addressing-the-ball, hitting-the-shot captain, and while he undoubtedly overdid it at times and got up some eminent noses on his own team, the overall inspiration he provided was probably the decisive factor. There is not much between the teams these days – there has not been since 1983 – and external influences like this particular captain can be important.

As usual, the final day singles were hugely dramatic. It looked as though Jose Maria Olazabal would produce the fairytale finish, from wheelchair to Ryder Cup hero in less than 12 months but Lee Janzen, who played superbly throughout, won the last three holes to deny him.

It fell eventually to Langer, who had suffered so at Kiawah, to retain the cup amidst almost unbearable excitement. He took the two putts he needed to beat Brad Faxon on the 17th and the crowd went crazy. Ballesteros, however, was not satisfied. He wanted to win in Spain. It all hinged on Colin Montgomerie's match with Scott Hoch, all square at the 18th. The Scot hit a superb drive down the middle and an equally good second on to the green and was certain of a par four. Hoch needed to hole from 20 feet for a four and Ballesteros, knowing he had the half point he needed, suggested that Montgomerie concede the putt.

It was a gesture in keeping with the spirit of the Ryder Cup, although the bookmakers did not appreciate it. It meant that the score was 14½–13½, rather than the probable 15–13 and there was rather more money staked on the closer result than the more emphatic one.

However, Ryder Cups are not played for bookies and it was a European rookie who summed up why they are played. Ignacio Garrido got into the team 18 years after his father, Antonio and Ballesteros had become the first Europeans to play Ryder Cup golf. Ignacio played well and showed himself smitten with the whole thing. 'The atmosphere,' he said, 'cannot be written, neither could it be read. You have to experience it. We could play 100 holes and we would not be tired – the spectators would carry us in their arms.'

SOLHEIM CUP

On the eve of the first Solheim Cup, at Lake Nona in Florida in November 1990, Joe Flanagan was a frantic man. Flanagan, executive director of the Women's Professional Golfers European Tour (WPGET), a body very much in need of the oxygen of publicity, knew the match against the Americans was a good thing. Indeed he had been adamant that it should go ahead when it began to look as though enthusiasm elsewhere was waning. But he also considered the inaugural event a necessary evil, something that had to be got over and done with, for he harboured the secret fear that his players, hopelessly outclassed on paper, would be thrashed, that they would not score a single point and that their confidence and credibility would be shredded.

Flanagan did not voice such worries publicly but there were many who did. They saw the event as a non-starter, a mis-match of such epic proportions that it was not worth putting on. The women professionals of the United States were just so far ahead of their European counterparts that the critics were convinced that such a contest would be premature for years to come and that staging it too early would set back women's golf, not advance it.

It had been agreed at a meeting in March 1990 that the match would be played, that it would be held in the USA later that year and that the format would be similar to that of the Ryder Cup. There were upheavals within the LPGA – Bill Blue, the commissioner appointed in November 1988, was not at Lake Nona – and many doubted that there was enough time to organize an international event, however low key. The first meeting of the Solheim Cup committee did not take place until August, at Wykagyl Country Club, New Rochelle, New York, during the JAL Big Apple Classic. Miraculously, however, with the backing of Ping – then more formally known as Karsten Manufacturing Corporation – and some sterling work co-ordinated by Mike Milthorpe and Mike Waldron of the LPGA, the baby of the transatlantic team competitions was up and toddling.

The name of the cup had been the subject of some debate – Zaharias, Wethered and Atlantic were suggested; Ping was rejected as too commercial; there already was a Karsten Cup, for a competition at Moon Valley in Phoenix and so it came to be called the Solheim Cup. Essentially, it was a tribute to Karsten and Louise Solheim, stalwart supporters of the women's game or, in their own phrase, 'true believers'. They agreed to a suggestion from son John that their company should sponsor the first 10 stagings of the event, taking it up to the year 2008, the sort of long-term commitment that would allow the competition plenty of time to become established.

At Lake Nona, there was a lot of style – a 'Tie and Tennis Shoes' gala evening at Universal Studios; the Friendship Bowl, a competition for friends and sponsors from both sides of the Atlantic; a flag-raising and not least the trophy itself, a superb piece of handblown glass by Waterford Crystal, valued at £25,000 when it was created. As it turned out, the golf was quite classy too, and there was relief all round when everything passed off satisfactorily.

As expected, the Europeans were outclassed – only one of the 16 matches reached the 18th – and there were several drubbings but Laura Davies and Alison Nicholas ensured that there would be no whitewash when they defeated Nancy Lopez and Pat Bradley, Hall of Famers both, by 2&1 in the foursomes on the first day. Even though the competition was hailed as a major milestone in the history of women's professional golf, the result convinced many observers that it would be a long, long time before the Americans' pre-eminence was challenged.

It took all of two years. The eight Europeans who had arrived at Lake Nona as the underdogs, with too many of them overawed at the thought of stepping on to the first tee with the likes of Lopez, had no such feelings by the time of the second match, at Dalmahoy, near Edinburgh, in 1992. The format was the same – four foursomes, four fourballs, eight singles – but there were two extra players per side because all 16 players had had to play on all three days in Florida, with no spares available in case of illness or injury, let alone lack of form. Seven of the home team had played in the first match – Davies, Nicholas, Dale Reid, Pam Wright, Liselotte Neumann, Helen Alfredsson and Trish Johnson (only Marie-Laure de Lorenzi was

Marie-Laure de Lorenzi.

missing) – and six of them (Reid was the exception) played regularly on the LPGA tour and now realized that the Americans, though very good, were not infallible or unbeatable.

'I look at the video of Lake Nona,' Alfredsson said, 'and all I see is them holing chips and putts and us missing. But that is because they were aggressive, confident and we did not trust ourselves. We had an initial fear.'

There was no fear at Dalmahoy but there was fury. In the issue of the US magazine *Golf Digest* that was current at the time of the match, Beth Daniel had voiced the opinion, 'You could put any one of us on the European side and make it better. But the only Europeans who could help us are Laura and Liselotte.' It was tactless but by no means indefensible. At the time the interview took place (at the US Women's Open in July), Davies, US Open champion in 1987 and Neumann, US Open champion in 1988, were the only members of the European team to have won regular LPGA Tour events. Florence Descampe, a far from boring Belgian, joined them by winning the McCalls LPGA Classic in the August. Daniel denied making the remark but it was like lighting the blue touchpaper and the Europeans duly exploded. Mickey Walker, Europe's captain, had little call on her motivational skills thereafter.

The Europeans played like women possessed. Neumann and Alfredsson – Swedes based in America – jabbered away together in their native language, to the amazement and irritation of opponents who thought they knew them well.

The newspapers loved it and the Americans, who had five old Solheim hands in Daniel, Betsy King, Bradley, Dottie Mochrie and Patty Sheehan and five newcomers in Juli Inkster, Brandie Burton, Meg Mallon, Deb Richard and Danielle Ammaccapane, were on the back foot all week. They were not helped when Kathy Whitworth – their captain – had to fly back home at the beginning of the week because her mother had died. Alice Miller took over and conceded, 'It was a week of adversity.'

The weather was dark and dank, but the golf sparkled from the off. This was not to be Florida revisited. Seven of the first eight matches went to the 18th and Europe won three, lost two and three were halved. Nicholas and Davies, Europe's Little and Large, set the tone with six birdies in the first 10 holes against King and Daniel. The bookmakers, unsentimental beings that they are, had made the American team 6–1 on favourites but the fervour factor made a nonsense of the odds.

The Europeans played like women possessed. Neumann and

Alfredsson — Swedes based in America — jabbered away together in their native language, to the amazement and irritation of opponents who thought they knew them well. 'They're not like this on tour,' one of the Americans commented, indirectly acknowledging that there is nothing like team matchplay to get the juices flowing.

On the Sunday, the Americans were quietly confident – only a point behind, with 10 singles to come. What's more, Europe had to bring on Kitrina Douglas and Catrin Nilsmark to make their Solheim Cup debuts. Douglas, understandably nervous, never got going against Richard yet by the time the Englishwoman had lost on the 12th it was clear that something exceptional was happening: Europe were going to win. Eight thousand sodden spectators, reared on numerous Walker, Curtis and Ryder Cup disappointments, cheered themselves hoarse, scarcely able to believe their eyes. Blue (for Europe) was the colour dominating the scoreboards and only Richard, Inkster and Daniel, who was too wily for the excitable Descampe, finished in the red. Nilsmark had the day of her golfing life against Mallon. 'I had not fears, nor expectations,' the tall Swede said. 'I just went out to play every single shot as though it was the most important of my life.' By the 16th, she was three up and her point would seal the match. She hit a safe tee shot, arrowed a majestic three-iron over a chasm to a green surrounded by wildly beating hearts and two putts later had won the Cup. The green took a pounding as the Europeans cavorted crazily.

Walker called it 'one of the greatest sporting achievements of the century' and she'll get no arguments from anyone who was there (bar the odd American.) The newspaper and magazine reports still vibrate with the passion

Catrin Nilsmark's putt lips out during the second day foursomes.

and excitement of it all. But the television companies showed so little interest that those who weren't there, including former Ryder Cup captain Tony Jacklin, were reduced to following the matches on Ceefax, a teletext service.

Charlie Mechem, the urbane commissioner of the LPGA, was unfazed by the tumult and the shouting and took the long view, as was his wont. 'I thought the object of the exercise was to win,' he smiled in the middle of the European mayhem. 'But for me the single most important thing was that the quality of the golf was outstanding.'

> **But the television companies showed so little interest that those who weren't there, including former Ryder Cup captain Tony Jacklin, were reduced to following the matches on Ceefax, a teletext service.**

The Europeans were on a high for months afterwards – Alfredsson won the Dinah Shore the following March and Johnson won twice in April, their first wins on the LPGA tour. The 1992 Solheim Cup had given them the confidence that they could compete with the best the US Tour had to offer. Prior to 1990, only three Europeans had won on the LPGA Tour: Anne-Marie Palli in 1983; Davies, who had won four times and Neumann, who had won the US Open. But by the time of Dalmahoy that total of six wins had been increased to 10: Davies, Neumann and Palli had had another win apiece and Descampe had also won. Post-Dalmahoy, the wins flooded out – between then and the fourth Solheim Cup at St Pierre in 1996, there were 29 victories by Europeans. Davies and Neumann plundered 16 of them but nine other players also won, including Annika Sorenstam, yet another impressive Swede, who started hoovering up titles in 1995.

Come 1994 and the third Solheim Cup at The Greenbrier – styled as America's resort and so grand that Bing Crosby once joked that he washed and ironed his shirts before sending them to the hotel laundry – even television was taking an interest. There was live coverage in the UK and USA and several thousand spectators majored in map reading to find their way to a hilly corner of West Virginia that was as picturesque as it was out of the way.

Walker was captain of Europe for the third time and the US skipper was the outgoing JoAnne Carner, Big Momma herself, who had been the mother of all matchplayers in her amateur days. She won the US Amateur five times and did not lose a singles match in four Curtis Cups. Her only problem at The Greenbrier was the frustration she felt at not being able to play. Sporting a red, white and blue sequinned baseball cap that was all stars and stripes, Carner was affability personified, joshing with the Europeans, eating with them often but determined to win back the cup, which she duly did.

At The Greenbrier there were still 10 players a side but everyone played all three matches – the format having been adjusted yet again after Dalmahoy, when the US team had been horrified to discover that it was possible to travel thousands of miles to play only once. In 1994 there was also a travelling reserve – Michelle McGann for the US, Kathryn Marshall for Europe – in case of illness or injury. Neither was needed but they both proved willing cheerleaders.

Davies was not at her booming best at The Greenbrier but Dottie Mochrie was inspired, if bordering on the boorish, after a poor showing at Dalmahoy – 'The longest flight I've ever taken was the trip back from Scotland,' she said. The American, hair dyed fiery red, won all three of her games and in the singles Davies was buried daftly down the order at No. 7. By the time she lost to Burton, it was all over and the fat lady (Carner, as designated by Daniel) was holding the cup.

The Solheim Cup committee agreed yet another change of format for 1996, increasing the number of players, the number of matches and, inevitably, the chances of the stronger side. In many ways the 1996 Solheim Cup at St Pierre was a huge success, indicative of how far 'the Ryder Cup with lipstick' (Welsh journalist Tim Glover's memorable description) had come in no time at all. There was lots of live television and radio coverage; a tented village and hospitality packages; nearly 15,000 spectators on the last day; some high-quality and exciting golf, with Europe fighting back dramatically after a woeful first morning; impeccable play and behaviour by Dottie Pepper and an informal choir – the Spontaneous Orpheus – on the first tee to entertain players and fans before the matches teed off. The Swedes got blasts of Abba; de Lorenzi took the tee to the strains of the Marseillaise; Sheehan merited a burst of Yankee Doodle; McGann, who arrived one windy morning wearing a baseball cap instead of her trademark broad-brimmed straw, was asked 'Where's your hat? Where's your hat? Where's your hat?' and Davies, then the world No. 1, was greeted with a football-style chant of 'Number one, number one, number one,' to Sousa's march *The Stars and Stripes For Ever.* It was all wonderful – except the result from a European point of view.

The Americans won the first series of foursomes, a format regarded as the European forte, by 3½ to ½. Davies and Nicholas lost for the first time in foursomes, albeit on the last green and that marked the break-up of an inspirational partnership. In the afternoon fourballs, Europe fought back to win two of the matches, halve one and lose one.

Saturday was phenomenal. Incredibly, the US won only one match all day – late in the afternoon, when Robbins and King beat De Lorenzi and Joanne Morley, making her debut, 2&1 – and halved two. From 5–3 down the Europeans had surged ahead, 9–7. The spectators, let alone the players and captains, were exhausted, exhilarated and shell-shocked. Walker, in charge of Europe for the fourth time, had been stung by a wasp in the morning and looked like a casualty from the Crimea with her head swaddled in bandages. Judy Rankin, the meticulous, thoughtful US captain, who had replaced Carner earlier in the year because the latter's husband was in ill health, was just glad the day was over.

On Sunday, the Americans depressed the home side and silenced the crowd, turning the scoreboards into a sea of red. The Americans won all but three of the singles, losing only the top match – Sorenstam, unbeaten in five matches, defeated Bradley – and halving two. It was an impressive display of their much-vaunted strength in depth and was achieved with scoring that was, in the main, solid rather than spectacular. In a victory that boosted US morale enormously, McGann was at most two under par in beating Davies, who had been immense on Friday afternoon and throughout Saturday but could not muster a single birdie on Sunday.

'What's happened to Laura today?' asked someone who had witnessed the world No. 1's strangely lacklustre performance. The answer, very simply, was that she had run out of steam and it summed up Walker's main problem. She had had to ask too much of her best players. Sorenstam, Davies, Johnson and Neumann all played five times and that is wearing, physically and mentally.

Nilsson was to prove a painstaking captain, but not one capable of reversing the trend. Although the European Ryder Cup team had triumphed at Muirfield Village in 1987, the women of 1998 could not repeat that historic victory.

Rankin, with stronger resources, was able to husband them better and only Robbins played five matches. Bradley was the only American to play just twice – the minimum possible under an unnecessary edict that insisted that everyone had to play at least once before the singles, a decision that should be left to the captain – but Lisa Hackney, Morley and Reid were used as sparingly by Walker, further reducing her options and putting the squeeze on her top players.

The number of talented, battle-hardened Europeans is increasing and

Walker, who put her heart and soul into the matches, handed over to Pia Nilsson, a cerebral Swede, for the 1998 match at Muirfield Village. Walker retired with an OBE and a unique badge of office presented by Louise Solheim. It was a specially commissioned gold necklace, featuring a miniature Solheim Cup in white gold and set with four diamonds, one for each year of captaincy. All captains have necklaces but Walker's is the most diamond encrusted.

Nilsson was to prove a painstaking captain, but not one capable of reversing the trend. Although the European Ryder Cup team had triumphed at Muirfield Village in 1987, the women of 1998 could not repeat that historic victory. In fact, they were never ahead in the whole match, losing 16-12.

The format, constantly changed to suit the Americans, features too many matches for the Europeans, who have yet to develop the strength in depth to contest 28 points. A radical rethink – or rapid European maturation – is required if the Solheim Cup is to become consistently competitive.

WALKER CUP

Americans are not currently known for understatement, but this has not always been the case. Take, for example, a report of the proceedings of the second Walker Cup match, which was played at St Andrews in 1923. The US team officials, returning victorious, duly turned in a summation of the proceedings to the executive committee of the USGA. In dry and dusty fashion, Harold F. Whitney, chairman of the International Matches and Relations Committee, recorded that, 'Your committee is of the opinion that international competition in golf has done as much for the development of the game as any other factor.'

As understatements go, that takes some beating. What Whitney was not to know, of course, was that the Walker Cup would be only the first of the cups. The Ryder and Curtis Cups would follow shortly and they would add immeasurably not just to golf and its development but to the world's sporting scene overall.

The Walker Cup was the first truly international team event and for almost 20 years it was a biennial highlight. Some of the most dramatic struggles in matchplay golf took place between the gentlemen golfers of that period and the world watched, because this at the time was the best against the best.

In those early days the Walker Cup was wholly amateur. It remains so in theory, but not in practice. When the USGA decided that golf scholarships did not contravene the amateur regulations and that those receiving them could carry on playing in the Walker Cup, two things happened: American superiority was further underlined and the whole emphasis of the match was subtly altered. The participants still wanted to beat hell out of each other but for those outside the teams and officials, and particularly outside America, there was reduced interest. This occurred because the Americans were, essentially, already professionals, being paid through their scholarships for doing little else all day but play golf. The Americans therefore completely dominated the Walker Cup, which became known as the Walkover Cup. Since the resumption of golfing hostilities after the Second World War, the USA lead the series by 22 ½ matches to 4 ½ (by 1999), which is a bad enough record.

It is a sad story and one that, for a time, had a parallel with the Ryder Cup before Jack Nicklaus intervened. The R&A, who have authority over the GB&I side, have set their face against any change, citing the difficulty of picking a team – but that is a specious argument. It would have taken no great selectorial wisdom to choose Jose Maria Olazabal nor Per-Ulrik Johansson and the difference just one outstanding player can make was perfectly illustrated by the effect of Severiano Ballesteros on the Ryder Cup team.

After they had been defeated by the record margin of 19–5 at Interlachen, Minnesota in 1993, a former team captain of GB&I conceded that maybe they needed some help, carefully adding, 'It won't happen in my lifetime.'

The pro-European argument was dented at Nairn in 1999 when a very good GB&I team, shrewdly captained by Peter McEvoy, who was bullish about their chances long before the match, hammered the USA 15-9. It was a record defeat for the Americans, who won only two matches (out of 12) on the last day.

Jack Nicklaus, Muirfield. 1959.

The victory meant that GB&I had won three of the last six matches of the century but which was the aberration? Nairn or Interlachen? It is surely the essence of matchplay that in order to be exciting, matches must first of all be close and very few Walker Cup matches have been. Admittedly, if all matches were like those at the Peachtree Club in Atlanta in 1989, the series would be unbearably, not to say fatally – in the case of the more elderly officials of both sides – exciting. That was the year that the home team included Phil Mickelson, Robert Gamez and Jay Sigel. For once, however, GB&I managed to play their game when it mattered and by the final singles the US needed seven points from the eight matches – they only got 6 ½ of them. At one stage the visitors were losing every match and it was amid terrible tension that three of them clawed back a half, to scrape victory overall.

That year some of the home selectors had hopes of a victory and wandered out to the practice ground to run an eye over the visitors. They watched Nicklaus for a minute or two, turned in silence and went straight back to the bar. They knew there was no hope again that year.

Andrew Hare came from dormie two down against Doug Martin; Eoghan O'Connell received some assistance from Mickelson, who of all people three-putted the 17th and the mighty Sigel, duffing chips under the strain, contrived not to win from two up with three to play against Jim Milligan, who was engulfed by his team-mates. They had just become the first GB&I Walker Cup side to win in America.

The Walker Cup had started out of a desire for more frequent contact, and competition, between the two principal golfing nations of the time. Individuals had started to travel to America or Great Britain in search of the various championships and in 1920 the American participants were accompanied by officials seeking to confer on the rules of golf with their opposite numbers at the R&A. Among them was George Herbert Walker – the president of the USGA – who had been educated partly in Britain, at Stonyhurst. He was keen on the idea of an international contest so he put up the USGA International Challenge Trophy. The press soon dealt with that unwieldly title.

The matches were an immediate success and why not, given the names that appeared? Bobby Jones played until his retirement in 1930, Francis Ouimet and Jess Sweetser were in most of the early teams, as were Roger Wethered and Cyril Tolley, and the roll call ever since has been hugely impressive. The Americans have had the likes of Lawson Little, Charles

Yates, Willie Turnesa, Frank Stranahan, Dick Chapman, Charles Coe, Bill Campbell, Gene Littler, Ken Venturi, Harvie Ward, Billy Joe Patton, Tommy Aaron, Deane Beman, Lanny Wadkins, Vinny Giles, Tom Kite, Jay Sigel, Scott Simpson, Gary Hallberg, Scott Hoch, Hal Sutton, Corey Pavin, Davis Love, Duffy Waldorf, Scott Verplank, Billy Mayfair, Phil Mickelson, Robert Gamez and Tiger Woods.

A number of names are missing deliberately from that list. Nicklaus played, of course, and his appearance at Muirfield in 1959 gave rise to a lovely story. That year some of the home selectors had hopes of a victory and wandered out to the practice ground to run an eye over the visitors. They watched Nicklaus for a minute or two, turned in silence and went straight back to the bar. They knew there was no hope again that year.

It was probably worse still in 1975 at St Andrews when what is almost certainly the strongest Walker Cup team ever came over. It included Jerry Pate, Craig Stadler and Curtis Strange, who all went on to win major championships; George Burns, Jay Haas and Gary Koch, who all won on the US Tour and the lifelong amateurs Vinnie Giles, Dick Siderowf and Bill Campbell, who all won the British or American amateur titles.

The list of outstanding GB&I players is necessarily shorter, although Bernard Darwin and Leonard Crawley – two men who saved the face of golf writers by being able to turn their hands to golf as well as a nifty paragraph or two – had some success. Great players came from all the contributing countries: Ireland produced the likes of Jimmy Bruen, Joe Carr, Cecil Ewing, Philip Walton and Ronan Rafferty; Wales chipped in with John Llewellyn Morgan; Scotland had Ronnie Shade, Reid Jack, Charlie Green, Sandy Lyle and Colin Montgomerie; while England produced Ronnie White, Michael Bonallack, Clive Clark, Peter Townsend, Peter Oosterhuis, Peter McEvoy, David Gilford and David Marsh.

It was Marsh who hit one of the most famous shots in the history of the Walker Cup, at least as far as the GB&I side were concerned. It came at St Andrews in 1971, at the 17th. This could be the hardest hole in golf even in a friendly but in a Walker Cup match when your country is trying to win for only the second time in nearly 50 years, it becomes all but impossible. Marsh was in the penultimate match in the final singles, against Bill Hyndman III, a player good enough to reach the final of the Amateur in 1969 and 1970, only to lose to Bonallack each time. Playing captain of the 1971 team, Bonallack lost to Lanny Wadkins but the next six GB&I men won. That meant if Marsh won, GB&I would win the cup and he knew it. Standing over his second shot to the treacherous 17th green, he twice had

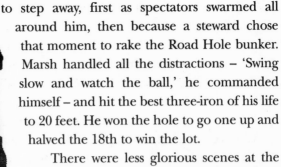

to step away, first as spectators swarmed all around him, then because a steward chose that moment to rake the Road Hole bunker. Marsh handled all the distractions – 'Swing slow and watch the ball,' he commanded himself – and hit the best three-iron of his life to 20 feet. He won the hole to go one up and halved the 18th to win the lot.

There were less glorious scenes at the 17th in 1926 when the home pair of Tolley and Andrew Jamieson were playing Jones and Watts Gunn, who eventually won the hole with a seven after Jamieson had started the comedy of errors by driving out of bounds. In 1930 at Royal St George's the figures were more impressive. James Stout – known as Bill – a dentist from Yorkshire, was seven up with 13 to play against Donald Moe. Stout continued to play well but Moe had five threes in six holes and birdied the last to win the match. A spectator summed it up, 'This is not golf, it's a visitation from God.'

Leonard Crawley – able to wield a golf club and pen with equal efficiency.

In 1932, at Brookline, the match was played during a total eclipse of the sun and Stout managed a half with Jess Sweetser. The only GB&I player to win was Leonard Crawley, who beat George Voigt one up. Crawley was a character and later in life, as golf correspondent of the *Daily Telegraph*, he was given to wearing outrageous hats and an awful ginger-coloured suit that suggested he might be colour-blind. His Walker Cup career spanned 15 years, even though it was on that first appearance in 1932 that he managed to make his mark on the trophy, so to speak. It was on display at the 18th and an errant Crawley shot put a dent in it and necessitated urgent repairs.

Players of Crawley's quality were rare in the GB&I side in the 1920s and 1930s, so much so that the suggestion was seriously made in *The Bobby Jones Story* that maybe Joyce Wethered could have played for the team. It was the candid opinion – off the record – of British critics that she would have been in the team at No. 3 or No. 4, no worse. Charlie Yates, who won the Amateur in 1938 and was on the US Walker Cup teams in 1936 and 1938, played with Wethered and said it was 'the first time I played 14 holes as a lady's partner before I figured in the match.'

In June 1938, the match was at St Andrews again and GB&I won for the first time. The captain, John Beck, held trials – almost as unheard of as practising – but as a result there were more of the right players in the team. One of them was Charlie Stowe, a wonderful artisan player from Wolverhampton in the English Midlands, with huge hands and an accent that was almost incomprehensible. He forced his way into the side through the sheer quality of his golf. When one of the selectors asked him for his telephone number, he was incredulous. 'Telephone?,' he said. 'We ain't even got the electric yet.'

Stowe played a central part in the match. Bernard Darwin, of *The Times*, was also working for the BBC as a commentator, but the commentary was fraught with problems – the chief of which was that he had almost no way of knowing what was going on. He walked with some of the matches early on but 'then I had to traipse back to my eyrie'. He had formed the opinion that Stowe's match against Charles Kocsis was 'the most critical' and when a piece of paper was put in front of him saying, 'Stowe at the 17th,' he believed the GB&I man had won.

'Well,' Darwin wrote, 'what would anybody take that to mean? I fancy most people who watch championships would think that Stowe had won at the 17th. At any rate, that is what I thought and with my last words through the microphone I tell the public that Stowe has won and that now the match is as good as ours. Then, when I have finished, my informant blandly remarks that all he meant was that Stowe was on his way to the 17th.' Much to Darwin's relief, Stowe won, heroically, at the 17th and a little later Cecil Ewing, the big Irishman from Rosses Point, wrapped the matter up. After all those years of defeat, Darwin was ecstatic and Sam McKinlay, of the *Glasgow Herald*, also a former Walker Cup player, was just as content. 'Well, Bernard,' he said, 'we have lived to see the day.'

Such days remained few and far between. America produced sides of a consistently high standard, while in the years after the Second World War, GB&I struggled to find teams capable of competing.

Among many great post-war players, perhaps two from each side stand out, the first of whom is Jay Sigel. When Sigel performed so poorly at the end of the Peachtree match in 1989, having been placed at anchor man precisely because of his experience, there were mutterings from the visitors' camp that it had been 'a match too far', that his nerve for the team occasion had gone. There was an element of wish-fulfilment, wanting finally to be rid of a man who had caused them such grief over the years and Sigel knew better. He was chosen for the next two Walker Cup teams and by winning five matches out of six showed that he was still capable of turning on the style.

No one has played more Walker Cup golf for the Americans than Sigel. In nine contests he has had 18 wins, 10 losses and five halved matches, a record that suitably embellishes the fact that he has twice won the US Amateur championship and the Amateur once. It was something of a shock when he turned professional at the age of 50 but no surprise at all that he won nearly US$5 million in his first five seasons on the Senior Tour.

Sigel's impact on the Walker Cup was only marginally greater than that of Bill Campbell, who first played in 1951 and was still in the team 24 years later, a record for longevity. He competed in eight matches during that time, never losing a singles. Campbell had a lovely, almost drowsy swing which may have been formed, at least subconsciously, by the experience of playing with Sam Snead in a pro-am aged 15. Something of a Renaissance man, Campbell went to Princeton University where his studies were interrupted by the Second World War. He was an infantry captain and, having survived, became a qualified pilot and a member of the West Virginia legislature. That he was able to reach the final of the Amateur in 1954, win the US Amateur 10 years later and play Walker Cup golf in three different decades is a tribute to an enduring swing.

The man who played in the most Walker Cup teams of all, though, was the slashing, dashing Irishman Joe Carr. He played in 10 matches, once as a playing captain and was non-playing captain on

Michael Bonallack – played in eight Walker Cups.

another occasion. He scored only 5½ points from his 20 games but brought a wonderful enthusiasm that helped all those around him. At Muirfield in 1959, he was playing Charlie Coe, one of the giants of American golf, when a pupil from Loretto school stepped on his putter and broke it. However, Carr was used to discarding that putter, because it had a mind of its own, and using a three-iron he still won 2&1.

The Bonallack swing was unorthodox – like heaving a sack of coal into the cellar was one unkind analogy – but he possessed enormous concentration and the ability to hole out from all over the green, particularly when it mattered.

However, modern amateur golf in the British Isles has had no better player than Michael Bonallack, and the R&A – whose secretary he was between 1983 and 1999 – has rarely been better served. The Bonallack swing was unorthodox – like heaving a sack of coal into the cellar was one unkind analogy – but he possessed enormous concentration and the ability to hole out from all over the green, particularly when it mattered. On one occasion at Portmarnock a television crew filmed the famous putting stroke. Bonallack was asked to hit six 10-foot putts but, while the crew got their angles right, the first six were only for practice. He holed one or two. Then they did it for real, and he holed the lot. David Kelley would believe that. In the 36-hole final of the English Amateur championship at Ganton in 1968, he was level par, or maybe one over, after 18 and 11 down to Bonallack.

Bonallack played in eight Walker Cup matches, twice as playing captain and won eight matches in 25 games, losing 14 and halving three. His last appearance was in 1973 but his career should have finished on the winning high at St Andrews in 1971. As playing captain his most important contribution – and one that only he with his towering reputation could make – was to imbue his side with confidence, telling them time and again that they were good enough. They were, too. They produced the most stirring fightback ever associated with a GB&I side, winning after giving the US a two-point start in the final singles. The Walker Cup had been won in what was then Bonallack's spiritual home and became his actual home.

The demise of the career amateur, on both sides of the Atlantic, has been gradual ever since. In America, only Sigel and Giles have fulfilled that role at the highest levels as, towards the end of the century, the rewards for even modest success as a professional proved too difficult to resist. Peter McEvoy occupied that niche for GB&I and overtook

Bonallack as England's most-capped player and most prolific points scorer. In 1978 he was the first British amateur to play all four rounds at the Masters and in 1988, when GB&I won the Eisenhower Trophy – the men's world amateur team championship – McEvoy was the leading individual and arguably the best amateur in the world. He played on five Walker Cup teams, from 1977 to 1989.

GB&I won in 1989 but the match reverted to custom with the US winning comfortably in 1991 and overwhelmingly in 1993 at Interlachen, Minnesota.

Two years later though, at Royal Porthcawl, with a team arguably not as strong, against an American team possibly stronger than at Interlachen, GB&I won. They were inspired by a smiling giant of a player, Gordon Sherry, 6 foot 8 inches and extrovert with it. He helped create an extraordinary atmosphere which led his team-mates to believe they could win. Tiger Woods, the best American player, was totally unable to compete with Sherry in this particular area, nor was he able to beat Gary Wolstenholme in a vital singles match. They came to the last hole level and, after good drives, Wolstenholme had a three-wood to the green and Woods a nine-iron. The Englishman hit the green and Woods, incredibly, dragged his shot out of bounds.

In 1997, though, the American team avenged themselves in familiar fashion. The match moved to Quaker Ridge, in New York and, despite being the best-prepared GB&I team of all time, the visitors were thrashed. You can, of course, prepare everything very thoroughly but, if the ingredients are substandard, the results will be as unappetising as the GB&I record over the years.

Nairn was a brave riposte but the thought persists that it was just a fluke and that the Americans will administer another thumping at Ocean Forest, Georgia, in 2001. To ensure a consistently competitive contest, Europe should be involved. It is still the obvious route for the Walker Cup to take.

CURTIS CUP

In 1986, Danielle Ammaccapane was a pert, dark-haired young miss from Arizona, unskilled in the arts of tact and diplomacy but with a sound-enough grasp of historical fact. 'We always win this thing don't we?' she said to Judy Bell, her captain, on the eve of the 24th Curtis Cup match, at Prairie Dunes in Kansas.

In fact, Ammaccapane exaggerated – but only a little. The United States had won the previous 13 matches, and since the match began in 1932, Great Britain & Ireland had won only twice, in 1952 and 1956, and tied twice, in 1936 and 1958. There had been some close encounters of the gallant-loser variety but it wasn't much of a record, and in the early 1980s the Brits lamented, 'Perhaps it's just a phase we're going through.'

The phase ended dramatically in the heat of the Kansas summer. Anything under 37°C (100°F) was a welcome relief but the visitors didn't sizzle, they scintillated. They cut their hosts into little pieces and stir-fried them, winning 13–5, one of the biggest margins in the cup's history. Their upturn in fortunes continued. Of the next five matches, GB&I won three, tied one and lost one. The Curtis Cup had become a contest.

Diane Bailey, the GB&I captain at Muirfield in 1984 when the Americans had won by a single point, expected her team to win at Prairie Dunes and they shared her conviction. Others did not. Enid Wilson, winner of the Ladies' British Open Amateur championship in 1931, 1932 and 1933, a member of the first Curtis Cup team and for many years women's golf correspondent of the *Daily Telegraph*, was characteristically trenchant. In her view anyone over 30 belonged in a sepia print in the clubhouse, not out on the course in the heat of battle. Since the average age of the GB&I team was 31 (the US average was 23 ½) Wilson was appalled. 'It's a case of bring out your dead, isn't it?' she said. 'I think it's wicked that these people keep on turning out instead of saying, "I made such a balls of it the last time, get somebody else in and give them a chance." We've lost before we even set foot on the plane.'

She undoubtedly had in mind Belle Robertson, the Scot who was competing in her seventh Curtis Cup at the age of 50, and Ireland's Mary McKenna, only 37 but setting a GB&I

Mary McKenna played more Curtis Cups for GB & I than anyone else.

record of nine appearances, all consecutive. Jill Thornhill, the English champion, was 43, but it was only her second Curtis Cup and Vicki Thomas, aged 31 and seemingly champion of Wales in perpetuity, was playing for the third time in a row. Between them at Prairie Dunes they played eight matches, losing one, halving two and winning five. They sent Wilson a souvenir programme, signing themselves 'The Living Dead'.

Claire Hourihane, another Irishwoman, aged 28, had played at Muirfield in 1984 and there were three suitably fresh-faced newcomers. England's Trish Johnson, playing out of the Pyle and Kenfig Club in Wales, was 21 and became the first GB&I player to win all four of her matches since the format of three 18-hole foursomes and six 18-hole singles on each of the two days was adopted in 1964. Lillian Behan, a 21-year-old from Ireland, won three of her four matches and Karen Davies, also 21, of Wales and the University of Florida, did not lose a match, winning both foursomes with Johnson and halving her two singles.

The phase ended dramatically in the heat of the Kansas summer. Anything under 37°C (100°F) was a welcome relief but the visitors didn't sizzle, they scintillated.

The Americans fielded eight debutantes. Their captain, Judy Bell, who first played in the cup in 1960, knew the opposition better than she did her own side. From the moment Dottie Mochrie duffed her drive at the first in the opening match and Ammaccapane, her partner, ignorant of the rules, built a stance in a bunker to forfeit the third and go two down, there was only one team in it. This was an upset on an epic scale by a potent mix of youth and experience. It was the first time a US team, male or female, amateur or professional, had been beaten at home and it set a precedent that was followed in the Ryder and Walker Cups. 'I think we were better than our effort,' said Bell, an honorary member of Prairie Dunes, 'but they were the best prepared British & Irish side I've ever seen over here. They did everything right.'

Four years before, on the 50th anniversary of the match at Denver Country Club in Colorado, GB&I did almost everything wrong. They lost the first hole of every match on the first day and were beaten 14½–3½, their heaviest defeat of the modern era. Maureen Garrett, the president of the LGU, and a former player and captain, put a brave face on things. 'I'm asking them if we can play the next Curtis Cup at Disneyland,' she said. 'Wonderful, unexpected things always happen there.'

In 1962, at the Broadmoor, also in Colorado, the last time matches were played over 36 holes, the United States had won 8–1. Bell was roundly beaten by Diane Bailey, who spearheaded the GB&I revival and continued to jinx the amiable American when they captained their respective sides in 1986 and 1988. Bell confessed, 'I'm the only US captain with back-to-back defeats,' and added, 'I make the record books in a lot of funny ways.'

The ritual slaughter of the British and Irish aside, the match at Denver in 1982 encapsulated the spirit of the Curtis Cup. The USGA invited all former players and captains to a reunion and 47 attended, including four people from the first match at Wentworth in 1932: Enid Wilson and the Americans Glenna Collett Vare, Maureen Orcutt and Dorothy Higbie. For Peter Macdonald, co-chairman of the Prairie Dunes Curtis Cup committee, it was a chance to meet some of the heroines of his youth – Jessie Valentine and Patty Berg were two. He wrote in the *Hutchinson News*, 'Anyone who attended the closing dinner will never forget it. It lasted until midnight, with reminiscences, little speeches full of love and laughter, a permeating spirit of goodwill and friendship and the total absence of excuses or despair on the one hand, or arrogance and superiority on the other. That night my chauvinism melted away.'

The Curtis sisters, Margaret and Harriot S., who presented the cup, could not have wished for a greater tribute. They came from Boston, Massachusetts and were good golfers themselves – Harriot won the US Women's Amateur championship in 1906 and Margaret won it in 1907, 1911 and 1912 – and their uncle Lawrence Curtis was president of the USGA in 1897 and 1898. There was a lot more to them than golf: Harriot was a civil rights activist and Margaret, who headed the American Red Cross bureau for refugees in Paris during the First World War, did a lot of work for charity.

The sisters and several other Americans had travelled to Britain in 1905 for the British championship at Cromer. They played a match that was billed as 'America versus England', with the home side, represented by a mixture of Scots, Irish and English, winning 6–1. Over the years there were other informal matches but it was not until 1932 that the official contest was inaugurated. A few years earlier the Curtis sisters had tried to hurry things along by donating a trophy, a silver Paul Revere bowl, 'to stimulate friendly rivalry among the women golfers of many lands.' Since finance was always a stumbling block, in 1928 Margaret wrote to Cecil Leitch, four times the British champion, with a generous offer, 'I will give a guaranty of US$5,000 per match for the first ten matches played, to be used in defraying the expenses of the members of such team or teams as cross the Atlantic Ocean to compete. This will help out Canadian, British, French teams, etc., as well as American ... There is only one condition attached ... complete anonymity.'

The French and the Canadians have yet to compete in the match but the Curtis persistence paid off eventually and thousands of spectators turned up on 21 May, 1932 for the first match, over the East Course at Wentworth. Marion Hollins, who made – and lost – millions on various ventures, was the American captain (non-playing) and her team was Glenna Collett Vare, Opal Hill, Virginia Van Wie, Helen Hicks, Maureen Orcutt, Leona Cheney and Dorothy Higbie. The home side of Wanda Morgan, Enid Wilson, Molly Gourlay, Doris Park, Diana Fishwick, Elsie Corlett and Mrs J B Watson (better known as Charlotte Beddows), led by the legendary Joyce Wethered, were expected to win but they scuppered their chances by losing the three foursomes. They also had to survive on scraps at lunch-time because the spectators had beaten them to the food. Wethered, Wilson and Fishwick won in the afternoon and Gourlay halved her match with Hill, but a trend had been set. Wethered, the foremost woman golfer of the day, admitted to shortcomings as a leader. 'I was the captain and not a very good one, alas. I was very much an individual and I tended to treat the team as being the same. I gave them no sort of instruction and also I personally played very badly in the foursomes. I putted poorly.'

The Americans also won the second match comfortably but in 1936, on a damp, dreich day at Gleneagles, there was the first tie. The heroine was Jessie Anderson, a 21-year-old local from Perth, who secured the tie by holing a 20-footer at the last to beat Cheney – who wore a heavy tweed coat between shots because of the cold. Anderson, who became Mrs Valentine, played in seven Curtis Cups, two in the 1930s and five in the 1950s. However, it was in the 1940s, during the Second World War, that wee Jessie had most reason to be grateful to the Curtis Cup. She was worried about her husband George, who was a prisoner of war, and contacted Margaret Curtis, who used her Red Cross connections to ensure that food parcels reached him.

After the war, the Americans, fielding players like Louise Suggs, Peggy Kirk Bell and Barbara Romack, continued where they had left off and won the next two matches. At Royal Birkdale in 1948, they were so horrified by the pitiful, post-war, rationed state of their opponents' equipment that most of them left their clubs behind. In 1950, at the Country Club of Buffalo in Williamsville, New York, they were less than charitable on the golf course. Frances Stephens, known as Bunty, of the GB&I side won her foursomes (in partnership with Elizabeth Price) and halved her singles and that was the visitors' total: 1½ points.

Stephens, Price, Valentine, Jean Donald, Philomena Garvey and Jeanne Bisgood, who played at Buffalo, were also at Muirfield in 1952, along with Moira Paterson and Kitty McCann. The captain was the redoubtable Lady Katharine Cairns and the home side won the foursomes 2–1 and, at the halfway stage of the singles (the matches were 36 holes), they were ahead in four and level in one. Victory seemed a formality but the Americans proved typically durable and it all came down to the match between Price and Grace DeMoss. Price, a diabetic, was one up playing the 14th but looked a little weary and, into a fierce wind, was in a bunker short of the green in three. DeMoss was just short in two and a spectator said, 'The only thing that can save us now is a shank.' DeMoss duly shanked, then had a hack in the rough and then another shank. Price won the hole, won the match 3&2, and the British & Irish won the Curtis Cup for the first time, 5–4.

As for Grace DeMoss, she married a Mr Smith and recovered her game sufficiently to play in the match at Merion in 1954, beating Valentine in the singles as the Americans won 6–3. It was their last victory for six years and it was another Mrs Smith (née Stephens) who was to determine the destination of the cup in 1956 and 1958.

Bunty Stephens, a member of Birkdale, the host club in 1948, won all her matches in the trials that year but was excluded from the team. She had a far from classic swing, with a pronounced pause at the top of her backswing, but her ability was not in doubt: it was her background that was frowned upon. Her father, Fred, who coached her, was the professional at lowly Bootle and it is generally accepted that snobbery was the real reason Bunty was not selected. She made no fuss about the decision and simply determined to play so well that she could not be left out in future.

She never lost a singles match in the Curtis Cup and in 1956, in dreadful weather at Prince's in the deciding match, she won the last hole to

Diana Fishwick, circa 1930.

beat the extrovert Polly Riley, who had won her previous four singles with consummate ease. It was to be 40 years before the British & Irish won the Cup outright again but they retained it at Brae Burn in 1958 and again the result came down to Riley versus Smith, Polly versus Bunty.

Riley was a tough competitor – in the 1948 Women's Texas Open she had beaten Babe Zaharias 10&9 (over 36 holes) – but she could not get the better of Smith. One up playing the last, the Englishwoman knew she needed to win to tie the match and retain the trophy. Riley bunkered her second shot and Frank Pennink wrote of Smith, who had driven down the middle, 'Once more rising in her might, she smote a three-iron of sublime quality five yards behind the flag.' It was not until 1962 that Smith lost to Riley, when they were the non-playing captains and the USA won 8–1. 'It's the first time I've got the better of Bunty,' Polly said, 'and I needed eight others to do it for me.'

Smith formed the backbone of the successful GB&I teams of the 1950s, along with Valentine and Price, the only other players to play in all five matches that decade. They would have been joined by Philomena Garvey, of Ireland, but for a row over the blazer badge in 1958.

The name of the team has run the gamut from Great Britain through the British Isles to Great Britain & Ireland, but Garvey drew the line at wearing a badge that depicted only the Union flag. In 1948, when Garvey first played there were no badges, simply a tie, and later the badge was representative of the four home nations. However, having decided on a change, the LGU refused to budge and Garvey, who had won the British championship in 1957, withdrew, pointing out perfectly reasonably, 'As I am an Irishwoman and we have a flag here of our own, it would look strange if I wore a flag that was not the flag of my own country. The whole thing is very regrettable.' Bridget Jackson, the first reserve from Handsworth in Birmingham, was called to the colours. One of the ironies of the situation was that Daisy Ferguson, an Ulsterwoman, was president of the ILGU and backed Garvey's stand – 'Miss Garvey, in an impossible situation, will have our greatest sympathy' – but was also captain of the team and ended up bringing the cup back home.

The matter of symbols was duly resolved and Garvey was back in the team in 1960. Nowadays the Irish Tricolour – usually the right way round – and the Union Flag – not always the right way up – are raised alongside the Stars and Stripes at the opening ceremony. In 1988, at Royal St George's, the home team had non-regulation, unofficial issue, pink sweatshirts emblazoned with the initials GB&I, all except Claire

Hourihane, the only Irish member of the side, whose sweatshirt read, 'GB and me'. That match indicated that the victory at 1986 Prairie Dunes had been no fluke but the 1960s and 1970s were barren years for the British & Irish.

Overall, the Americans were just producing too many strong players to back up outstanding talents like Barbara McIntire and JoAnne Gunderson (later Carner): people like Clifford Ann Creed, Ann Casey Johnstone, Carol Sorenson, Nancy Roth Syms and Jane Bastanchury Booth (whose daughter Kellee played in the matches in 1996 and 1998.) GB&I had some very good players in that time and there were still individual flashes of brilliance and moments of high excitement.

In 1964, at Royal Porthcawl, Gunderson and Marley Spearman played one of the great matches. On the first day, playing beautifully, Gunderson had beaten Angela Bonallack for the third successive match. 'She says she never plays so well as she does against me because watching me makes her swing slower,' Bonallack said.

In the afternoon, Pat Ward-Thomas was enraptured. He wrote in *The Guardian*, 'The abiding skill and sustained courage of Mrs Spearman will live as the supreme memory of the match. Few British players in the history of the competition with America have achieved a performance comparable to hers. She played top, with all the responsibility of that position, in all four matches.' Spearman and Bonallack won both their foursomes and Spearman halved her singles with McIntire – the US champion – and Gunderson, rated the most formidable amateur in the world. At the 18th, with Gunderson one up and eight feet away in two, Spearman holed from nine feet for a birdie three. Ward-Thomas wrote, 'They laughed at each other. Such was the spirit of the match. The American's putt licked the hole and a magnificent contest was halved as by every possible right it deserved to be.'

The USA also won another tight encounter at Royal County Down in 1968, with the home side's Ann Irvin and the American Phyllis (Tish) Preuss winning 3 ½ points each. Vivien Saunders, ever the Renaissance woman, then a student at London University, sat her psychology exams in Belfast on Monday and Thursday and played in the cup on Friday and Saturday. She won 1 ½ points and passed her exams.

The match at Western Gailes in 1972 was also close: Mickey Walker, who later became Europe's Solheim Cup captain, won 3 ½ points out of four and was the only player to finish the match unbeaten, but there were too many 'if onlys' and the USA won 10–8. In 1976, at Royal Lytham and

St Annes, the Americans sent what was perhaps their strongest side ever, including future professional stars Beth Daniel and Nancy Lopez, who was played only twice, and the match took on the look of a no-contest. It was not until Muirfield in 1984 that the British & Irish side realized that losing was not necessarily their birthright.

There have been new heroines since then: Linda Bayman on her cup debut, on her 40th birthday, on her home course at Royal St George's, holing an outrageous putt of 35 yards from off the 18th green to halve her match with an astounded Tracy Kerdyk; Brandie Burton – and most of the other Americans – putting the lights out on the fast, undulating greens at Somerset Hills as the USA regained the cup; Caroline Hall, aged 18, surrounded by thousands of people at Hoylake in 1992, hitting the four-iron of her life to the 18th, to beat Vicki Goetze in the deciding match to win the cup back; Janice Moodie, blonde, bustling and businesslike at the Honors Club in 1994, revelling in the responsibility of having to beat Carol Semple Thompson to secure the tie that would retain the cup – and hitting a majestic six-iron to four feet at the last to do just that; Alison Rose, a quiet bank official from Stirling, brimming with a self-belief long subdued, becoming only the second GB&I player ever to win all four of her matches, at Killarney in 1996 and at Minikahda in Minnesota in 1998, Barbara McIntire, recalled as captain 22 years after her last time in charge, inspiring her side to their first victory in six years, helped no end by Kellee Booth and Brenda Corrie Kuehn, who both won four points out of four.

Thompson, one of an increasingly rare breed – the career amateur – played in her tenth Curtis Cup that year, setting an American record that, given the lure of the professional game, is unlikely to be beaten – except by her. Ann Quast Decker Welts Sander, whose collection of husbands could not quite keep pace with her collection of Curtis Cups, played in eight matches, and her record will certainly not be overtaken, for she represented the United States in five different decades. She played in 1958, 1960, 1962, 1968, 1974, 1984 and in 1990, when at the age of 52 she became the oldest player to compete in the Curtis Cup. In an inspired pairing with Goetze, then 17, Sander won the two matches she played and maintained her record of never having been on a losing side, a feat that no American now takes for granted.

Prairie Dunes saw to all that.

CHAPTER 7

THE WORLD'S GREATEST COURSES

WHAT'S THE BEST COURSE YOU HAVE EVER PLAYED? That is the single most repeated question any golf writer ever hears and it is quite impossible to answer. Is there a best painting in the world, a best book? It depends, of course, on your taste and of the entire corps of golf writers that I know, none would choose to play their last round of golf – the ultimate test – on the course that I would choose, Brancaster, otherwise known as Royal West Norfolk. Which is why the list of great courses which follows is in alphabetical order.

Many tests determine whether or not a golf course is great. Some of the less well-known ones include the following: Do you, on hearing that an invitation is available, take the best golfing slacks to the cleaners? Do you begin to gloat over less fortunate friends? Do you – crucial test this – clip your toenails and fingernails and get your hair cut? Do you gloat after you have played, regardless of your score? And do you keep the sweater you bought, with logo of course, for far longer than its useful life?

All these things and more are caused by the thought of playing a truly great golf course, one that

is not normally available to you, and one that you know you will cherish. A sense of anticipation builds that demands you give yourself the best chance, for chances like this do not come often.

Not many courses can induce this kind of respect. Cypress Point can, as do Augusta National, Muirfield, the Old Course at St Andrews, Pine Valley, Seminole and maybe Royal Melbourne. These are some of the defining tests of golf worldwide – the courses that set the standards by which others are judged. These are the courses that architects today strive to emulate, knowing that no matter how good they are, no matter how

St Andrews, the home of golf.

good the ground available, no matter how many railway sleepers or ties they use and no matter how much tartan festoons the clubhouse, it would take a minimum of 50 years to attain that atmosphere.

AUGUSTA NATIONAL

It is, as it was intended to be, The World's Wonder Inland Course. The description, complete with its capital letters, is that of its architect, one of the finest the profession has known – Dr Alister MacKenzie.

The course, Augusta National Golf Club, in the southern state of Georgia, was built at the behest and with the collaboration of one of the finest of all golfers, Robert Tyre Jones jnr – Bobby as he was known – and together the two men set about creating something unique.

Jones' aim was, 'to develop a golf course and a retreat of such nature, and such excellence, that men of some means and devoted to the game of golf might find the club worthwhile as an extra luxury where they might visit and play with kindred spirits from other parts of the nation.' Some 30 years later he was happy 'that the club apparently has adequately fulfilled this mission.'

He can say that again. By the end of the twentieth century, few clubs had clung on to their original founding precepts as tenaciously as Augusta while hosting one of the most famous events in the sporting world, the Masters.

If there is one course in the wide, wide world of golf that everyone wants to play, it is Augusta National and it is one course they cannot. There is an armed guard on the gate, such is the privacy this exclusive club insists on but, in fact, it is no more private than a dozen other clubs around the country. The difference is that this course is exposed annually on television to millions of viewers. They see a place of supreme beauty and, understandably, would like to experience it. There is the famous example of Nick Faldo, who only took up golf because he put on the telly one night and saw Jack Nicklaus winning the Masters. 'I think I'd quite like to do that,' thought Faldo, then a teenager and he has since played Augusta often – and rather well.

> **If there is one course in the wide, wide world of golf that everyone wants to play, it is Augusta National and it is one course they cannot.**

The course he plays is much changed from that first envisaged by MacKenzie and Jones. When he first saw the land, a former nursery, Jones said, 'It seemed that it had been lying there for years just waiting for someone to lay a golf course on it.'

Magnolia Lane

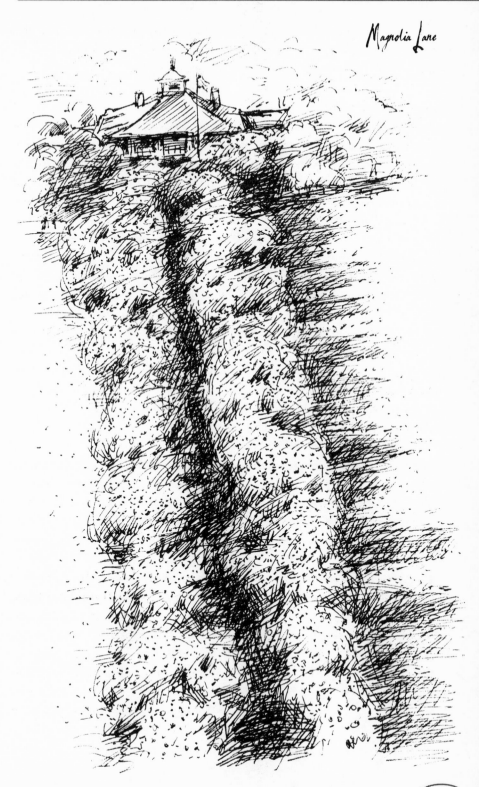

MacKenzie proceeded to do just that and his first routing is, overall, remarkably similar to what now exists. In detail it is very different; indeed, it changes almost every year in some degree.

In one respect it has altered not at all. The design philosophy was to build a course for 'the most enjoyment for the greatest number'. *In Golf is My Game* Jones said, 'Our overall aim at the Augusta National has been to provide a golf course of considerable natural beauty, relatively easy for the average golfer to play and at the same time testing for the expert player striving to better par figures. We hope to make bogeys easy if frankly sought, pars readily obtainable by standard good play and birdies, except on the par fives, dearly bought.'

When he first saw the land, a former nursery, Jones said, 'It seemed that it had been lying there for years just waiting for someone to lay a golf course on it.'

Long before reading that I had thought that if you set out with the intention of taking no more than five on any hole, you might, with luck on a good day and with the possible exception of the short 12th, succeed. With this as their guide, the handicap player need never feel that their score is getting wildly away from them.

The par fives, in essence, present little problem for the player content with a five. Collectively, and as presented to the professionals, they are as good a selection of long holes as exists anywhere in the world. In modern parlance, the risk-and-reward element is so strong that almost every professional feels the need to go for the green in two, knowing full well that a bogey or worse awaits if he fails. The challenge at the second is to carry or pass the fairway bunker on the right. With that accomplished, hitting the green should be relatively simple. If, in going for that little bit extra you drive into the bunker or the trees, you have a struggle for par. The eighth requires a strongly hit second but if, in trying for it the professional pulls it into the woods, he will be really fortunate to make par. The 13th and 15th holes are renowned worldwide as two of the best of their type, both requiring good accurate drives and then a precise carry over water. Curtis Strange lost the 1985 Masters at the 13th and Ballesteros the 1986 Masters at the 15th, both by finding the water. At all four holes the terror is taken away if you decide to lay-up and take three shots to reach the putting surface.

Ah, the greens. Those at Augusta are faster, truer and to the unwary more treacherous than can possibly be imagined. They are probably

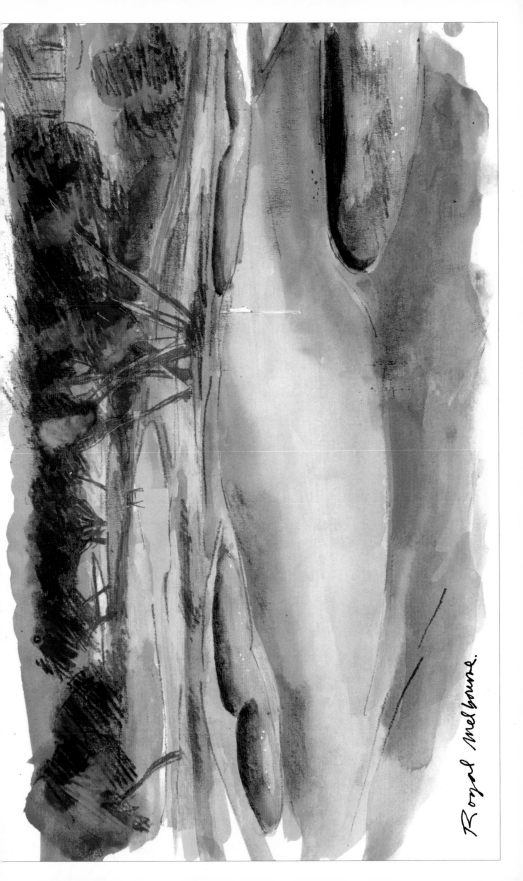

Royal Melbourne.

Royal Corwalis Dawn.

Royal West · Norfolk

Leopard Creek.

Taryaiho, Japan

St. Andrews

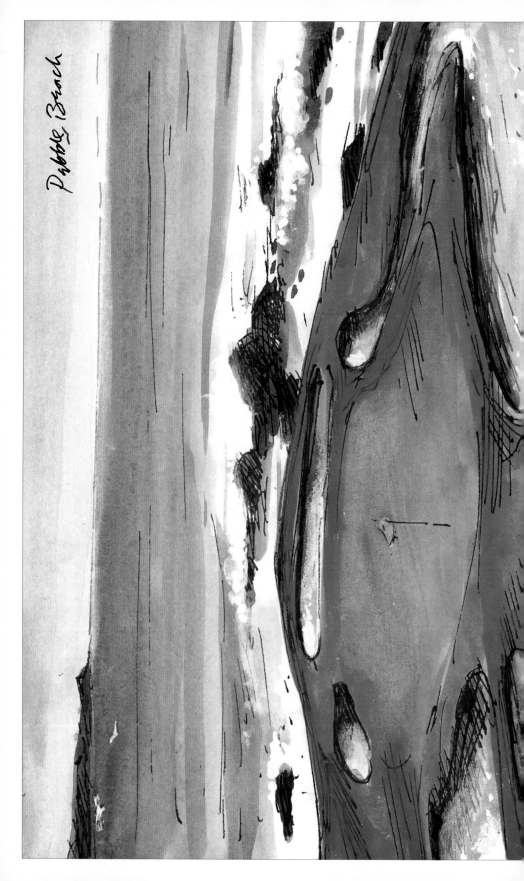
Pebble Beach

faster, too, than Jones or MacKenzie envisaged when they built into them some of the severest contours to be found on any course. That was in the early 1930s before modern agronomy brought course conditioning to its present level and before technology gave players greater length and accuracy and brought scores tumbling. Augusta now needs its Ferrari-fast greens and its ice-like slopes to protect it from modernity. The professionals, of course, get used to fast greens and learn to cope with the extra element presented at Augusta. Many of the players are, for example, good enough deliberately to hit shots that stop below the hole. For those unused to such speed or without such skill they can present an intractable problem. It is entirely possible on almost every green at Augusta to hit what you think is a good putt and see it, eventually, slither to a halt somewhere off the green. That need happen only once or twice early in the round for the putter to become an instrument of torture, totally useless for the purpose for which it was designed.

Traditionally, short holes have the most challenging greens and the four par threes present the biggest danger to the handicap golfer. The fourth is, at 205 yards, simply a very big hit, followed by some delicate putting on a green that slopes from back to front. When Sandy Lyle won the 1988 Masters he chipped in from the back fringe for a two. It was a superb shot, rolling very slowly when it hit the pin but had it not gone in it would have carried on rolling very slowly and finished off the green 30 yards from the hole. The sixth is shorter but if the pin is back right, on a sort of dais, it is to all intents and purposes invisible. There is no point in knowing where it is because you cannot get there. Jose Maria Olazabal once went for the pin when it was in this position, missed to the right and twice left little chips short. Then he hit the third one too hard and it rolled to the front of the green. The likelihood is to take three putts from there, so Olazabal recorded seven, a record high for the hole and lost the 1991 Masters by a shot. Just try and hit the green – anywhere.

That is the advice at the 12th, too, but this hole strikes terror into the heart long before you get there. Jack Nicklaus called it the most dangerous hole in professional golf and Tom Weiskopf once took 13 there. This is an exceedingly difficult green to hit, demanding extreme precision to carry Rae's Creek, then the front bunker and then stop it on the bootlace masquerading as a green. If you don't, you're in the bunker at the back – staring at Rae's Creek again. Calamities are common here but Weiskopf's double act with his caddie was a tragi-comic routine: hit, splash, new ball; hit, splash, new ball …

Part of the problem of the 12th is that the winds swirl in this opening in the pines and you are never sure when to hit. In 1992 Fred Couples got it minutely wrong, his ball pitched on the bank of the creek and began its inevitable roll towards the water. Then, for no discernible reason, it stopped half way down, defying the laws of gravity. Treading gently, Couples pitched and putted for a par that was obviously meant to be. He went on to win the tournament.

The 16th is nearly all carry over water. The tee shot is not as demanding as at the 12th but the formidable green pitches and rolls like a drunken sailor. It is essential not to go past the pin and, if you miss the green and find the bunker on the right, be prepared to take lots. On her one visit, my wife Patricia holed a 10-footer for her three and rushed off to phone her mother back home in the UK.

What manner of man – there are no women although they can play as guests – takes on the challenge of Augusta National and becomes a member? The short answer is those who are invited. It is the only way in and always has been. It was not just a rich man's club when it began – although in 1989 the net worth of the 300 or so members was put at US$10 billion. Early on, Jones himself had almost no money at all but as the best-known sportsman in America – two tickertape parades in New York – the great man had a worth far beyond actual cash.

The club was set up during the Depression – one member-to-be lost US$10 million overnight in the 1929 Wall Street Crash but others took care of his subscription – and was known as 'Bobby's Club'. However, it was Clifford Roberts, a wealthy man and a devoted friend of Jones, who made it all work. At an early membership meeting, Grantland Rice, a sportswriter much more famous than most of the people he wrote about, proposed that Augusta National be run by Jones and Roberts in any way they saw fit. The suggestion was unanimously agreed.

Jones, who died in 1971, became President in Perpetuity; and Roberts, who committed suicide in 1977, is Chairman in Memoriam. The club is packed with chief executive officers, heads of this and founders of that but the chairman is still the boss, in keeping with the autocratic Roberts tradition. Dwight D. Eisenhower was an active member of Augusta National – a hot line to the White House was installed in his cabin at the club – but even he could not persuade Roberts to cut down the tree that invariably impeded the presidential progress at the 17th. It is still there – known as Ike's Tree.

BALLYBUNION

Tom Watson set a trend some years ago. To avoid any fuss or hassle, he decided to set sail for the Open early, to explore with a few well-chosen friends, the links courses where golf originated. The first place he chose to play was Ballybunion, on Ireland's west coast, a course that stands comparison with the best links in the world.

He loved it all: the wildness of the setting; the jumbled dunes that run east–west as well as north–south and the quality of the challenge and stiff breezes that enhanced it. He enjoyed it so much he has been back many times since, for Ballybunion is a place for golfers to go. It is only necessary to set foot on the land to realize that the best possible use has been made of it. Many famous names have made the pilgrimage, including Jack Nicklaus, Byron Nelson and Nick Faldo, with Nelson bemoaning the fact that he hadn't discovered it 50 years earlier.

Golfers have been making special efforts to play Ballybunion for a great many years including the inimitable Patrick Campbell. In 1936, he set off on a golfing journey around Ireland and recorded the subsequent adventures in the *Irish Times*. He seems to have hit upon Ballybunion on one of those grey days when the wind blows hard and the whole of your being is concentrated on just getting round.

At any rate, he had little to say about the glorious stretch of holes by the Atlantic, or about the overall quality of the par fours – some of the best anywhere – and instead talked about the two par fives, which used to comprise the finishing holes. 'These,' he said, 'are two of the longest fives I know. At the 18th I hit two enormous wooden shots with my eyes shut, topped a mashie niblick (a six-or seven-iron) so that it bored its way two feet from the ground into the teeth of the wind, and I still only reached the edge of the green.'

Campbell was an accomplished golfer, so there must have been some breeze blowing but he was right in dismissing, with faint praise, the holes that now comprise the fourth and fifth. They are principally the only way of getting from the third to the sixth and by a distance the least interesting aspect of the course.

The biggest change to the course since Campbell's day has been in the positioning of the clubhouse, which has forced a change in the order of the holes. It means, fortunately, that the course no longer ends with those par fives but it was not done for that reason. In the 1970s the club, with great foresight, bought the land adjoining them, consisting of dunes that are, if anything, even more spectacular than the ones on which the existing course is built.

The club then decided to build another course, the New, and the result just goes to show how wise the founders were when, back in 1896, they decided to use the tract of land that hosts the Old Course. The land on which the New is built is somehow too precipitous, too spectacular, with the result that the player is either on the fairway or in very considerable trouble. It is too hard a course for all but the very good players and it looks furthermore as if it has been imposed on the land rather than blended into it.

The building of the New meant a new clubhouse, so that it could serve both courses and now the Old starts at what was the 14th. This is an extremely happy accident because it creates a fascinating first: one that offers a par four if only the player avoids his or her customary slice so early in the round. For to slice here means that you are dead, in a manner of speaking. There is a graveyard on the right, well within range of even a half-decent shot.

At 392 yards the first offers a chance of a par but the second, at 445 yards, demands some playing. The green, like many at Ballybunion, is elevated but the second shot has to be struck straight and very true to fly between a gap in the dunes that seems absurdly narrow so early in the round. If that's not demanding enough, the next hole is 220 yards long and one look tells you that your ball had better be on the green if par is required.

Seventh, Ballybunion

Now the golf course starts in earnest, demanding nothing but truly struck shots, particularly to the greens. You could imagine someone like Peter Thomson, who always said that the shot to the green was what made a golfer, glorying in the remaining holes. The sixth dog-legs out to the sea, the seventh runs along the coastline and the eighth is a short hole of such quality that you start thinking how on earth to play it long before you get there. It is only 153 yards long and has its back to the sea. This means that when the wind is from the Atlantic there is almost no known way of stopping the ball on the green, even if the bunkers are avoided, which is difficult. The inland ninth is simply tremendous while the 10th echoes the sixth in length and direction. The green is out by the ocean and there, right next to it, is the 11th tee.

This is one of golf's great tees, with, on just an averagely windy day, the sea crashing all around you and often some spray to contend with. In front of you is a drive that must be placed just left of centre and then – in one of the most photographed vistas in golf – the fairway disappears into a chasm and reappears at the other side, leading the eye to the green, which is framed by dunes. Beyond the green, a range of sand-hills and beach and sea, in their turn framed by more sky than you ever dreamed existed: it can be literally breathtaking. It is 450-odd yards from the back and around 400 from the easier tees, so your second-shot game had better be sharp.

Three of the next four holes are par threes: the 12th, 14th and 15th. It is the last of these that is the attention-grabber. If a 216-yard shot to a two-tier green, surrounded by bunkers, presents no problems, then here is your hole. For most it is a par three-and-a-half – at best. The 16th funnels inland, with yet another elevated green at the end of it, but after a short sharp climb to the 17th tee, there's the Atlantic again, distractingly so, since the tee shot has to be carefully played. It must be long enough to get past the mountainous dune on the left but not long enough to run out of fairway.

There are those who say that the 18th is not a worthy finish for Ballybunion and they may have a point, for the green is hidden by a huge bunker, making it a blind second shot. But a shot is only ever blind once, and in every other regard the 18th is a challenge and in view of what has gone before it will do for me – as for many a better judge.

CYPRESS POINT

The Monterey Peninsula houses two courses which, by any standards, are great: Cypress Point and Pebble Beach. They got a head start simply by being where they are, a place Robert Louis Stevenson called the 'greatest meeting point of land and sea in the world'. Even in the jet age his judgement stands. The sea is the Pacific Ocean, the coastline ruggedly beautiful and the Peninsula a fantasy forest of twisted, fantastically contorted, cypress trees.

The road winding in and around all this is called 17 Mile Drive and at one point there is a modest little sign announcing the Cypress Point Club. A modest little road leads to a minuscule car-park, where people usually change their shoes. For all its exclusivity, Cypress has its municipal moments – not many, though. If you want a coffee in the clubhouse, wear your jacket and tie.

The clubhouse is tiny and so is the professional's shop, which may be the last place in the Western Hemisphere that does not take credit cards. The members just charge things to their account but it comes as a shock to the visiting logo locust who wants that cypress tree motif with the legend 'Cypress Point Club' on the left breast. In the mid-1990s a quite ordinary sweater cost around US$120.

In the early 1920s, before the golf course, the Salinas area was known as the Valley of Green Gold and many of the fine houses on 17 Mile Drive were built on the proceeds of the lettuce crop. However, it's the cabbage that's the problem if you're playing badly at Cypress Point. The target areas are wide enough to be fair but if you miss them you're in trouble.

In the early 1920s, the Salinas area was known as the Valley of Green Gold and many of the fine houses on 17 Mile Drive were built on the proceeds of the lettuce crop. However, it's the cabbage that's the problem if you're playing badly at Cypress Point.

The first hole features an odd drive over a hedge, which has to be kept to the left and, if accomplished, leaves you with a mid-iron to the green. It is a reasonably relaxing start because the second, played to its par of five, is also accomplishable. Try for a four, though, and good players need two very good shots. This is often a characteristic of a great course – to score five on any hole is relatively easy; to score four is frequently very difficult.

Cypress continues with a sand-surrounded short hole, then a par four that winds its way uphill, delineated all the way by stretching splashes of sand, and a demanding dog-leg where a big draw off the tee gives the good player a chance to get up in two. By now you have been forcibly reminded that the course is not just the pretty face presented by the 15th, 16th and 17th holes, the ones that appear in all the photographs with the Pacific crashing all around them – what are now called 'signature' holes. The inland holes provide a superb test, reminiscent in their undulating way of Augusta National, Alister MacKenzie having had a large hand in both. In 1929 the US Amateur was held at Pebble Beach and Bobby Jones, having heard that the recently completed Cypress Point was something to be seen, played there and was hugely impressed. A year later when Jones found the land for his dream golf course, he sent for MacKenzie.

Cypress Point epitomizes MacKenzie's belief that the architect's chief object was 'to imitate the beauties of nature so closely as to make his work indistinguishable from nature itself'. In *Golf Architecture* he enumerated 13 principles that should feature in an ideal golf course, one of which was the 'heroic carry from the tee', with the option of an easier route for the less skilled. Lewis A. Lapham, MacKenzie's guinea-pig, recalled, 'I was, by 1927 standards, a long hitter and, by any year's standards, a very wild one. However, the Doctor [MacKenzie] was a patient man and used me to measure the extent of the "heroic carry". The Doctor had a small portable mat for me to hit from and two men out yonder to measure my drives. He would put the mat down, seat himself on a shooting stick and tell me to hit away, laddie. My first three or four tee shots were usually in the spinach but when I finally flushed one he'd move the mat 5, 10, 15 yards right, left, up, back, or wherever, and we'd go at it again.'

Lapham must have been particularly valuable at a hole like the eighth, where a 'heroic carry' is available, while perdition awaits those who do not make it. The drive must carry 210 yards on an exact line and the penalty for failure is to land in a bunker so big – it must be 60 yards long and 30 yards wide – and so soft and embracing that you might end up as bleached bones before getting out. The reward for those who make the carry is a tiny pitch to a green so severe that it requires the most delicate of shots to get close. Should you choose not to be heroic and take a line to the left of the bunker, there is still only an eight-iron or so to the green but on this putting surface you may start with the putter, then have a chip back. Most people hole out eventually.

Elevated tees are a feature of the course, as at the 15th, a hole that anywhere else would be the star of the show. It has everything. The tee is perched out by the shore, waves crash into rocks and run on into the inlets where the seals lie, pelicans practise their formation flying and a fishing boat head-butts its way towards Monterey to complete the picture-book perfection. In front of you lies the sharply sloping green. Surrounding it, sand. Surrounding the sand, ice plant – that rubbery vegetation from which it is impossible to move a golf ball. The whole is framed by phantasmagorical cypress trees and, depending on the wind, the club is anything from a four- to a nine-iron. It is a wonderful, wonderful golf hole and yet is not regarded as the best, nor probably even the second best, hole on the course. The 15th is a bit like being, say, Bobby Kennedy – successful, famous but with a big brother.

The JFK of Cypress Point is the par three 16th. This may be the most photographed hole in golf, a spectacular amalgam of the elements, a perfect illustration of what MacKenzie meant when he said that 'a course should have beautiful surroundings and all the artificial features should have so natural an appearance that a stranger is unable to distinguish them from nature itself.' Intellectually, you know that the green at the 16th has not been there since time began but, emotionally, you know it was meant to be.

Lapham was used extensively at the 16th and the result is the most heroic carry in golf. It is over 200 yards – 200 yards of ocean, rocks and ice plant. Mostly it demands a driver, for a mishit simply will not make it and failure means you now face it all again, or back down and hit a five-iron to the left, the bail-out area for the less-than-heroic. Or you might just hit the tee shot too well, run out of landing area and plunge into the Pacific on the left of the green. MacKenzie, worried that he might have made the hole too heroic, thought of presenting it as a par four. Fortunately, he did not and the 16th occupies a unique place in the golfing firmament: it is perhaps the best-known hole in the world despite the fact that hardly anyone ever plays it.

It is a simply spectacular spot. Shortly before the 1981 Walker Cup two of the club's employees were looking for the most beautiful place they could imagine for their wedding and they chose the 16th tee. The club gave permission but stipulated that, should any members arrive at the time of the service, the couple had to be temporarily put asunder and the golfers called through.

More often than not you will leave the green to the sound of honking noises that get louder the closer you get to the 17th tee. This is sea-lion territory and there always seems to be a touch of derision in the honks – particularly when you stand and stare at what lies ahead. The carry, again over rocks and rolling breakers, is not so intimidating in itself, although you must hit a stout shot of at least 180 yards, but for it to be any good to you the line must be perfect. A controlled power fade is best and if you could call on Lee Trevino or, nowadays, Colin Montgomerie to hit it for you that would be ideal.

Any idiot can drive well left off the tee to avoid the ocean at the start but that brings it into sharper relief for the second shot, which is exceedingly difficult from the left. From the middle or right-hand side of the fairway, it is only very difficult. You have to play over some old cypresses, gnarled and nearly keeling over, supported by arboreal Zimmer frames – like a crotchety ancient aunt, they cling on defiantly, making life as difficult as possible.

The green is tiny and, if hit, the satisfaction quotient is immense. If the ocean has been avoided, the ancient aunts carried, the green held and a par four achieved, you ought to be able to shake hands, say, 'Thanks for the game' and go and contemplate the round with a civilized whisky or two. But this is only the 17th green and, although you have just completed the most spectacular and challenging stretch of golf anywhere in the world, it is a sad fact that there is still one hole left to go.

The club gave permission but stipulated that, should any members arrive at the time of the service, the couple had to be temporarily put asunder and the golfers called through.

Sandy Tatum, a member and a former president of the USGA, called Cypress Point the Sistine Chapel of golf, which makes the 18th, unfortunately, the aisle that leads to the church doors. There is nothing wrong with the 18th, except that it should not be there. In Sistine terms, the anthems have been sung and the soul uplifted but now you have to chant a few automatic responses – long-iron, short-iron, two putts, par – before you leave. It's a better hole than that but you don't feel that it is.

There is a splendid house just to the right of the 18th tee and that's where the course should finish. The wit, wisdom and wealth of the membership should be able to locate another hole in that fantastic forest and enable us all to leave the chapel with the choirs in full voice.

MUIRFIELD

What is the first thing that comes to mind when mention is made of Muirfield? Is it that Jack Nicklaus, no less, regards it as the best links course in the world? Is it that some of the greatest Open championships and Amateur championships have been held there? Or is it its great reputation as a golf course the average golfer simply cannot get to play on?

The answer, of course, will vary according to status in the golfing world, but it should be said straightaway that Muirfield is unfairly maligned in the matter of getting on: it just takes time and the courtesy due to all private clubs. The home of the Honourable Company of Edinburgh Golfers will open its doors if the bell rope has been pulled correctly.

In 1991, Payne Stewart, then US Open champion, was refused a tee-time but it was a genuine misunderstanding. When Stewart arrived for the Open at Muirfield the following year, John Prideaux, a secretary as affable as some of his predecessors were rude, was on hand. 'What the devil do you think you're doing?' he blustered. 'You don't think you're going to play, do you?' Stewart caught on at once. 'Hell, man,' he pleaded. 'At least let me play this week.'

There is no club more worth the effort. While there may be clubs with as demanding yet fair a test and others with as much if not more natural beauty, there is not one that combines those qualities with the history that is attached to Muirfield. This is a club without parallel in the golfing universe.

It may be the oldest club in the world. Others would dispute this, principally Royal Blackheath, Royal Burgess and the R&A and, of course, it all depends on the definition of oldest. Muirfield maintains, with some justification, that in order to acknowledge the existence of a club there must be some written evidence to prove it and by that criterion they are indeed the oldest. The first records of what were then called the Gentlemen Golfers of Edinburgh were written in 1744, over 10 years before anything surfaces – in written form – about the R&A. Not that

Muirfield, 17th.

concessions are about to be made. *The Golfer's Handbook* revealed that Blackheath still regard themselves as being founded in 1608 and Royal Burgess in 1735.

There is the stuff for erudite argument but essentially it is inconsequential. What is important is the current existence of a magnificent golf course, in the custody of those who think it important not only that it should be kept in the best possible condition but also that it should host, from time to time, the game's great celebrations. By the late 1990s they had, for example, accepted 14 Open championships and nine Amateur championships; the Walker and Curtis Cups twice each but the Ryder Cup, strangely, only once.

And what a list of champions. If it is true that a great course produces a great champion – a dubious proposition – then the proponents of that argument can always point for justification to Muirfield. Of the 12 champions, only one, Alf Perry in 1935, could be described as a lesser player, the others being: Harold Hilton (1892), Harry Vardon (1896), James Braid (1901 and 1906), Ted Ray (1912), Walter Hagen (1929), Henry Cotton (1948), Gary Player (1959), Jack Nicklaus (1966), Lee Trevino (1972), Tom Watson (1980) and Nick Faldo (1987 and 1992).

With winners like that it is clear that, down the years, Muirfield has been full of Open moments and one of the most pleasant was that Cotton won the last of his three Open championships there. Sir Henry thought Muirfield to be the best course and wrote, 'It was always in perfect condition – and cruelly fair.' That phrase has real poignancy – there are no excuses, no hiding places at Muirfield.

Cotton, who also won the championships of 1934 and 1937, might have been indisputably Britain's best-ever player had not the Second World War intervened. His triumph in 1948 came very largely courtesy of a second-round course record of 66, before which he was introduced to King George VI on the first tee. Then, 'With the Royal touch still fresh upon his hands,' as Bernard Darwin wrote in *The Times*, Cotton hit a drive and three-wood into the first green and holed from 12 feet for a birdie three. He eagled the long ninth, was out in 33, back in the same number and Darwin concluded, 'Neither I nor anyone else has ever seen him play better, more calmly, or more confidently.' He won by five strokes.

In 1959, the Open was won by Gary Player, who arrived two weeks early to practise. There was much negotiating before Colonel Brian Evans-Lombe, the club secretary, allowed Player 18 holes a day. The club also hosted the Walker Cup that year and in it played one Jack Nicklaus, who in 1966 used that experience to win his first Open. 'I knew Muirfield,' he said, 'and I knew it well. With its splendid turf, its moderate undulations – it was my kind of course.'

But he could not have expected what he found. The championship committee, as they do from time to time, took leave of their collective senses and let the rough grow to the point where the fairways were largely invisible. It looked like a wheatfield. Doug Sanders announced that he would accept the hay and lost ball concession rather than any prize money but then played in more mature fashion to finish joint second with Dave Thomas.

Nicklaus decided that if anyone could handle it, he could. 'After all, I was an old Muirfield man' he commented. And with the driver effectively confined to the bag, there was always going to be only one winner, for, with the possible exception of Sandy Lyle, no modern player has played the one-iron so well as Nicklaus. He won by one shot, birdieing the 17th, a hole of 550 yards, downwind. He hit a three-iron off the tee followed by a five-iron which Pat Ward-Thomas of *The Guardian* described as 'deathless'. Nicklaus hit another one-iron off the tee at the 18th and a three-iron into the green, to complete a career Grand Slam, the first of three.

Nicklaus was second in the Open of 1972, the 11th to be held at Muirfield, but had little more than a bit part in one of the most sensational finishes to any championship. The starring roles were shared by Lee Trevino, Tony Jacklin and that 17th hole. The two were level on the 17th tee but Trevino hooked his ball into a bunker and was lying so badly he had to come out sideways. Jacklin's drive split the fairway. Trevino hit a poor third into the rough on the left and as they walked up the fairway he said, 'It's all yours.' His body language mirrored his words and when he hit his fourth shot on to a steep grassy bank through the back of the green, he had obviously given up. Jacklin, 15 feet away

Lee Travino celebrates chipping in, Muirfield. 1972.

in three, had no chance to mark his ball before Trevino played his fifth. He snatched a wedge out of the bag, did not take a practice swing or any care at all over the shot – and holed it for a par five.

Jacklin has always claimed that the three putts that followed were not a result of shock but of aggressiveness but he has never denied the effect of failing to win that championship. In *The First 40 Years*, he said, 'The heart was ripped out of me. I stepped off the 18th green a shattered man, broken by what had happened … I was honestly never the same again.'

The principal reason, perhaps, that Muirfield is so perfect as a championship venue is that, unlike so many links courses, it is not an out-and-back layout with nine holes stretching into the distance, and then returning. Muirfield has, in effect, outer and inner nines, which has two immensely important effects: the wind is almost invariably blowing from a different quarter on each successive hole, and no one hole is very far from the clubhouse. The first of these effects is to challenge the very good player and to confound those of lesser ability, while the second comes into its own at tournament time, for the spectator can very quickly join whichever group he or she wants to see.

It is also a true links. There are no trees and a complete absence of water.

> **'The heart was ripped out of me. I stepped off the 18th green a shattered man, broken by what had happened ... I was honestly never the same again.'**

There is only one blind shot – the drive at the 11th – but nowadays that is accounted a blessing. It also has the best set of bunkers of any course in the world. They are deep and steep, almost exclusively one-full-shot-penalty bunkers and there are times when they are more than that. In the 1979 Walker Cup, in the foursomes, the Americans Doug Clarke and Mike Peck found themselves in the huge cross-bunkers at the 17th. They both left the ball in once and Clarke looked to the heavens and crossed himself before his second attempt. The ball stayed in and Peter Alliss, commentating on television, said sadly, 'You can't trust anyone these days.'

Nicklaus has called the 18th the best hole on the best Open course. It is made by the fairway bunker on the right, which catches all those shots whose sole intent is to avoid the fairway bunkers on the left. Having succeeded in finding the fairway the second still has to be carried, and precisely at that, on to the green, for there are bunkers short, to the right and to the left. It is a fine, and fearsome, finish – one befitting the stature of Muirfield.

PEBBLE BEACH

Pebble Beach is, in some ways, America's St Andrews – it can be played by anyone and Jack Nicklaus has described it as a 'shrine'. It is situated on the Monterey Peninsula, near Carmel, a picturesque little town whose most famous mayor was Clint Eastwood.

The peninsula is prime golf and real-estate territory – other wonderful courses there include Spanish Bay, Spyglass Hill and Old Del Monte – and was originally developed by Samuel Morse, an early environmentalist who was related to the inventor of the telegraph. He instigated the building of Pebble Beach and Cypress Point, the former being laid out by Jack Neville, with later alterations by Chandler Egan and Nicklaus.

Nicklaus said, 'I fell in love with it immediately. It remains my favourite among the 600 or so courses I have played around the world.'

Architecturally it is the spectacular married to the sound; aesthetically it is beautiful but not without blemishes and as a test of golf it goes from demanding to dull. Pebble Beach, perhaps because television loves it and concentrates on the first of these qualities, has an enormous reputation that is not wholly justified in every particular. However, it has a high percentage of great holes, so, on a one-off basis, it is probably worth paying the enormous sums now demanded and putting up with a round of five hours or more. After all, this is the course of which Nicklaus said, 'I fell in love with it immediately. It remains my favourite among the 600 or so courses I have played around the world.' He was reflecting on the 1961 US Amateur championship, which he won by beating Dudley Wysong in the final and he was 20-under par for the 112 holes he played that week.

Pebble Beach is regularly voted one of the top five golf courses in America, although in 1995, when *Golf Magazine* divided their panellists into four categories to assess their votes, it was the architects, the group least likely to ignore some of the lesser features, who placed it outside the top five. Admittedly, they ranked it sixth.

There is nothing sensational about the start at Pebble – the first and second are pretty dull and the third, while difficult, is nothing special. There is no hint of what is to come. The fourth is the first of the eight holes on the cliff edge and it is a very good short par four, needing precision to hit a tiny green, a trademark at Pebble. But it is at the sixth that the course gets into its stride – the second shot has to be struck truly because it has to find an elevated green and is usually into the wind. Almost everybody finishes short first time.

The short seventh is simply sublime. It is one of the most photographed holes in the world, along with the 16th at Cypress Point, and the big problem is what club to hit. The hole is only 107 yards long but, if the wind is howling in from Hawaii, it can be a teeth-clenching four-iron. Mostly, it is between an eight-iron and a wedge hit from an elevated tee and the vista encompasses masses of light blue sky, the deep blue of an ocean perennially plundered by hordes of diving pelicans, some sea-lions and, on dry land, a cluster of silver-sand bunkers and a heart-shaped green that dispenses few favours to its fleeting visitors. It all caused Fuzzy Zoeller, practising for the 1992 US Open, to stop his customary whistling and burst into song. 'Oh, what a beautiful morning,' he warbled. The temptation is to stop all 'the flailing about' and just sit and enjoy the view.

Three more of the best holes in golf follow immediately. The 431-yard eighth has what is easily the most dramatic second shot in golf and Nicklaus called it his 'favourite'. It has to carry a canyon filled with sea, sand and scrub – from rim to green is 180 yards, a longish iron or fairway wood for most. A slight mishit or a weak slice means doom but there is a

Pebble Beach. 18th

wide expanse of land to the left, for the lay-up and a safe bogey. Absolute accuracy is also essential because there are five bunkers awaiting as well as a horrid little bank on the left, which offers what seems to be a minuscule area of putting green for a masterly shot and a vast amount of cliff edge for anything slightly thin. Trust Nicklaus to love a challenge like this.

The ninth, at 464 yards, is by definition a par four, but normally yields a five. In the Pebble Beach Pro-Am, the best players in America averaged 4.36. Coming after the eighth, average 4.4, and before the 10th, 4.32, that produced a stronger-than-average annoyance quotient. The problem is that the ninth is cambered towards the sea, which means that instinctively the ball is kept towards the left, where the rough has been grown in and the bunker lies. All in all it is probably best to go quietly. Ditto at the 10th. It is shorter but the fairway bunker is huge and the green itself is tightly bunkered. By now the handicap golfer is beginning to feel slightly bemused, maybe wishing that he had stayed on that seventh tee.

In the third round of the 1992 US Open, Gil Morgan was 12 under par, seven ahead, when he reached the eighth tee. He said to his caddie, 'The golf course starts here,' and his scores on the next three holes – the terrible triumvirate – were 6,5,6. The title slipped from his grasp. He was also four over par for the next four holes although from the 11th to the 15th Pebble Beach is solid rather than spectacular. The holes are all inland and do nothing to raise the pulse, barring the 14th green, which is so severe that Paul Azinger once five-putted it.

The 16th, though, is a wonderful dog-leg, with big bunkers in the elbow of the hole, which are an automatic one-stroke penalty. The second has to carry a tangled mess of tufty grass and the green slopes viciously from back to front. It is another hole where par is a very good score and is the start of a finish that is as strong as anything in golf. Carnoustie's may be marginally harder but Pebble's is prettier.

The 17th plays at around 209 yards – it can be stretched to roughly 220 – and it needs anything from a driver to a mid-iron. There is nothing but rough and sand in front of the green, which is narrow and has a ridge running from tee to sea, effectively dividing the right and left portions of the putting surface. For a shot hit too long there is sand, then rocks and sea; if ever there was a short hole where the player might wish for a stroke in hand, this is it.

The 18th, at 548 yards, is simply a great hole. It has provided architectural inspiration for seemingly hundreds of other 18ths, which bend themselves round water on the left, challenging the player to cut off as much as he dares. The tee is perched out in the Pacific Ocean, with breakers pounding all around and a breathtaking view of stark hills beyond the green; Nicklaus called this 'one of the greatest places in golf'. The problems are to choose, then achieve, the best line from the tee, avoiding the rocks on the left and hoping that the bunkers on the right are also out of play – and not forgetting the cluster of trees on the right-centre of the fairway cluttering up the second shot. Only the mightiest hitters can carry the front bunkers and reach the green, and anything over-drawn results in an undignified scramble among the rocks plus a likely seven.

PINEHURST

Pinehurst is a place of many parts and is much, much more than the sum of them. The golf course count is huge and still rising, which is no bad thing as the surrounding area is outstandingly suited to it.

Pinehurst is one of the world's true golf resorts. There is not a great deal to do other than play and, with such a selection available in such a small area, why would anyone want to do anything else? There are up to 40 courses within a comfortable drive of the village centre and most of them are not just good – they are excellent.

This is not an accident. When the eminent golf architect Donald J. Ross took his first look at the pine forests and the soil strata, he said, 'Of all the land I've surveyed for courses, none compares to the sand barrens around Pinehurst, North Carolina.' What's more, he moved to Pinehurst and lived there for the rest of his life.

No area of land is better suited to its name. The dominant tree is 'pine' and 'hurst' is an old English word with meanings ranging from a hillock to a sand-bank in the sea to a wood or wooded eminences. Pinehurst has plenty of woody and hillocky bits and, given its sandy soil, was obviously under the sea in another age. The site was, and is, perfect for the construction of golf courses and Ross must have been thrilled when he realized that this vast quantity of land – 5300 acres bought for US$1 an acre – was just waiting for his touch.

Although Ross was a good enough player to finish eighth in the 1910 Open at St Andrews – and his brother Aleck (or Alex) won the US Open in 1907 – he became famous throughout America as a designer of golf courses. Ron Whitten, architectural editor of *Golf Digest* magazine, dubbed him 'the first superstar of American golf', pointing out that in 1925, an era when the Hagens and the Sarazens were playing for purses of US$1000,

Ross was earning US$30,000 a year running a company that employed 3000 men on course construction and maintenance. A poster of the late 1920s and early 1930s showed an elderly Ross urging people to visit Pinehurst – US$110 for eight days all-in, including railway fare – where they would be able to meet the man himself. It was the start of the 'big-name architect' syndrome.

Golf architects should surely be like referees or umpires – if they've done a good job, they don't impinge – but Pinehurst gained some notoriety from the Ross connection and he enjoyed living there. It also gave him the chance to spend 30 years perfecting one of the nation's greatest courses: Pinehurst No. 2.

The original No. 2 course was 5860 yards long, with browns instead of greens. Now the course has grown to 7028 yards, with grass greens 'rumpled into interesting contours' as Ross put it and the areas around the greens have become world famous. No. 2 is renowned for the pressure it places on the second shot, for Ross was a firm believer that the good player should drive the ball to the correct side of the fairway to have the chance of hitting the green with a firmly struck shot. He also believed that, if the green was missed, the recovery shot should be as tricky as he could make it. 'The contouring around a green makes possible an infinite variety in the requirements for short shots,' he wrote, adding, 'you will be interested to see how many times competitors whose second shots have wandered a bit will be disturbed by these innocent-appearing slopes.'

The course is widely acknowledged throughout America as offering one of the fairest tests in golf. The terrain undulates but it does not heave or plunge and, while a stance can be uneven, it is unlikely that this will be a permanent condition. A handicap player once commented that he enjoyed it because he didn't lose a ball. The first hole is, in some ways, a microcosm of what is to come, despite the out of bounds road on the left, which, paradoxically, defies one of Ross' design precepts. 'It is a beastly nuisance when starting off play and before getting limbered up, to drive a ball out of bounds,' he said. 'It generally means delay, loss of a ball, vexation and even profanity.' Even so, on No. 2, the 414-yard first gives the player a chance to open with a par.

The eighth is a lovely hole, diving away from the tee into a valley at the end of which is a green that is slightly elevated, like so many Ross greens. It spurns anything but the best of second shots and par here produces a little swagger. In fact, so does par on most holes on Pinehurst No. 2. The best players will be looking for a birdie at the long 16th – if only to provide insurance for the 18th. There the tee shot, over an expanse of scrub and uphill, must be well struck and straight to give a clear sight of the green, which, while big enough, is surrounded by bunkers and those inevitable slopes. It is also back in front of the clubhouse where a balcony of sceptical players can watch your efforts to finish respectably.

Ben Hogan won his first pro tournament, the 1940 North and South Open, at Pinehurst and Sam Snead also made a name for himself there. He was invited for a practice round by Dutch Harrison, an established player and gambler, who quickly realized that he was not the hustler but the hustled. At the end, Harrison was blunt, 'Kid,' he said, 'from now on you work your side of the fairway and I'll work mine.'

In the 1951 Ryder Cup, the USA won 9–2 on No. 2 and in his match against Charlie Ward, a pugnacious bantamweight from the Midlands of England, Hogan hit a shot that amazed even him. One up at the 28th – the 10th the second time round in those days of 36-hole matches – Hogan seemed certain to lose the hole after hooking his tee shot into the rough and hacking out. Instead, he crashed a brassie on to the green and holed from 60 feet for a birdie four. Later, he went back to pace off the shot: it was 305 yards.

No. 2 hosted the world amateur team championships for men and women, respectively the Eisenhower Trophy and the Espirito Santo, in 1980. The United States won both titles and I met my wife there. I beat her in the final of the chipping contest at the Pine Crest Hotel, where they have a chipping board leaning against the wall, near the bar. The board is a large green sheet of wood with a hole in the centre and the object is to chip the ball into the hole from 15 feet or so. Even those staying at the luxurious Pinehurst Hotel wander down to try their luck.

In 1999, Pinehurst No. 2 hosted the US Open and proved itself fit for the best. The occasion sanctified the whole resort and was the ultimate recognition of a man who might in the true sense of the word be called the father of American golf – Donald J. Ross.

PINE VALLEY

If it came down to a ballot of players, Pine Valley, that visually stunning golf club in the backwoods of New Jersey, would certainly rank as an all-time great. No political party, no pop group has ever won more popularity contests than this very private members' club, which, despite the fact that it has never hosted a major championship, is almost permanently rated the best golf course in the world. Architects admire it, professionals proclaim its excellence, journalists drool over it and whenever magazines of whatever nationality come to list their top 100 courses – or whatever number they choose – Pine Valley is the No. 1. This is quite extraordinary. It seems to indicate a massive and permanent outbreak of masochism among those whose job it is to rate and rank golf courses, for what they are regularly nominating is a layout that is almost impossible for the average golfer to get round. Furthermore, the club is proud that it is next to impossible to play and will lay considerable amounts of money against the first-time player, with a handicap of 10 or more, breaking 100.

Alister MacKenzie, of Cypress Point and Augusta fame, was once told in admiring tones of a new golf course where no one had ever broken par. His response was, 'My goodness, what's wrong with it?' Well, what is wrong with Pine Valley is that it is too darned difficult. It's not the intrinsic design, nor the speed of the greens, nor the narrowness of the fairways, all of which are fine. It is the penalty for playing a bad shot that is out of all proportion.

The rough is of the sort where platoons of invading soldiers could secrete themselves for weeks without anyone noticing them and to miss the rough and find the trees is to risk getting lost altogether. Without the dire warnings beforehand most golfers would not take enough golf balls – maybe could not take enough – with them to complete the round. Wherever there is not fairway, there is heather and gorse and deep tangled grass – unless there is sandy waste, hardpan or bunkers.

What is certain is that if you are not on grass that is cut quite short, you will have extreme difficulty finding your ball and playing a shot, which does not strike me as being fair or enjoyable. Architects are fond of saying that if they designed a golf course like St Andrews today, they would be run out of town by their employer. But at least St Andrews, eccentric though it may be in the modern age, is playable. Pine Valley, except for the very good player who can keep it on the fairway all the time, is not.

Alister MacKenzie, was once told in admiring tones of a new golf course where no one had ever broken par. His response was, 'My goodness, what's wrong with it?' Well, what is wrong with Pine Valley is that it is too darned difficult.

Pine Valley was the brainchild of George Crump, a Philadelphia hotelier, who, in essence, laid it out. A note in the programme for the 1985 Walker Cup explained that he believed that a course should 'box the compass', in other words test every shot in the bag. Tellingly, however, 'more than anything else he believed that a good shot should be rewarded – and a bad one penalized, even if severely'. He certainly achieved that.

They boast about this sort of thing at the club. In the same programme, they proudly quoted Dan Jenkins, a writer who knows his golf. 'Man knows that this is the golf course with the largest sandtraps and the funniest footprints in the world, and knows that Pine Valley – just the *sound* of it can make you shank – has more bushes, trees, Scotch broom, poverty grass, hawthorn and mountain laurel lying around those traps and in them, than any course ever devised. And he knows that success depends on which way your shots bounce off the pine trees. Fail, and you tear up your score card and retire to the gin-rummy table for the afternoon.'

Golf, as we know, is not meant to be fair but it is not meant to be deliberately unfair either and Pine Valley, in many places, reaches that level. Fancy being proud of a course where 'success depends on which way your shots bounce off pine trees.' Jenkins, incidentally, rates it as his favourite course.

There is no doubt, though, that Pine Valley is a lovely place to be. The aforementioned ingredients make it the most

Pine Valley

pleasant of places to walk, particularly if you're not having to hit a golf ball at the same time. It must also be admitted that the good players are not as afflicted as the handicap golfer. The only problem Jack Nicklaus had when he first played there was that he was on his honeymoon and his wife Barbara had to sit outside in the car – women are allowed into the club only on Sunday afternoons.

What a wonderful thing it would be if you could just round up the best 150 players in the world, dump them in County Down and tell them to come back four days later having decided on a champion. Whoever it was would be a worthy one.

In the 1985 Walker Cup, in the foursomes on the first day, Peter Baker and Peter McEvoy completed nine holes in an approximate 31 and, not surprisingly, won the point. The visiting side also included Colin Montgomerie and David Gilford, who like Baker went on to become Ryder Cup players. However, the United States won narrowly, 13–11, thanks in no small measure to Davis Love III, who beat McEvoy easily in the singles on the last day. Love was a much longer hitter then than 12 years later, when he won the US PGA championship and by the not-so-simple expedient of birdying three of the first four holes, he was four up. So you can get round Pine Valley but you have to be good.

The late great Peter Dobereiner was a member at Pine Valley and, although his golf game was constitutionally incapable of getting him round the course, he always argued vehemently that it was a great one. However, in a career that has allowed me to play nine of the 10 courses generally accepted as the best in the world, including Pine Valley – and 30 of the top 50 – the New Jersey layout is the one at which I would least like to have to try and maintain a handicap. It is just too difficult for the common man.

ROYAL COUNTY DOWN

One of the most evocative songs in a land famous for them, has the line: 'Where the Mountains of Mourne sweep down to the sea...' Sing this, in the company of an expatriate, golfer or no, and watch the tears well up. If a golfer, watch them flow the more freely, for the memories that song will bring back are those of what is, scenically, the most spectacular of the world's great courses, Royal County Down.

Some would argue for Pebble Beach, or Cypress Point, maybe even Turnberry but while those courses all have a great empathy with the sea, none has what is arguably the most beautiful backdrop in the world, the

Mountains of Mourne, which do indeed sweep down to the sea. Backdrops of themselves mean nothing but when they are allied to a course of the quality of County Down, the effect is to produce a place in which it is a massive pleasure to be and to play golf.

This course of major championship quality will never host an Open, because its ancillaries are insufficient but what a wonderful thing it would be if you could just round up the best 150 players in the world, dump them in County Down and tell them to come back four days later having decided on a champion. Whoever it was would be a worthy one.

This archetypal links course is built among dunes which have barely been disturbed because, when Old Tom Morris laid it out in 1889 (for a fee of £4), there was nothing to disturb them with. This means that some shots are blind, which in turn results in some modern-day bleating about 'unfairness'. Of course, the five blind tee shots are blind only once and on each of the holes – the second, fifth, sixth, ninth and 15th – there is plenty of fairway to land on.

The first three holes run along towards the north, with a ridge of dunes separating the player from Dundrum Bay. The long first proffers a par but the second and third, at 424 and 468 yards respectively, offer nothing but hard work. You then turn back towards the south, where the fourth tee reveals an irresistible vista, in this case of mountains, with the spires of the town rising up below them. The fourth is a short hole of some 211 yards, with not much but gorse between you and the green should you fall short. Waver just a little off line and there are 10 bunkers around the green, so a three sends you on your way rejoicing.

The dog-leg-to-the-right fifth is another tester. A blind drive across oceans of rough has to be kept right to avoid a bunker on the left – but if you are too far right, you will still be in the rough. The hole is 440 yards long so a successful drive is essential but, if the wind is anywhere but behind, the second is still going to be a long club of some sort. Few quarrel with a bogey five.

The seventh is a short hole where much of the putting surface is hidden by a big front bunker, which also hides the fact that, if you should miss the green to the left, your ball will hurtle down a severe slope and the chip back will be one of the hardest shots of the day.

But it is the ninth tee that commonly brings first-time visitors to a halt and has them scrabbling about in their golf bags for the camera. The tee is on a ridge of dunes, below lies the fairway bordered by more dunes that narrow down to the green almost 500 yards away. Above it all is *the* backdrop, with Slieve Donard, the highest of the mountains, imposing itself on the eye. It is all just magnificent.

The second nine is of the same character, albeit with different challenges, as the first. The 10th, a short hole of some 200 yards, is where my career as a golf writer nearly came to a premature end. In the final of the 1970 Amateur championship, which provided Michael Bonallack with his fifth – and last – title, his opponent, Bill Hyndman, shanked a shot off the tee. The ball flew, at head height, through the crowd and nearly took my nose off. It was part of the reason Bonallack, who had beaten Hyndman in the previous year's final at Royal Liverpool as well, went on to win by 8&7.

The 11th, 13th and 15th, all par fours, are all around the 450-yard mark so, on the first two, you had better hope for the wind to blow from the south. In one international match, the wind was so turbulent that eight holes were out of reach, for the best amateurs in the country, with two full-blooded whacks.

The 14th, at 216 yards, belies its description as a short hole, especially if the aforementioned breeze is from the north, but at least the 16th and 18th offer chances for redemption. The 16th is a par four of 267 yards, drivable in the right conditions, while the 18th is a rather plain par five and a bit of a letdown after what has gone before.

Years ago, I was offered a place in a fourball that was to play at County Down. One of the four had a small private plane in which we flew to Belfast; another, a professional racing driver, drove us to the course and the third was a stockbroker whom I had entrusted with a few unremarkable shares. As we walked down the first fairway I thought, 'Here I am playing golf with my personal pilot, my chauffeur and my stockbroker.' Inevitably, I took seven, puffed up pride was instantly banished, and the overwhelming charms of Royal County Down took over.

ROYAL DORNOCH

Royal Dornoch is a place of pilgrimage. It is not a place a golfer comes across accidentally, for it is not on the way to anywhere and is, indeed, a long way from anywhere. It demands a definite determination to visit but is one of the sport's high altars, on which has been sacrificed many a fragile game.

Set in a stunningly beautiful place, it is the most northerly first-class course in the world, at 58 degrees, on the same latitude as Hudson Bay and Labrador. Yet, given a little luck and a warm sweater it is playable throughout the year.

The first time I played the course I drove almost non-stop for 10 hours from Birmingham and the next morning met a solitary golfer looking for a game. 'I hope this is as good as it's cracked up to be,' he said. 'It took me 10 hours to get here.' He had flown from New York to London, from there to Inverness and driven the remainder.

The pilgrims flock to Dornoch to see what golf architects and designers the world over have hailed as the best and about which Tom Watson said, 'This is a course that can set par for them all. I have played none finer, a natural masterpiece.' Herb Warren Wind, the American golf historian, said that it 'may be the finest natural golf course in the two hemispheres – and more than that, an experience that reaches deep inside a man for certain reasons hard to define.'

'I hope this is as good as it's cracked up to be,' he said. 'It took me 10 hours to get here.' He had flown from New York to London, from there to Inverness and driven the remainder.

Certainly Sandy Tatum, a former president of the USGA, found them hard to define. On one occasion at Dornoch with Watson, the pair had completed 18 holes before the heavens opened and rain, driven by a gale, all but blotted out the course. After lunch, to Tatum's amazement, Watson announced he was going to play another 18. Foul weather or not, he just had to experience Dornoch again.

The club was founded in 1877 and played a major part in the survival of Dornoch town itself, which had become what one commentator described as 'an old-fashioned, outlying, outlandish grey nest to which no stranger ever thinks of going, except the sheriff of the county.' The late Donald Grant, recorder of the club's history, recounted how 'two young Dornoch men made a pact with each other.' Hector Mackay, a lawyer, went to John Sutherland, an administrator and scratch golfer, and said, 'John, this old town is quiet, is almost in decay; but we have many assets here. The town is well built on different levels, we also have the cathedral and Dornoch links. I will take care of the affairs of town and parish if you will stay and look after the golf club and the golf course.' The deal was done. Mackay became town clerk, Sutherland the secretary of the club, and remained so for 53 years.

Sutherland was a good player, among other good players and it was their combined excellence that eventually put Dornoch on the golfing map. It came about through what was to become known as the Dornoch Invasion, which, while sounding fearsome, was nothing more than six members of the club 'making the sally south' as Grant put it, to play in the 1909 British Amateur championship at Muirfield. It was to make them and their club famous. What these six men did was to beat six of the best golfers in the world and their exploits had the wires humming not just in the United Kingdom but also all across America.

In the first round, Jerry Travers, the reigning American champion was playing Capt W. Henderson. Travers had won the US title in 1907 and 1908, would win it again in 1912 and 1913 and would win the US Open in 1915, but he lost 2&1 to a Dornoch man. If that was a shock, what happened to John Ball was a sensation. Quite possibly the best player in the country, Ball had already won the Open once and the Amateur five times, but he was beaten on the 18th by Tommy Grant, a baker with no left thumb and the hooker's grip of all time.

There was more to come. Alick Morrison beat Johnny Low, a famous St Andrews golfer and runner-up in the 1901 championship and Sutherland beat Harry Colt, the golf course designer. All the Dornoch men lost in the next round except Sutherland. He beat J.L.C. Jenkins, who was to win the title in 1914 and then took the biggest scalp of all, defeating Harold Horsforth Hilton at the 19th. Hilton remains the only British golfer ever to win the US Amateur, in 1911, when he was also the Amateur champion. That year he was also joint third in the Open, having won the championship in 1892 and 1897. However, on one day in 1909, he was not as good as the secretary of Royal Dornoch.

Sutherland was a good player, among other good players and it was their combined excellence that eventually put Dornoch on the golfing map.

As a result, the invaders were themselves invaded. Hilton and Ball made the pilgrimage north to see for themselves the quality of the golf course that had fostered such players and the resultant publicity helped make Dornoch. What they found is not what the visitor would see today. In fact, Dornoch's most famous son, Donald Ross, the most venerated of golf architects, would not recognize all the course, for six holes became a 'dispersal airfield' and disappeared during the Second World War. The course – created variously by nature, Old Tom Morris and Sutherland – was rebuilt by George Duncan and the current sixth to 11th holes are his work. Regardless of who put them there, the 18 championship holes are nothing short of magnificent. The course is fit to hold any championship, although the pity of it is that it is so far away and so short of accommodation that the Open championship could not realistically go there. The Amateur did once, in 1985.

All the holes at Dornoch are memorable, with the exception of the seventh, which seems out of character. The fifth was the favourite of Tom Watson, with its drive from an elevated tee to a course that bends away beneath towards a massive bank of whins, or gorse, which, in May, is blindingly yellow. The sixth is a great short hole, with a bunker on the right that has to be re-made periodically, so frequently is it used. The hole that caused the trouble in the 1985 Amateur was the 14th, only 459 yards long but played that week mostly into a substantial breeze. The players had problems reaching it, not least because it bears a Ross trademark – a plateau'd green. To go for it and miss it means an exceedingly difficult chip, which is precisely what Ross had in mind.

> **'Modesty forbids me saying more than it is the most beautifully situated links in the world, and that no American golfer should omit to go there'. Donald Ross**

In his book *The Confidential Guide to Golf Courses*, Tom Doak, an architect himself, gave Dornoch a perfect 10, but the last word should go to Ross. Looking back fondly on his home course after many years in the United States, he said of Dornoch, 'Modesty forbids me saying more than it is the most beautifully situated links in the world, and that no American golfer should omit to go there, where he will find the best golf, a royal welcome and no rabble.'

ROYAL MELBOURNE

No one who has played there ever forgets Royal Melbourne. It is one of the greatest courses, one of golf's masterpieces. As Peter Thomson, five-times Open champion, said, 'By any judgement, Royal Melbourne must have a strong claim to be the equal of anything on earth.'

If you go as a punter you will not play the course on which the professionals compete, for that is a composite of the 36 holes there. It matters not. Play the West, the better of the two but do not miss out the East, which suffers only in comparison with its big brother.

For the purposes of this piece, the composite course has been considered, for this is the mixture that is held to be magical by the rest of the golfing world. It is the course that is consistently placed among the top 10 in the various rankings. It consists of 12 holes from the West Course and six from the East Course, an arrangement only necessary come tournament time and made in order to avoid having to cross a busy road. It has to be said, though, that on balance it does improve matters.

The course was laid out by Alister MacKenzie in late 1926 and, according to the American historian Herb Warren Wind, it 'made his reputation'. Wind said, 'He had at his disposal an ideal tract of tumbling duneland, some of it wooded. He made the most of it. Almost every hole presents the golfer with an appealing problem to solve … If a golfer plays a sturdy round on Royal Melbourne it gives him immense satisfaction for he has to think his way around a demanding course and come up with a succession of well-played shots.'

MacKenzie's enormous reputation rests principally on his design of three courses – Royal Melbourne, Cypress Point and Augusta National – and Melbourne was the first of these. He was commissioned to lay out the West Course, then known as the MacKenzie Course, as it should be again. For this he was offered a fee of 1000 guineas – an enormous sum for the mid-1920s – but the canny Australians, aware that their man was going to do other work while in Australia, demanded a percentage of those other fees.

MacKenzie advized on or drew up plans for 19 other clubs while there, so in effect Melbourne got its course for free. Better than that, MacKenzie made considerable use of the services of a man called Alex Russell, a former Australian Open champion, in the laying down of the West. Russell in turn made much use of his new expertize and laid out the East. The club had, effectively, got two for the price of none.

Royal Melbourne signature hole, par – three tifth.

Before MacKenzie started work at Melbourne he asked for a list of the members, with their ages and handicaps, for he wanted to be sure that everyone would be able to play the finished article. He then produced a course which provides ample room off the tee but one which demands that if the best approach to the green is to be made, then the drive should ideally finish on a certain part of the fairway. That design principle is notably present at his most famous creation and Royal Melbourne is for some an Augusta National with rough.

There is another strong similarity. At Augusta the greens, because of their speed, dictate the way every hole is played. It is no good just being on a green there: in order to be sure of two-putting it is necessary to be on the right part of the green. The greens at Royal Melbourne are just as quick as their American counterparts, probably more severely sloped and make the same demands. Hale Irwin, playing in the 1978 Australian PGA championship, made the point, after successive rounds of 64 and 75, when he said that the only difference was that in the former round he was consistently below the hole, in the latter above.

The greens, particularly when a hot northerly blows in from the tropics, can become almost impossibly fast and on one infamous occasion led to a mass walk-out of players from the 1987 Australian Open. It was led by, of all people, the amiable Sandy Lyle, a man much given to the proprieties of the game. The protest led to the postponement of Sunday's final round, which was replayed on Monday.

Through a series of mischances, the hole on the sixth green had been cut on a severe slope. Some of the very early starters managed to hole out but a 50-knot northerly began to blow and putting became impossible. A club professional, Russell Swanson, took eight putts to hole out; an American, Mike Colandro, had a 20-footer which four times rolled back to his feet before he holed the fifth one and when Lyle got there, he refused to play on.

Lyle was backed by most of the players, including Greg Norman who, overnight, led by seven shots. Eventually the Australian Golf Union, responsible for the pin position in the first place, had to agree but then they made another mistake. They refused to refund the day's entrance money and the mood of the spectators, robbed of their golf and their money, turned ugly. The police suddenly found themselves called on to protect officials. On the Monday, order restored, Norman went on to win by 10 shots.

That sixth hole is one of the greater glories of Royal Melbourne. It is 428 yards but the second shot can be substantially reduced if, from the elevated tee, the courage is similarly heightened and the ball flown over the mass of scrub and sand that inhabits the dog-leg. Fail and you are in there for ever; succeed and a precise shot to the pin awaits.

There is also a big element of risk and reward at the eighth (the 10th on the West). At 305 yards it represents a good long hit, particularly when there is a huge and ravenous bunker awaiting failure. 'It can be driven,' said Thomson, 'and often is but in this lie the seeds of destruction.' Of the bunker he said, 'A man feels small indeed standing in there, trying to play out.'

To tempt the player, the forward tees are sometimes used, presenting a hole of 270–280 yards, but the challenge is still the same and it was accepted long ago by one Harry Williams – one of Australia's most talented players in the 1930s. Williams was a left-hander and, playing with a member, he drove the green, fading the ball in perfectly. 'Bet you couldn't do that again,' was the instant challenge and the instant response was to do so. 'The hole sets up for a left-hander's fade' was the response to that, so Williams promptly hit a high draw over the trees and drove the green twice more.

One of the more extraordinary members of Royal Melbourne was the Hon. Michael Scott who, in 1933, won the Amateur at Hoylake at the age of 54. He spent 11 years in Australia, from 1900, winning the country's Open in 1904 and 1907 and the Amateur title in 1905, 1907, 1909 and 1910. But it was the winning of the 1907 Open that stirred a controversy that, had it occurred in later years, might have been every bit as ferocious as the 'Lyle Strike'.

On the 12th tee in the second round, Scott mistakenly drove from in front of the markers, a mistake made by a number of other players that day who were confused by a new system of marker discs, when they had been accustomed to sandboxes. The committee invoked equity because 'the ground was not as clearly marked as it should have been' and then, when a furore broke out, appealed to the R&A. A Sydney newspaper, no lover of things Melbournian, claimed Scott should have been disqualified and castigated the ruling: 'The committee have established a very bad precedent and their decision would be laughed to scorn by the Rules of Golf Committee.' It duly was but by then it was too late.

Perhaps the most difficult hole at Royal Melbourne is the par-four 14th, controversial in that the drive is blind, over a group of bunkers on the skyline. This is one of the 'heroic carries' of which MacKenzie was so fond and in 1974 Lee Trevino, in the Chrysler Classic, did not make it. He took nine and then walked off mumbling about the greens. Make the carry, though, and there is still a 200-yard-plus shot to the green, over rough and, by the green, numerous bunkers. The green itself, said Thomson, 'is a mass of subtle slopes,' adding, 'this is a hole where making par brings all the satisfaction of a birdie.'

The course finishes strongly, with a long short hole, the 16th, at 210 yards but playing more because it is uphill with bunkers short of the green. The 17th is a long long hole, 575 yards and unreachable for the majority without a gale behind, and the 18th is a long par four, on which three putts are simple, given the immensity of the green.

In short, Royal Melbourne is a marvellous test of any player's skill and temperament.

ROYAL PORTRUSH

An obsession is a terrible thing.

In the mid-1970s, when most people were giving Northern Ireland a wide berth because of the Troubles, an American arrived at Royal Portrush, presented a letter of introduction to the secretary, paid a green fee, hired a caddie and strode off in the direction of the first tee. Once there he kept on walking, leading the way up the 16th fairway and on up the hill that is the 15th. He was gone for about 30 minutes. When he came back, he paid his caddie, packed his clubs in the car and prepared to leave. Before he drove off, he revealed the purpose of his mission. 'I read somewhere about the best 18 holes in Europe and I've set about playing them. Your 14th is one of them. I've just played it twice and made a three and a four. Now I'm off to the ninth at Royal County Down.'

It is to be hoped that he at least approached the course via the scenic route, along the Antrim coast road, past the impressive ruins of Dunluce Castle or, even better, over the top from Ballymoney, bucketing across country until he could see a great sweep of Atlantic, the town of Portrush off to the left and the vast rolling mass of some of the best golfing territory to be found anywhere. Imagine seeing all that and playing just one hole.

Calamity, as the 14th is called, is a great hole all right but only in the run of what has gone before. The other holes contribute vitally to its notoriety and, taken out of context, Calamity is just a long difficult par three, with a vast chasm plunging down to the fourth fairway of the Valley course on the right. On the left of the green there is a little saucer-shaped depression known as Bobby Locke's Hollow because that is where Locke's percentage, hooded tee shots ended up during the 1951 Open championship, when he was attempting to win his third consecutive Open.

The fifth is a lovely par four, almost driveable in some conditions by some people, with views of the White Rocks, Dunluce castle, the Skerries, Benbane Head and Inishowen and its green perched precariously above the beach – in fact, all too precariously. After a series of winter storms in the early 1980s a Coastal Erosion Fund had to be set up, massive boulders were put down at the base of the cliffs and a never-ending battle was begun.

Fred Daly, the first Irishman to win the Open, learned his golf at Portrush. So did Rhona Adair, twice a winner of the Ladies' British Open Amateur championship and once, in 1900 at Lytham, winner of a long-driving competition with a blow of 173 yards, two feet. Portrush was also the home club of the Hezlet sisters, May and Florence, who met in the final of the 1907 British championship, and in the finals of the 1905, 1906 and 1908 Irish championships, with May unkindly winning all four.

'I read somewhere about the best 18 holes in Europe and I've set about playing them. Your 14th is one of them. I've just played it twice and made a three and a four. Now I'm off to the ninth at Royal County Down.'

Portrush has been host to numerous women's championships, won by some of the great names: Lady Margaret Scott, Joyce Wethered, Jessie Valentine, Catherine Lacoste, Julie Hall. It is seen as a driver's course par excellence. Its fairways are not wide and favour curves, not straight lines. It relies more on humps and hollows than bunkers to protect its greens, and the rough, likened to wire wool by one competitor in the 1993 Amateur, is augmented by gorse, sea buckthorn and rugosa roses.

Joe Carr, who won the last of his three Amateur titles at Portrush, in 1960, could be wayward on occasions and once drove miles right into the boondocks at the ninth – a par five with an elevated green. He waded in with his four-wood, found the ball and smashed it on to the green. 'Brute force and ignorance, Madam,' he explained cheerfully to one open-mouthed, unbelieving witness.

It was another 33 years before the Amateur returned to Portrush and the final was a close affair. Iain Pyman beat his fellow Englishman Paul Page with a par four at the 37th after they had shared 21 birdies between them in a scintillating battle that matched the surroundings.

Two years later, in the Senior British Open, there occurred one of those lovely moments that sport occasionally grants us. On the third hole of sudden-death against America's Bob Murphy, Brian Barnes holed a monstrous, 50-foot putt to take the title. The win was a wonderful achievement but more wondrous still was that the first man to congratulate Barnes was his father-in-law, Max Faulkner, then 79, the first – and so far the only – man to win the Open in Ireland. Faulkner was attending his first professional event in many, many years and had only gone to Portrush in the hope that just maybe his son-in-law could complete a unique family double.

That Open of 1951 was the official seal of approval for Portrush. Bernard Darwin, who had not previously seen the course in its revised form – designed by Harry Colt and opened in 1933, with a couple of changes in 1946 – was duly impressed. He said, 'It is truly magnificent. Mr Colt has built himself a monument more enduring than brass … I find it hard to imagine a more admirable test of golf.'

The Giant's Causeway and the Old Bushmills Distillery are just up the road but the course has a beauty and spirit of its own, captured by Patric Dickson in his ebullient book *A Round Of Golf Courses*. He says, 'I have never seen a links which so invites adjectives of nobility and size; of space and height. Sometimes in dreams one has the sensation of flying or gliding gently and easily as a gull from the cliff-side. Portrush is flying golf – one longs to take off after the ball and indeed the air from the Atlantic is so fresh that such levitation does not seem impossible.'

ROYAL ST GEORGE'S

Almost every day almost everybody in the Western world mentions, in passing, the name of a tiny town in southeast England. In asking for, or eating, a sandwich they unconsciously celebrate Sandwich, in Kent, which has two enormous claims to world fame.

The first is that it was once the home of John Montague, the 4th Earl of Sandwich (1718–92), who, as the tale is told, was such an inveterate gambler that he refused to leave the card table to eat. The practice grew that meat would be brought to the table, between rounds of bread, and thus the sandwich was born.

The second is that Sandwich remains the home of one of the finest links courses anywhere in the world. Royal St George's, named after the patron saint of England in response to Scotland's St Andrews, is the epitome of linksland golf, built amid a marvellous dunes system which has been designated a Site of Special Scientific Interest, so variegated is the wildlife and plantlife. Here are bar-tailed godwits, short-eared owls, ladies bedstraw and clove-scented broomrape, plus nine varieties of orchid. If it were not such a joy as a golf course, Royal St George's would be a joyous place just to be, given half-decent weather. Given a gale, it can be hell on earth.

The land was discovered by a Scot, Dr Laidlaw Purves, who was working in London but decided he wanted to replicate the kind of golf he knew at home. He is said to have walked from Rye to Ramsgate looking for linksland: he would have saved himself a lot of walking had he started from Ramsgate, just up the road. Work began in 1887 and by 1892 word had filtered north. A committee at St Andrews recorded, 'We have been informed that there is an extraordinary new course being built at Sandwich which might well be suitable for big tournaments.' Two years later, Royal St George's hosted the first Open in England. It was not notable for the Scottish entry, despite the railways offering cheap fares. That championship was won by an Englishman, J.H. Taylor, the first of his five. He did not break 80 in any round and in fact 79s by Douglas Rolland and Andrew Kirkaldy were the best of the championship. The last man failed to break 90 in any round, took 102 in his second round and totalled 388 – some 62 shots behind Taylor.

There was a school of thought in the 1880s which believed that real golf was simply a matter of finding a series of sand-dunes, the bigger the better, whacking your ball over the top and then going to find it. Another school of thought viewed this as anything but golf because it allowed luck too large an influence. Bernard Darwin, writing in 1910, in

If it were not such a joy as a golf course, Royal St George's would be a joyous place just to be, given half-decent weather. Given a gale, it can be hell on earth.

that wonderful book *Golf Courses of the British Isles*, after Royal St George's had hosted three Opens, said, 'The course was heralded with much blowing of trumpets and, without undergoing any period of probation, burst full-fledged into fame. For some time it would have ranked only a degree below blasphemy to have hinted at any degree of imperfection. Then came a time when impious wretches, who had the temerity to think for themselves, began to whisper that there were faults at Sandwich, that it was nothing but a driver's course, that the whole art of golf did not consist of hitting a ball over a sand-hill and then running up to the top to see what had happened on the other side.'

The club, to their credit, listened to the better-informed of their critics and began to remove some of the more outrageous features. It was a slow process and by the time Jack Nicklaus got there, to play in the 1959 Grand Challenge Cup, there were still a few blind holes, and blind shots, left. He concluded that he did not much like the course because there was too much left to chance.

When the Open returned to Royal St George's, in 1981, after a 31-year absence because of Sandwich's inaccessibility, the notorious short third, previously completely blind (as it was when Goldfinger played James Bond in their fictitious match at Ian Fleming's thinly disguised Royal St Mark's), had been opened up and the course itself was a lush green colour. This seemed to be a transparent attempt by the authorities to take the bounce out of the course and they were duly lambasted by Tom Watson, who pointed out that links courses were supposed to be brown and bouncy. Sprinklers had been installed on Sandwich. Deal, next door, was baked a lovely ochre.

Royal St George's.

Bill Rogers won that Open and Sandy Lyle won in 1985, the first Briton to do so since Tony Jacklin in 1969. Lyle was a beneficiary of the weather, going out early in the first round and late in the second and missing most of the gale and rain. Lyle capitalized and reached the 72nd hole thinking he needed a par to win. His second, well struck, was unlucky to run down into a small swale called Duncan's Hollow and unluckier yet to find a thick patch of grass which almost hid his ball from sight. A stab with a wedge brought him to his knees and the ball failed to stay on the putting surface. Lyle was convinced that that shot had lost him the Open but he putted the next one to two feet and holed out. He waited and watched but no one matched him. The next day, the Open champion put up a marquee in his garden, ordered vast quantities of Chinese food for his friends and spent much of the time in the kitchen, washing up.

Over the years, Royal St George's has reorganized and recovered itself, becoming one of the great tests of the game and, in all the reconstruction, one formidable, frustrating, even frightening obstacle has been left: the great wall of sand, masquerading as a bunker, that confronts the player at the fourth hole. This mountainous monstrosity demands a carry of 220 yards and while there is a safe (well safer) line to the left, the prevailing wind comes from the left, too. It is roughly 50 feet high, quite possibly the biggest in Britain and could be known as Ollie's Folly. Practising for the 1993 Open, Jose Maria Olazabal went in there just to see what it was like. Taking a nine-iron from the foothills, he hammered the ball into the wall of sleepers, causing his caddie, his partners and a marshal to duck sharply as the ball flew backwards into waist-high rough. Assuming he ever found it, he would then have been faced with trying to carry the bunker out of the tall grass to a green still some 270 yards away. 'I will not,' said Olazabal, 'be going in that place.'

One man who did, in competitive circumstances, was Reg Glading, who was playing extra holes in an English championship. His ball plugged near the top, he could not climb in from the peak for fear of dislodging it, so he had to climb up, without ropes or crampons, from the bottom. It took ages and when he got there, he was exhausted. He took a waft at the ball and, to the helpless hilarity of all those watching, overbalanced and fell, base over apex, all the way down again. The ball inexorably followed him down and inevitably added insult to indignity by hitting him and costing him the match. Glading over, down and out.

Darwin, who knew Royal St George's so well, and saw it approaching maturity, should have the last word.

'Throughout all this controversial warfare,' he said, 'one fact has remained unchanged, namely that whatever they may think of its precise merits as a test of golf, most golfers unite in liking to play there ... Sandwich has a charm that belongs to itself and I frankly own myself under the spell.'

ROYAL WEST NORFOLK

The moment you turn off the main road, the world takes on another tint. Suddenly all is sepia and faded at the edges; this is altogether another, older world and one that takes you back to when golf began. It is only a short drive from the village of Brancaster to the clubhouse of the Royal West Norfolk Golf Club but in travelling it you go from the end of the twentieth century to the end of the nineteenth.

Royal West Norfolk is a living museum piece, pretty much perfectly preserved, a salutary and yet wholly welcome reminder of what golf was and at Brancaster still is. Given one last round of golf to play in my life, this is the place I would go to play it.

Perhaps nowhere in the world is there a more proper golf club, by which I mean a club that exists purely for the playing of golf that our forefathers would recognize. The modern-day appurtenances and abominations of golf – the luscious lie on manicured sward, the machine-raked bunkers, the putting-green tees, the Stimpmeter-speed greens and the motorized caddie cart – are not known at Royal West Norfolk.

This is not a 'Golf and Country Club'. There are no tennis courts, no croquet lawn and no swimming pool, just the neighbouring North Sea which is always cold, often angry and occasionally determined to destroy the course

This is not a 'Golf and Country Club'. There are no tennis courts, no croquet lawn and no swimming pool, just the neighbouring North Sea which is always cold, often angry and occasionally determined to destroy the course, which lies precariously between saltmarsh and sea. Changing tide patterns and the rapacious North Sea are threatening invasion by simply sweeping away the sand-hills, a thought that hardly bears thinking about. The club is limited in what it can do as those environmentalists who say that nature must have its way gain increasing influence.

Brancaster is links golf in its purest form. From the moment that you plough your way through the sandy path that leads to the first tee there is no doubt as to what the course is based on and, although the founders had difficulty making sufficient grass grow in such surroundings, that has now been overcome. As you stand on the first tee the best views are still to come, but to the city-dweller or the sad suburbanite the sheer magnitude of that vast expanse of sky, seemingly limitless and yet wrapping itself all around you, is overwhelming. Royal West Norfolk, on that first tee, can seem to be the most agreeable and peaceful place in the whole of the golfing world.

Ray Kimber, the club professional for almost 30 years, described 'one of those rare, sunny, windless days when the tide is right in ... As you play the first nine you look over the flooded saltmarshes to the villages of Brancaster, which seems to nestle in the trees and Brancaster Staithe with its harbour full of brightly coloured boats. On the back nine you have equally pleasant views of the sea and Scolt Head. Everything is peaceful and golf is a really easy game.'

It is rarely thus. There is usually a breeze and it is usually brisk. If the wind is coming from the east, there will have been nothing to stop it since it left the Ural Mountains and it will pose golfing problems later on, for some of the most demanding shots will have to be played directly into it. Then you will appreciate why Alastair Cooke claimed Brancaster had been designed by Lady Macbeth.

One of the most extraordinary things about golf's founding fathers is the severity of some of the challenges they gave themselves. Most of the earliest courses in the United Kingdom evolved when clubs were made of hickory, the gutty ball was in use and later the Haskell. It was simply not possible to hit the ball either as consistently or as far as the modern equipment allows and yet there are shots at Brancaster which are desperately difficult, even today.

The Clubhouse,
Royal West Norfolk.

The first to make you quail is the shot to the green at the third with a putting surface perched high on a plateau, invisible from the fairway. No shot should be regarded as blind once seen once, but somehow this green and this pin are always farther away than you thought and if your third shot is a putt you can be pleased. The short fourth demands precision, for the green is supported and defined by railway sleepers, surrounded by sand, and the drive to the fifth, again blind, can be intimidating into the wind. It is not that the carry is too demanding, just the thought of what awaits if you do not make it – which is likely to be some thrashing about in sand or infernally long grass, or both.

By the time the seventh is completed you may well feel ready for anything, which is just as well, for the eighth and ninth holes are, when the tide is in, two of the best holes anywhere in golf. They are made so by the intrusion of the marshes, hitherto away to the right and awaiting a slice. On the eighth tee it slithers, like a serpent's tongue, directly in front of the tee and consternation sets in. Again, it is not so much the carry demanded – for a well-struck shot should be safe – but the possibility of being in close proximity to the flora and fauna of Brancaster.

The 10th has a somewhat less threatening drive, but atones for this with a second shot that is so demanding it can at times appear impossible. In front of the green is the marsh, bordered by a sleepered bunker; at the back a large bank of thick grass; all of which leaves the player with only one option – hit the green or else. It is at this end of the course, with estuary and marsh intertwined, sea and sky seemingly limitless, that you can feel as if you are in one of those wrap-around, 360 degree Cinemascope theatres. There is nowhere like it in golf.

There are many more challenges and delights on the way home and the clubhouse itself is a delight. Clubhouses should be, must be, old and musty. There should be a smell of leather from vast and commodious armchairs in the lounge. One day a week there will be a smell of the polish used to put a sheen on the huge oak tables that abound, covered with golf magazines, some of which may be as little as two years old. There should be a few battered, dog-eared books scattered about and there should always be a Suggestion Book. It will be full of the hrrumphs of the ages, indignation should be rife, change will always be resisted and that damned secretary should spend more time putting things to rights than putting his own game on the right foot.

There should be honours boards and lists of presidents, captains and secretaries and portraits of some of the more colourful. There should be floorboards and preferably they should creak. The lockers should have the varnish of the ages blistering and peeling from them and they should contain a collection of discarded sweaters, waterproof jackets bought for a younger slimmer figure and several putters that have not seen the light of day for many a year.

There should be a bar which, as a primary duty, sells proper beer, real beer, hand-drawn beer. It should also have bottle upon bottle of whisky, with strange unpronounceable names, all of them ordered by members who only ever had a tot or two and have long since died. Behind the bar there should be the facilities for making, year-long, enough sandwiches for a small army and, in the winter, the only meal fit for a cold and weary golfer – poached eggs on toast and a huge pot of tea.

Many, if not all, of these conditions exist in the clubhouse at Royal West Norfolk. But then again, they should, for this is a proper clubhouse, at a proper golf club where the things that matter are done properly.

RYE

It is best to go a day or two early to Rye. It is important, too, to have made your arrangements to play, for this is not a course for the casual visit. Having obtained permission, try to arrive in this glorious little throwback of a town with time to browse: few places repay it better.

Rye is built on a hill and was once an important harbour. In Tudor times there was a 400-strong fleet based there and Queen Elizabeth I dubbed the place Rye Royal; but the sea has receded, the harbour is no more and one of Britain's best links courses has been built where once there were waves. Rye wraps itself around great and glorious sand-dunes and the fundamental difficulty of the holes is heightened because the stance is almost certain to be uneven and the wind is practically certain to be blowing. Par is 68, a target as tough as some of the tiny greens at the end of the five short holes that are such a feature.

There is a famous line that the hardest shot at Rye is the second to the short holes, and this has sufficient truth to remove the smart-alec element in it. Only one of them, the 17th, is not fascinating. The second has deep bunkers on the right that must be avoided; the fifth is surrounded by severe slopes; and the seventh substitutes sand-hills for slopes. The 14th has the most unusual, and occasionally the most frustrating, obstacle in railway sleepers that project themselves some two feet out of the ground, bulwarking a mound and preventing any suggestion of a Texas wedge, or even a low pitch and run, to the green.

Bernard Darwin, in his *Golf Courses of the British Isles*, extolled Rye. 'The holes are so contrived,' he said, 'that the prevailing wind which comes off the sea is always blowing across us … For the few who are artists in using the wind Rye is a paradise; for the majority who are not it is a place of trial and disillusionment.'

Darwin lived in the dormy house at Rye for many years, testimony to his affection for the place, which is echoed by Donald Steel, the golf course architect, international golfer and golf writer. In *Classic Golf Links of Great Britain and Ireland*, he said of Rye, 'It is a magical place, unique in the world of golf. It is a model of what a true seaside links should be, a test of imagination and ingenuity.' Steel knows Rye well, having played for many years in what Darwin called 'one of the few really sacred festivals of golf.'

The President's Putter is a compulsive reunion of the members of the Oxford and Cambridge Golfing Society attracting competitors from all over the globe. It is a four-day event played in the first week of January, which makes it if not eccentric then at least a little whimsical, a mid-winter exercise of camaraderie in combating cold and consuming Kummel.

There was a time when the Putter field contained most of the best amateurs and therefore the best players. Its winners included Laddie Lucas and Leonard Crawley, both Walker Cup players; Cyril Tolley, Amateur champion in 1929; and Roger Wethered, who in 1921, lost a play-off for the Open championship to Jock Hutchison. Then there was the annual glimpse of the *Boy's Own Paper* game of Ted Dexter, the former England cricket captain; of Freddie Brown, another England cricket captain, who unlike Dexter, customarily lost in the first round, once after being four up; and for 36 years, there was the late Gerald Micklem, the most dedicated of British golf administrators, with an enduring swing that took him through 111 matches. He won 76 and stopped before people began to be surprised at him getting through a round.

Nowadays the entry is less formidable but the Putter remains a guide to a man's fortitude both in playing in extreme conditions and in surviving the social combat course in various public houses like the Mermaid, the Ship and the Hope Anchor. The last's motto for the week: 'you can never have enough Kummel in stock.'

The weather is a constant topic and a factor in every match. Some people function better than others under three sweaters and waterproofs, but strangely the Putter more often than not runs its course in its allotted time. In 1964 they had to play the fifth round, the semi-final and the final over 12, 12 and 18 holes respectively on the same day, leaving Donald Steel a slightly breathless winner. Steel, who has won the Putter three times, is the Association of Golf Writers' (AGW) member who salvages the self-respect of all the rest of us by actually being able to play the game.

Each winner is required to attach a ball to the Putter, itself a venerable old instrument once used by Hughie Kirkaldy when he won the Open championship at St Andrews in 1891. It was bought by John Low, the Society's first president, who used it to reach the final of the Amateur championship in 1901. The attached golf balls are a piece of potted golf history, ranging from battered old Silver Kings of Spaldings to sleek Dunlop 65s and modern Titleists.

Rye, of course, is the perfect venue for an event. The area survives winters better than most, the course is a hardy creature and there is the town itself, replete with history and hostelries.

ST ANDREWS

St Andrews makes no grandiose claims for itself, although it is perhaps the one place in all the golfing world that justifiably could. It does not proclaim itself Golf Capital of the World, nor does it claim to have the Most, or the Biggest, or the Best. But it is undeniably the Home of Golf.

Golf, in a recognizable form, was nurtured in this place and has been played over the same acres that now comprise the Old Course for much of the last five centuries. For much of that time, too, golf has been administered from St Andrews, mostly by reason of the benevolent dictatorship of the R&A. They make the rules by which the world – outside of the North American continent and Mexico – plays its golf and, perhaps more importantly, they preside over the spirit of the game. Golf has more rules and definitions of those rules than any other game but it is a sport that depends wholly and completely on the honesty and integrity of the player and is governed by one over-riding consideration: equity, or fairness.

Appropriately, St Andrews possesses in the Old Course a test that is unique. Quite apart from its idiosyncratic bunkering and its vast double greens (which always add up to 18: second and 16th, third and 15th, and so on), it finishes right in the middle of St Andrews itself. A shanked second shot at the 18th could finish among the coffee cups in the lounge of Rusacks Hotel or in with the cashmere 'seconds' at the Woollen Mill shop.

The first and 18th holes occupy a piece of land which, if it were in an English village, would be a cricket pitch, or, maybe in this modern era, a supermarket or mall. But the fact that the town encroaches so closely illustrates perfectly how interwoven sport and commerce have become in this place. Golf and Gown, too, have become interdependent, for St Andrews is also a university town, with 6,000 students studying everything from metaphysics to a cure for slicing. There are cobblestoned streets and tea shops but it is not a tawdry, twee, touristy town, stuck determinedly in the past. It bustles and would still be a thriving metropolis even if there were no golf.

Golf permeates St Andrews, however. In the grounds of the cathedral, the heroes of the past are buried, including Allan Robertson, Willie Auchterlonie and his son Laurie, and Old and Young Tom Morris. The father has a plain grave but the son is laid to rest under a relief of himself, holding a club and taking up his stance, left foot and left shoulder drawn well back. Over the last few years, the custom evolved of leaving some small tribute and there are dozens of wooden tees from around the world as well as pencils, markers and even a tattered leather glove.

The reason for it all is laid out behind the famous beach (a starring role in *Chariots of Fire*) and a line of rather scruffy dunes, not the imposing and impressive barriers that feature at places like Royal Birkdale, Royal St George's, Ballybunion or perhaps best of all Portstewart, but it is the land that makes the most famous 18 holes in the world of golf – plus 54 more of almost the same standard.

It is linksland, which because of its sandy base is useless for agricultural purposes. It is land

A shanked second shot at the 18th could finish among the coffee cups in the lounge of Rusacks Hotel or in with the cashmere 'seconds' at the Woollen Mill shop.

that is full of humps and hollows, it pitches this way and that, full of undulations so constant and severe that to ride a buggy on it for any length of time is to invite seasickness. The particular stretch is also full of bunkers, some of them very deep, some very small as well; almost all in places that cannot be seen from any reasonable distance. They gather in what looks like a good shot down the middle and most of them are at least a one-shot penalty, even for the professionals. The unwitting amateur can totally ruin his card – and his temper – with just one visit.

The names are evocative. It is possible to be up the Principal's Nose, to be in the Lion's Mouth, in Coffin, Grave or in Hell – the bunker that spreads itself across the direct line to the 14th green. In the 1995 Open, Jack Nicklaus spent four shots trying to get out of there and holed out in 10. The 17th also has its share of bad bunkers. It is fairly easy to dump the second shot into Scholar's, well short of the green and from there it is not difficult to find the bunker a few yards in front, which has the name-with-a-sneer. It is called Progressing, as in 'Well-at-least-you're-nearer-the-green-than-you-were-before.' And in front of Progressing is the most infamous of all bunkers, the Road Hole bunker.

There are several problems, which, collectively, make this the most dastardly trap in creation, the first of which is its accessibility. As the player faces up to the second shot, with anything from a three-wood to a seven-iron, the 17th green itself runs at an angle that represents 10 to 4 on a clock face, with the bunker half way down, on the left. The green itself is raised some three feet high and at the back is a metalled road, running parallel with the green, which gives the hole its name. The last place a player wants to go is into a bunker with sides so high and so steep that they can barely be seen over but to go right is to risk the road. A further problem is that the contours at the front of the green help guide the ball towards the sand and it is entirely possible for a golfer who has played short to chip, or even putt, into the bunker.

Once in, it requires real skill to get out, for the ball has to be hit hard enough to get the requisite height and yet softly enough not to run on to the road once it hits the putting surface. To have two or three failures raises not an eyebrow in any bar in St Andrews; it needs six or seven before anyone will listen, with an air of world-weariness that suggests this sort of thing happens every week of the year. The bunker is occasionally called the Sands of Nakajima after Tommy Nakajima, who once took five attempts to escape but perhaps the costliest failure, and certainly the one

Hell Bunker. St Andrews.

seen by the most people, was that of Costantino Rocca, in the four-hole aggregate play-off with John Daly for the Open of 1995. The 17th was the third hole, Rocca was two behind when he went into the bunker and when he took three to get out he had effectively handed the Claret Jug to Daly.

The Road Hole bunker has a sadistic appeal, indulged by the R&A during that Open. With malice aforethought, they sanctioned the installation of a tiny television camera between the revetted sods of grass that make up the wall of the bunker. The BBC were then able to show very clearly the sheer scale of the shot required and viewers could watch the ball hitting the face and falling back in, transfixed by the discomforture of some of the world's best players, yet appalled by the scale of difficulty of the shot.

Then there is Ballesteros, having just holed the putt that won him the 1984 title. His fists are clenched, his teeth bared in the broadest of smiles and his eyes are ablaze. His body language tells you that this is the thing he has wanted all his golfing life.

Not everyone likes the Old Course. It took Bobby Jones some time to learn to like it – although when he did he loved it and played the greatest match of his career there; he beat Cyril Tolley, the defending champion, at the 19th in the fourth round of the Amateur championship of 1930, the year of the Grand Slam. Sam Snead, raised in the wooded valleys of West Virginia, loathed the plainness of the place and the lack of definition, and in the modern era Scott Hoch has made no secret of his dislike. 'It's the worst piece of mess I've ever seen,' he said. 'I think they had some sheep and goats there that died and they just covered them over.'

Hoch hates links golf so much he won't play in the Open at all but to win an Open at St Andrews was the self-confessed career highlight of Jack Nicklaus and Severiano Ballesteros, and they have the pictures to prove it. The photgraphs of them on the 18th green as they celebrated their achievement have become two of golf's most re-created images. In 1970, Nicklaus, in a rare release of emotion, spontaneously threw his putter high in the air and the camera caught him as he ducked, suddenly realizing that what went up must come down. Then there is Ballesteros, having just holed the putt that won him the 1984 title. His fists are clenched, his teeth bared in the broadest of smiles and his eyes are ablaze. His body language tells you that this is the thing he has wanted all his golfing life.

The challenge of the Old Course depends not just on its intrinsic difficulty but also on the weather. Like many a long-established links, it needs a wind to protect it, preferably a strongish one at that. In general terms, the drawer of a ball will prosper, while a fader or a slicer is likely to be in gorse going out and out of bounds coming in.

Realizing that anyone who hit huge high hooks as a matter of course could do well, Michael Bonallack, then secretary of the R&A, predicted that one John Daly would have an exceedingly good chance of winning the 1995 Open. His four-round score of 282, six-under par, was fairly conventional but the weather that week varied from breezy on the first day to fairly strong winds on the second, breezy again on the third and very windy on the fourth. By contrast, when Nick Faldo won in 1990, with a score of 270, the course was baked brown by constant sunshine and the breezes, if any, were light. Three years prior to that, Curtis Strange had carded a 62, admittedly in a meaningless third-place play-off in the Dunhill Cup, but it was evident that the Old Course needed some help.

In 1997, the R&A unveiled half a dozen new tees which lengthened the course by 161 yards, to 7094. They might have expected some clamour at this tampering with an Old Master, but in fact such objections were strangely muted. Even the most ardent opponents realized that, with the advance of technology, the Old Course was being brought to its knees in benign conditions. Aware of the heritage they had in their hands, Bonallack commented, 'If we changed any of the bunkers, or any of the greens, we would be shot and deservedly so. But by building some new tees we are trying to bring back into play the hazards and problems that existed years ago and which recently have become endangered.'

Some see that as an admirable objective; others feel that St Andrews should be for ever unchanged as a monument to the past and, perhaps, as a means of measuring how the game has, and will, change. Rightly or wrongly – and perhaps on balance rightly – the R&A have decided to preserve as much of the old Old Course as they can while maintaining it as a living, breathing, growing, prospering challenge that will test future generations as it did all their forefathers.

SEMINOLE

The driveway that leads to Seminole lacks drama. There is a high concealing hedge on one side, a few trees and houses on the other – Magnolia Lane it is not. It's dull but it doesn't matter and it is very definitely the last time you will be bored at Seminole. Once the drive turns 90 degrees to the left, total fascination sets in. Seminole is superb, it is scintillating – and that's before you get to the golf course.

The clubhouse is understated, as all the best clubhouses should be, but the first glory of Seminole is about to be discovered. The late Dave Marr, who once worked here and whose later pronouncements on golf carried almost papal authority, proclaimed the men's locker-room the finest in the game and there are no arguments from this quarter. Nowadays it would be called open plan but it was conceived as a great congenial barn, full of warming wood, cooling drinks and congenial chatter. Lockers line it; big wooden tables and large comfortable armchairs are scattered about; golf books lie around; coffee and other drinks are dispensed at a nod; and the honours board of club champions looks down. You could live your life in this locker-room and this clubhouse – and no one would blame you if you did.

They have – and have had – some great players at Seminole, which is hardly surprising, given the quality of the course. The club champion in 1995 was Vinnie Giles, or Marvin M. Giles III as he appears in the R&A records book as the winner of the 1975 Amateur championship at Hoylake. Giles was a Walker Cup player and had been US Amateur champion in 1972 but it was some field he beat at Hoylake. It included Nick Faldo, Sandy Lyle, Nick Price, Curtis Strange, Craig Stadler, Jerry Pate, Gary Koch, George Burns, Jay Haas, Michael Bonallack, Peter McEvoy, Dick Siderowf and Mark James, the other finalist. In 1996, in defence of his club championship, Giles scored 68,85 – it can blow a bit in that part of Florida – and lost to Buddy Marucci, another Walker Cup player, who shot 72,74. Marucci has his own slightly unwelcome place in history – he is part of the Tiger tale, having been beaten by Woods in the final in the second of the prodigy's three consecutive US Amateur

Once the drive turns 90 degrees to the left, total fascination sets in. Seminole is superb, it is scintillating – and that's before you get to the golf course

championship wins. Bob Sweeny, who won the Amateur in 1937 at Royal St George's, was also a member. A cosmopolitan figure, he won a Blue at Oxford, a Distinguished Flying Cross with the RAF and was known to give Ben Hogan shots in their regular games at Seminole.

Hogan used to practise there in preparation for the Masters and Marr recalled, 'You could set your watch by him. He would tell his caddie he would be there by 10 and at 30 seconds to you would hear his spikes on the steps. He would practice till 12. One hour hitting balls and one hour short game. But he hated doing short game, he much preferred seeing the ball go through the air.' One day, Hogan said to Marr, 'Dave, call me Ben. Don't ever call anyone Mister you may have to play.' Marr admitted, 'I would never have called him Ben without that.'

Conveniently, Seminole's practice ground is right outside the locker-room. Although Hogan could have found those facilities almost anywhere, he could not have found Seminole anywhere else. The course is quite simply astonishing. You can see most of it from the practice ground and I doubt that there is such a small tract of land with so many high-class holes packed on to it anywhere else in the world. It doesn't look like much at first sight, with one coral ridge to keep the sea out and another, further inland, to keep the traffic out. The land in between is, in places, below sea level and must have looked very unpromising. What it needed was a genius and it got one in Donald J. Ross. He created a course that is endlessly fascinating and always subtly challenging.

Tom Doak got it spot on in The Confidential Guide. 'Because of its popularity as a retirement capital there are more than 1000 courses in Florida today,' he said. 'I'll take Seminole, you can have the other 999.'

Many of the greens are elevated and all of them are quietly but sufficiently contoured, so much so that the first-time player simply cannot make sufficient allowance for the break. The fifth is a big dog-leg, which features a large and obvious shelf on the green, determining the way the hole must be played, but mostly you would be wise to take a caddie – and listen very carefully.

The eighth was a Hogan favourite for it demanded skills not many possess – a drawn drive and a faded second, both hit very precisely. The 15th was another favourite. It features a large fairway split into two and to reach either piece requires a carry over water. The second shot is another carry but this is unusual because water is rarely part of the scheme of things at Seminole.

My notes are splattered with phrases such as 'be precise; needs solid shot; excellent hole'; but, when you play a new course, it is the feeling that counts, the sudden dawning that the course has all your attention, that you are engrossed by it. That feeling came very quickly at Seminole and Tom Doak got it spot on in *The Confidential Guide*. 'Because of its popularity as a retirement capital there are more than 1000 courses in Florida today,' he said. 'I'll take Seminole, you can have the other 999.'

CHAPTER 8

SNAPSHOTS OF A WORLDWIDE GAME

SPLENDOUR, SPLENDOUR EVERYWHERE
MICHAEL BLAIR

G EOGRAPHICALLY AND GOVERNMENTALLY, Cornwall is in England. Historically and spiritually, it is a country all its own. In the Halzephron Inn in Gunwalloe, not far from the Lizard, a local commanded that Cornwall be called the Far West but this is about golf courses not politics.

John Betjeman wrote about golf here and so did A.P. Herbert. Compton Mackenzie lived in Gunwalloe and his little house, Toy Cottage, is on the way to a magical clip of coastline featuring a string of coves bitten out of Als Yr Yffarn (The Cliffs of Hell, in Cornish). At the bottom of the lane, on a stretch of land called Gwills Towans, there is Mullion golf course, where A.A. Milne played several times a year and nearby there is a miniature church of such age and beauty as to touch the soul. Mackenzie became a lay reader and once preached a sermon with the text, 'Sin if you feel you must but above all do something.'

The 'something' to do is play golf. Mullion, formed in 1895, is Britain's southernmost club, in a setting that is majestically exceptional. On a blue clear day, with the larks exalting, the view down to the sea from the 14th fairway takes the breath away.

Breath is something of which you can be very short when negotiating

Mullion. Ideally, you need a hang glider to get down the sixth and a ski lift to climb the ninth. There are some rather ordinary holes but the seventh, a long par four playing up to Church Cove, is stunning and you will need your best drive to take on the four elevated bunkers that guard the approach to the green.

Herbert was so entranced that he was inspired to write his *Song of Mullion*, with a last verse that goes,

Now will I take my newest ball
And build a mighty tee,
And waggle once or not at all
And bang it out to sea.
And hire a boat and bring it back
And give it one terrific whack
And hole it out in three,
Or nine – or 10 – or twenty-five –
It matters not; to be alive
At Mullion in the summer time,
At Mullion in the silly time,
Is good enough for me.

To the east of Mullion there are other, newer, Cornish golf courses that one day may earn a lore and a few legends of their own but we take the old romantic trail to the county's north coast, to a place so revered by Betjeman that he asked that his remains be put down there. The poet is buried in the tiny ancient church of St Enodoc, which stands in a glorious stretch of golfing country alongside the Camel Estuary. You come across it as you play along the spectacular valley of the 10th and you play away from it down the short 11th, skirt it again on the 12th and you look down on it from the 13th. Then you talk about it at the 19th.

Mrs Hoskin, who owned the land, banned golf on the church loop on the Sabbath but relented just prior to the English Ladies' championship in 1937, when the club agreed to give her 20 per cent of all visitors' green fees.

St Enodoc is one of the most perfect, most natural places where golf is played. Small wonder it moved Betjeman to write,

Lark song and sea sounds in the air
And splendour splendour everywhere.

He said, 'A beautiful course like St Enodoc is bound to have favourite spots for each of us, even for so bad a player as I am. I would put as my own favourites the view from the eighth tee and the prospect of the fairway from the 12th with the sound of the Atlantic on the shore behind.'

The course was 100 years old in 1990 and in all its years its sixth hole has been feared by those who gaze on the Himalayas Bunker. This is a steep hill directly facing you, the whole of the front of which is hollow and covered with sand. It is no longer designated as a bunker; it is not regarded these days as being fair as the ghosts of golfers long dead will concur; but you are not considered to be a true St Enodoc golfer unless you have spent a significant part of your life in it.

If St Enodoc is everything a links lover could ever want, then at our next stop we find some of the game's oldest roots. We take the long winding road up the coast and come upon Royal North Devon Golf Club at Westward Ho! This is the oldest club in England still playing on its original site. There is evidence of golf having been played here in the mid-1850s.

The club was founded in 1864 by the Rev. I.H. Gossett as the North Devon & West of England Golf Club. Old Tom Morris was one of its earliest distinguished visitors. He, like the members, would have changed in a room in nearby Beers Farm and been taken to the first tee by horse and buggy. Later a bathing machine, dragged into place by the coastguard, was used for changing and then – the height of sophistication – came the club's famous tin hut, which was positioned on a pebble ridge. The members endured these primitive facilities until the clubhouse was built in 1888 and it is still in use, a wonderful monument to the game and its history.

If you think of modern clubhouse design and then imagine an opposite, you come up with Royal North Devon. If you think of the designer courses that are being created the world over, with the accent on water and lushness, then there is simply nowhere further removed from that concept than Royal North Devon. It is unique. A vast spread of flatland, behind the pebble beach beyond the sea. Sheep graze on it and horses roam. Time has stood still.

Apart from one green, the fifth and one elevated tee, the sixth, the land is exceptionally flat and its features are its fairway undulations, the awesome bunker that stretches across the fourth to catch the drive and the sea reeds that grow in abundance. They make the dog-leg 10th a fearsome hole and, beware, they are as sharp as needles. Every fairway lie is as tight as tarmac and the greens are as hard as bone and fast. They survive the ravages of nature and equine invasion like few others could and it is the eternal testimony to the care with which they were originally laid.

The club received its royal patronage in 1865 from Edward VII, Prince of Wales and three years later North Devon's ladies' section was formed. Trish Johnson, the Curtis Cup and Solheim Cup player, is among the club's proudest products. Dozens of the game's greatest players have visited here but none was more famous than the giant who rose from within the parish. The influence of J.H. Taylor prevails to this day and is manifest in the portrait that stands in the clubhouse museum and the memorabilia that has been assembled to mark his vast achievements.

Taylor was born in the village, caddied at the course and went out into the world to become one of the greatest players of all time. He won five Open championships and a handwritten letter dated 12 June 1909 started, 'My Dear Taylor. I must congratulate you on your wonderful play … I expected you or James Braid to win but never thought you would have so much in hand.' It is signed by W.G. Grace, a giant of another game. Another letter, signed by Rudyard Kipling, concluded, 'Your autograph is going to make a friend of mine very happy.' In 1957, at the age of 87, Taylor became the club president, an honour he accepted after much searching of his conscience. A deeply religious man, he was not happy that the club allowed golf on a Sunday.

Northwards again, over the Torridge and the Taw, to another stretch of Devon heaven – Saunton. Linksland unsurpassed, this superb terrain is passionately adored by a club that was 100 years old in 1997. Fifty years before that, Taylor wrote, 'It is going to be one of the great courses,' Darwin described it as 'The real thing,' and asserted that it transcended St Andrews or Sandwich – 'or anywhere' – as a true home of seaside golf. James Braid was asked what he thought of the course and replied that it was not a course. It was a links.

Saunton is all the things that its eulogists insist – and more. It is a place with a soul, a course (sorry, links) that seems to respond to those who love it best. When a sou'wester is up, it is a mighty test but, unlike some links you can think of, it is a fair test. What you see is what you get. The fairways invite the bravest drive and, if you make it, the reward is not denied by some evil bounce or sinister hidden bunker. On a day like ours, not a wisp of cloud or a breath of wind, Saunton is the ultimate golfing pleasure and a joy for the naturalist, too. Wild orchids grow among the 350 varieties of flowers that the botany department of Bristol University have identified as bejewelling this land.

Except for a spell during the Second World War when the American Army took it over as a training area (and laid mines in the dunes which German prisoners of war were later despatched to clear) golf has been played continuously at Saunton. It began as a nine-hole course, was redesigned by W. Herbert Fowler in 1919 and although a great effort was required to restore it, and the clubhouse, after the American 'invasion', the character of the East Course has changed little since the first days.

Saunton also has a West Course which, for a number of years, was regarded as a mere diversion; somewhere you went to kill time or to sharpen your game in readiness for Darwin's 'real thing'. That is not the enduring impression of Saunton II. Much effort and expense have been invested in raising its status and when the secretary asks you which of the courses you would prefer to play, he does so in the certainty that Saunton II is a comparable test of golf. It is shorter than Saunton I but tighter.

The club hosted the English Women's Amateur championship and the Brabazon Trophy in its centenary year and is a favourite venue for such top amateur events. In 1984, the R&A took the St Andrews Trophy there and GB&I beat the Continent of Europe 13-11, with Peter McEvoy defeating Jose Maria Olazabal by 2&1. Another memorable moment that week was when a herd of cows plodded up to the 18th, where they were confronted by the captain of the R&A and a past secretary of Saunton, red flags in one hand, gin and tonics in the other.

That epitomizes the spirit of golf in Devon and Cornwall. We are left with memories of splendid courses and something else. Golf clubs can be still and forbidding places, cold and indifferent to the visitor. Not here. And how much more pleasant the game is to play when you have been welcomed at the gates.

* Michael Blair is the golf correspondent of the *Birmingham Post* and an ardent and occasionally adept practitioner of the game.

THE FAIREST OF THE ISLES

A SNAPSHOT OF SCOTLAND

IAN WOOD

Golf in the Western Isles is different. Even on the aircraft from Glasgow to Stornoway on the Isle of Lewis, I was aware that the Scotland I knew was being left behind. To begin with, I was seated beside a family who were conversing animatedly in a strange tongue. This, then, was the start. The Gaelic. Here was I, a Scot, an alien in my own land.

It was an odd feeling to know that these people represented the real Scotland and that I was the fake, the Lowland interloper. I was trying to cope with these and other deep philosophical musings when I discovered that the family was, in fact, Swiss.

It was a small misunderstanding, the forerunner of many that were to attend my sweep through the Outer Hebrides, which took me from Stornoway to Barra, by way of Harris, North and South Uist and Eriskay.

I would commend anyone going to the Isles to forget the car and just go. Don't worry about getting anywhere because something will turn up. There will be times, when you're standing on some deserted jetty peering out to sea and there isn't a soul in sight, far less a ferry, that you'll wonder if life as you've come to know it is about to peter out amid a tangle of tarry ropes and seagulls. Fear not. It won't. There'll always be a white knight, like Norman, the taxi man at Stornoway. He fixed me up with excellent bed-and-breakfast at Mrs Slater's and then I was off to visit Stornoway Golf Club.

Stornoway celebrated its centenary in 1990 and in all honesty it did awfully well to make it. Originally sited near the aerodrome, it was taken over by the Ministry of Defence at the outbreak of the Second World War and, with the compensation that was doled out, a course was constructed on ground in the lee of Lews Castle. The course originally comprised 18 holes but, when some of it began to sink, it was reduced to 12 holes. Since those somewhat erratic beginnings, it has been gradually extended, first to 16 holes with two holes being played twice to make the 18, and finally to its present 18-hole, 5252-yard splendour.

Gus Matheson, who had been greenkeeper in the 1970s, recalled the heady days of the club's development. He waxed quite lyrical about the course's signature hole, the 11th, a 551-yard monster called the Dardanelles, where the line for the second shot over a ridge was indicated by a distant war memorial. Any wind here and the fourth shot will have to be given a healthy clip. At the 12th, the line was indicated by an old lamp-post, one picked up by Gus on his way home one night. It had been snapped off at the base but exactly how or why escaped him.

As Mrs Slater didn't do an evening meal, I sought sustenance and wound up at the Star Inn at South Beach. I chose the home-made steak pie with that feeling you get in pubs that the chances of either home or steak being remotely associated with the dish are slim in the extreme. It was delicious – wonderful beef done in beer –and I whiffled off back to Mrs Slater's, happy and replete. The next stop was Harris.

I went by bus and this was the start of a love affair with the Isles buses. There was something about the way they just crop up. Also, as the bus rumbled along roads which ranged from narrow to unlikely, the driver would occasionally wave to some dot on a hillside who would wave back. On the Isles people are aware of other people and not a vehicle will pass you on the road without the driver giving you a wave. Soon you're waving back.

I was heading for Scarista in South Harris and the road took us through gaunt, rugged countryside dotted with crofts, each with its little peat stack in the garden. The route down the west coast winds round Luskentyre, a vast bay of emerald sea and silver sands. This breathtaking sight sets up the traveller for Scarista itself, a quirky little nine-holer set out along another idyllic stretch – flanked by open sea – which runs between Borve and the Toe Head peninsula.

One result of this use of crofting land is that the Outer Isles courses tend to be somewhat homespun. Grazing land is just that and you can, as I did, find a dead sheep in a bunker. I gave myself a free drop.

There has been a course at Scarista since James Braid laid one out after the First World War but the links fell into disuse during the Second World War and the ground was lost to golf. Finlay Morrison, the former professional at Bruntsfield in Edinburgh and a Harris man himself, began to lay out the present course in the early 1980s. Now the Harris Golf Club (motto: 'Perseverance') fight the good fight over the 2014-yard, par-31 layout whenever they can, but never on Sunday. There are stern notices to that effect.

The captain, Willie Fulton, the art teacher at the Sir Edward Scott School in Tarbert, told me that there were 350 life members from all parts of the world. Life membership cost £50 and the only condition was that the recipient must not be an islander. Visitors pay £5 a day. Nick Faldo once played the course, and signed his note, which was duly framed and put up for annual competition as the Faldo Fiver.

Like most of the courses in the Outer Isles, the land is leased from crofters and when I arrived Donald John MacSween was busy moving 100 lambs with the aid of Ben, a young dog he was breaking in. MacSween didn't play golf himself but was about to lease some land to the club to build a clubhouse. It also transpired that he and his wife ran the excellent Sandview guest house where I was staying. One result of this use of crofting land is that the Outer Isles courses tend to be somewhat homespun. Grazing land is just that and you can, as I did, find a dead sheep in a bunker. I gave myself a free drop.

The next morning, I caught the ferry from Leverburgh to Otternish in North Uist and headed for Askernish in South Uist, by bus from Lochmaddy. Askernish is on the west coast some five miles north-west of Lochboisedale and the club was founded in 1891. The course, which was designed by Old Tom Morris, fell into neglect until 1956, when Dr Kenneth Robertson arrived. He became the driving force behind the club, which flourished until 1981 when he retired to Edinburgh. Askernish's fortunes declined again but the members were hopeful of a revival.

The course is a nine-holer varied on the outward and inward halves by the use of different tees. It measures 2553 yards on the first nine and 2489 yards on the second, 5042 yards in total. The first hole, a 347-yard par four which sweeps towards a ridge beyond which lies the Atlantic, is a good one and this is a pretty course in dire need of tidying up. However, it's the members who carry out the maintenance – as they do at Scarista – so it doesn't do for visiting townies to get too pernickety.

This is also true of the six-holer at Eriskay, which for sheer golfing gall takes a bit of beating. You can see it from the little ferry boat which takes you over from Ludag Jetty at the southern tip of South Uist, but you don't believe it. The brainchild of Willie Rusk, the ferryman, the course is ingeniously spattered over a hillside. A six-hole sprint takes the golfer along the coast, up the hill, round a house, past a football pitch and back again (the footballers must have nerves of twisted steel), down the hill and back to the sea. You can do this three times for a fiver.

It was built in 1994 on grazing land which had gone wild, more or less willed into existence by Paddy Forbes the postman, Father MacLellan the parish priest and Rusk. The views are ridiculously beautiful. I'd spent the best part of a week travelling through the Outer Isles where stunning scenery is pretty well standard, but Eriskay was sensational. Barra was much the same.

The club there was founded in 1992. The course was built on high ground and calls itself 'the most westerly' – the members claiming that their nearest neighbour in that direction is Labrador. From the heights you look out to the Atlantic and take in a panorama which includes seven gleaming beaches. Leslie MacKinnes, the greenkeeper, has produced some good firm surfaces, but his life is made difficult by rabbits who delight in boring holes in the greens.

The course, another nine-holer, measures 2396 yards and the usual fiver gets you on. It starts gently with two par threes before getting serious with a 512-yard number which swings round the base of the hill you will be required, subsequently, to go up. The climb is rendered not just bearable but utterly memorable by the view of Seal Bay below and it is tempting to sit down, relax and stop all the flailing about. This, the torpor of the Islands, is an ever-present danger. You find yourself waiting for ferries and not really bothering whether they turn up or not.

The news that Caledonian MacBrayne, the ferry people, were being threatened by strike action hastened my departure from the Craigard Hotel – excellent cockles with garlic – and I headed for the airport. On Barra, that means the beach.

When I arrived, no one was there except the fire crew. I was told that the girl would be along in a minute and once she arrived things really began to happen. Some hikers stopped in to buy Mars bars and the fire engine moved off to shoo some cattle from the beach. The plane arrived dead on time, which is important at Barra, for you don't want to arrive when the tide's in. I went aboard with my fellow passenger, had a brief chat with the crew and off we thundered towards the open sea. As we settled on our course for Glasgow, I realized, with a pang, that the next person I waved to in a passing car or lorry would be most unlikely to wave back.

* Ian Wood brings a wonderfully subtle, and often oblique, sense of humour to his golf writings. His column, the Last Word, has enlivened the sports pages of *The Scotsman* since 1987.

THE GREENEST OF GREENS

A SNAPSHOT OF IRELAND

Ireland is altogether too much. There is more concentrated great golf on this island than in any country of comparable size on earth and it would take a lifetime to appreciate it all. All over the world there are great golf courses and great places to play golf and the two things are not necessarily synonymous. But in Ireland, in more cases than not, they certainly are.

Everywhere in Ireland there are courses, some of them famous, some scarcely heard of, where, once seen, you could live happily ever after. The vast majority of them are genuine links courses, situated in stunningly beautiful places and developed over the years into magnificent tests of golf.

Nor do you have to go cap – or letter and handicap certificate – in hand to the secretary and beg to play. Nowhere on the planet makes visitors more welcome than an Irish golf club and, it has to be admitted, many a schedule has been ruined by that very welcome. Nowhere is it easier for a glass to become two or three than in an Irish bar.

You will be able to play many of these courses peacefully, without being pushed or held up and without taking out a second mortgage. Indeed, on many you will be able to play all week for what it might cost to play for a day at one of the snootier clubs in another land.

So why does not the whole golfing world spend all its time playing golf in Ireland? Well, there are drawbacks, not all of them connected with the hospitality. For many people Ireland is a long way away and even for those who live close, some of the best courses are fairly inaccessible – yet it is that very inaccessibility which makes many of them such a joy. There is also the weather. It is not true that it rains all the time in Ireland but the colour of the grass and the nickname, the Emerald Isle, should tell you something. Then there is the wind, particularly on the west coast, the Atlantic coast.

All over the world there are great golf courses and great places to play golf and the two things are not necessarily synonymous. But in Ireland, in more cases than not, they certainly are.

There are some rough and ready guides as to whether the elements are too severe to play golf in Ireland and the first is that, if you can hold the car door open long enough to get out, you can play. It is important to check too, before going out, that the pins still have their flags on them; indeed, that there are still pins in the holes. The wind can be quite a factor in Irish golf, as it howls over the contours of the course. But really bad days are rare, confined mostly to the winter, and even on a trip in October I found golf demanded only a single sweater on 12 out of 14 days.

The world and his wife rightly know all about the Ballybunions and the Portmarnocks of this world but some 40 miles north of Dublin is a wonderful course, Baltray, more properly called County Louth, which has escaped mass attention. This only makes it the more desirable and, after a first meeting, more desirable still.

Baltray is a classic links, built for the most part in a dunes system and its hinterland, and it offers every traditional test. The third green, for example, would be despised and rejected if it were to be created now, for it is blind, the putting surface is like a switchback and an apparent good shot will not necessarily prosper. But once you know what you are about and hit the correct part of the green, the ball will probably end up close.

From that green the course turns into the dunes proper with a lovely little drive and pitch, followed by a short hole with the biggest little bunker in the east. The green is elevated and most of the right side slopes down to a nasty little pit, which may be the most over-used patch of sand in Ireland. The popular modern phrase is 'collection' bunker but this one does not so much collect as devour. Be very precise with the tee shot or be prepared to be blasting out.

The green for the long sixth is upturned and tiny, as befits a target that is being aimed at by a wedge, and the short seventh illustrates the effect wind can have on these exposed places. It is 145 yards long, all carry, and even a moderate blow can demand a four-iron or more. By the 12th the course has returned to the dunes, playing in the lee of a great green ridge of marram grass and all the holes on the homeward stretch are wonderfully attractive.

There is a typical links-style hut just below the 13th tee, open-sided and square, but with the walls running X-ways, so that the shelterer is protected from rain from any quarter. I played the 12th in shirt-sleeve sunshine, hit a drive off the 13th tee and saw to my right lovely blue and white skies, a balmy scene. To my left, though, was an ugly curtain of black being blown inexorably towards the 13th and retreat was the only option. Such storms typically last 10–20 minutes and the vista off the elevated 14th tee, over the beach and bay, through freshly cleared air, was worth a wetting.

The 14th is a great drive and pitch, again to a green that must be hit precisely; the 16th, a great par four, is a hugely demanding driving hole and, if successful, equally so with the second shot; and the 17th and 18th serve to deliver the player to a great drop of Guinness in the clubhouse.

The visitor with unlimited time and a mind that is prepared to be permanently boggled could do worse than follow the coastline northwards from Baltray, in an anticlockwise direction, around Ireland. The Royals – County Down and Portrush – would be the next courses to crop up and then a lovely surprise. Portstewart has lived for a very long time in the shadow of its near-neighbour, Portrush, and for most of that time had 11 magnificent holes and seven more in a field. Now it has 18 holes of a standard quite comparable with anything in Ireland, the club having gone back, literally, to grass roots and built seven holes where they should have been initially.

There is a great range of sand-dunes that sweep away from the town and down to the mouth of the River Bann – tall, angular, imposing and perfect for nothing but golf. For years visitors would stand on the elevated first tee at Portstewart, quite possibly the finest first tee in the entire world, with beach and sea to the right and the fairway spread 50–60 feet beneath you and wonder why the golf course did not go further into that range of dunes. Now it does. After that great inviting drive and a second shot carefully faded around the south face of an Eiger-like dune and, hopefully, two putts, the course continues into the sand-hills.

As it does you enter an almost silent world, with only the elements, the wind and the nearby sea and its seabirds, to listen to, for the dunes drown out any other noise. The club laid out the course 'in-house' and a magnificent job they have made of it too.

Further up the coast in Donegal lies Cruit Island which is next to impossible to find without one of the Discovery Series maps produced by the Ordnance Survey of Ireland. The Cruit Island Golf Club is a stunningly beautiful nine-holer, situated in one of the loveliest and most remote places in the whole of Ireland. It is a very real test of golf, at the very end of the back of beyond. Should you happen to find roughly the right part of the mainland, cross the bridge to Cruit and just drive on – do not give up. Eventually you will run out of island. The moment that happens you will be greeted by the clubhouse. It is likely to be shut. Don't worry. Find the honesty box, insert the £7 it costs per person and climb to the first tee.

The view from there is fantastic: all rocks, other islands, turbulent seas beating on a battered coastline and vast expanses of sky, stretching away to Newfoundland. In a place like this it wouldn't matter much what the golf was like or even if there was any at all but the big bonus regarding Cruit is that it is a totally respectable course. It has four very good holes and it has one that says, very simply, eat your heart out Pebble Beach.

It would be worth going to Cruit simply for the sixth, a short hole of 139 yards, facing into the prevailing wind. As you stand on the elevated tee there is the sea behind you and to your right, while in front there are two rocky inlets with the sea rushing into and through them. Both have to be carried and, if the normal gale prevails, it requires something like a five-wood to reach the green. That is what it took the day we played and, perfectly struck, it travelled about 130 yards. The same club at the short eighth, 206 yards, travelled 240 yards downwind.

On and around, down the coast or across the country, Rosses Point is not just golf. The poet William Butler Yeats was enchanted and inspired by the beauty of the area around Sligo and is buried in the churchyard at Drumcliffe under 'bare Ben Bulben's head'. It is a place of myths and legends, from the burial cairn of Maeve, Queen of Connacht, on top of Knocknarea Mountain to the megalithic Stone Age cemetery at Carrowmore.

The course is a wonderful, mystical masterpiece in its own right with views that take the breath away and, usually, a wind that makes the eyes water. Perched on its point, five miles north of Sligo, battered by the Atlantic gales, the links has been bewitching golfers since the County Sligo Golf Club was founded in 1894.

Redesigned by Harry Colt in the late 1920s, the course is remote enough to be unspoiled by overuse, yet hosts the West of Ireland championship every year and has been played by the best. Walter Hagen and Joe Kirkwood came to smell the flowers, taste the Guinness and play an exhibition in 1937, Norman Von Nida and Bobby Locke arrived in 1947 and Sir Henry Cotton in 1951. It was the first links course that Bernhard Langer ever saw – he came for a round and stayed two weeks, which is par for the course in Ireland.

Eventually you will run out of island. The moment that happens you will be greeted by the clubhouse. It is likely to be shut. Don't worry. Find the honesty box, insert the £7 it costs per person and climb to the first tee.

If you still do not yearn to play Rosses Point for yourself, read *Get to the Point* by Steven Reid and then spurn playing if you can. As Peter Dobereiner wrote in the foreword, 'Reading his treatise I felt the sting of the salty Atlantic breeze on my cheek, heard the cry of the distant plover and detected the faint whiff of peat smoke in the air.'

It is almost criminal to pass by, in a literary sense, on the other side of Lahinch and Tralee, both of which exalt the name of golf and could never be passed by in reality, no matter the penalty. But we have to get to Ceann Sibeal (pronounced Kee-own Shivail) Golf Club, at Ballyferriter, near Dingle in County Kerry. Sibeal is the westernmost golf course in Europe, and to play it is to experience those ultimates in golfing joys: a superb course in a desolate place, surrounded by magnificent scenery and silence. It is also surrounded by the Gaeltacht – the area of Ireland where Irish is the mother tongue.

At 6440 yards Sibeal is not quite long enough for first-class pretensions, although when a breeze is blowing (remember where you are) that is sufficient golf course for most people. It is almost always in wonderful condition. A former president of the Golfing Union of Ireland sighed and said, 'It's the best sod you'll tread in Ireland.'

The fairways undulate as they should, the greens pitch and roll like the tides in the bay and there is a stream – a devil's ditch more like – that wanders its way through and round the course. It comes into play on 11 holes, a constant menace, a perpetual worry. The sea is rarely out of sight and never out of earshot, the course is surrounded on three sides by soaring hills and, when the sun begins to set over the Three Sisters and Smerwick Harbour, be prepared to have your breath taken away.

Then there is Dooks, only 15 miles away as the seagull flies, albeit 40 or so miles by road, which is quite probably the most beautiful little course in the world. If you can contrive to play this place on a bright afternoon, late in the year, as the sun is starting to go down, it may be that you will have to give up the golf altogether and just stand there, pulverized, at what is around you.

Certainly I have never been more totally surrounded by superb scenery than at Dooks, nor have I heard that scenery better described than by the Irishman in our fourball. 'There's only one way to describe it,' he said, 'and that's that it is indescribable in every direction.' To the north are the Brandon Mountain and the Slieve Mish mountains with, beneath them, all the shades of silver and blue as Castlemaine Harbour turns into the deep waters of Dingle Bay. To the south are the Macgillycuddy's Reeks, providing the most dramatic backdrop possible for the course in general and the short 13th in particular. This is an original, a throwback hole of only 150 yards but once on the green the problems start. It pitches this way and that, as if laid out by a drunken sailor and no putt is safe and certainly not sure. No modern architect would dare design it and this is a classic example of a green lying where it fell and all the better for it.

'When the visitor finally gets home, sometimes only two or three days overdue, he will reflect that the Irish way of golf is the best and that the best of Irish courses are the best anywhere ...'

The course is only just over 6000 yards, but that is deceptive. Not only will the inevitable breeze make things that much more difficult but there is also the problem of what to do with holes like the third. This is only 300 yards long and, as it is down the prevailing wind, a good drive gets quite close to the green. But that green is perched above you like a top hat and you have to decide whether to pitch to it and run over the back or bump-and-run-it and fail to get up and have the ball run back to your feet.

Problems like this are merely those of golf. A much greater problem at Dooks is how to continue to play, when all around is attention-demanding scenery, the grandeur of which simply points up the futility of what you are trying to do.

Resisting the pull of Waterville, we head east again to what is perhaps the most romantic golf course story in all Ireland's long history. The European Club, at Brittas Bay, between Arklow and Wicklow, 40 miles south of Dublin, is the creation, in every respect, of Pat Ruddy, architect and activist, designer and dreamer.

Ruddy, practically single-handedly, is responsible for finding the land on which the course lies, for deciding on its design and, most importantly, for creating the entire ambiance of the place. 'What I want here,' said Ruddy, 'is to arrive at a situation where those fortunate enough to play at The European will enjoy their golf on one of the finest links in the world in the uncrowded atmosphere that was part of the game in the 1950s ... The policy at the club is to have the clubhouse warm and bright and the kettle on when the first players arrive at 8 a.m. and to keep the welcoming glow going to dusk each day.'

Ruddy is a proper man of golf and he is able to impose these proper conditions because he owns the place and has a feel for what is right in the game. There will be no carts or cart-paths at The European; there will be no five-hour rounds – or at least no one will do it twice; there will be no gin-palace clubhouse; and there will be no corporate memberships with the consequent corporate cloggers-up of the course. There will be just as many people on the course as Ruddy thinks fit, for he knows after a year or two in operation that there will always be sufficient cashflow to sustain club and course. This is a benevolent dictatorship, with the accent firmly on benevolent. He glories in the creation of a course that may eventually rival the long-established greats of Irish links golf.

In any established dunes system there are likely to be natural golf holes all over the place and the trick is finding them. Ruddy revealed an eye for such things and the result is a wonderful course, full of challenges and rewards. In addition to the dunes holes there are three that run along the foreshore, with the sea and beach a constant hazard to the right. But it is invidious to pick out individual holes on a course chock-full of them. This is a course that needs to be experienced. It took Pat Ruddy seven years to build it, a labour of love in its most literal sense, and now all he asks is that you go there, play it and enjoy it.

As Peter Dobereiner, who had a passion for Irish golf, once wrote 'When the visitor finally gets home, sometimes only two or three days overdue, he will reflect that the Irish way of golf is the best and that the best of Irish courses are the best anywhere ...'.

THE HWYL AND THE HIRAETH

A SNAPSHOT OF WALES

Wales is not the first place that golfing visitors to Britain think about – which is not to say that they shouldn't. Scotland and Ireland perhaps understandably have a higher profile for golfers but that often means overcrowding and five-hour rounds in the more famous places. Try taking five hours on a Welsh course and there are certain to be ructions.

Welsh golf has three principal assets: Royal Porthcawl in the south; Royal St David's in the north and Ian Woosnam, who plies his trade worldwide. Woosnam has brought an awareness of Welsh golf to the rest of the world and when he won the 1991 US Masters he became one of the country's best-known visitors to the United States since Madoc ab Owain Gwynedd. Madoc who? Well, it is quite possible that he was the first white man to discover America, long before Christopher Columbus, Amerigo Vespucci and assorted Portugese, Icelanders or Norsemen.

Woosnam was born in Oswestry and played his early golf at the border town of Llanymynech, which has 15 holes in Wales and three in England, and is affiliated to both the English and Welsh golf unions.

As a course Llanymynech is best described as 'sporty', offering a sufficient challenge to the golfer and stimulating the senses in every way possible. On a fine day there are stunning views for over 50 miles in any direction and it is a lovely place to be and to play golf.

Like so many countries though, Wales' finest courses are around its coast, and the best of these is Royal Porthcawl, home to four Amateur championships, a Curtis Cup and, in 1995, the Walker Cup. It could undoubtedly host an Open, but there are not enough ancillaries. Porthcawl is a magnificent links course, of which Downing Gray, the American Walker Cup captain, said before the matches started that he wished he could roll it up and take it home. Two days later, after a rare American defeat, he might have preferred just to roll it up. Dick Chapman beat Charlie Coe in an all-American final in the first Amateur held there in 1951, a championship in which Bob Hope played but lost in the first round. Another American, Dick Siderowf, won in 1973 beating Peter Moody, who was almost reluctant to stay for the final: he had arranged to umpire a cricket match at the school at which he taught that day.

Royal Porthcawl, founded in 1891, was originally at Lock's Common but remained there for only a few years before the club moved a few hundred yards to their present site, one from which the sea is visible from every hole. The first three all run alongside the Bristol Channel and are protected by a line of sand-dunes and pebbles from the prevailing winds. The pebbles are almost all perfect oval shapes and one sits on my desk, a natural paperweight, reminding me of where my drives often finish.

The prevailing wind blows left to right for the opening holes, not a friendly direction at the start of a round and to stand on the fourth tee with only one shot dropped is an achievement. Those first three, and then the last four holes, are central to good scoring at Porthcawl. Three of the last four are par fours, averaging 430 yards, two of them across the prevailing wind and the 18th directly into it.

It is a lovely hole running downhill to the sea at the end of which awaits some of the best 'real' beer in the country, in one of the most welcoming clubhouses in golf.

There are other wonderful courses in the area, Pyle and Kenfig, Ashburnham and the clifftop course at Southerndown where they used to have a clubhouse dog called, with malice aforethought, Shank. A friendly animal, he used to accompany visitors around the course to the total detriment of their golf. The effect on a golfer's short game of constantly calling out, 'Come here Shank,' scarcely bears thinking about.

Harlech Castle was built in 1258 'to put down the malice of the Welsh' but since then the sea has retreated and now on the sheep-grazing land, amidst the sand-dunes left behind, lies the golf course. Built in 1898, Royal St David's,

Welsh golf has three principal assets: Royal Porthcawl in the south; Royal St David's in the north and Ian Woosnam, who plies his trade worldwide.

with its incomparable setting, has five times hosted the British Ladies' championship, a tournament absolutely perfect for the course. It is testing and only twice do two holes in succession play in the same direction. Anything over a breeze will cause trouble. The Royal prefix was granted to the club in the early 1900s and in 1935 the Duke of Windsor, then Prince of Wales, made a special journey to the club to play himself in as captain.

Harlech, incidentally, is in the county of Gwynedd from which the intrepid explorer Madoc came. So too is Aberdovey – or Aberdyfi, the town's correct Welsh spelling. This was the favourite course of the world's first notable golf writer, Bernard Darwin of *The Times*. He used to say that if he had one course left to play in the world it would be Aberdyfi, adding,

'About this ... I am a hopeless and shameless sentimentalist and I glory in my shame.'

Those emotions stemmed from the fact that his uncle, Colonel Ruck, 'laid out' the course in 1886 by borrowing nine flower pots from a woman in the village and cutting nine holes in what was then marsh. 'Proper' golf arrived in 1892 when the first medal was held and the young Darwin won it with a score of 100.

Since then at least three architects have had a hand in changes to the course – Harry Colt, James Braid and W. Herbert Fowler, a distinguished cast list – and now it is a delight. The 16th is the hole that remains in the minds of most. A good tee shot needs to avoid the railway on the left and the huge dunes on the right and only an excellent one will be on the exceedingly narrow fairway. It is only a short par four of some 288 yards, but the green is so tiny that even a wedge shot can miss it.

There are other worthwhile courses in Wales. In the south, the undiscovered gem that is Pennard; Borth and Ynyslas, also redesigned by Harry Colt and in the far north the magnificent Conwy course, covered in broom and heather and within a mile of the town and another incredible castle. Golf has been played on that site since 1869 and a more natural spot for the sport could scarcely be imagined.

Go and play in Wales – play with what the Welsh call 'hwyl' (fervent emotion) and experience the 'hiraeth' (sweet longing). You will find nowhere better.

GREAT GOLF ON GOLDEN ISLANDS

A SNAPSHOT OF THE UNITED STATES

There are at least two ways of looking at the Intracoastal Waterway, that fantastic 2455-mile passageway that enables boats to sail the entire eastern seaboard of the United States without ever once venturing into the Atlantic Ocean. It is either the greatest boon ever to sailors or the longest lateral water hazard in the history of golf. Similarly Interstate 95, the concrete ribbon that stretches from Miami to Maine could be called the best and most varied road in America or simply the longest cart path in golf. One thing is certain: the conjunction of these two features continues to be a huge boon to the booming game that is golf on that enormous continent.

The barrier islands are a geographical accident, agriculturally insignificant but scenically superb, often with great stands of oaks and pine. Usually on the Atlantic side there is a large amount of dunesland and on the Waterway side are vast stretches of wetland and nothing much in between. Farmers have generally taken one look and gone elsewhere. The I-95, which links the great cities of the east – Miami, Jacksonville, Savannah, Washington, Philadelphia, New York and Boston – is also the main feeder road for the islands, a huge commercial artery. If you are a golfer, with a serious interest in some of the finest courses anywhere in the world, you will come to know it well. The islands were quickly discovered as wonderful retreats for the monied classes.

When the railways opened up America, people like the Rockefellers and the Carnegies fled the northern winters and travelled to the Carolinas, Georgia and Florida, building vast mansions wherever they went. Sometimes they built golf courses too. There used to be one on Cumberland Island, a lovely place accessed by ferry from Fernandina Beach, right at the top of Florida. In 1750 its population was described as 'an assemblage of pirates, smugglers and ruthless raiders' but now it is largely left alone for wild horses to roam. There is just one tiny Inn, Greyfield, where the late John Kennedy jnr had a miraculously quiet wedding in 1996.

There was once 'a large quantity of live oak and pine fit for ship building' and the island was stripped, the timber cut down by slave labour. The remains of their cabins are still visible, especially from what used to be the golf course, built on Sassafras Field for William Coleman Carnegie, brother of Andrew. There were nine holes, built around six greens, one of which was named, with striking indifference, Chimneys, because it was right next to the brick-built chimneys that had housed the fires for the slave cabins and are all that is left of them. It requires a close look around the field to find any evidence of a course but it is there. There are slightly raised and flattened areas that could only have been greens and some small circular indentations surrounded by crushed shell, which served as bunkers.

The clubhouse is still there, too, although nowadays it is the home of 'Betty', a former policewoman who does several jobs on the island. When she arrived, in the early 1990s, what is now the living-room still had benches all round the walls where the players would change and her bedroom still has the original lockers. They are used as dressers and cupboards and still function perfectly.

Golf has died on Cumberland Island but it is developing furiously elsewhere in a region that is so suited to it. In Florida, most golf courses exist to sell houses and a must is plenty of palm trees and colourful flowers, shrubs and bushes to inspire evocative, property-selling names such as Hibiscus Trace or Tamarind Hollow. Top of the pops are Coral Anything and Anything Haven, Osprey fly frequently, and Something Creek and Something Cove abound. Perm any two and combine with Palm, Pine, Lakes, Shores or Waters and you have the name – there's a computer programme somewhere churning them all out.

It's not just the conditions on the ground along the southeast coast that are so perfect – climatically everything is just right too. All the different and necessary types of grass grow; there is sand and water there naturally and golf is never better than when a good breeze blows, which happens all the time on this coast.

Ecology now plays a large part in the building of courses and at Amelia Island, 13 miles from Jacksonville, they are proud of the wildlife that co-exists on their property. The ocean is home to grouper and tuna and the Waterway to the extraordinary manatees who, when they are not feeding (eight hours a day), are mostly resting (12 hours a day). There are also loggerhead turtle, whose eggs are protected from humans and other wildlife; and in autumn the Northern Right Whale moves into the Waterway to calve. Only 350 of this species are believed to be left and this area is their only calving ground.

The short fourth has a railway-sleepered green across water but is only a short-iron and, unlike the 11th, it does not have an alligator.

The natural beauty of Amelia has been used by some of the world's best architects to create 90 holes of golf. Long Point, designed by Tom Fazio, is hugely difficult, especially for a resort course, which ideally should moderate its challenge to the likely potential of its probable customers.

The Golf Club of Amelia Island is a very different story. Water comes into play on 14 holes but, importantly, the average player does not feel intimidated – there is always somewhere to go that is safe. It was designed by Mark McCumber and Gene Littler and is the only golf course attached to the super-swish Ritz-Carlton chain. The course is literally on the beach and a short wooden bridge leads from the hotel to 12 miles of flat, shell-filled strand. The beaches can be wild and windy but outside the Ritz they are smoothly machine-raked – luxury living the American way.

The first, 100 yards from the sea, is an ease-yourself-in opening hole but the second is daunting. It dog-legs left round trees and water and needs two solid hits before leaving a six- or seven-iron to the green. The short fourth has a railway-sleepered green across water but is only a short iron and, unlike the 11th, it does not have an alligator. These creatures have been known to swallow golf balls and the only way to get them back is when they are returned naturally. That's a long wait but the pace of play at some points may encourage you to consider it.

The 18th, with its large fairway and large green, is designed to leave the golfer with a feel-good factor and this is a sensible resort course, combining fear and incentive in the right measure, in a stunningly beautiful place.

There is little point in trying to pinpoint the best course in Myrtle Beach, not least because they may well be building it at this very second.

The islands off the Georgia coast are known as The Golden Isles and, in the setting sun, it is easy to see why. There was also a short period when they represented gold, literally, for some of them were prolific producers of cotton, none more so than Sea Island. Having given its name to one of the finest varieties of cotton, it now gives its name to some of the finest golf.

Sea Island attracts big names. George Bush spent his honeymoon there in 1945 and returned 50 years later to celebrate his anniversary. He planted an oak outside the main building in the tradition of Calvin Coolidge, Dwight Eisenhower, Gerald Ford, Jimmy Carter – and Margaret Thatcher. Most of the presidents were golfers and the Sea Island Golf Club has four separate loops of nine holes of varying vintages. The Plantation nine came into being in 1927; the British architects Colt and Alison did the Seaside nine in 1929; while the Retreat and Marshside nines were built after the Second World War.

Colt and Alison, the foremost designers of their time, left behind a loving experience. There is playability everywhere, long avenues of live oaks and sweeping panoramas over the marshes to the mainland. You must use a cart – unless you can get in early and snap up one of the few caddies or use some cunning. If you play after four o'clock, not only do you get that lovely evening light illuminating one of the world's beautiful places but also you will be allowed to walk and enjoy it all the more.

Given that everything exists for golf to flourish, it is hardly surprising that several conurbations of courses have sprung up, with whole counties consumed by the sport. One of the most famous is Myrtle Beach, which had around 150 courses in the Grand Strand area in late 1999 but that total could be up to anything by the time you reach the end of this sentence. It is said that you could play golf on a different golf course every weekend for a year and still not see them all. There seems to be no reason why there should not be 220 courses – or 440 – because the land is perfect – and perfectly useless for anything else. It is flat, dotted with marsh and lake and studded with great stands of trees, pines and hardwoods. So far the investors keep making money. Golf has brought prosperity to the area.

In the 1920s Myrtle Beach was a village of around 250 people and in an effort to attract businesses their owners were offered seaside homesites, with the plot next door thrown in free. Now fortunes are being made by the industries servicing golf and golfers. Property developers do well, so do hoteliers and less traditional companies like the one specializing in booking tee times at courses in the area.

Even night spots flourish because of golf. The Doll House has the subtle slogan, 'A Gentleman Always Chooses The Right Club'. Parked outside was a car, presumably staff, with the licence plate, 'I TEASE' and two others, presumably belonging to customers, read, 'TEE 4' and 'AT A MTG'. Golf pervades the place. At Myrtle Beach they talk about golf as they once talked about textiles in the Lancashire mill towns or coal in the Rhondda.

The Golf Writers' Association of America played its part in the expansion. In 1954, the writers were invited to play The Dunes, the granddaddy of Myrtle Beach courses, the week before the Masters at Augusta. They wrote about this place with the wonderful weather and unlimited potential and *voilà*. The GWAA still plays its annual championship at Myrtle Beach, with at least one round at The Dunes, the course built by the original Robert Trent Jones. Its instantly recognizable trademark is the Horseshoe Hole. The tee and the green are about level with each other but there is a huge lake intervening, which means that the player has to describe a horseshoe shape to get to the green. It's the ultimate 'wow-I'd-like-play-it' hole and has been pictured in every US golf magazine *ad infinitum*.

There is little point in trying to pinpoint the best course in Myrtle Beach, not least because they may well be building it at this very second. Also, it is hard to find a bad one because there are so many good ones; no course can afford to be bad. The same holds true for the resorts that cling to the Intracoastal water hazard along the Interstate 95 cart path. High standards have been set and the itinerant golfer can be grateful.

SO GOOD, BUT SO FAR

SNAPSHOT OF AUSTRALIA

The Nepean Highway, which leads out of Melbourne's city centre to the suburbs, like many of its kind, is hugely unattractive in its early stages. As the road progresses, however, it jettisons the tawdriness, replacing it with suburbia and, eventually, countryside. And it is that countryside which ultimately makes travelling the Nepean Highway a delight. For this, if anything ever was, is a road to golfing glory. It takes you to the Sand Belt, site of many of the magnificent clubs which, in sum total, are probably the finest collection of courses in any city in the world. As far as golf goes, Australia in general and Melbourne in particular has courses of a quality that cannot be beaten anywhere.

Royal Melbourne is the jewel among them but it almost beggars belief that there could be so many others, so near, that would themselves be outstanding in another place. Kingston Heath, for example, is superb; and so too are Yarra Yarra, Commonwealth and the Metropolitan Club. There is also Victoria, literally just across the road from Royal Melbourne, set up by those unable to get into the Royal when it was founded.

Victoria is a wonderful amalgam of a dozen different varieties of tree, separated by a course sufficiently challenging to have produced Peter Thomson and Doug Bachli. they have a

As far as golf goes, Australia in general and Melbourne in particular has courses of a quality that cannot be beaten anywhere.

unique achievement to their credit, for in 1954 Thomson won the Open and Bachli the Amateur championship. For almost a year the trophies were on display in the clubhouse, over 12,000 miles from their origins.

If Royal Melbourne did not exist, Kingston Heath would probably be the celebrated Australian course. For the first-time visitor who has already played the Royal, there is something eerily familiar about Kingston Heath. Both courses are set among the same types of tree but it may not be until the ball is bunkered that realization dawns, for the bunkers at both courses are the work of Alister MacKenzie. Accuracy is all at the Heath. Miss a green and a fearsome shot is certain to result, either out of sand (preferably) or from scrubby bushes in which the lie varies only from difficult to impossible. Thomson has said that the second shot, the shot to the green, is 'the art of the game' and nowhere is it more necessary to be the complete artist than at Kingston Heath.

Golf in Melbourne is not confined to the Sand Belt area. At the end of the Mornington Peninsula, the left arm that embraces Melbourne harbour, is a place called Cape Schanck where Robert Trent Jones jnr built a golf course and a spectacular creation it is. Wild and wonderful are the words that come to mind and 'are there any more balls in the bag?'

Before reaching the Cape, there is the lovely Portsea course, situated

New South Wales, Sydney.

in a part of the peninsula once described as 'beautifully picturesque, swelling in gentle elevations of brightest verdure, covered by a profusion of flowers.' Those words were written in 1803 by Lieut. James Tuckey, an officer on board HMS *Calcutta*, who could not have forseen the day when some of those 'gentle elevations' would provide the land for Portsea Golf Club.

HMS *Calcutta* had entered Melbourne harbour and turned right. Had they turned left, they would have saved themselves months of privation and thirst. They would have found water and fertile land, not difficult, dry scrub; they would have found the land that now houses the Barwon Heads Golf Club, another gem.

Barwon is almost, but not quite, genuine links. It looks like a links but there is not a blade of fescue, for example, nor the fine sand that characterizes so many real links. The highlights are probably holes 11–14, a loop that brings into play dunes and marsh as well as trees and bushes. The 13th is a truly great short hole, with its raised green and deep grass bunkers, making accuracy absolutely essential. The clubhouse is in a time warp, with a great late 1920s feel. They have rules about where you may go with and without a jacket and tie, including a bar that demands both those things. There is, fortunately, another bar which overlooks the 18th green, enabling members to watch their peers and there is also that epitome of golfing tradition, a dormy house.

Championship golf is centred mainly around Melbourne and Sydney, with Adelaide, Perth, Brisbane and Hobart making occasional appearances, but corporate golf has its home very largely in Queensland. Here golf is mostly a cash cow, the courses decorating resorts to help sell homes and holidays. Not that some of them aren't very good courses or, for that matter, resorts. It is just that the emphasis is different. Making megabucks is the preferred option and the target is the tourist who is not necessarily a good, or even competent, golfer.

Golf is the perfect sport for an area that wants to develop its economy through tourism. The building of the course brings in millions of dollars in itself, the building of the houses that surround it millions more and the marketing and promotion of the resort yet more. The Gold Coast, or as it is rapidly becoming, the Golf Coast, discovered these facts early, taking the lead from places like Palm Springs in California and the whole of Florida.

Much of the early impetus for expansion came from Japan, just eight or so hours away to the north. Japanese companies funded the development of the resorts and then fed in large groups of players. For most of them it was and is cheaper to fly to Australia two or three times a year, stay for a week or two at a resort and play every day than it would be to join a club at home – even if they could find one with memberships still available. Some Queensland travel companies specialize in bringing Japanese golfers to the region, providing Japanese-speaking guides, and business booms.

The quality of the courses may not be the first consideration of the developer but it is necessary that they should be sufficiently challenging to maintain the interest of the golfer and to bring him or her back for more. Several resorts manage this quite comfortably, with Sanctuary Cove and Hope Island leading the way. The former is the home of the 1991 Open champion, Ian Baker-Finch, and the latter hosted the Johnnie Walker Classic, won by Ernie Els, in 1997.

Hope Island claims the impossible and almost brings it off. They say the course is 'rich in the traditional features of the great courses of Britain and Ireland', although the inhabitants of those places would certainly be surprised by play-ing the game in temperatures nudging the early 30°Cs (90°F). But by creating humps and hollows in the fairways, making the bunkers proper bunkers and not waste areas, incorporating some marshy areas and building swales around elevated greens, they have succeeded in bringing

Playing from an elevated tee it is important to get the right club because if you get it wrong and run through on to the rocky seashore behind, your penalty drop, not nearer the hole, will be in Tierra del Fuego.

about a course that has at least a touch of Europe about it – without its weather.

Much farther south is Tanunda, in the Barossa Valley, the area just above Adelaide that forms the mainstay of Australia's wine industry and it is a course that gladdens the heart. This is not solely because it possesses a multitude of extremely beautiful trees or some of the most fascinating bird-life to be seen and heard on any golf course or because some of the panoramas are fit to be compared with any in the world. Tanunda possesses one wonderful and nowadays almost unheard of attribute: it is developing from a patch of raw terrain where golf took place into a really good golf course by the literal sweat of its members' brows. It is developing as golf courses used to 100 years ago. The members decide what needs to be done and then band together and go out and do it. Just as an example, in October 1996 some of the older members formed themselves into a kind of Dad's Army and in that one month put in 1000 hours of work, all unpaid.

In the past couple of years the browns and the sand greens have become grass greens, the fairways have gone from having 20 per cent grass cover to 80 per cent and whereas the rough used to be mostly dirt, the grass now flourishes to the extent that some members are complaining that the fairways are too narrow. What money has been needed has come mostly from the members or from local wineries, some of whom have been persuaded to sponsor a hole in return for a sign proclaiming their product. That means you are constantly being reminded of some of the great names in Australian wine, making thirsty work thirstier.

Roughly halfway between mainland Australia and Tasmania is King Island, a spot so tiny most Australians have never heard of it. For as long as ships have been sailing, it has been the function of King Island to wreck them and a chart of 1806 described its coast as 'foul ground'. It is dissected by the 40th parallel and swept by the Roaring Forties, some of the fiercest winds in the world, which frequently exceed 60 miles per hour. King Island is the only bit of land for 15,000 miles and if, as the policemen say, you proceed in a westerly direction, you will step ashore in South America.

Still, they play golf on King Island – there are 35–40 active members – and the course far exceeds expectations. It has 12 greens but only 16 distinct tees and this happy arrangement enables you to have two goes at the hole which is the fifth first time round and the 14th later. There are two greens, both set on the other side of a rocky bay and the golfer is required to assess, very precisely, just how much he is going to try and cut off. There is plenty of room on the right for the cowardly, but if you are brave and good you might just drive the green on the direct line.

The short third is, depending on whether the winds are roaring or not, a three-wood or a wedge. Playing from an elevated tee it is important to get the right club because if you get it wrong and run through on to the rocky seashore behind, your penalty drop, not nearer the hole, will be in Tierra del Fuego.

The 18th, another short hole, demands a tee shot that will carry a huge chasm to a plateau green some 170 yards away and behind that green is the clubhouse, full of those who have safely finished, beer in hand, watching your futile efforts. Humiliation apart, it is reassuring that there are few more welcoming places than an Australian clubhouse.

GOLF GROOMED IN JAPAN

A SNAPSHOT OF JAPAN

By 1903 the Open championship was 43 years old, the US Open was nine years old and golf, although not yet huge, was a growing game. The hugely significant developments of the time included the establishment of clubs like Shinnecock Hills in the United States and the club at Pau in France. Away on the other side of the world another enormous step was being taken that would eventually establish golf as a truly global sport: the game was being introduced to Japan. The subsequent explosion of interest owed its beginnings to a quite remarkable man, not sufficiently celebrated for his part in the game's growth.

Arthur Hesketh Groom, a big burly Englishman from Stanmore in London, arrived at Kobe in 1868, the first year that Japan was open to foreigners and fell in love with the people and the place.

Groom, who began as a tea trader before diversifying into silk and then hotels, lived in Japan for the rest of his life. He indulged in 'huntin', shootin' and fishin'', adored painting and drama but above all loved hiking, especially in the steep forested mountains that form the backdrop to Kobe port. They range up to 3000 feet high and provide relief during the humid summer months for those who can reach the summit. Groom formed a particular attachment to Mount Rokko, which affords spectacular views over the bay of Kobe and in 1900 he decided that a plateau close to the summit would be an ideal place for a few holes of golf. He and a few friends hiked to the top armed – as the bemused locals saw it – 'with swords and scissors' and eventually cleared out sufficient undergrowth for four rudimentary holes, complete with sand greens. They were ready for play in 1901. Golf in Japan was about to begin.

At first, it was a game for expatriates. Groom built a villa nearby and entertained friends there before and after the golf. That became so popular that he built some more villas, in the Western style and sold them. It became a tiny but influential resort for the FRs (Foreign Residents) as they were known. So highly regarded was Groom at this time, especially by the locals who had become unexpectedly prosperous, that in 1913 they erected an obelisk in his honour. It was destroyed by Japanese soldiers during the Second World War but was rebuilt in 1955.

Very quickly four holes was not enough. By 1903 there were nine holes and by 1907 the full 18. That was the year that Shotaro Kokura became, in all likelihood, the first Japanese person to play golf. He was invited to play at Kobe; sadly, history does not record his score.

Groom was undoubtedly the Father of Japanese golf and his influence lingers on. There is a lovely bronze of Groom in the clubhouse, a wonderful old building which is furnished in a style that you might expect to find in a golfing backwoods in, say, the Welsh Border country or the Highlands. It is untouched by the modern era, the furniture is rattan chairs, the walls and floors are of wood, the locker-room is properly musty.

If that, to those with long memories, is familiar, Kobe golf in general is not. The visitor will be told that he cannot play with the bag, or the full number of clubs, with which he arrived. He has to select 10 of his allotment of 14 clubs and put them in a smaller, tubular-style bag, provided by the club. The reason is simple. You are required to take a caddie: caddies are in short supply, so each one has to carry all the bags of a fourball, two on each shoulder. At least nowadays the caddies do not also have to carry the members up the mountain by sedan chair. There is an alpine-style, hairpin-corner road and a cable car to the top of Mount Rokko.

There are times on the Kobe course when you are grateful that it is on average 6°C cooler than the port. It is a hilly course with holes like the 11th, which is a five-iron short hole, completely blind from the tee, over a huge hill, down a steep slope to a flat circular green. There is no way of knowing whether you are on it until you arrive, panting, at the top of the rise.

Kobe is a museum piece and a treasure. It is truly golf from a bygone age and if it seems scarcely right to designate a hole of 183 yards

Arthur Hesketh Groom, the father of Japanese golf.

as a par four, as is the third, then it has to be realized that the green is probably 50–60 feet above the tee and even with modern equipment it requires a mighty smite to carry the ball on to the putting surface. The 18th is what would be called the signature hole these days. An elevated tee looks over a tree-filled ravine, with a carry of 200 yards or so to the fairway, with the green a further 25 yards. There is a safe route to the right but that is usually treated with contempt. Instead, that ravine is filled with balls: this is Japan where 'face' is everything and no one wants to be a wimp.

The Japanese customarily play nine holes and then stop for lunch. If you book 18 holes you will get two tee times, allowing an hour or so for lunch – perhaps fried octopus and stewed tripe, followed by beef curry. This being Kobe, famous throughout Japan for its beef, the meat is superb. The cattle are fed with beer and have their hide vigorously brushed each day, to produce a marbled fat effect that makes the beef incredibly tender. It is also incredibly expensive, at US$69 a pound.

The lunchtime tipple is served in glasses bearing the following inscription, in tiny gold lettering.

A glassful of drops
Each drop is tomorrow's dream
Sip your dreams by drops.

Very Japanese.

If Kobe represents nostalgia, Kitago, on the southern island of Kyushu is everything that golf has become with the aid of modern equipment. What they have done, in effect, is slice the top off several mountains, to create sufficient flat land for a golf course. This sort of thing is necessary in Japan, where most of the natural flat land is required for agriculture, but inevitably attracts criticism from environmentalists. Most districts allocate a certain percentage of their land for golf development, usually one or two per cent. When that is filled, there are no more courses. However, golf is such a lucrative market that there is a constant danger of corruption. In 1992, one builder decided to 'square' the mayor of a particular district so that the regulations might be 'eased'. He paid him over 1200 million yen (US$10 million). Not surprisingly the course was built; also not surprisingly the mayor and contractor were found out and ended up in jail.

At Kitago the developers consulted with all the objectors at every point and the local population were solidly behind the creation of the golf course. Before it came along unemployment was endemic; now 90 per cent have jobs; a dozen new businesses have moved into the area, among them food suppliers, taxi and bus companies, transport companies, a post office and a garage. There are 400 permanent jobs where none existed before. It took 2 $1/2$ years to build the course, three million cubic metres of earth were moved and it cost 5 billion yen (US$400 million), plus 7 billion (US$560 million) for the hotel that goes with it. Membership costs 8 million yen (US$65,000).

Faith, and the bulldozers of golf architects, can move mountains and what they have created is a very good golf course, with some stunning views. It is also quite possible to walk the course, accompanied by a caddie driving a motorized cart with all four sets of clubs on it. At the points where it gets tricky, on the back nine, moving walkways have been installed to lift you from one carved-out hole to the next. There is a moving rubber belt between static handrails and the golfer stands on the belt, presses a starter and a recorded voice, in Japanese, advizes you to 'look after yourself'. Here the course resembles those mountain terraces of the Himalayas and elsewhere where, over the centuries, locals created fields out of rock with their bare hands. In Japan, with sophisticated machinery, they have created fairways out of thickly forested slopes in days.

Some of the principal beneficiaries of the emergence of Kitago Golf Club are the caddies, many of whom have been trained specifically for this course and have never before worked in golf. Many of them are women, all are good and ours was unremittingly cheerful. If a shot was any good at all, she said 'Ni' sha' (nice shot) and if it was really not up to much but not down a ravine she would produce a big smile and say 'Safe'. She trotted everywhere, carrying handfuls of clubs for every possible shot and, with the aid of a notebook, told her clients exactly how far it was to the green. She would write down, say, 165 Y, and then give you your choice of a four, five- or six-iron. At the end of the round all four players were asked to fill in a caddie-ratings card. Japanese friends guided us to the section we were looking for in all four categories: 'Excellent'.

In Japan, caddies are often armed with walkie-talkies, to keep in touch with their colleagues in front, to confirm that they are out of range if the next shot is blind. At short holes, they perform a little ceremony when their players have putted out. They replace the pin, face the tee and bow to the group behind, shouting 'Hai dozo', which in this context roughly means, 'Thank you for waiting, the green is clear now.'

It is an expression of a golfing culture that is very different from that in Europe or, even, America. The Japanese golfer has anything that might be construed as hassle removed from his path from the moment his car is surrounded by white-gloved attendants, his clubs removed and delivered, usually on an automatic trolley, from the front of the clubhouse to the back. There they will be polished and transported to the first tee by the allocated caddie, to await the emergence of their owner from a locker-room so well-appointed that some visitors might be reluctant to leave it. There are showers, a steaming communal bath and heated lavatory seats. To clean your shoes, there is a high-pressure air pipe that blasts away the dirt, bringing to mind Dylan Thomas's lovely line in *Under Milk Wood* when the houseproud housewife warns her husband before he draws the curtains in the morning, 'And before you let the sun in, mind it wipes its shoes.'

On the other side of the mountains from Kobe lies Hirono, one of Japan's finest courses, founded in 1930. There is, after a few holes, an almost eerie sense of *déjà vu* if the visitor has ever played golf in the sand-and-heather belt of Surrey and Berkshire, for Hirono could be a combination of Sunningdale and The Berkshire; an American might be irresistibly reminded of Pinehurst; a European of Chantilly. The holes are lined mainly with pines, interspersed with other varieties, the fairways are reasonably broad, there are lots of gentle dog-legs and the greens are surrounded with British-style bunkers that look exceedingly familiar. It is not surprising because Hirono was designed by Charles Alison, a partner of Harry Colt, who built Sunningdale. Those bunkers – with faces half turf, half sand – were popular in the 1930s and, to distinguish them from the flat, more open versions common in the 1990s, are still known in Japan as Alison bunkers.

Japanese caddy.

Perhaps the greatest glory of Hirono lies in its selection of short holes, three of which demand a carry over water, although never an impossible one. Of the four, though, the only completely dry one, the seventh, is probably the star. Alison built it to play at 200 yards, but this has now been shortened, albeit by only five yards, to make the carry more reasonable. The shot has to travel over a deep gully – where the land is contorted in every fashion possible – over some front bunkers and stop on a green that slants away from the player. A three is a real achievement and a hole-in-one highly unlikely.

In Japan, to hole in one involves an expensive ritual. You have to buy drinks and presents for everyone at the club at the time, then you have to do the same for all your friends, whether or not they were there. Furthermore, the club will expect to be bought a tree to mark the occasion, so an insurance policy is a snip at 450,000 yen (US$3,600) for a once-only payment.

Hirono's clubhouse, reminiscent of the 1930s with its mock-Tudor frontage and imposing honours boards, is a place of privilege. Not everyone can play there, a situation common in a country where there are hundreds of thousands of golfers who have never set foot on a course. Clubs are expensive to join: Koganei, which is popular because it is near the business districts of Tokyo, costs over 250 million yen (US$2 million); the average is 33 million yen (US$260,000). No wonder players, fully equipped with the latest gear, frequent the driving ranges that sprout in every town and city and soar up to three tiers in Tokyo.

As the twentieth century draws to a close, Japan has around 6000 driving ranges and 4000 courses. A survey in the early 1990s revealed that, exclusivity notwithstanding, there were, in one year, 105 million 'visits' to courses, a fantastic figure and one that is growing annually. Suitably 'Groomed' from the start, the Japanese have become addicted to golf like no other nation.

AFRICA EMERGENT

A SNAPSHOT OF AFRICA

One of the great anomalies in golf is that South Africa, with all its advantages of climate and terrain, has actually produced more world-class golfers than world-class golf courses. It has, in the Durban Country Club, a course of undoubted international quality and, in Leopard Creek and the Gary Player Country Club at Sun City, others that are close to it. Thereafter, while there are lovely places to play and some courses containing more challenge that many can cope with, there is no course of such consistent quality that it could be ranked with the best of the world.

This is strange because there has been a stream of fine strikers of a golf ball emerging from the country, and there was that wonderful year in 1994 when Ernie Els won the US Open championship, Nick Price the

It is another of golf's great places: a place where the temptation to call a halt to all the futility and to stay and absorb the sensations of Africa becomes almost an imperative.

Open and the PGA championship and Simon Hobday the US Senior Open. Add to that the fact that Gary Player is one of only four men ever to have completed a career Grand Slam and that Bobby Locke won

three Open championships in four years – and four altogether – and you have a solid tradition of great African players.

Leopard Creek golf course at Malelane, in Africa's High Veldt, 260 miles from Johannesburg is well worth a detour. The aptly named Crocodile River, which forms one of the course boundaries, is home to some of the most enormous specimens of that predatory beast.

Game abounds here and the day I played the Leopard Creek golf course a hippopotamus wallowed, as hippos are supposed to do, in the lake to the right of the 15th. Now a hippo-pot-ay-mus, as we were told by Flanders and Swann in those pre-politically-correct days, is no ignoramus, and this one, ejected by its herd, had happened on one of Africa's most delightful spots as home. Furthermore, it will be able to watch Ernie Els play the odd shot, for the South African star has a house on the other side of the fairway, complete with thatched roofs and built in African style. Els, in turn, will see abundant wildlife, for elephant, rhino and a broad range of the monkey family all make frequent appearances. A leopard still has its territory here and there is a story of the time some rock-blasting was necessary during the building of the course, to clear a certain area. When the dust settled, there were three rather aggravated lions who had been awakened from their day-time slumbers by the noise.

Many modern architects like watery obstacles on their courses, for the holes dug out for the lakes provide earth for mounding elsewhere; the water is both a defining feature and a hazard and, of course, a source of irrigation. Water holes are often overdone because of all this but not at Leopard Creek. Although strictly speaking water comes into play on eight holes, the average golfer is not generally asked to hit other than a

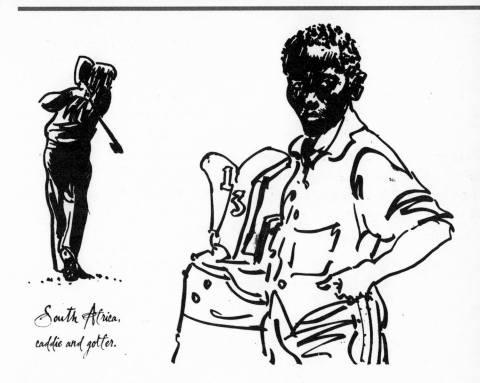

South Africa,
caddie and golfer.

fairly short iron to make the carry demanded and, if you can't hit a green with one of those, you probably don't deserve to.

The fifth is a short hole with water all down the left but plenty of dry land on the right and is deceptively long. If the pin is on the back and your ball on the front you will need to pivot on the putt, on what is a huge St Andrews-style double green – the largest in Africa. When I was there, the greenkeepers were clearing some dead reeds out of the lake. They knew about the small croc that lived there but not about the 10-foot monster that suddenly appeared. Work stopped instantly.

The 13th is the hole that everyone remembers from Leopard Creek. It is a par five and a stream runs the length down the left, turning into a small but strategically important pond just in front of the green. The land gathers down to it, making both stream and pond much bigger than their actual size and influencing every shot, right from the drive. Most members will have to lay up short of the hazard and then pitch to an inverted 'L'-shaped green – and then prepare themselves for one of the most spectacular greens anywhere in the world. It is perched on a cliff some 70 feet above the Crocodile River, which runs away, with hills and bush, into the distance – an African panorama both beautiful and dangerous. It is another of golf's great places: a place where the

Durban Country Club.

temptation to call a halt to all the futility and to stay and absorb the sensations of Africa becomes almost an imperative.

Durban Country Club is a proper golf course in every sense, with the kind of emphases that we are in danger of losing elsewhere in the Western world. At Durban there are plenty of caddies, ample tee times and a clubhouse in which service is immaculate and everything first-class. In short, it is redolent of another age.

The course itself is pure, proper golfing pleasure. Built on what were originally grassy sand-dunes it is now a hummocky heaven with exotic tropical trees and is populated by families of monkeys who make a wonderful diversion. The first is a good starting hole, a drive and a pitch, and the short second requires you to blank out the bush-filled depression in front of you. The third is a celebrated par five, so narrow and so dangerous that it is on the mind long before you get there.

Prince Edward, Earl of Wessex, is alleged to have taken 17 at the short 12th and, as you stand on the tee, this seems entirely possible. The pin is on a pimple of a green, with a run-off of about 60 yards if you miss.

The two closing holes are possibly the best. Both have fantastically contorted fairways which require absolute accuracy or the ball will run away to snake country. The 17th is, at 387 yards, a drive and a pitch while the 18th is a wonderful hole at 274 yards. The temptation is to try and drive the green and the reality is that you will come off the shot and disappear for ever down the steep drop-off to the right.

Despite the beauty and quality of these two courses, I would not complain if I had to play the rest of my golf at either the Player course or at Fancourt, a resort of considerable class near George, in the south. Sun City and Lost City, twin resorts, are incredible concepts, costing billions of rand and designed to ensure that no one wants for anything. Both have golf courses designed by Gary Player but while the one named after him is traditional in form and a joy to play, the Lost City course is a modern abomination. It is deliberately created for carts, which means that walking is next to impossible and it is all sharp edges, which means you are either on the fairway or in deep trouble. On one hole you could even be dead if, on hitting your ball into the hazard in front of the green, you went in to retrieve it. There are 40 or more crocodiles in a pit in front of the green at the short 13th – and hundreds of abandoned golf balls.

The golf is totally contrived and a complete contrast to the Player course, which is intrinsically superior and allows you to walk and to take a caddie. Caddies are, almost without exception, marvellous, although it is entirely possible that yours will be able to play better than you. This with minimal coaching but maximum ability to mimic the swings of the good players. Not only does a caddie take up to an hour off the playing time of a round, but he also provides instant knowledge of what is required on a strange golf course.

Nowhere was this more evident than at the Wild Coast Country Club, in the Transkei, a course that is built in, on and around a series of hill-tops and chasms and would be utterly unplayable without both a cart and a caddie. The cart is required because some of the walks from green to tee are necessarily of packed-lunch length and the caddie is needed because someone has to be sufficiently eagle-eyed to spot the precise point at which your ball disappeared into the alien corn or the tumbling chasm.

The Wild Coast is aptly named: it can blow with Irish ferocity and the Country Club gets in the way of most of it. But when the weather is right, the views are sensational and the golf is an experience.

The whole of Fancourt Hotel and Country Club is also an experience – one that Ernie Els and his family have opted to enjoy frequently as they have bought a holiday home there. Fancourt is on South Africa's Garden Route, the road that runs round the bottom of the map and leads to Cape Town. This is just about as beautiful an area as you can find anywhere in the world and Fancourt caters for those who want to enjoy the mountains, beaches and vineyards, which are in close conjunction.

The golf course is parkland and beautifully wooded. Player has made an interesting course out of some rolling terrain, interspersing water hazards where the trees don't offer sufficient challenge. It is, in fact, just about perfect for a resort course, demanding enough but with the opportunity to play that little bit better than you think you can.

Cape Town saw the first of South African golf, when six holes came into being at a nearby army camp in 1882. The first recorded monthly medal was not for another four years – a Lieutenant Gardiner of the Royal Scots wisely allowing Lieutenant-General Sir Henry Torrens, Officer Commanding Her Majesty's Forces at the Cape, to win, with a score of 94 to 99.

Golf was mostly played on 'browns' in those early days, which perhaps explains why the game was slow to take off. Even the South African championship was played on sand greens as recently as 1913. The early events were won mostly by expatriates – and mostly Scots at that – and it was 30 years before a South African professional won his country's Open. At least Messrs Locke, Player and Els have put a stop to all that.

SAND, BUNKERS AND YET MORE SAND

A SNAPSHOT OF EMIRATES

The vehicle was totally, immovably, stuck. Half way up a towering sand-dune the jeep had spun its wheels, dug itself into the sand and a lot of hot and increasingly frantic digging had only succeeded in embedding it further into its own tracks. Melodramatically, the prospect of dying in the desert crossed our minds. From the top of a dune you can see a long way in the desert and there was definitely nothing there.

Our small exploring party had set out from Jebel Ali, just outside the City of Gold, Dubai and we were about to inspect what we had in the way of provisions when suddenly, like a genie, another jeep materialized. In it were three men and a falcon, the latter hooded and tethered but ready for action.

These were true men of the desert and they were out hunting – falconry, one of the great pre-occupations of the Middle Ages, lives on in Arabia. They took one look at our situation, quickly deflated all four tyres, pushed the jeep until it faced down the dune, engaged the four-wheel drive and ... we were free. They even blew the tyres back up for us and four relieved golf writers breathed again.

Of all the unlikely places for golf to alight, the Arabian desert is high on that list. It is hard to imagine a more unnatural activity than playing golf on green grass in an area which, left to itself, would be given over to sand-dunes and scrub.

The Maktoums, the rulers of Dubai, are renowned in the world of racing and are more interested in the winner of the Derby than of the Open but early in the 1980s they deemed that golf was a financial imperative in order that the huge numbers of businessmen being attracted to the region by the 'black gold' – oil – would have somewhere to relax. The Emirates course, designed by the American Karl Litten, was duly built. It is magnificent, not only fit for a sheikh but also for the world's best players. Winners of the Dubai Desert Classic include Severiano Ballesteros, Fred Couples, Ernie Els and Colin Montgomerie, with totals, on this 7101-yard course, ranging between 12 and 20-under par.

The magic factor, of course, is water and to cause the desert to bloom requires vast amounts of it. It would be ecologically objectionable if what was needed were to be drawn from the limited supplies available naturally so the rulers of Dubai came up with an ingenious solution. In another part of town, Dubal, one of the world's leading makers of aluminium, was producing huge amounts of water from its own desalination plant. The water they took from the Arabian Gulf would have been returned to it but is now pumped to the four golf courses that exist in the area. Each needs around 600,000 gallons a day throughout the year but that is not a problem. The Dubal plant can produce over 30 million gallons a day.

This supply allows the existence of more than 30,000 trees and shrubs on the Emirates course. More than 2000 casuarinas line the perimeter while within there are date palms, hibiscus, oleanders and coconut palms. Within that greenery, in turn, are the birds. When the ground stood as pure desert no more than ten species were spotted. Since the coming of grass and water there have been more than 230, including single sightings of the oriental pratincole and the white-throated bee-eater, plus the more regular migratory birds like the little crake, the marsh sandpiper and hypocolius.

The course is full of risk-and-reward challenges. The par fives are all reachable by the top professionals, but there are big penalties for failure. The best-known of all is the 547-yard 18th, which dog-legs left from the tee. After a good drive the players are almost always on the limit of their ability if they want to go for the green in two, for there is a large lake in front of the green.

In 1996, for example, Colin Montgomerie needed a birdie to win the Desert Classic. He stood 251 yards away from the pin, contemplating whether he should go

Golf in the desert.

for the carry, or rely on pitching close to the pin with his third. The dilemma produced the Canon European Shot of the Year. Despite the fact that it was his first tournament after a three-month lay-off and the fact that the breeze was against, he decided to take his driver, caught it right out of the middle and finished 15 feet from the hole.

Conversely, in 1997 Ian Woosnam needed only to par the hole to win the tournament. He duly laid-up safely short of the water with his second and had a mere 73 yards to the pin. He took a wedge, hit the ball 60 yards and saw it hit the bank and trickle back into the water. That single shot, a candidate for European Dunce of the Year, cost him US$90,000, for he found himself in a play-off with Australians Richard Green and Greg Norman. Green won at the first extra hole.

The trophy, or Dalleh, a gigantic silver coffee pot of traditional Middle Eastern design, is unique and so is the clubhouse. It shimmers in the heat but is no mirage. It has

Of all the unlikely places for golf to alight, the Arabian desert is high on that list. It is hard to imagine a more unnatural activity than playing golf on green grass in an area which, left to itself, would be given over to sand-dunes and scrub.

been called Dubai's answer to the Sydney Opera House and is a modern representation of a Bedouin encampment, with seven interconnecting 'tents' made of glass, concrete and steel. No expense has been spared and the players are unanimous in their praise of the facilities and of the course – the locker-rooms, the practice ground and the greens that Norman has rated in the world's top three.

The desert itself is also a great attraction and several companies run safaris or offer a night out among the dunes complete with traditional dress, camel rides, belly dancers and traditional fare like lamb-in-a-pit. Dig a hole in the sand, light a fire, insert lamb (in a huge cauldron) and leave for a very, very long time. Dubai is different and deliciously so.

CHAPTER 9

GREAT PLAYERS

THE TRIUMVIRATE: VARDON, TAYLOR AND BRAID

HISTORY HAS GIVEN UP ON HIERARCHICAL NICETIES such as the comparative status in the game of Harry Vardon, J.H. Taylor and James Braid. Three of the most influential figures in golf generally, and in the evolution of professional golf especially, they have become simply and for ever – The Triumvirate.

Born within 14 months of each other, between 1870 and 1871, in their fruitful prime from 1894 to 1914, they won 16 Open championships. Vardon won six, Taylor and Braid five each. Vardon also won the 1900 US Open. Taylor was the first non-Scottish professional to win the Open, on the first occasion it was held outside Scotland – at Royal St George's, Sandwich. Braid was the first man to win five Opens.

Probing further into the minutiae of their achievements, it is seen that Braid twice broke 300 in winning his titles and Taylor once. Vardon, for all his six titles, never got below 300, which does not prove a great deal. Scoring generally was higher in those days and when these three giants were in their pomp, tournament golf was a rarity. The scale of their accomplishments is more clearly seen in the matches that they played against each other, against the best of British and the best that an infant American game could put against them.

All three are credited with more than 500 exhibition matches in their careers and, long before the Ryder Cup was introduced, appeared in fervently contested England–Scotland clashes. Along with his contemporaries, Vardon also played in 'big money' matches (the stakes being as high as £50), which sometimes attracted crowds of 10,000.

Interestingly, as well as being close in the matter of Open championships won, there was not a great deal to separate the three of them in the matchplay arena, either. Vardon played Taylor 47 times, won 26 times and halved twice; Vardon met Braid 83 times and was beaten 40 times, with seven games halved; and, in more than 74 head-to-heads, Braid and Taylor won 31 times each and were all-square on the other 12 occasions. So much for their playing records.

As a presiding figure in the game overall, Vardon exerted an influence that is unsurpassed. He instructed the world on how a golf club should be gripped and how it should be swung. Walter Hagen, no less, was an imitator. He was, as Bobby Jones, Ben Hogan and Jack Nicklaus were later, a truly international champion. The first of them all.

Vardon was born in the village of Grouville on the island of Jersey. He had the classical start in golf: he was a caddie. He left school at the age of 12 and tried a variety of jobs before joining his younger brother, Tom, an assistant professional at St Annes, in Lancashire. Vardon was taken on at Studley Royal, then Bury and he seemed to have found his niche when he became greenkeeper and professional at Ganton, in Yorkshire.

He finished fifth and ninth behind J.H. Taylor in the 1894 and 1895 Opens and, if Taylor was not aware of him then, the following year Vardon introduced himself with a jolt. He beat

Harry Vardon.

Taylor 8&6 in a match at Ganton and relieved the more famous golfer of his Open title after a play-off at Muirfield.

By the time of the 1914 Open at Prestwick, Vardon, Taylor and Braid had five Open championships each. It was the last championship in which any of them would appear as likely winners: Vardon and Braid were 44 and Taylor 43. Vardon and Taylor were drawn together for the last two rounds and on the last day there were only two strokes – in Vardon's favour – between them. After a second round 82, Braid was out of it, so this was a straight Vardon versus Taylor fight for the title. A record attendance responded to the drama of one of golf's great confrontations.

In his later years, Vardon's putting veered towards the unreliable. Not so Taylor's. And with that advantage, Taylor turned a two-stroke deficit into a two-stroke lead, which became three after the opening hole in the final round. Taylor then missed a putt of less than three feet and it disturbed him – though not as much as what happened next. How the Colin Montgomeries of the modern game would sympathize with Taylor, a thoughtful, sensitive man, more highly strung than the placid, pipe-smoking Vardon. Taylor told the story in *Golf: My Life's Work*.

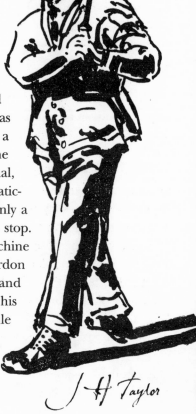

'As I walked back towards the third tee, the thought struck me that a three-stroke lead against Vardon was a slender and insubstantial lifeline and about as reliable as throwing a rope made of cottonwool to a drowning man. It was my honour towards the bunker pontifically known as the Cardinal, when at the top of my backward swing a lunatic-looking youth clicked an infernal camera only a few yards away, which brought me to a full stop. Strung up as I was, the snap of the machine completely upset my mental balance. Vardon rubbed it in by taking the bold, short and courageous line over the Cardinal with his second shot, getting a well-deserved four while I had to be content with a normal five. My lead was disappearing and my thoughts became more apprehensive.'

The fourth, Pow Burn, Taylor described

J H Taylor

as the greatest tragedy of his golfing life. The 'clever' Braid had been asked to tighten up the course and had installed a couple of bunkers at the range of a good drive. Vardon missed them, Taylor did not. From the bunker he went on to the burn, took seven to Vardon's four and by now Taylor's nerves were shot. He four-putted the fifth and later wrote, 'From then until the end I fought a losing battle and I was fairly and truly licked.'

Taylor was born at Northam in North Devon, caddied at the Royal North Devon Club at Westward Ho!, learned his golf and became a professional there and then moved up the coast to Burnham, where he was greenkeeper-pro. He played his first Open in 1893, won it the next two years and was on his way to immortality. Great golfer and intense competitor though he undoubtedly was, he was not the classicist.

At 5 foot 8 inches, he was considered small. His swing was ungainly and 'punchy' but when he planted his big feet he could cheat a wind as well as anyone. His temperament was sometimes his foe – it certainly was at Prestwick in 1914 – but no golfer ever tried harder than Taylor and no one can detract from his record. He was a figure of some stature in the game and played a large part in the setting up of the PGA (Professional Golfers' Association). He left school at 11 but loved Dickens and Boswell and *My Life's Work* was all his own work. He was also renowned as a clubmaker, public speaker and designer of golf courses – Royal Mid-Surrey bearing his signature.

It was then, as now, highly fashionable for famous players to enter the design business. None in his day – and few since – did so with greater industry and creative instinct than Braid. Bernard Darwin in his book *James Braid* wrote, 'I believe James loved golf with an intense, whole-hearted love the capacity for which, whatever its object, is not given to many people. He loved not merely the playing of it, but everything to do with it, certainly not least the making of new courses and the mending of old ones.' He had a good eye for country and the most famous course with which his name is connected is probably Gleneagles.

Braid was brought up at Elie, in Fife, and came to golf in the usual way, as a caddie. Darwin related how Braid's boyhood passion for the game was inflamed by a meeting with Jamie Anderson, the then three-times Open champion. Anderson had travelled from St Andrews to play a match at Elie, and the 13-year-old Braid had followed him round with 'adoring, dog-like eyes'. So touched was the famous golfer that he invited the boy to play a few shots. Then play them again. Anderson told Braid to play as much golf as possible, practise as hard as he could and one day he would be an Open champion.

In 1901 the prediction came true – a little later, perhaps, than Braid had expected because he was by then 31. The delay may be accounted for by the fact that he had enjoyed a distinguished career as an artisan amateur – with a handicap of plus three – and he had a trade in joinery to pursue. He passed on to professionalism as a clubmaker at the Army and Navy Stores and once he had won that first Open, at Muirfield, he was away. For the next 10 years he is said to have 'sparkled brilliantly' and five Open titles in that span support the lavish praise.

He went to Muirfield as holder of the Musselburgh Open, a 36-hole event that he won with the 'fantastic' total of 140, yet if he was the form man in the field it was not immediately apparent. Braid hooked his first tee shot over the wall and started with a double bogey. He was out in 43 but battled manfully against a strong wind to return in 36 and this was only two shots behind Vardon. Although Braid and Vardon were level after two rounds, the pundits had by then made Vardon a 3–1-on favourite, odds that were rapidly altered when Braid played a decisive third round of 74. Despite snapping his cleek at the 18th, he beat Vardon by five shots.

The Triumvirate split up when Vardon died in 1937 and in 1950 Braid and Taylor were elected honorary members of the R&A, along with Willie Auctherlonie, the first professionals to be so distinguished.

FRANCIS OUIMET

With an honesty and a modesty that was totally characteristic, Francis DeSales Ouimet at the end of his career wrote, 'I always viewed my victory of 1913 in the light of a huge fluke.' In a play-off, the young and unheralded American had beaten two of the game's greatest players – Harry Vardon and Ted Ray. Bernard Darwin, however, that equally honest chronicler of *The Times*, had an altogether different viewpoint regarding Ouimet's win in that year's US Open. Darwin was the marker in that play-off and said it was 'the most momentous win in all golf history.'

That verdict is the one that has been accepted by history. For Ouimet's victory pointed the way for all America and all American golfers. They had been shown, in the most forceful manner possible, that the acknowledged giants of the time – the British – could be beaten. One man had shown the way and others poured through the open gate.

Ouimet won that play-off rather easily, by five strokes from Vardon and six from Ray, but if there was a fluky factor about the win it lay in the manner of his entry for the championship. The USGA were looking for a good amateur field for the event, which was to be played at Brookline

Country Club, the course beside which Ouimet and his family lived. They were not wealthy: Ouimet had learned the game through caddieing at the club and although, at the age of 20, he had become a good player, he still had to work for a living. In his book *A Game of Golf*, Ouimet said, 'The president of the USGA thought I should enter ... I argued with him about the folly of such a thing, and he won the argument. I was employed by Wright and Ditson in the sporting goods business, I had taken my vacation for the National Amateur championship and I did not have the courage to ask for more time off to play the Open.'

Ouimet, though, had been entered by the USGA and when the pairings appeared in the paper his boss said, 'Well, I see you are now going to play in the Open.' Ouimet admitted, 'I was embarrassed. I said I had no intention of playing but if he would be good enough to let me wander out to Brookline and see Vardon and Ray perform I should be ever grateful to him. With a gleam in his eye, my chief said, "As long as you have entered, you had better plan to play." This was an order. I needed no further instructions.'

As a former caddie himself, Ouimet employed a 10-year-old, hardly bigger than his bag, who might otherwise have struggled for employment that week. His name was Eddie Lowery and on the 72nd fairway, with the US Open championship at stake, he handed his master an iron with the words, 'Keep your eye on the ball and hit it.' Ouimet did precisely as he was told.

Lowery did such a good job that when, the next morning, the time came for the play-off, he was able to beat off all offers for his job. 'On the way to the tee,' said Ouimet, 'my good friend Frank Hoyt asked me if I would not permit him to carry my clubs. I told him he must see Eddie. He made one or two offers of money,

Francis Ouimet.

but they did not tempt Eddie in the least ... he positively refused to be bought off. Finally Hoyt appealed to me. I looked at the 10-year-old Eddie; his eyes filled and I think he was fearful that I would turn him down. In any event he seemed so sincere I did not have the heart to take the clubs away from him.'

It was as well he did not. Lowery obviously had none of the bashfulness that often afflicts boys and on the first hole of the play-off he was there with his advice again, 'Be sure and keep your eye on the ball.' Ouimet went on, 'He kept telling me to keep my eye on the ball. He cautioned me to take my time. He encouraged me in any number of different ways.' When, at the eighth, Ouimet hit a sensational second shot to a blind green, Lowery said, 'Your ball is stone dead.' Ouimet said, 'I wanted to think it was, but I wished to prepare myself in case it were not.' But Lowery was right again. It was only a foot from the hole.

That settled any nerves Ouimet might have had, it made him all square with his illustrious opponents and, in fact, he led all the way from there in. The following year he won the US Amateur and, 17 years after that, won it again.

Ouimet had a distinguished career in golf, playing in seven Walker Cup teams, captaining six and, in 1951, being elected captain of the R&A, the first person not of British nationality to hold that office. He was honoured off the course in America, too. He served on the USGA executive committee, was the vice-president and had a portrait of himself painted by President Eisenhower, which now hangs in the clubhouse at Augusta National.

But it is perhaps the legacy of his behaviour towards Lowery that will ensure his reputation for ever more in American golf. In 1949 the Francis Ouimet Caddie Scholarship Fund was started, to provide financial aid for higher education for a number of caddies. By 1992 over US$6 million had been given away to young men and women in Massachusetts who had served as caddies, helped in the professional's shop or worked with the green superintendent. Among the contributors to the Fund was Lowery himself, who won the Massachusetts Junior championship twice running, before moving to California where he became a successful businessman.

Ouimet died in 1967, at the age of 74 and Darwin, who was so taken by Ouimet's demeanour during the US Open play-off that he found himself hoping for an American win, paid tribute to the man in *Life is Sweet, Brother*. He said, 'He had plenty of ambition and stern resolve, for no great game player can do without them, but with them he combined a genius for playing his game for fun. His was a very rare gift.'

Faldo study page.   Practising at St Andrews late into the evening as the sun sets.

Open Championships 1990.

x Watching the hours of practise it occurs to me that Faldo has developed a method of 'sharpening' his game by acquiring a procedure to check his

① short-game ② chipping
③ putting
④ Bunker skills
⑤ Swing
He continually goes through these procedures.

x I don't know any player that 'stands' to the ball as well as Faldo. He seems to seek balance and control without any tension! His grip is firm yet never 'strained'! The grip is subtle and 'feeling' rather than 'tight'!!

Nick listened when he was told that he had to work on the inconsistencies of his method. Faldo had to develop a swing that would repeat under pressure. David said he had to stabilise the swing with a 'passive leg action', and in doing so create a 'resistance' to the rotation of the trunk. Like Winding a spring, to learn to coil the upper body over the resistance of the knees and hips, to create 'TORQUE' energy and then be released to drive the downswing through the ball.

Nick Faldo

Bobby Jones

arnold Palmer

Jack Nicklaus

greg Norman

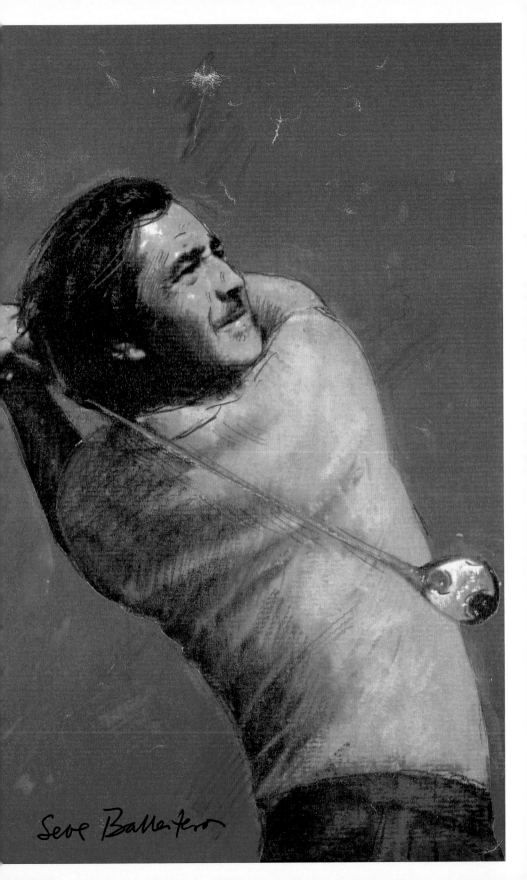

Seve Ballesteros

Tiger Woods.

WALTER HAGEN

Walter Hagen did not prevaricate: he took up golf, he said, for the money and made a million. Hagen defined professionalism in sport and, at the same time, was and still is professional sport's most glorious contradiction.

He was flash and brash, one of sport's first 22-carat showmen and, of all the things said of him and by him, Herbert Warren Wind summed him up most perfectly. 'Great as he was as a golfer,' wrote Wind in 1948, 'Hagen was even greater as a personality – an artist with a sense of timing so infallible that he could make the tying of his shoe-laces more dramatic than the other guy's hole-in-one.' Hagen would probably have settled for that as an epitaph.

His own summation of his life and times was the famous, 'I never wanted to be a millionaire – I just wanted to live like one.' But underneath the nonchalance, flamboyance and apparent throw-away attitudes was another characteristic – indelible assurance – which Hagen displayed throughout his golfing life. Only Jack Nicklaus exceeds Hagen's haul of 11 major championships. He won five US PGA championships, four of them in a row from 1924.

Margaret Seaton Heck crammed numerous tales of the man's golf and of deeds extraneous into *The Walter Hagen Story* but could not fit them all into the book – because of lack of space and, she noted, 'Boston censorship'. As Heck put it: there were no intrusions on Hagen's time, only welcome interruptions. He believed in not doing today what he could put off for three weeks. During the years – yes, years – that she worked on Hagen's book, Heck despaired of those interruptions. 'There have been many days,' she wrote, 'when we have worked for 20 minutes and entertained his friends and admirers for four hours.'

Hagen began as a caddie at the Country Club of Rochester, New York, playing the game with clubs given him by members. Duly smitten, he was rarely to be seen without one of them in his hands. He even fashioned his

Walter Hagen.

own four-hole course in a cow pasture. Champions, he was to say later, are made, not born, and Hagen made himself what he was by the sheer volume of his work in his cow pasture. Talent, he conceded, was important but only practise could transform flair into reliable method. By the time he was 15 he claimed that he had played more golf and practised more shots than the average 21-year-old.

Hagen, 21 years of age, was US Open champion. He was so impressed with his own achievement that he informed the Phillies that he would not, after all, be attending their trials.

Hagen, for all his later fame and the magnitude of his presence in the game, had the sort of basic grounding that club professionals all over the world would recognize. When he was 12 years old, he had sat in his school classroom, watched golfers outside at play, jumped through the window and virtually put an end to his formal education. He tried a variety of jobs from wood finisher for a piano manufacturer, to car repairer to apprentice mandolin maker. At one stage, he was a budding taxidermist. But it was golf that gave him his solid start in life. He learned the club professional's trade and was skilful enough to assemble his own golf clubs. He won two US Opens and a French Open with clubs that he made himself.

He played his first championship, the US Open at Brookline in 1913, aged 20. After all, if he was going to make a name for himself, he had better get started so off he went to take on the best. Harry Vardon, the best player in the world, was in the field and 'As I expected to become the best, I decided to keep my eye on him.' Hagen noted that Vardon had 'a much more compact swing than I'd ever seen' and he set about emulating some of its characteristics.

In the last round, a calamitous start of 6,5,7 meant Hagen was quick to put the Vardon method to practical use. He hit his best drive down the fourth fairway, flashed a five-iron to the concealed green and holed for a two. Then he birdied the fifth ('my Vardon drive was good to see') and the sixth when his too strong second shot got caught in the folds of the flag and dropped into the cup. He was four-over par after three holes and level after three more.

Hagen was a contender again until the 14th, where he took seven and so was finished. He had lost a tournament but had gained, or so he thought, the proper perspective on his sporting career. He was not a golfer but a baseball player at heart and in substance. Invited to the Philadelphia Nationals' training camp the following winter, he had got rid of his 'temporary' obsession with golf. 'If I could wangle a contract with the

Phillies I'd be headed for the big time in baseball. After all, that had been my original ambition.'

The following summer he was sitting in the pro's shop at Rochester explaining to his fellow professional, Dutch Leonard, how he was going to electrify the world of big-league pitching, when Leonard asked him if he was going to enter the US Open. Hagen thought not. 'I'm going to work harder in baseball and let up on golf.' The editor of the local newspaper overheard the conversation and virtually shamed the young man into changing his mind. That process was dramatically assisted by the offer to pay all Hagen's expenses. Hagen had three weeks in which to get himself ready. He confessed that he had never worked harder.

For the rest of his life he wondered how he made it to the first tee for the 1914 US Open for, on the night before, he developed food poisoning. By dawn he was so weak that he could scarcely stand to play a golf tournament. Leonard persuaded him to go to the course and see how he felt at start time. How he felt was sore. He had difficulty swinging the club yet he played – and won in a style that laid the foundations of the Walter Hagen legend.

Hagen, 21 years of age, was US Open champion. He was so impressed with his own achievement that he informed the Phillies that he would not, after all, be attending their trials. He worked on his golf instead. Back at Rochester, he watched the shop, gave lessons and mended and made clubs but his horizons were widening.

His ability 'to put on a good performance increased through time and experience'. Competition was his lifeblood and he always claimed to play his best game under pressure. 'When I was short of cash, I could always win. When I needed a title to enhance my value in exhibitions, I went out and got it. The healthier my economic situation, the lousier I played.' That observation does not bear serious scrutiny because Hagen's economic situation was vastly enhanced the following January when he won the Panama Exposition championship at Ingleside, San Francisco. It carried the first US$1,000 prize in the history of American golf. He played the first nine holes in 30.

A cheque that size made Hagen financially sound for the rest of the year and his confidence was soaring. A.G. Spalding & Bros made him an offer to play their ball and he was now a genuine 'big shot'. If he endorsed a product, he used it and for a period he stayed faithful to a brand he knew was inferior to one used by many other pros – even though he claimed it cost him many shots.

In 1918, Hagen was persuaded into the pro's job at Oakland Hills, near Detroit and was immediately aware of the social changes that were taking place in the game. In the years to come, he was to play his part in the acceleration of this process. Detroit, he discovered, was a boom town and clubbist niceties had been overwhelmed in the lusty growth of the place, which was full of millionaires. 'They took me in as one of their own,' said Hagen, 'I was a golf champion and a good fellow and that was enough for them.' A professional had to know his place in those days, even in the United States, but Hagen was to help change all that. At Oakland Hills he was welcomed into the clubhouse – unlike at Rochester.

Having played in the Florida tournaments of 1919, Hagen came up fit and fresh for the US Open at Brae Burn. He talked of his 'iron man' physique and how well it had served him on the course and – especially – off it. His friend Al Jolson and his company were in Boston and Hagen partied every night. He and the local favourite, Mike Brady, tied for the championship and, the night before the play-off, Hagen partied with particular zest at Jolson's farewell shindig.

> 'They took me in as one of their own,' said Hagen, 'I was a golf champion and a good fellow and that was enough for them.'

When Hagen arrived at Brae Burn for the play-off, Brady had been hitting practice balls for more than an hour and had his shirt sleeves rolled up. Hagen advized him to roll them down lest the gallery should see his muscles quivering. As he suspected it would, this caused Brady to hook into the trees at the second and he took six to Hagen's four. There were a couple of rules spats – both players being penalized two shots – and they reached the 17th with Hagen ahead by two but struggling to stay awake. There followed another incident over Hagen's lost and found ball and his right to clean it and he took five to Brady's four. There was one in it at the 18th, which both played in four.

Hagen was US Open champion for the second time, his fame was greater than ever and there were increasingly insistent reminders that if he was all that good he had to play the Open to prove it. He gave up his club job and became, according to his job description, 'a full-time businessman golfer'.

Hagen said later that his trip to England was an education. At the time it was one bewildering incident after another, starting with the newspaper article that portrayed him as an upstart, leading to a famous altercation at the 1920 Open at Deal. As a professional, he was not allowed into the clubhouse so he changed in his limousine, parked ostentatiously in front of the club. It was also his first experience of playing a links course in a gale and his first round in Britain amounted to an 85.

He played the rest of the championship in a frenzy of unrewarded determination. 'I tried to keep fighting,' he wrote. 'I suppose I should have picked up my ball as most golfers would. I've never done that and I intended to show the British that I could take a beating and still smile. I took the beating all right. George Duncan won with a not-too-creditable score of 303. I trailed in 53rd, in a field of 54.' A British sportswriter captured the essential Hagen when he wrote that Duncan made his exit as though he had lost. 'Yet there was the American, Hagen, finishing with his head up as if he himself had won instead of finishing far down among the also-rans.'

On the eve of the 1922 Open at Royal St George's, Hagen was loath to retire and, about two o'clock in the morning, someone reminded him that most of the opposition were in bed. 'Maybe they're in bed but they're not sleeping,' was his famous retort. Hagen took 300 shots over his four rounds and, despite George Duncan's heroic attempt to catch him, that was good enough to make him the first American-born professional to win the Open.

He won golf's oldest major again in 1924, 1928 and 1929. He also won five US PGA championships, and a total of 60 tournaments. Add to that magnificent record his lifestyle dress sense and towering personality and you come up with a giant. 'It was Walter who made professional golf what it is,' said Gene Sarazen.

Hagen had his setbacks. He struggled with the memory of his first Open championship for the rest of his life; he was numbed by his defeat by Archie Compston in a challenge match in 1928 (18 up with 17 to play); and he nearly died of malaria in India. 'Yet, somehow,' he wrote, 'when I put the plus and minus things together, the minus seems to make the plus better and more worth winning and seems to make the victories sweeter.'

GENE SARAZEN

Gene Sarazen, born Eugenio Saraceni, was demonstrably one of the greatest golfers the game has known. Along with Jack Nicklaus, Ben Hogan and Gary Player, he won all four of the game's major championships – The Open, the US Open, the Masters and the US PGA. That he won the Masters when it was only in its second year and had hardly established itself is, in the context of his career, unimportant. He was certainly good enough to have won it when it became recognized as a major event.

Sarazen was a perky, shoulder-rolling, eye-twinkling, little man. He stood, stockily, only 5 foot 4 inches tall and entered golf in the classic manner, by caddying at a local club in Harrison, New York. The family needed the money, for his father, Federico, was a poor businessman only rarely in funds. Sarazen graduated from the caddyshack to the professional's shop simply because he revealed a flair for the game, and throughout a long career he depended more on talent than technique.

That talent, though, was sufficient to make him two fortunes. Having amassed one in the 1920s, he was wiped out by the stockmarket crash and, when he needed the miserly sum of US$1,000 to compete in the 1932 Open at Prince's, Sandwich, he had to borrow the money from his wife. It was as well she had it to hand, for Sarazen then won his only championship on that side of the Atlantic. It was at a time when British professional golf was not particularly strong and he won by five shots, easing up from another American, Macdonald Smith.

Appropriately, Prince's shares a boundary with Royal St George's, where Sarazen was invited to watch the 1993 Open. The field for that event was the strongest assembled hitherto and all the top players played at or close to their best, producing a finish of breath-taking quality. When the smoke cleared, Greg Norman was the man left standing, having produced a final round of 64. Nick Faldo, Bernhard Langer, Corey Pavin, Nick Price and Ernie Els were all gunned down. Invited to say a few words at the presentation ceremony, Sarazen, a fiercely combative man in his youth, revealed himself as being capable of appreciation too. 'I never thought I would live to see golf played like that,' he said. 'What Greg did out there was incredible.'

The game had certainly changed from Sarazen's early days. Norman had in attendance his coach, manager, wife and personal pilots to fly him back across the ocean. Sarazen picked up the game by watching other players. 'No one gave me lessons,' he once said. 'I'd go miles and miles to watch tournaments. My favourite was Walter Hagen.'

But the legacy of no lessons was a grip that would frequently let him down. He was always in danger of hooking out of bounds and he invented a heavy club that could not be swung properly unless it was gripped in the

Gene Sarazen.

conventional pattern. It was an idea copied from the leaded baseball bats that Ty Cobb used in that era to keep loose.

Sarazen's most famous invention was the shape of the sand wedge as it is used to this day. In Al Barkow's book *Gettin' To The Dance Floor*, he explained that he used to mix with Howard Hughes, before he became reclusive. Sarazen took flying lessons from him and during the course of them realized that 'when I took off I pulled the stick back and the tail went down and the nose of the plane went up. Something flashed in my mind, that my niblick should be lowered in the back.' So he put some solder on to some regular wedges. 'What I did was put a flange on the back of the club and angled it so the flange hit the sand first, not the front edge, which was now raised. Now I could hit behind the ball and explode it out.'

That invention revolutionized bunker play and present-day professionals think about holing out rather than just getting out of the sand. 'I guess the sand iron would have to be one of the most important contributions I've made to golf' Sarazen said. 'I think the club saves everybody six shots a round.'

He did not get a penny piece out of his invention. The clubmaking company he represented, Wilson, had it in the fine print that all such benefits accrued to them but Wilson, with whom Sarazen stayed all his life, were good to their illustrious client. He was still signing lucrative contracts to represent them when well into his 90s.

That sand iron played a major part in one of Sarazen's more incredible feats. In the 1932 US Open he played the last 28 holes in 100 shots, an average of 3.57, an amazing thing to do with the equipment and course conditions of the time. When he came to the short 12th, he hit a thoroughly bad tee shot in the rough, 50 feet from the hole, with a bunker between him and a pin set tight to the sand. It would have been easy to get the ball to 20 feet but, by taking his sand iron and a big chance, he cut the ball up, landed it softly and saw it trickle to two feet. The sand iron was used again at the 16th and 17th and finally at the 18th where he exploded to eight feet and holed the putt to win by three shots – shots arguably saved by the sand iron.

Sarazen's most famous shot – which he always called 'lucky' – was the four-wood he holed for a two at the 15th at Augusta to deprive Craig Wood of the 1935 Masters. It was heard around the world but, at the age of 71, invited back to the Open at Troon, Sarazen hit a shot that was *seen* around the world. At the tiny Postage Stamp, the tiny Italian American, a little portly in his plus-fours, holed in one. The next day, he was bunkered off the tee but it was no problem for the inventor of the sand iron – he holed out for a two.

BOBBY JONES

As the arguments rage across the ages, interminable and incapable of being determined, as to who was the best ever, perhaps only one thing is certain: Robert Tyre Jones jnr was the most-loved golfer of all time. No one has ever stirred the sentiments of so many people as this handsome figure with a gift for lighting up golf courses and the lives of everyone he met.

He did more, in less time, in the matter of winning championships and spreading the gospel of golf than anyone before his time, or after. He compiled an eight-year record in which he won the US Open four times, the Open three times, the US Amateur five times and the Amateur once. He signed off with the most fantastic flourish in the whole history of sport, let alone golf, when in 1930, he completed the Impregnable Quadrilateral – the Grand Slam – by winning the Amateur, the Open, the US Open and the US Amateur. Furthermore, he achieved it with style and grace and a charm that would now be called charisma.

Jones played all his golf as an amateur but he won seven professional major championships – as many as Arnold Palmer, Sam Snead, Gene Sarazen and Harry Vardon. Only Jack Nicklaus, Walter Hagen, Ben Hogan, Gary Player and Tom Watson have won more.

Nor was he just good at the playing of the game. He retired two months after that momentous and monumental achievement of the Grand Slam and proved himself to be a gifted teacher of the game, a lucid and extremely literate writer on the subject and, later, one of the most courageous of men. On 15 August 1948, Jones played what was to be his last game as the following day, in hospital, he was told that there was damage to the spinal tissue and that an operation would be needed.

It was unsuccessful and not for another year or so was a proper diagnosis made: he had syringomyelia, a rare condition that attacks the spine. The condition was, and is, incurable. It withers the muscles, dulls the sense of feeling yet brings intense pain. Jones suffered it for 23 years and when he died he had gone from his fighting weight of 170 lb to under 100 lb.

Jones wrote, 'On the golf course a man may be the dogged victim of inexorable fate, be struck down by an appalling stroke of tragedy, become the hero of unbelievable melodrama or the clown in a side-splitting comedy – any of these within a few hours and all without having to bury a corpse or repair a tangled personality ... The main idea in golf, as in life I suppose, is to learn to accept what cannot be altered and to keep on doing one's own reasoned and resolute best whether the prospect be bleak or rosy.' Such thoughts, if anything could, must have helped through the final years.

Jones, a sickly child, had been introduced by his father to the game, in the hope that it might help his health. It quickly became obvious that he had a talent for striking the ball, although it was to take some time before he translated that into scoring and still more before he learned how to win, although he did pick up his first 'cup' at the age of six. Jones' 'Boswell' was O.B. Keeler, an Atlanta newspaperman, and he coined the phrase the 'seven lean years' to describe the frustrating period of Jones' early career when he entered national championships and found dozens of different ways of not winning them.

He was, of course, very young and he had lessons to learn. One of these was at all times to play against 'Old Man Par', for Jones firmly believed that if you could equal or better golf's mythical man, you would win a great many more times than lose. He said, 'I thought of golf as a game at which to beat someone. And of course I did not know that someone was myself.'

Bobby Jones.

He was burdened with a temper, something that dogged him his entire career but he eventually learned to control it to the extent that he did not show it. In *Down the Fairway*, written when he was 25, he told of the time he entered his first national championship, the 1916 US Amateur, at the Merion Cricket Club in Philadelphia. He was 14 and in the first round drew Eben Byers, a former champion. 'Mr Byers and I played terribly,' said Jones. 'He was a veteran and I was a youngster but we expressed our feelings in exactly the same way – when we missed a shot, we threw the club away. At the 12th hole Mr Byers threw an iron out of bounds and would not let his caddie go after it … I think the main reason I beat him was because he ran out of clubs first. Someone playing behind us said later that we looked like a juggling act.'

Jones was not finally to control his temper until after the infamous occasion at St Andrews when, in the 1921 Open, he picked up his ball at the 11th in the third round. He called it a 'superbly childish gesture' and admitted his principal regret in golf was 'that I ever quit in competition'.

The lean years ended in 1923 – not before time. 'I had played 11 national championships,' said Jones, 'and I was still outside. The thorn was beginning to rankle in earnest. Was I a golfer or only one of those hapless mechanical excellencies known as a great shotmaker, who cannot connect the great shots in sufficient numbers to win anything?'

> He said, 'I thought of golf as a game at which to beat someone. And of course I did not know that someone was myself.'

The US Open at Inwood Country Club, on Long Island, New York, provided the answer. He was playing badly prior to the championship and took Stewart Maiden – the professional from whom he had learned his swing simply by imitation – along for consultations, possibly the first instance of a coach attending a championship in that role. Jones played reasonably well but with a chance to win outright he finished, as he said, 'like a yellow dog'. He dropped four shots over the last three holes, and tied with Bobby Cruikshank. In the play-off, Jones was one ahead at the 18th and both men hit bad drives. Jones was on hardpan, with a huge pond to carry to the green, over 200 yards away but, with no apparent hesitation, chose a two-iron and banged it to six feet. Francis Ouimet called it, 'The finest shot I have ever seen', but Jones' recollection was more hazy. 'I suppose I had to decide whether to play safe or go for it,' he said, 'but I don't remember it.'

From that moment on, Jones was a different man. He now knew he was a great golfer and he went about proving it, winning those 13 national championships from July 1923 to September 1930.

Jones may have been the most intelligent of all the champion golfers so far. In 1922, the year before his breakthrough, his preparation for playing in the first Walker Cup consisted of graduating as a mechanical engineer from the Georgia School of Technology and then, by way of a diversion from things practical, studying the arts in order to get into Harvard. On the train north, to Long Island and the National Links where the cup was being played, he was boning away at Cicero's *Orations Against Cataline* and trying to catch up on some Latin work. Later he qualified in law and had his own practice. He thought deeply about the game of golf and wrote about it compellingly.

Jones was totally unable to play competitive golf lightly. Every shot had to be played as close to perfection as could be and, although he once confessed that he expected no more than six such shots per round, he never ceased to try to make it more. He played with an intense concentration, once remarking that only God could know what some shots cost a golfer. He also admitted that physically it was hard to cope and if any clue were needed as to why he gave up the game at the age of 28, two months after bringing about its finest achievement, it lies in the fact that at Oakmont, in 1919, when he played in the US Amateur and was runner-up, he lost 18 lb during the week. He would regularly lose 10–15 lb during a championship, even though he could play 36 holes of friendly golf every day for two weeks and not lose an ounce.

Jones conceived the idea of the Grand Slam, a concept so grand that it could only bring about undreamed of pressure. He set out to do the thing that golfers of all standards and for all time have found impossible – to win a particular tournament on purpose. Furthermore he was going to do it four times in one year and, at a time when transatlantic flights did not exist, he was going to win two on one continent and two on another.

In *Golf is my Game*, Jones admitted to some little white lies about the 1930 Slam. He said he had frequently been asked if he had planned an attack on the four championships and 'did not feel like saying that I had, because I felt reluctant to admit that I considered myself capable of such an accomplishment. But,' he went on, 'at this point, separated from the fact by so many years, this reticence seems a bit silly. Actually I did make my plans for that golfing year with precisely this end in view, and so prepared myself more carefully than I had ever done before.'

His bid opened at St Andrews, in the Amateur. 'I soberly concluded that this was the most important tournament of my life,' he said, adding wryly, 'it is an inescapable fact that I could not win all four without the first one, and this first one had always been for me the most difficult.'

He had some heroic matches in that championship, the one against Cyril Tolley being of epic proportions. He also had to beat two of the finest American golfers – Jimmy Johnson, then US Amateur champion, and George Voigt, who had been in that year's winning Walker Cup team – and both were fiercely fought affairs. The final was against Roger Wethered, brother of Joyce and a fine English amateur who had tied for the Open in 1921, also at St Andrews. 'It was plain,' said Jones, 'that Roger thought golf championships were very nice things, but it was also plain that he did not want to win them as badly as I did.' Nor did he win this one, Jones triumphing easily, 7&6.

The Open was at Hoylake and after 36 holes Jones led by five over

Archie Compston. After 40 holes, Compston was level. Jones started 4,5,6,3 against Compston's 4,3,4,2 and at the end of the round led by one shot, 215 to 216. Compston, who frequently blew hot and cold, finished with an 82 and the only pressure on Jones came from himself. This he piled on in unprecedented fashion, with a seven at the eighth, taking five to get down from 20 yards short of the green. 'A kind old lady with a croquet mallet could have saved Jones two strokes,' commented Bernard Darwin. Jones staggered along, dropping shots but still unchallenged, until the 16th, Hoylake's most remarkable hole, which skirts the practice ground and offers danger to both drive and second shot. He put his second into the greenside bunker in a devilish lie, offering almost no stance. Another disaster looked likely until Jones fished out a club that would certainly be illegal now. It was a 'massive, concave sand wedge', which had been given to him by Horton Smith, and he almost holed it. The shot won him the championship, by two strokes from Macdonald Smith and Leo Diegel. Afterwards, scarcely able to hold his drink through the release of pressure, Jones told the man from Associated Press that it was all getting too much for him, that he would never play in the Open again, that it was 'all too thick for me'.

The US Open was at Interlachen, near Minneapolis, and it featured perhaps the only controversial incident ever to attach itself to the Jones name. He led by five shots after three rounds but, rather like Hoylake, he made a poor start to the final round and lost four shots to Macdonald Smith, and thereafter it was always close. Jones rallied and the incident, which would have caused a sensation in this day and age, occurred at the 17th, a long short hole of uncertain length: 262 yards in one account; 263 in another and 272 in yet another.

He now knew he was a great golfer and he went about proving it, winning those 13 national championships from July 1923 to September 1930.

Whatever, it was long enough and Jones hit a wild high fade so bad that it clattered into the spectators and was never seen again. There was however a marsh that lay in the general direction of where the ball, when last seen, was heading. It was not defined as a hazard of any kind and Jones did not know what to do. He asked the referee, Prescott Bush, whose ruling did not please everyone. Although neither Bush nor any of the spectators had seen the ball go into the marsh, he decided that 'the ball went into a parallel water hazard,' adding that 'you are permitted to drop a ball in the fairway opposite the point where the ball crossed the margin of the hazard.'

Not surprisingly, many people felt this was a partial ruling, that the ball should have been declared lost and that Jones should have been told to go back to the tee and try again – Gene Sarazen, among others, feeling that it rather spoiled Jones' victory. Jones accepted the decision and, from the fairway, took five, a score he could well have made even having to go back to the tee. However, he survived not only the incident but also any challenge to his good name and he won the championship by two from Macdonald Smith.

He set out to do the thing that golfers of all standards and for all time have found impossible – to win a particular tournament on purpose. Furthermore he was going to do it four times in one year.

Now only the US Amateur at Merion remained. Jones, as ever honest, said, 'With all due respect but at the same time with all frankness I had for a long time felt that the American Amateur was the easiest to win of the Big Four. To be completely honest I recognized that the major part of the problem would be behind me once I showed up at the tournament all in one piece and in a fit condition to play.'

And so what happened? Two things. Firstly, in a game of golf at East Lake he was caught in a thunder and lightning storm. Bolts struck all around him and his companions, scaring them half to death, and they fled the course. Just as they got to the locker-room entrance 'we were dazed by a monstrous explosion as a heavy bolt hit a big double chimney immediately above our heads. I did not feel a thing … but when I got back into the clubhouse someone discovered that the back of my shirt had been ripped down to my waist and I had received on my shoulder a scratch some six inches in length and just deep enough to break the skin.' Secondly, Jones was walking to a lunch engagement when he heard a 'look out mister'. A runaway car was heading directly for him and 'I made a broad jump that would have done credit to Jesse Owens.' The car passed directly over the spot he had just vacated.

After that, winning golf matches was relatively simple. He won both his 18-hole matches by 5&4, and his first two 36-hole matches by 6&5 and 9&8. He then beat Gene Homans 8&7 in the final. The 11th green at Merion is about 600 yards from the clubhouse and the journey to it took Jones a very long time. *The New York Times* called it 'the most triumphant journey that any man ever travelled in sport.'

On 18 November 1930 Jones not only announced his retirement but also added that he was surrendering his amateur status in order to make the teaching films, since turned into videos, that have become classics.

The New York Times ran an editorial on the retirement of a man who was more than a sportsman: he was an icon, a symbol of grand sporting achievement. They ended it with the words, 'With dignity he quits the memorable scene, on which he nothing common did or mean.'

In 1936 it was a St Andrews caddie who recognized that Jones was some goddamned golf player all right. Staying at Gleneagles en route to Germany for the Olympic Games, Jones decided that he could not be so close to St Andrews without playing and motored over. By the time he got to the starter's hut for what he had thought would be a completely informal game, there were 2000 people encircling the tee. He was not in practice, nor even playing with any regularity and yet because it was St Andrews, because those people had turned out to watch, the instincts of a great player took over. He went to the turn in 32, a score that included a birdie at the short eighth. He needed what he called 'a soft four-iron' which he faded gently, pitching it short so that it took the contours of the green, to finish nine feet away. It was a shot of surpassing skill, dragged back from the memory of times long gone. The caddie, who had never seen anything like it, blurted out an instinctive compliment which moved Jones more than anything ever written about him. 'My,' said the caddie, 'but you're a wonder, Sir.'

Jones famously replied, 'I could take out of my life everything except my experiences at St Andrews and I would still have had a rich and full life.'

Honours on and off the course were heaped on Bobby Jones throughout his active career and for long after he had ceased playing. Although essentially a modest man he was pleased when the Royal Lytham & St Annes Club decided to erect a plaque on the spot from which he hit one of the great shots of golf, to win the 1926 Open. It was at the 17th in the final round and Jones and Al Watrous were level on the tee. Watrous drove well, Jones badly, and when Watrous hit his second on to the green William C. Fownes jnr, then president of the USGA, commented, 'That's worth US$100,000 to him.' Fownes felt that given Jones' lie, he would be unable to reach the green and Watrous would therefore win the Open. The ball lay in a sandy waste and Jones could not see the green. 'The prospect was not precisely encouraging,' he said. He had to hit a shot with a carry of 175 yards and then stop it very quickly on the green – 'This, off dry sand, was a stiff assignment,' said Jones. He hit it perfectly and Watrous, unnerved, three-putted and lost the championship.

The mashie-iron with which Jones hit the shot was presented to the club and is the trophy in one of their premier competitions. A note from Jones reads, 'The plaque and the competition for my iron gave me much pleasure. I am so happy that the club have put this old implement to such use. I am afraid that it has thus acquired a dignity far beyond its worth.'

In 1955, the USGA instituted the Bob Jones Award, to be presented in recognition of distinguished sportsmanship in golf. It is the highest honour bestowed by the Association, honouring, 'not Jones' accomplishments as a player, or his contributions to the game, but rather his spirit, his qualities as a human being and his attitude toward the game and its players.'

Three years later, on 9 October 1958, came one of the most moving ceremonies ever witnessed in golf, when Jones was made a Freeman of St Andrews. He was in the city as captain of the American team for the first Eisenhower Trophy, the world amateur team championship, and was by this time mostly confined to a wheelchair. He was welcomed by the provost, Robert Leonard. 'We wish to honour Mr Jones because we feel drawn to him by ties of affection and personal regard of a particularly cordial nature, and because we know that he himself has declared his own enduring affection for this place and for its people. We welcome him for his own sake; we welcome him also as an ambassador in the cause of international understanding and goodwill; we welcome him, moreover, not only as a distinguished golfer but also as a man of outstanding character, courage and accomplishment, well worthy to adorn the roll of our honorary burgesses.'

Jones famously replied, 'I could take out of my life everything except my experiences at St Andrews and I would still have had a rich and full life.' He added, 'This is the finest thing that has ever happened to me. Whereas that little cup was first in my heart, now this occasion at St Andrews will take first place always. I like to think about it this way, that now I officially have the right to feel at home in St Andrews as much as I, in fact, always have done.'

JOYCE WETHERED

Joyce Wethered, the outstanding woman golfer of her generation, perhaps of any generation, was a modest soul, as befitted a well-bred girl born in the south of England in 1901, at the end of the Victorian era. However, her competitive achievements were far from modest and she had plenty of admirers who were only too willing to wax lyrical about her ability.

Even in 1997 at the age of 95, Gene Sarazen, alert and aware, had no doubts. 'Joyce Wethered was the greatest woman golfer who ever lived,' he said. No one else – not Babe Zaharias, Mickey Wright or Laura Davies – could topple Sarazen's contemporary, who died later that year, from her pedestal.

Bobby Jones, then at the peak of his powers, played with her in a match at St Andrews in 1930 and commented, 'I have never played golf with anyone, man or woman, amateur or professional, who made me feel so utterly outclassed.' He recalled that they played the Old Course from the very back of the championship tees, with a slight wind blowing off the sea and that Wethered, round in 75, holed very little but never looked like missing a shot.

By then, she had given up championship golf for good, having been tempted out of retirement the year before to play in the Ladies' British Amateur championship at St Andrews. 'There was a magic about St Andrews,' she said. 'I loved it and I couldn't resist when the championship was there. I had to come back.' She won the title for the fourth time, defeating Glenna Collett (later Mrs Vare), who was to win the US Women's Amateur championship a record six times but never the British, in a final that was watched by thousands and featured golf and tension of the highest order.

Bernard Darwin, golf correspondent of *The Times*, was entranced. 'Many epithets will be used to describe the fluctuations of the match and the quality of the play. I feel unequal to the effort, and will let stark figures, with adjectives, speak. Miss Collett went out in 34 and was five up. She came home in 41 and pulled down to two at luncheon. She went out in 42, lost six holes out of nine, and was two down at the turn in the afternoon. She did the next eight holes in 36, including a seven, got one hole back, and lost by 3&1. It was a great match greatly played … As to Miss Wethered, if she prefers now once more to retire into private golf she can do so with the knowledge that she has given as complete proof of surpassing greatness as any game player of either sex that ever lived.'

Wethered honed her game playing with her older brother Roger (who was still an undergraduate at Oxford when he tied with Jock Hutchison for the 1921 Open at St Andrews – Hutchison winning the 36-hole play-off) and his university contemporaries like Cyril Tolley, who ranked with the best players of the time. Wethered, a perfectionist, also watched and played with the best professionals and developed

'A yard putt to win faced me on the 37th, a thing I had always prayed not to have. It went in and I went and sat down on a hillock by the beach and everyone came and stared at me as though I were something in a zoo. I was dead tired. My legs had left me. Usually when you won, the elation would carry you on, but not that time.'

a beautifully balanced swing, with a rhythm modelled on that of Jones himself. Henry Cotton said of her, 'In my time, no golfer has stood out so far ahead of his or her contemporaries.'

She won the English Ladies' championship five times in a row, starting in 1920, when she was an unknown quantity and caused a huge upset in the final by beating Cecil Leitch, the defending champion, for whom the word redoubtable might have been coined. Leitch beat Wethered in the finals of the French and the British in 1921 but was never to beat her younger rival again in major competition, losing to her in the final of the British Ladies' in 1922 and in 1925, at Troon, at the 37th.

Wethered, the defending champion, retired after that victory and her description of the aftermath helps explain her decision. She wrote, 'A yard putt to win faced me on the 37th, a thing I had always prayed not to have. It went in and I went and sat down on a hillock by the beach and everyone came and stared at me as though I were something in a zoo. I was dead tired. My legs had left me. Usually when you won, the elation would carry you on, but not that time.'

She had developed the knack of being able to wrap herself in a cocoon of concentration and appeared nerveless, which she confessed she was not. 'I was told I always looked very calm but I was frightfully shaky.' In 1921, at the inaugural Worplesdon Foursomes, Darwin wrote, 'I have never seen any woman play such faultless and masterly golf as Miss Wethered did in the semi-final round. With all the respect to her brother, who played some shots that hardly anybody else could play, it was she who was the cement of the partnership.' The Wethereds defeated Darwin and his partner comfortably in that semi-final but lost the final. They won the foursomes the following year and then, in the face of her mother's disapproval, Joyce changed partners. 'I had a lot of friends and I wanted to play with them,' she said.

She loved foursomes and, even after she gave up championship golf, she played at Worplesdon and won the competition eight times with seven different partners. Darwin was one of them and Wethered admitted that playing with him was 'the bravest thing I ever did. He was very irascible and he was not a good loser. He wanted to win frightfully and some people could not play with him. But I was so fond of him, and I knew it would pass. He was the same in a friendly family foursome on holiday.'

In 1935, Wethered toured the United States as a professional, playing over 50 exhibition matches with the likes of Jones, Sarazen and Zaharias, who was still very new to the game. Wethered always cherished a remark made by Jones after a match at East Lake. He had obviously been singing her praises but a lot of his countrymen thought he was exaggerating – until she went round in 74. Charlie Yates had 76 and Jones had 71. 'I knew you wouldn't let me down,' he said.

In 1937, Wethered married Sir John Heathcoat-Amory and devoted herself to him and their house and garden at Knightshayes Court in Devon, which now belongs to the National Trust. Lady Amory died in 1997 but well into her nineties she was still taking an interest in the feats of Davies, Ballesteros and company. She was disinclined to reminisce about her own career, saying simply, 'It was all so long ago.'

SAM SNEAD

Samuel Jackson Snead, Slammin' Sam as he was perhaps inevitably tagged, had a swing that was admired, coveted even, by more top-class players than perhaps any golfer who ever lived. He appeared to be a complete natural, able to hit the ball vast distances, with a loose and easy action, that looked as if it required no rehearsal. 'Sam,' said an envious rival, 'just walked up to the ball and poured honey all over it.'

He was a complete contradiction, both in terms of swing and character, to his two great contemporaries, Ben Hogan and Byron Nelson. Hogan worked all hours of the day and the night to find a swing that worked, while Nelson was simply the most efficient scorer and winner of his day. But Snead, with his often casual air and tall dominating manner, attracted the galleries – and the women – throughout his career, which ended with him winning the Masters three times, the US PGA three times and the Open once. Only five professionals in the history of the game have a better record than that.

There is however one outstanding omission from Snead's list: he never did win the US Open. It was a failure that prevented him from being ranked alongside the four players with whom he naturally attracted comparison: the Grand Slam winners Gene Sarazen, Ben Hogan, Jack Nicklaus and Gary Player. It was a failure that he always insisted did not bother him but if it did not – and that is doubtful – it bothered a great many other people who felt that the exclusive club could only be enhanced by his presence.

Snead came from the backwoods of Virginia, from Hot Springs, where he maintained a home all his life. He learned the game the hard way at White Sulphur Springs, the resort to which he was attached in the early days. On one occasion he was playing well in a tournament when a fellow pro said to him, just before the final round, in an attempt to put him off his game, 'How do you expect to do well with that left elbow flying around like that?' Snead shot 80 but he learned to hustle and was himself no stranger to the black art of gamesmanship. Still, it was in that early period that his reputation for being slow on the uptake, for being the archetypal hillbilly, was created. He had just won a tournament in Oakland, California when he was approached by a photographer who took a victory picture. It was duly wired around the country and appeared in a New York newspaper. A few days later Snead happened to see a copy and said, 'Hey, how could they get my picture in New York, I ain't never been there.'

That unprompted remark travelled around the world of golf, causing giggles wherever it went. The man in charge of the fledgling US Tour, a natural publicist called Fred Corcoran, seized on it. He told Snead that the reporters of the time loved the idea of someone sneaking out from the sticks and playing great golf and the man himself later admitted, 'I got the notion that playing up the hillbilly thing wasn't a bad idea.'

If he was notoriously slow on the uptake, that did not prevent him from asserting his opinion once it was formed. Snead was the captain of the 1969 US Ryder Cup team at Royal Birkdale when the match was halved because of a famous and quixotic gesture by Jack Nicklaus. The American conceded a short putt to Tony Jacklin, which had it been missed would have meant yet another US victory. Most of the world applauded a wonderfully generous and sporting moment but Snead, to whom it meant that he was not now a winning captain, seethed. Furthermore, he let Nicklaus know that he seethed.

On an earlier visit to Britain, Snead won the 1946 Open at St Andrews but he never liked the Old Course and, heresy or not, he didn't care who knew it. He got away with almost everything during one of the most durable careers golf has ever seen. He was, most of the time, an amiable man, a man's man, with a fund of stories that were very definitely not for mixed company. He won around 140 tournaments during his career, the exact number difficult to gauge, depending on what constituted a proper tournament during his early years.

His swing was generally admitted to be the most graceful of them all – Bobby Jones said he couldn't see how Sam could ever shoot above 70 – and it enabled him to become the oldest man ever to win on the US Tour. He took the Greater Greensboro Open in 1965 at the age of 52 years, 10 months and, perhaps the most incredible feat of all, produced rounds of 67,66 at the age of 67 in another tour event, the Quad Cities Open. In his later years beating his age became an almost daily event.

BABE ZAHARIAS

There's never been anyone like the Babe in the world of golf. People loved her or loathed her but no one ever ignored her, and there's no denying that the multi-talented, extrovert Texan, the toughie with the heart of gold, was unique.

The athlete of the century was a label the lady would have had no hesitation in bestowing on herself, for there was no false modesty about her. She was boisterous, brash, up front – and with good reason, for she excelled at almost everything bar humility. Even today, when women run marathons and only the fundamentalists are allowed to tut-tut out loud, she would be a sensation. In the 1930s, she was out of this world. She lit up the Depression and beyond and her feats became woven into myth and legend.

Mildred Ella Didriksen (Babe changed the spelling to Didrikson, more American) was born in 1911, although even that is not as simple and straightforward a statement as it should be, for several reference books give the date as 1914. Babe could be economical with the truth when it suited her and was never one for letting the facts get in the way of a good story. What is not disputed is that she developed into an exceptional athlete, fast, strong and combative, excelling at everything she turned her hand to, from baseball and bowling to basketball and rollerskating. She played a mean harmonica too, occasionally at the same time as knitting argyle socks on four needles. She was a one-woman track-and-field team and at the Olympic Games in Los Angeles in 1932 she won gold medals in the javelin and the hurdles and tied for first in the high jump before being disqualified because her head-first style, previously uncriticized, was declared illegal. This daughter of Norwegian immigrants was a national heroine and kept the press and public entertained with a sharp wit that rarely owed much to diplomacy. Golf was never quite the same genteel game when the Babe was around.

At first she tried to beat the ball to death and, when she played in a couple of exhibition games with Joyce Wethered in the mid-1930s, she liked to boast that she could outhit the Englishwoman off the tee with a two-iron, although at that stage she was not in the same league as a golfer. 'I've often thought how lucky I was to play my golf before she came on the scene,' Wethered said, with the sort of modesty that was completely alien to Babe.

Hitting the ball a long way was never a problem for Babe and she loved the effect her power had on onlookers, who were amazed that this relatively slight figure could pack such a punch. It took her a little longer to appreciate the nuances of the game

Babe Zaharias.

and Gene Sarazen wrote, 'When Babe Didrickson was first turning to golf, her desire to be a sensationally long hitter retarded her development. Babe would close the face of the seven-iron and toe it in and belly the ball 170 yards. When Babe stopped kidding herself and began playing a seven like a seven and not like a two, she started to develop a grooved swing and a glorious golf game.'

A lot of hard work and devoted practice turned the Babe into a formidable competitor but not everyone approved of her and the USGA rescinded her amateur status because she had been a professional athlete and played other games as a professional. It wasn't until 1943 that she was reinstated, by which time she was Mrs Zaharias, having married George, a large wrestler billed as 'The Crying Greek from Cripple Creek.'

In 1946, Babe won the US Women's Amateur and the following year she took Scotland by storm when she won the British Ladies' Amateur at Gullane, watched by huge crowds, herded by white-coated stewards. She was the first American to take the title and George, whose eye for publicity was as sharp as his wife's, loaded a tug with reporters and photographers and steamed out to meet her on her return to New York.

The myth has it that Babe won 17 consecutive events in 1946 and 1947 but her streak lasted a mere 13 – she and George conveniently forgot a first-round defeat in the US Women's Open, then a matchplay event, a case of over-egging the legend. Babe turned professional again and in 1948 won the first of her three US Open titles, now strokeplay. Managed by Fred Corcoran, she played numerous exhibitions, raking in the money at a time when most people thought there wasn't much of a living to be made from golf.

Babe also provided a focal point for the fledgling women's professional tour. Patty Berg, a stylist and showwoman in her own right, was overshadowed like everyone else but she was a fan who appreciated that Babe drew the crowds and did not resent her hogging all the attention. 'She had so much flair, colour and showmanship,' Berg said. 'We needed her.'

Not everyone was so enamoured. No saint and a congenital exaggerator, Babe would claim to have gone round in 68 in practice when everyone knew it was 74 or more. It was good for business but some players called it lying – quietly, of course. She also had an irritating habit of breezing into the locker-room and asking who was going to finish second that week. It was not entirely tongue-in-cheek and served its purpose if it ruffled the opposition. Babe hated losing, and the official LPGA handbook credits her with 31 victories out of 128 events. She was one of the four original inductees into the LPGA Hall of Fame in 1951.

Babe's greatest triumph was the US Women's Open of 1954, the year after she had surgery for cancer of the bowel. At the time of her operation, which received widespread publicity, it was thought that she would never play championship golf again. But normal rules did not apply to Babe and she recovered to win the Open by 12 shots – with nothing more than a five on her card in the 72 holes – from Betty Hicks, with Louise Suggs a further four shots behind. Babe won four other tournaments that year and she also won twice in 1955, but her health started to deteriorate again and even her indomitable will could not stave off the disease. She died in 1956, at the age of 45.

The Tour nearly died with her – Babe was the person most people came out to see – but it survived and perhaps that's the best legacy of all.

BYRON NELSON

If it were possible to tack together the talents of, say, Tiger Woods with his extreme length and Phil Mickelson with his wonderful short game and amalgamate them in one athlete, it might well be that the combination would win a few tournaments and a fair bit of money in one season. But do you think that even such a massively-gifted mythical figure would win 18 tournaments, 11 of them consecutively, come second in seven more, and take home US$10 million in a single season? The odds could well be against it. Only one person has ever won that number of tournaments in a season and he actually won only US$63,335 worth of war bonds for his trouble, which since it was in 1945 would be worth the aforementioned millions now.

The man who did it was Byron Nelson, known to television viewers only as the avuncular, kindly-looking, old man who annually opened proceedings at the Masters with Sam Snead and Gene Sarazen by hitting a single shot off the first tee. No one has come even vaguely close to equalling his remarkable achievement and no one ever will.

'The Streak' as it has become known in America has never really received true recognition, in the States or the rest of the world. This was partly because communications were not brilliant at the time, partly because most of the rest of the world was still pre-occupied with other matters, and partly because there was the suspicion that it had been achieved against less than full-strength opposition.

The last point receives short shrift from Jackie Burke jnr, who won four tournaments in a row in 1952, the next-best since The Streak. 'I don't care,' said Burke, 'if he was playing against orang-utans, 11 straight is amazing.' And so it is. Winning at any level requires a level of commitment and concentration and a willingness to go through psychological pain barriers that few people possess. To do it 18 times in a season beggars belief. It also drained the man himself.

One year later, aged only 34, he retired from golf and, with the money he had made, bought a ranch in Texas. It was what he had always wanted for, unlike the majority of great champions who are obsessive about their golf, the competitive game was really a means to an end for Nelson. As soon as he had enough money to stop, he did so and pretty much remained stopped thereafter.

Winning at any level requires a level of commitment and concentration and a willingness to go through psychological pain barriers that few people possess. To do it 18 times in a season beggars belief. It also drained the man himself.

Nelson has always been criticized for that decision on the grounds that he did not fully exploit his talent. But a substantial clue as to why he did it is contained in Al Barkow's *Gettin' to the Dance Floor*. In 1944, the year prior to The Streak, Nelson realized that he did not always concentrate hard enough. He went on, 'The truth is when you're playing well you quit concentrating. You can get a little complacent if you're playing good, good, good. It can get kinda boring when you're playing as well as I was – and then all of a sudden you quit paying attention.'

Having resolved to concentrate and work on his chipping, Nelson proceeded to his year of years. In 1945 he had no fewer than 25 rounds of 66 and, having averaged 69.67 during 1944 (winning six Tour events), he brought that down to 67.92 in 1945. At a time when the prize money list was only 12–15 places long he made money in 113 consecutive tournaments, an indication not only of his brilliance but also of his consistency.

The Streak began in March, in Miami, in a fourball competition. Nelson played with one of his lifetime friends, Harold 'Jug' McSpaden, and in the quarter-finals they beat Ben Hogan and Ed Dudley. Sam Snead was also in that field and, like Hogan, featured in almost all the tournaments that made up The Streak.

The richest event of the year was the Tam O'Shanter Open in Chicago, with US$60,000 in war bonds as a prize fund. Nelson with rounds of 66,68,68,67 won by 11 shots from a man billed as Lieutenant B. Hogan. Gene Sarazen was joint second. By that time Nelson had already won the US PGA championship, during which he survived a real threat. He recovered from two down with four to play to beat Mike Turnesa, one of seven brothers, all pros, who was seven-under par for the match. 'How are you supposed to beat this man?' Turnesa asked.

It was almost as if Nelson could not help himself. After winning seven in a row he could feel the pressures building to the point where he was fed up with success. He said to his first wife, Louise, before the first round of the eighth event that he felt like blowing up and 'getting it over with'. When he came in, Louise said, 'Well, did you blow up?' 'Yeah,' he said wearily, 'I shot 66.'

Not all Nelson's best golf was played that year. In 1937 he won the Masters despite being four behind Ralph Guldahl with only seven holes to play. Two years later he won the US Open at the Philadelphia Country Club, taking charge of the play-off with Craig Wood and Denny Shute by holing a one-iron second shot for an eagle two at the fourth.

Altogether Nelson won five major championships: the Masters in 1937 and 1942, the US Open in 1939 and the US PGA in 1940 and 1945. Including those events he had a total of 52 victories, including the 11 in succession. 'Nowadays,' he said, 'people don't play 11 in succession, much less win them.' Typically he went on, 'I prefer to be remembered as being friendly and a good Christian man rather than as a golfer. I got sick and tired of competing. Nobody understands it, but I never did feel I quit too soon.'

BEN HOGAN

The chronicler must get close to his subject to do it thorough justice and, as Ben Hogan was almost as famous for being publicly gestureless as he was for his golf, personal close-ups and human interest stories concerning the great (greatest?) golfer do not abound. Much has been said and written about Hogan's inability or refusal to communicate with all and sundry and there were some who even called him surly. Byron Nelson knew him as well as most and said of his inclination to stay clear of the media and of strangers generally, 'Ben was naturally shy and enjoyed his privacy,' adding, 'he was the most dedicated man to his profession that I ever met.'

There is therefore one context, one only, in which history can evaluate or even discuss the man – championship golf. Immediately we start with superlatives. Was Hogan the best there ever was? To ask that question, or to argue it, is the biggest compliment that we are able to pay. It is asked of only one other man, Jack Nicklaus – or two, if you include Bobby Jones. Nicklaus amassed 18 major titles, while Hogan 'only' won nine, so is it reasonable to conclude that, as the major tournaments are the true test of greatness, Nicklaus was twice the golfer that Hogan was? As nobody has ever argued that, then we may remove mere statistical elements from the debate.

And yet … At some stage we must judge a golfer on the things that he wins and if we throw in Nicklaus 18, Hogan nine as a measure then we have to counter by mentioning 1953. In that momentous year, Hogan won three major championships and did not play in the other. That proves his greatness. That makes him unique. In all his career, he claimed 63 US tour victories. Only Sam Snead (81) and Nicklaus (70) won more. Nicklaus, Jones and Willie Anderson were the only men to match Hogan's four US Open victories and only Nicklaus and Walter Hagen (11) won more majors.

'Record? Oh! that's nice,' said Hogan, 'but I was only trying to win a golf tournament.' And when Hogan tried to win a golf tournament in that extraordinary year, he almost always did.

When golfers are gathered together between, say, the Masters and the US Open, the conversation frequently turns to the possibility of the new Masters champion going on to win the other three majors. Speculation is usually dead by the last day of the next major championship. For it has happened just five times that the winner at Augusta has the four-timer still in his sights after the US Open. The last time that it happened was in 1972 when Nicklaus won in Georgia and then at Pebble Beach. Before that, in 1941, Craig Wood won the Masters and the US Open, at Colonial; Hogan completed the double at Oakland Hills in 1951; and Arnold Palmer rounded off a neat little pair at Cherry Hills in 1960.

Ben Hogan

Two major championships in a season have been beyond nearly all of the finest golfers yet seen. All four – the Grand Slam – is believed to be an achievement beyond any golfer. But three, right next door to the impossible … that was done by Ben Hogan in that wondrous summer of 1953.

The year before Hogan had played a poor Masters and he finished tied for seventh. Next he finished third in the US Open at Northwood and this was only relatively good because he had tied the US Open record with a half-way total of 138 only to finish with a pair of undistinguished 74s. He may well have spent the winter pondering his fallibility and it is typical Hogan that the memory enhanced the resolve.

At Augusta the following April, he played what he described as the best golf of his life. This amounted to an aggregate score of 274, which broke the old record by five shots, and he won by five from Porky Oliver.

'Record? Oh! that's nice,' said Hogan, 'but I was only trying to win a golf tournament.' And when Hogan tried to win a golf tournament in that extraordinary year, he almost always did. He played only six events, won five of them and finished tied for third in the other.

In June, he was at Oakmont for the US Open. If his first round, a five-under 67, which gave him a three-shot lead, suggested a dawdle, it was nothing like that. This was a championship to be hewn rather than taken by divine gift. Sam Snead was after this title, too and his second-round 69 closed the difference to two shots. At the start of the fourth round, Hogan's lead had dwindled to one. Prophetically, he told the media that the tournament could come down to the last three holes and, when he came to them, Hogan was one-over for the round. He knew he was in the lead but not its extent. He did appreciate, though, the capability of Snead, who was playing behind him. Was Hogan to play in safely or did he require some extra insurance? He answered the question some time later. 'All you can do in a situation like that is try to play as well as you can, one hole at a time' and, one hole at a time, he was utterly brilliant.

'I've had a lot of blessings in my life and one of them was watching Ben Hogan hit balls.' Ben Crenshaw.

He waved an imperious two-wood away to the 234-yard 16th. Par. Then on to Oakmont's old 17th, a 292-yard par four, all uphill – and mind those abyssal bunkers. In three rounds Hogan had played short of them and budgeted for certain pars. Now he took his driver and aiming for the narrow gap to the green, put himself within 30 feet of an eagle two. He 'settled' for the birdie.

Oakmont's 462-yard 18th is fairly widely accepted as one of the finest closing holes in golf and Hogan's drive accounted for the first 300 yards of it. He paused for a drag on his cigarette, plucked a five-iron from his bag and laid the ball eight feet from the pin. He had finished 3,3,3 and beaten Snead, the only other man to get below 290, by six shots. It was his fourth US Open in six years.

His CV now read: two US PGA titles (1946, 1948), two Masters triumphs (1951, 1953) and four US Opens (1948, 1950, 1951, 1953) – yet it was incomplete. It did not include the Open championship. Hogan was reminded, from inside and outside Britain, that greatness would elude him, that he would have but a toehold on the pantheon, if he did not win golf's most venerable trophy in the heartland of the game.

He journeyed to Scotland for the 1953 Open at Carnoustie, where he conducted an autopsy in advance of slaying it. He learned so much so thoroughly about the intricacies of the course that he was able over the four rounds to post descending scores of ascending excellence: 73,71,70,68. He won by four shots. On his return from Europe, Hogan found a tickertape welcome awaiting him in New York. Three days later, there was a celebratory parade along the streets of his home town, Fort Worth.

Four men have won all the world's major championships: Hogan, Nicklaus, Gary Player and Gene Sarazen. None has won them consecutively. That Hogan should go closest sets him apart and also raises the question of why, in a year in which he was uniquely dominant, did he not even try for the Grand Slam? For some, that question has not been answered entirely satisfactorily. The notion that the scheduling of the US PGA and the Open precluded his playing in both has apparently been rejected. The widely accepted reason is that because the PGA was at that time a matchplay event, Hogan because of the effects of a bad road crash in 1949 did not have the physical resources to play two 18-hole matches a day before a possible 36-hole semi-final

Four men have won all the world's major championships: Hogan, Nicklaus, Gary Player and Gene Sarazen. None has won them consecutively. That Hogan should go closest sets him apart and also raises the question of why, in a year in which he was uniquely dominant, did he not even try for the Grand Slam?

and a 36-hole final. History will excuse the man on those utterly reasonable grounds.

However, 36 holes a day was not uncommon in those days. Had not Hogan played every day, hitting three balls at every hole, in the fortnight prior to the Open? Including the qualifying rounds, had he not played 108 holes in the championship? And can we not wonder if a strong reason for Hogan not playing the US PGA was a basic dislike of matchplay golf? Americans after all have a national aversion to that form of the game.

That said, Hogan was to play a significant part of his career under extreme physical duress. He was at the height of his powers when he had that head-on car crash with a bus on his way home to Fort Worth. On impact, Hogan is said to have thrown himself across his wife, Valerie, to save her from certain death and he received injuries so severe that the last rites were read. The local radio stations even announced his obituary.

Fortunately, those reports were premature but his multiple injuries were such that there were genuine doubts that he would ever walk again. That he should play golf again, any kind of golf, was not a thought that occurred to his closest medical advisers. Which is how the real Ben Hogan story became a Hollywood story, duly made into a film in 1951 entitled *Follow the Sun* and starring Glenn Ford. Even Hollywood does not get too many plots as unlikely as this one.

Later in the year of the crash (1949), Hogan had travelled to Ganton, in Yorkshire, to captain the American Ryder Cup team. Within 12 months of the accident he was playing tournament golf and was beaten in a play-off for the Los Angeles Open by Snead. One month later, Hogan won an 18-hole play-off to lift his second US Open. He was frequently in pain and he blamed his failure to win the 1955 US Open on the fact that his undercarriage had failed him.

Pain and more pain and through it all Hogan played perhaps the purest golf that has ever been seen. He was, according to a very insistent lobby, the greatest striker of the golf ball of them all and Nicklaus said 'hear, hear' to that. Talent he obviously had but, from all the accounts that survive, it was sheer dedication that put him apart from the rest.

Born in Dublin, Texas, in August 1912, he was nine years old when his father committed suicide – he shot himself while Ben was in the room. He and his brother and sister were then taken by his mother to live in Fort Worth and it was there as a 12-year-old that he became a caddie. In his spare time, after a false start (he was a natural left-hander), he became a golfer, turned pro at the age of 19 but had to wait nine years for his first victory and 15 years for his first major.

Through his younger days, Hogan was in conflict with a hook. He had a ruinous tendency to over-swing and he took years to find the knack of hitting the ball consistently straight or, better still, to order. Hogan always insisted that there was no such thing as a deliberately hit straight shot. There is fade, there is draw but, he insisted, 'you only hit a straight ball by accident'. This from a man who may well have spent more time on the practice range than any other before or since. The game accepts that he invented the modern concept of practice and when his recorded views on the subject are trotted out there is invariably a reference to a Gary Player anecdote.

'Young man,' Hogan said to Player, 'you're going to be a fine player. Do you practise a lot?'

'Oh, yes, Mr Hogan,' Player replied, 'I love to practise'.

'Double it,' said Hogan.

The leading players of Hogan's day, and many of those who followed him, queue up to endorse the legend of his skills and attitude. 'I've had a lot of blessings in my life and one of them was watching Ben Hogan hit balls,' said Ben Crenshaw. 'He was as close to perfection as any human being has ever been hitting a golf ball,' added Dave Marr.

Inevitably there were a few myths with which to embellish the essentials and one of them was that Hogan had a secret, the secret of the golf swing. And it was known to few, if any. The word secret could well have been used in the wrong sense: it was not a secret but the knack of hitting a golf ball that Hogan acquired to a degree unmatched by any other player and he possessed that knack because he searched longer and harder than any other man to find it. The best place to learn about Hogan's supposed secret is in his instruction book, *The Fundamentals of Modern Golf.* It remains one of the most helpful manuals ever printed.

MICKEY WRIGHT

Ben Hogan was not prone to hyperbole, so when he said that someone had the best swing that he ever saw, it was praise not bestowed lightly. The object of his admiration was a tall blonde Californian called Mickey – Mary Kathryn – Wright, who started to dominate the LPGA Tour in the late 1950s and was well-nigh unbeatable in the early 1960s – when golf was just wild about Arnie Palmer and Jack Nicklaus was starting to make a mark. Wright was a quiet reserved person in the Wethered mould and her idea of the ideal round was to tee off at dawn all by herself, play her round, come in and go home. All that helps explain why she is not better known, despite a record that ranks her as an indisputable great, a player whose contemporaries were in awe of her talent and unstinting in their admiration.

Wright won 82 tournaments in a professional career that started when she was 20 and from 1961 to 1964 she was without peer, heading the money list for four successive years and winning 44 individual tournaments. Kathy Whitworth, she of 88 wins, is a devotee bordering on the evangelical. 'To my mind, and in many people's mind, Wright was the greatest player that ever lived. She certainly had the greatest golf swing and Hogan, Nelson and Watson said the same thing. Her execution was just so near perfect in such an imperfect world. The pity is that people didn't realize it and, of course, now they never will. But when you could actually hear the ball leave the club face and see it, you just were dumbfounded, it was so great to watch. You knew you were playing with someone far superior.'

Betsy Rawls, another noted technician, whose record of four US Women's Open titles was matched by Wright, was also lavish in her praise. 'Mickey set a standard of shotmaking that will probably never be equalled. Her swing was as flawless as a golf swing can be – smooth, efficient, powerful, rhythmical and beautiful.' Harvey Penick, who taught Rawls and Whitworth, also helped Wright and said he didn't dare change her swing because it was too perfect. He remembered that her favourite pastime was to go to Fort Worth and sit and watch Hogan practise. The great man told her he didn't mind, 'as long as you don't say anything'.

The respect between Rawls and Wright, nearly seven years younger, was mutual. They were soulmates – students of the game and highly intelligent people of the utmost integrity. Wright, who dislikes public speaking (despite the priceless asset of a warm, deep, resonant voice) and detests the limelight, even agreed to speak at the USGA's annual meeting in 1996 when Rawls, a rules buff, was presented with the Bob Jones Award and Judy Bell, another remarkable woman, was elected president.

Whitworth will regale you for ever with tales of Wright's shotmaking prowess and used to love it when her heroine got into trouble, for it invariably meant a jaw-dropping demonstration of control and skill that defied belief. What's more, it was all done with a Lyle-like insouciance that made a difficult shot look the easiest thing in the world. There was a minimum of fuss, no prowling and head shaking à la Ballesteros. 'That's not to say Mickey didn't take great pride and get a great thrill when she hit a good shot,' Whitworth said. 'It's just that there was no fanfare whatsoever.'

Born in 1935 in San Diego, Wright won the US Girls' Junior championship in 1952 (the only matchplay title she could recall winning, being a devotee of technique and the demanding discipline of strokeplay). In 1954, she was the leading amateur in the US Women's Open, tied for fourth with Rawls, 17 shots behind Babe Zaharias, with whom Wright played the last 36 holes. She admitted she was terrified but broke 80 in both rounds on what was an extremely emotional occasion, since Zaharias had had an operation for cancer the year before.

Wright spent a year at Stanford, studying psychology, before joining the Tour in 1955. She won her first tournament, the Jacksonville Open, in 1956 and won three times in 1957. In 1958, she served notice that she would fulfil all the great expectations when she won five events, including the US Women's Open and the LPGA championship, the first time any player had won both titles in the same season. Wright, who was 23, remained the youngest winner of the Open until Catherine Lacoste superseded her in 1967, but her record-winning total of 290 lasted only a year. She beat it herself by three shots in 1959, despite having so much trouble with her putting that she had to make several SOS (save our score) calls to short-game guru Paul Runyan during the championship.

In 1960, Wright added six more victories to her tally, and in 1961 she moved into overdrive – and stayed there for four years. She won 10 times in 1961, including three of the four major championships, the US Women's Open, the LPGA and the Titleholders. In 1962 she won another 10 tournaments, including four in a row and in 1963 it was 13, including another run of four straight. In the Titleholders, she lost an 18-hole play-off to Marilynn Smith, who rated it the highlight of her career. Wright, Smith pointed out, was at her peak, 'She had beautiful mechanics, wonderful tempo and rhythm and a deep desire to win.'

In 1964, Wright could still do no wrong and won 11 times but the strain was beginning to tell. She put a lot of pressure on herself to perform and in many eyes she carried the tour: if she didn't play, sponsors wanted to know why; and if she didn't win, everyone wondered what was wrong. She had ulcers, did not sleep well and began to have trouble with her wrist and her feet. In 1965, she decided to go back to college but that didn't work and she returned to play the tour, more or less full-time, until the end of 1969. She won her last tournament in 1973 but in 1979, when very much an occasional competitor, she was one of five to tie for the Coca-Cola Classic. Nancy Lopez, the new sensation, won the play-off.

The mantle had been passed on but Wright had reminded everyone of the stuff of champions.

ARNOLD PALMER

Golf has raised no greater celebrity than Arnold Palmer. In his playing career he did most of what there was to do, but by far his greatest achievement was to become an American folk hero, accepted as such by all those with even just a passing interest in the sport.

Few men ever made more money out of golf than Palmer and his image was used to sell almost every conceivable thing, from cans of oil to tractors, from Cadillacs to Rolexes, from private banks to batteries and the money poured in – but he was always unimpressed by wealth, his own or anyone else's. Because of his tremendous successes and his incredible popularity he has, in his time, been urged to run for almost every office, up to and including President of the United States, but has not considered any of them. For this is a man who is happiest at home, down in his den where he has a Rolling Rock beer dispenser, or tinkering in his workshop. He has always been at his happiest with a few close friends, sipping a few beers and telling the tale.

Palmer still lives in Latrobe, the small Pennsylvania town in which he was raised. His father, Deacon – Deke – was the professional and greenkeeper at the golf course there and remained so, even when his son bought the place, until he died. He instilled into his son the virtues of hard work and honesty, of straight dealing and plain speaking. For decades now Palmer has been applauded on to every green and every tee of every golf course he has played. His response has been to wave or smile, sometimes to wink and then, unconsciously, hitch up his trousers. It became his trademark – the Palmer 'hitch'. Women have been known to swoon.

The hitch has been a habit all his adult life and arose from his build. Palmer is built like a middleweight, with exceptionally broad shoulders and a wasp waist, and the shirt has not been made that is broad enough to cover those shoulders and sufficiently narrow to stay inside a pair of his trousers. As a result his shirt is always half out of his trousers – even as a young boy Palmer was always being chided for it by his mother.

The legend of Palmer the home boy has always said that he loves nothing more than to spend an hour or two fiddling with his golf clubs, lead-taping the head, perhaps, or in the old days, putting on a fresh whipping. Palmer is certainly a happy man at home. But the reluctant-legend theory loses its credibility when it insists that he would have traded celebrity for a quiet life in Latrobe. For Palmer is one of life's great competitors. He had a fierce and raging desire to be successful at golf, which was so powerful that had it been denied expression in that particular sport it would have taken him to the top in some other field.

Larry Guest, in his book *Arnie: Inside the Legend*, told the story of when Palmer found himself drawn for the final round of the 1980 Masters with Jack Nicklaus, a man with whom he had a rabid rivalry for many years. It had begun at Oakmont in the 1962 US Open, when Nicklaus, pudgy-faced, double-chinned and apparently arrogant, had the temerity to beat Palmer in front of regiments of his Army. 'Go back to Ohio, Fat Jack,' they yelled and 'Arnie you ain't' in an unseemly display of favouritism.

Palmer didn't like it but there was not much he could do about it and he liked even less the fact that he was being beaten by some kid rookie. It was the start of a relationship that has ranged from friendly to hostile over the years and has always had to accommodate the soaring ambitions of both men and has not always succeeded.

At Augusta in 1980 the two were one stroke apart after three rounds and the draw brought them together. At this stage Palmer had not won a major championship since 1964 and had not won on the regular US Tour since 1973, when at the age of 43 he took the Bob Hope Desert Classic. Nicklaus, on the other hand, had won a major in the last 12 months and was to win another, the 1986 Masters. It should have been no contest. When Palmer heard about the draw, he punched the air in delight and shouted, 'I'll whip his ass.' Prior to that round Palmer had not broken 70 in his last 18 attempts at Augusta but, as wife Winnie observed, 'Arnie plays good when he's got something like this to light his fire.' That day he was round in 69, to the 73 of Nicklaus, and his grin was as wide as could be.

Palmer is besotted both with the game and with Augusta and when, in January 1997 he got the telephone call that all ageing men dread, to tell him that he had prostate cancer, he straightaway asked his doctors, 'If I have immediate surgery, how long is the recovery period?' The answer was 42 days and with a quick mental calculation Palmer worked out that he could be fit enough to play in the Masters if all went well. It did, and not only was he well enough to play Augusta but he also competed in his own Bay Hill Invitational in Orlando, Florida, three weeks before.

He was practising for that event the week before when who should stroll on to the practice ground but a new resident of the Orlando area, Tiger Woods. Aware of the young phenomenon's hitting prowess, the 67-year-old Palmer waited until he got a drive flush out of the middle of the club, which even so might have finished 80 yards behind a Woods special and turned and growled 'Watch out Tiger'. The two all but collapsed with laughter.

They had a brief conversation. Palmer asked Woods if he was enjoying his new life on the US Tour, and the young man said, 'Yeah, because the thing is I love to play golf.' It was exactly the right thing to say. Palmer responded, 'Well, that's good. I know something about that. It's a problem I've had for about the last 60 years.'

Palmer's passion for, and childish delight in, the game itself has always communicated itself to crowds who created for themselves that loosely knit, wholly unorganized, completely instinctive body called Arnie's Army. It marched wherever Arnie went, to the beat of the Palmer drum, but unlike other armies, when their general lost his ability to win, they did not disintegrate or slyly or sadly slip off home. Even when the head told them that tournament victories were no longer likely, the heart insisted that they stay.

For watching Palmer has always engaged the emotions. To the men he is a fighter who, rather than walk on to the first tee, clambers through the ropes, strides over to the red corner and starts shadow boxing. He is about to go 18 rounds with an opponent that simply has to be smashed to smithereens.

The women, it seems, sense the strength and feel the magnetism and yet detect a vulnerability, too. There have always been a high proportion of female members of the Army, attracted perhaps in the early days by the almost cherubic countenance combined with a ferocity of style that was, and is, unique.

Palmer was for ever in trouble. That slashing swing, with its windmill finish, could not be guaranteed to keep the ball out of the trees, nor did it. Jim Murray, the great Los Angeles sportswriter, told the story of being on the course one day. 'Arnold knocked the ball way into the rough. It was in a pile of twigs and leaves and I think there was a dead squirrel and a beer can in there too. Anyway he walked over and stared down at his ball. And then he saw me standing there and asked, "Okay wiseguy what would your idol Hogan do here?" I told him "Hogan wouldn't be here."'

Palmer, Birkdale.

When Palmer found the trees, instead of the sagging shoulders, he embraced the trouble he found; he went deep into the trees with his head held high – literally, for he was looking for every conceivable escape route. 'Trouble,' he once said, 'is bad to get into but fun to get out of. If you're in trouble, 80 per cent of the time there's a way out. I suppose,' he added, 'that there's a place to play it safe but as far as I'm concerned it's not on the golf course.' Revealingly, he also once said, 'The only really unplayable lie I can think of is when you're supposed to be playing golf and you come home with lipstick on your collar.'

Because of the way he played, fuelled by intensity and in sporadic spells of brilliance, the word that attached itself to his game was 'charge'. Palmer became known for his last-round charges from several strokes behind to the victory podium and it was never better illustrated than at Cherry Hills in the 1960 US Open. Just before the final round Palmer was sitting talking to Bob Drum, a sportswriter with a blunt perspective on life. Drum thought that Palmer had no chance of winning and said so. Palmer thought that a little 65 might have a chance but Drum was dismissive. Then Palmer went out and drove the first green, all of 346 yards, went out in 30, was round in 65 and won his only US Open. The 'charge', first seen that year when he finished birdie, birdie, birdie at Augusta to win the Masters, was enshrined.

Not that it always worked, of course. That same year, in the US PGA, Palmer took eight at one hole and that championship became the one he never won, the one that kept him from joining the most exclusive group in golf history, those who have won all four of golf's majors.

He made his first trip to the Open in 1960, driven by the thought that if he wanted undiluted international acclaim as the best player in the world, he would have to prove it outside the United States, and principally in Scotland, birthplace of the game. The Open, the Centenary Open, that year was at St Andrews, the home of golf: what better place, and what better time, to win? That he did not is a thoroughgoing comment on the occasional unfitness of things. Once again there was a charge, but it was left too late, for Palmer was four behind with six to play and could not catch the Australian, Kel Nagle.

Palmer won the Open at Birkdale the following year and defended successfully at Troon in 1962. There is a plaque to him at Birkdale, to mark one of his trademark recoveries. In the final round, his drive at what is now the par-four 16th kicked into a patch of tangled heather and gorse and most pros would have taken a penalty drop. Palmer waded in with a six-iron and slashed the ball on to the green. He won by one shot from Dai Rees.

Palmer won his last championship in 1964, his last tournament in America in 1973 and his last in Europe in 1975. Since then there have been more farewells than from Dame Nellie Melba or Frank Sinatra. In 1980, for example, at the Muirfield Open, Palmer openly speculated that this might be his last visit. Pat Ward-Thomas, *The Guardian*'s golf correspondent and an ardent fan of Palmer, wrote, 'The first two days of this championship may have been Palmer's farewell to competing in the Open. He looked so fit and alert that I could hardly believe 20 years had passed since he played so great a part in starting the modern era of championship golf.' Privately, Ward-Thomas, who retired a year or two later, was more direct. 'Keep going,' he urged his hero, 'at least see me out.'

Palmer was to do that comfortably. The man who loves competition and golf in equal, and huge, measure could not tear himself away from the game. He was back for the 1984 Open at St Andrews, he was back for the return there in 1990 and he played one last US Open in 1994, at Oakmont. If ever there was a place to bring down the curtain on his career in national Opens, this was it. He missed the cut by 11 and there was an emotional farewell – on the course and off. Every time he got half way through a sentence, he broke down – and the towel he had draped over his shoulders because of the extreme heat and humidity was working overtime. Palmer managed a few, choked thoughts, 'It's been 40 years of … fun … work … enjoyment …' and there was a very, very long pause …

GARY PLAYER

There is a famous criticism of Mozart: too many notes. In the case of Gary Player perhaps it should be too many visions, for surely nobody in all golf history has had so many visitations from above, assuring him absolutely that he would win that week.

This small but perfectly formed golfer from South Africa makes no secret of his allegiance to the Lord, and indeed why should he? He ascribes a large part of his incredible success to Him and out of all the people he has met in one of the most-travelled lives of our times says that the evangelist Billy Graham is 'the finest man I've ever met'. Whether or not this is the secret, the fact is that Gary Player became only the third man in history to win all four of the principal championships in his career.

But Player knew he was going to do it. In *Grand Slam Golf*, he revealed, 'I got the message. It is an indescribable feeling, which I have had four or five times in my life, the positive, powerful feeling, indeed certainty, that I was going to win the championship. Before the Masters of 1961 I said I would win it and that I would win all four major championships because I had been given a message by God.'

He won in 1961 all right but he had already won the 1959 Open at Muirfield with the help of what the irreverent might claim was an outside agency. Before the final day's play – all 36 holes of it – Player told his clubmaking representative that, despite being eight shots behind the leader, he was going to win. He said, 'Tomorrow you're going to see a small miracle. In fact you're going to see a large miracle. I'm going to win the British Open.' He did, too, despite a double-bogey six at the last hole, which reduced him to tears and the certainty that he would be caught. He wasn't.

Player got some terrestrial help from Arnold Palmer in winning the Masters in 1961, having told manager Mark McCormack at the start of the week that he was going to win. 'I said to him in complete sincerity that I was going to win the Masters because I was sure that God wanted me to win it,' said Player. In the end, Palmer needed a par at the last to win and took a double-bogey six.

Player's third major arrived a year later, when he won the US PGA at Aronomink, a Donald Ross course in Pennsylvania. 'Again,' he won he said, 'in a manner which makes me convinced that from time to time I really am blessed and that my life in some mysterious way is pre-ordained.' This time Player had been through what he called 'a period of despair' during which he lost a play-off for the Masters after being three ahead and then simply gave in at the Open at Troon. He admitted that he did not appreciate the hard bouncy conditions, so much so that during the back nine of the second round, 'I reached the point of thinking that the whole thing was useless and pointless and I just batted the ball in over the last few holes.' After this un-Player-like behaviour, the South African rang manager McCormack. 'I don't think I can go on with this ridiculous life ... chasing around the world like an idiot ... living out of a suitcase.' It was the depression of the long-distance traveller and no one has travelled further in pursuit of golf's grand titles than Player.

Player did, however, go to Aronomink and was mighty glad that he did. 'Here was a marvellous course,' he said, 'green and ripe, with lush fairways, dazzling white bunkers, holding greens, lovely trees everywhere. The whole setting was so peaceful and sympathetic to me, after the brutalities of Troon, that I felt happy and relaxed and invigorated.'

There was only one left for the Slam but Player had to wait nearly three years for that, for the US Open at Bellerive near St Louis, Missouri in 1965. 'An extraordinary thing happened before the championship,' he said. 'By the first tee there was a big scoreboard which included all the names of the previous US Open winners. The first time I walked past that scoreboard I saw in beautiful gold letters that it said '1965 G-A-R-Y P-L-A-Y-E-R.' Every time I passed that board from then on, it said the same thing.'

Perhaps the only golfer not to read that scoreboard that week was Kel Nagle, a pragmatic Aussie who would have assumed that someone was messing about had he seen any gold lettering. The two men tied and Player won the play-off. 'As I fished the ball out, after the final putt, I paused and gave thanks to God.'

Player's Christianity was presumably of the muscular variety, for in *Grand Slam Golf* he revealed himself as an outspoken supporter of apartheid. 'I must say now, and clearly, that I am of the South Africa of Verwoerd and apartheid … I just wish that the people who criticize my country would make a little effort to understand it more fully, because I am proud of it.' By the time *Gary Player: To Be the Best* was published in 1991, his views had been tempered.

He admitted he was once of the Verwoerd persuasion but found it astonishing that he was regarded 'as a spokesman for apartheid'. He could not understand why he was vilified for not taking a stand when Sewsunker Sewgolum, a Cape Coloured, had to stand outside in the rain after winning the Natal Open in 1963. 'I knew nothing about the incident,' Player protested. 'I did not even play in the event.'

He was 'astounded' when he had a glass of iced water thrown in his face during the 1969 US PGA and was called 'a damned racist'. He never did appreciate that the sins of omission hurt as much as those of commission. Many people who called themselves Christians condoned apartheid and Player now believes that it is 'a terrible system'. He also believes that 'I have played a significant role in trying to eradicate apartheid in my country.'

Be that as it may, there is no doubting Player's on-course achievements. To have won nine major championships as a professional in the era of Nicklaus, Palmer, Trevino, Miller, Floyd and latterly Watson is a huge achievement and it took all the combativeness and aggression that a little man – Player is 5 foot 8 inches in his spikes – can summon. The last of the majors – the Masters – was in 1978 and it required him to play the last nine holes in 30, for a final round of 64, which equalled the then course record. He birdied the 10th, 12th, 13th, 15th, 16th and 18th (he holed from at least 15 feet at the last) but, during that incredible run, the crowds were mostly elsewhere watching those they assumed had more chance of ultimate success. Player remarked to Severiano Ballesteros, his playing partner, 'You know, these people think I can't win this,' and, thus fired up, he did.

If Player's beliefs can seem contradictory, it is fair to say that controversy has followed him on the golf course as well. He is, without doubt, one of the great matchplayers of all time. It is a format that provides him with the perfect outlet for his eagerness to take on the world and all its works, and his five World Matchplay titles won at Wentworth are eloquent testimony to his abilities in that direction.

Matchplay is also the perfect vehicle for gamesmanship, something that seems to occur naturally in Player. He claimed, in *Gary Player: To Be The Best*, never to have used it but went on, confusingly, 'A man who complains about gamesmanship is a sissy.'

Johnny Miller once had to wait several minutes before an important putt in a match against Player because the South African was assiduously raking a bunker. In the semi-final of the World Matchplay in 1968, Player and Tony Jacklin were at the 37th in front of a biased, parochial crowd. 'Miss it, miss it,' someone said as Player was over his putt. He holed it, then immediately started haranguing the crowd, leaving Jacklin to wait until the row died down. Jacklin missed and Player was loudly and roundly booed.

For nearly 20 years, from 1959 to 1978, Player was one of the Big Three – that McCormack-inspired marketing tool involving the South African, Palmer and Nicklaus. In that time Player won his nine majors, Palmer six of his seven and Nicklaus 13 of his 18. They dominated golf and monopolized the headlines – and each of them did it in his chosen way.

JACK NICKLAUS

Jack Nicklaus has lived his life on the leader-board, in the full glare of all the glory golf can offer. He is demonstrably the most successful golfer that ever drew breath. He won 18 professional major championships, two amateur championships and had, by 1996, won 80 other events, a grand total of 100. Given that golfers, by the consent of both them and us, are measured by their majors, Nicklaus is pre-eminent and given that it took him 24 years to compile his championship wins it will necessarily take anyone attempting to, a long time to overtake him. Nicklaus' achievements stand alone since records began with the 1860 Open championship.

What he has achieved is wonderful and we should all be thankful for it. For Nicklaus was a great deal more than just a successful golfer. In addition to being the greatest winner, he was also the greatest loser, being runner-up in major championships an almost unbelievable 19 times. It became commonplace to see Nicklaus standing on the last green, shoulders squared, making full eye-contact and shaking hands with another player, and the marvellous thing about it was that no one could tell from his manner whether he had just won or lost.

At least twice he had to give best to Tom Watson, for example, once after what is probably the greatest championship ever, the 1977 Open at Turnberry. He had played the last two rounds in 65,66 and the disappointment of losing after playing so magnificently must have been crushing but, sure enough, Nicklaus immediately went to his conqueror and congratulated him.

In the press tent, in the aftermath, neither man would reveal just what Nicklaus had said. An hour or two later, after he had indulged in some clubhouse celebrations, I bumped into Watson who was about to carry the trophy up the interminable steps to the Turnberry Hotel. More in hope than expectation I asked the new champion what had passed between them and he said, 'Oh, I don't know, something like you've seen my best and you've beaten it.' Nothing Jack Nicklaus could have said could have been better than that – the world's best had played his best and it had not been good enough. No wonder Watson glowed.

Five years later Watson beat Nicklaus again in a championship the Bear would dearly have loved to win – the 1982 US Open. That was the occasion of Watson's amazing chip-in at the 17th hole at Pebble Beach, a shot widely held to be impossible. Nicklaus, who moments before had been silently certain that he had another championship won, now knew that he had not, and yet, by the time Watson came off the final green, Nicklaus was waiting for him. 'You little sonofabitch,' he said, 'you're something else. I'm proud of you.'

Those are not isolated examples and golfers who grew up and played the game in the second half of the century are unbelievably fortunate to have had him as a role model. This is a man who curses not, neither does he spit; clubs are not thrown; officials are not bawled out; opponents are not abused and rules are not broken.

In all the years, all the newspapers have not been able to find one scurrilous or scandalous story about him and he has mostly been able to leave his game in the front porch and be an admirable, and admired, family man off the course. He has also, it has to be said, been able to leave family matters back in the home, thanks to a wife, Barbara, who has an almost uncanny ability to cope not only with Jack and a travelling life but also with four sons and a daughter and now myriad grandchildren.

Nicklaus was not a natural in the sense that people think of Snead or Ballesteros, gifted with grace and a swing from the gods. Nicklaus, particularly in his youth, was a big powerful man who, off a relatively wide stance, took a full swing and simply smashed the ball unheard of, undreamed of distances. In his early days he had the advantage that first John Daly and then Tiger Woods and, among the women, Laura Davies, had over their contemporaries of being 30–40 yards longer than the next-best, and more if required.

It was not an effortless advantage. Nicklaus hit the ball so viciously in the 1960s and 1970s that it always seemed possible that he would burst something, either ball, club or maybe even a muscle. At the moment of impact when going for a big drive the veins stood out, the face was contorted and the body seemed to strain every sinew; it was an obvious and massive effort, but oh how it worked. The reason it did so was that the basics were correct and Nicklaus was a great one for basics. At the

Nicklaus, cocooned in concentration, hardly registered them while the beaten Palmer could only say, 'I didn't think he was good enough. I didn't think he could drive it straight enough for Oakmont. I didn't think ...' It was the last time that anyone thought that Nicklaus might not be good enough for any situation.

start of every season he would spend a week with the late Jack Grout, just going over the grip, the stance, posture, over and over, until he was sure everything was in place.

There was nothing beautiful about the resultant swing. The thrill was in the hit with Nicklaus, an always solid smack which rocketed off the clubface miles, straight. He was over a sustained period of time, say 20 years, the longest, straightest driver the world has known. There was never any need for theatricals with Nicklaus. If he was slow – and he was – it was because the checklist had to be ticked off. He approached each shot in exactly the same way, as if he were the pilot of the plane on a pre-flight routine, making sure he clicked all the switches. The contrast with say Ballesteros, who was often also slow, was that the Spaniard always seemed to be stalking his shot like a predator waiting to pounce.

Nicklaus always knew precisely what he could do and when Deane Beman revealed that he had started pacing yardages on tournament holes it was like a Damascean revelation to Nicklaus. It fitted perfectly with his philosophy and his own yardages became his bible, to be kept, treasured and re-read. They were as priceless to him as anything that came from Gutenberg. He has kept every one he ever compiled.

His first win as a professional was the US Open at Oakmont in 1962. He beat local boy and world golfing god Arnold Palmer in a play-off that has become notorious for the partisan spectators holding up placards by bunkers saying, 'Hit it in here Fat Boy.' Nicklaus, cocooned in concentration, hardly registered them while the beaten Palmer could only say, 'I didn't think he was good enough. I didn't think he could drive it straight enough for Oakmont. I didn't think …' It was the last time that anyone thought that Nicklaus might not be good enough for any situation.

That win did more than just give Nicklaus his first major championship. It announced a talent so monstrous that the golf world blinked and shook its collective head – no one was supposed to do what Nicklaus had done.

Such ability needed strong mental foundations as well as physical skills and so clearly did Nicklaus see the game and so easily did he pinpoint the problems that it took him time to learn that not everyone had that same ability. To be able to suffer fools, or anything he considered foolish, did not come easily to him. He had to work at it and he did but, before that happened, it was easy to find yourself at the wrong end of those piercing blue eyes staring with seeming contempt straight through you. One example: the Carnoustie Open of 1968.

During the days before the championship the wind was from the north or the east and either way the 18th green was out of reach for normal human beings. On the Wednesday evening, in the pressroom, I asked Nicklaus if he would be going for the carry, over the Barry Burn that runs directly in front of the green. 'Whaddya mean?' he demanded, as if it were a terribly complicated question. I repeated it, with a few 'ers', 'wells' and 'you knows' thrown in and he just continued to glare before replying, 'Of course I'll be going for it,' in the most dismissive tones imaginable. I felt then it was a reasonable question – I still do – but Nicklaus did not like being asked a question that related to human beings of only normal accomplishment.

Such curtness was tempered by success and maturity but Nicklaus loves a practical joke, which is why I knew I could rely on him back in 1990 when he was to make his debut on the Senior Tour in The Tradition at Desert Mountain in Arizona. The co-author of this book, my wife Patricia, had just won a national championship but was shy of claiming great credit for it as there were no single-figure handicappers in the event that year.

She was going to be at Desert Mountain and, as the principal pre-tournament interest was bound to be the Nicklaus reaction to being 50, both she and he were bound to be in the same press conference. A couple of weeks before, with malice aforethought, I gave Nicklaus a note and he readily agreed to the plot. The conference had been going for a while and there was discussion about whether Lee Trevino, who was winning a lot, was *really* dominating because he was usually winning by just the odd shot. Trevino, who was there, said he wasn't aware that sponsors paid more to those who won by more than one.

Suddenly, out of nowhere, Nicklaus produced the note I had given him and said to an audience of almost exclusively male American pressmen, 'I was kinda wonderin', I received a little note here, is there someone in this room won the Barbados Ladies' Open championship this year? Hmmm?'

The men looked baffled and a tape of the conference tells that there was a long embarrassed silence – until Patricia identified herself. There was loud laughter and Trevino yelled, 'How many did you win by?' 'I won by 10,' she confessed. 'Hey,' said Nicklaus and Trevino, almost in unison, 'she dominated. There's domination, right over there.' The tape is still, proudly, in the family archives.

In the early years Nicklaus' all-embracing concentration made him seem totally impassive to fortune good or ill and appeared to exclude expressing emotion. By the end of his career he was still not exactly Jumping Jack Flash but he had had his moments. There was the time when he almost brained poor Doug Sanders on the 18th green at St Andrews when he had finally won an Open at the home of golf and, to express his 'sheer, uncontrollable joy', flung his putter in the air, heedless of where it landed. In his book *On and Off the Fairway* Nicklaus said of that championship, won after an 18-hole play-off, 'Rightly or wrongly … I felt a victory here, in the cradle of golf was critical to being regarded as being at least a "complete" golfer and probably essential to ever being rated the best of one's time … I've rarely been closer to heaven than I was here at the end of it.'

Then there was the 1975 Masters, arguably the greatest championship ever played in America, depending on whether Nicklaus' win in 1986 counts more with you. The 1975 event was possibly the purest theatre, given that it had the three best players in the world at that time – Nicklaus, Tom Weiskopf and Johnny Miller – all at their peak and contesting the championship between them. It boiled down in the end to a matter of will, and in that there was only one winner. It took until the 16th before Nicklaus imposed himself irrefutably, with a 45-foot putt that was in the hole a long time before it actually got there. Nicklaus knew that it was in, too, and the abiding memory is not of the amazing leaping finale of the putt but the almost unbearable suspense of watching the man himself crouching, staring, glaring, urging, willing the ball into the hole. He said at the time, 'It was the longest critical putt I've yet holed in a major and oddly enough I thought I might make it even before I'd stepped up to the ball, which doesn't happen very often from that distance.'

He holed another that was full of body language in 1986 and was later full of the plain language of amazement. 'I just don't understand putting,' he was to say. 'To draw the putter back and to hole something like that when it is difficult to even draw breath … well.' The putt was of some 20 feet, it was on the 17th, it was for a birdie and it was effectively for his sixth green jacket. As the putt neared the hole Nicklaus leaned forward, eyes intent again, daring the ball to disobey. When it went in the putter was raised aloft; there was a hole to play but he knew what it meant.

Late in 1996 Nicklaus won his 100th event as a professional, a fact which spoke of excellence sustained over four decades. He had won 38 tournaments while still in his twenties; 46 in his thirties; six in his forties; and 10 (and still counting) in his fifties. It is a formidable tally, especially given the manner of its compilation. There are two very good reasons why Nicklaus could have won more, maybe lots more.

The first is that the man himself admitted that in his early years he nursed himself. 'I paced myself very well throughout my career,' he said. 'I've always been as fresh at the end of the year as at the beginning. I could have won a lot more tournaments when I was young, but if I had I might not have been playing today.'

The second reason is that Nicklaus mostly won playing conservative golf, for the very good reason that that was usually all it needed. He knew that if he kept going, just keeping in touch with the leaders, more often than not they would stumble and he could step in. Nicklaus has always seen Bobby Jones as a man to emulate and it was Jones who wrote, in 1927 in *Down the Fairway*, that the key to success was, 'the stolid and negative and altogether unromantic attribute of patience.' Some 50 years later, in *On and Off the Fairway*, Nicklaus wrote about his first Masters win, 'Most golf tournaments are not so much won by opportunistic play as not lost when opportunity presents itself. It is a great realization for breeding patience and perseverance.'

Nicklaus, for so many years the best player in the game by miles, was able to adopt such a policy, so much so that when he won his first Open championship, at Muirfield in 1966, Herb Warren Wind remarked, in *Following Through*, that 'not once did he stray from his policy of non-attack.' That it was a successful policy is obvious but there were mixed reactions to it by some in the game, who thought that Nicklaus both could and should have been even more successful, especially in the championships.

Peter Dobereiner once wrote that he wished he could walk by the side of Nicklaus during an early championship round and simply inform him of the next shot he was going to play. It was a wish born of seeing what the great man could do when circumstances dictated that he attack, that he go for the aggressive shot and Dobereiner simply wanted to see that innate conservatism cast aside a lot earlier. In short, he wanted Nicklaus to dominate the field in the manner his game suggested he could.

Not unnaturally Nicklaus disagreed but the Dobereiner theory was given credence many times, notably at Muirfield in 1972 when Nicklaus was already the US PGA, Masters and US Open champion. The PGA title had been won in February 1971, but even so he needed only the Open itself to become the first man ever to hold all four professional major championships at the same time and the first since Ben Hogan in 1953 to have won the last three of those titles in the same year.

But Nicklaus played too cautiously; his intent was to avoid error. It had worked before, it could work again. This time, however, Tony Jacklin was playing inspired golf and Lee Trevino was chipping in, holing bunker shots and long putts all over the place and the two of them got clean away. After three rounds, when he was six shots behind Trevino, five behind Jacklin,

Nicklaus, 1969 Ryder Cup
Royal Birkdale

Nicklaus realized that something had to be done, so he cast aside dull care, went for everything and got round in 66. It was good enough for second place. If only, if only ... if only Nicklaus had done a Dobereiner, 1972 might have been the year of the professional Grand Slam. Then again, Nicklaus would argue that if he had done what Dobereiner wanted, he wouldn't have won the preceding titles.

Nicklaus could also look back on what is, using the word advizedly, an astounding record on the US PGA Tour. In his first 17 years as a professional he was always in the top four of the money list, although after that he never achieved it again, and from 1958 to 1995 on the regular tour he played in 546 tournaments, making the cut in 490 of them – another astounding figure. Everyone knew instinctively, just by watching him play golf, that he was the man to beat in any tournament, but for once the statistics also tell a truthful tale.

There is also no doubt at all that his instincts are completely in the right place in many matters. Sportsmanship, with which he is deeply imbued, means among other things giving the opposition a fair chance. In his attitudes to a proposed World Tour, and to the Ryder Cup up to the 1980s, these values are obvious. When the idea of a World Tour was first floated, by Greg Norman in 1995, Nicklaus was in Japan and he was wary of wholehearted support because he did not know the full details but instinctively he was for it. He knew that over the years the great, and potentially great, players from abroad had not been treated fairly: if it were possible to keep them off the US Tour, they were kept off; if it were possible to keep them out of the US majors, they were kept out; and all the time Nicklaus and the other really good players wanted to play them more, not less, frequently. He knew that the true test of a champion was to beat the best as often as possible and he also knew that there was an insufficient number of chances of doing that. The World Tour, potentially, offered more and so, in principle, he was in favour.

Then there was the Ryder Cup. By the late 1970s the match had become insupportable in a modern golfing world. Great Britain & Ireland were not a match for America and in 1977 Nicklaus told Lord Derby, then president of the British PGA, that 'reality must prevail if the event isn't to decline into an exhibition bout.' GB&I became Europe and 10 years later the Americans, captained by Nicklaus, were having the pants thrashed off them at Muirfield Village, built by Nicklaus.

At the 1969 Ryder Cup at Royal Birkdale, it was Nicklaus' innate sense of the correctness that made him concede Tony Jacklin's two-footer, which ensured a tied match, with the words, 'I don't think you'd have missed that but I wasn't going to give you the chance.' Again it was his instinctive fairness that instigated an action which in turn brought several of his team-mates, and his captain Sam Snead, to near apoplexy.

In all the arguments as to who is, or has been, the best, what is indisputable is that Nicklaus has had a longer and more successful career than anyone else. For his first 15 years or more, golf tournaments – particularly championships – were a case of 'beat Jack and win'. A golf writer's life was simple in those days. Demanding sports editors, who wanted a pre-tournament prediction of the winner, got Nicklaus every time and our success rate would have driven a horse-race writer to a quiet frenzy. Among the many highlights of his career, here are just a few more from among those not yet mentioned.

A golf writer's life was simple in those days. Demanding sports editors, who wanted a pre-tournament prediction of the winner, got Nicklaus every time and our success rate would have driven a horse-race writer to a quiet frenzy.

Nicklaus won the 1965 Portland Open for the third time in four years and got there by flying across the country 'about 5000 feet above the ground' in the first of the Air Bears, an Aero Commander.

Only 12 months later he had the first of what were to be three career Grand Slams when he won the Open at Muirfield. His vaulting ambition, though, hardly recognized the feat. He wanted to win all four in the same year – which at that time he believed could be achieved. It cannot.

In 1973 Nicklaus won the Tournament of Champions. He had lost that year's Masters with one of his over-cautious displays which left him eight behind the third round leader Peter Oosterhuis. He then embraced aggression, again it was too late and despite eight birdies in a final round of 66, finished two behind Tommy Aaron. He was so fed up that he wanted to withdraw from the Tournament of Champions but his wife Barbara said, 'You are going. Your plane reservations are here and this is when you are going to get there.'

Then there was the 1975 Masters which made Nicklaus a five-star general, beating the previous record of four wins set by Palmer in 1964. Nicklaus sincerely believes that nerve-wracking tussles like this one, which went to the final hole, are 'sheer fun'. He said, 'The fact of the matter is that the tougher and closer the competition, the more I enjoy golf.' For years this championship was his favourite recollection and not just because he won. 'Winning by easy margins may offer others kinds of satisfaction,' he said, 'but it's nowhere nearly as enjoyable as battling it out, shot by shot, down to the wire. I might add that this holds true even when I don't win because the next two most enjoyable tournaments I've ever played were the 1977 Masters and British Open.'

Nicklaus used to win tournaments by grinding the rest of the field into submission, not like Ballesteros with blindingly brilliant shots. But what happened at the 1975 US PGA? At the 625-yard 16th, Nicklaus drove into water and had to take a penalty drop. His next finished dead behind a tree and roving television commentator Bob Rosburg was already intoning the phrase that has come to haunt him, 'He's dead. He's got absolutely no chance.' Don't say that to Nicklaus. 'I knew I was staring at an eight,' he said, 'but I took a big cut at the ball with a nine-iron and lo and behold when I ducked out from the trees, there was my ball on the green, 30 feet from the hole.' Seve would always hole that putt; so did Jack.

He knew that the true test of a champion was to beat the best as often as possible.

In fact, many would say that over the years Nicklaus has been the finest pressure putter of them all and he admits that he won the 1980 US PGA championship at Oak Hill purely on his putting stroke. 'Prior to that event,' said Nicklaus, 'I hadn't been playing well and I hadn't been putting well. But my son Jackie gave me a lesson the Sunday before about moving the heel of my putter through the ball. I proceeded to hole everything. I can't remember ever putting that well in a major championship and I won by seven strokes playing mediocre golf.'

Winning the 1977 Memorial Tournament, the event he created which honours a different man or woman of golf each year, brought another form of satisfaction. Nicklaus feels a responsibility for everything at this event and frequently finishes the round with a golf bag stuffed full of sweet wrappers and fag ends, not to mention polythene bags that were littering the course. Despite distractions and a notebook full of Things To Do Tomorrow, he won what was only the second playing of the event.

Just as he won a major championship as the first of his professional triumphs, his first win in Seniors golf was also a major, The Tradition on a course he designed, Desert Mountain. Ever the perfectionist, he was not particularly happy about the timing of the tournament. It was played the week before the Masters; the week that had, throughout his career, been devoted to practice for that championship. Even at the age of 50 he entertained thoughts of proper golf, of proper major championships.

There have been more Seniors wins since then, but increasingly the man who has set the standards for all others to follow has turned towards course architecture. His design work has taken him, in the late 1990s, to the Far East and to Japan, and it was on a driving range at the Dunlop Phoenix event that he was practising when a young Englishman, a promising player called Lee Westwood, came and stood in the bay next to him. Instead of watching the great man, then aged 56, the 23-year-old Westwood took a metal-headed, graphite-shafted driver and began belting out drive after drive that carried 20 yards past where the Nicklaus efforts were finishing. The man of whom Bobby Jones once said, 'He plays a game with which I am not familiar,' looked up, smiled and shook his head with a touch of sadness. Golf, he knew, was renewing itself.

TOM WATSON

As Tom Watson stood to his second shot on the 17th hole at St Andrews in the 1984 Open championship, he had every hope of winning his ninth major championship. He had hit a perfect drive to the most difficult hole — bar none — in world golf, he had his yardage and he was confident he had the right club. Moments later his major championship career was in ruins. Not only did he not win at St Andrews but he was never to win another major.

What Watson did on that 17th fairway was called, by Mark McCormack, 'a decision that will live among the great errors of the game.' It is arguable that by making that error, he lost not just a championship but also, for ever, the confidence that enables great players to be great.

By the 17th in that final round, only Severiano Ballesteros and Watson were in contention. The Spaniard was in the group ahead of the American, but on the 17th tee both were 11-under par. Ballesteros went on to par the 17th; now it was Watson's turn.

He hit a perfect drive, for, having taken the risks with the out of bounds on the right, he was rewarded with the only view worth having of the 17th green, looking down its length of perhaps 60 yards. All he had to do now was pitch a mid-iron short of the putting surface and let it run up on to the green. A par is a birdie at the 17th at any time.

But somewhere in the surveying of that next shot something went drastically and dramatically wrong. From the more dangerous left-hand side of the fairway, Ballesteros, like Watson a long hitter, had hit a six-iron that landed short of the green and ran on. Watson computed that he had 210 yards to the hole and maybe, although he has consistently denied it, his mind went back to the 1983 Open at Royal Birkdale. On that occasion he had 213 yards to the pin and hit what he has always called the finest two-iron of his life to win the championship. He said of that shot, 'It was exactly what I had planned. The wind was right to left and I wanted to draw it slightly into that wind. It was right on the flag all the way except that I never did see it land because of the crowds. But I knew that when it came down it would be splitting the flag, not right, not left but right on it.' The similarities between what Watson did then and what he tried to do at St Andrews are uncanny but, if he had announced to the crowd at the 17th what club he was taking, they would have gasped in astonishment. Simply put, a two-iron was never the club. It was no more than a four-iron, probably a five. Watson hit the shot as he saw it and we saw it carry the green, bound over the road and finish a foot from the wall.

No one knows what Watson's thoughts were as he trudged up the 17th fairway, past the pin, over the metalled road and up to his ball. He must surely have known he had blown the championship, for now, in his present position, a six was about the best he could hope for. In the event he manufactured a brilliant little stab shot that got the ball back on to the green, but probably 35 feet from the pin, from where, given how sick he must have been feeling, he did well to two-putt. That bogey five was, however, enough to lose him the title he was defending.

That episode closed the curtain on Watson's championship career, which had been one of the most glorious in golf. He had, for example, won five Opens in Great Britain in nine years, including three in four years from 1980 – a record that completely demolished the previous best, which was Harry Vardon's five, out of six altogether, in 16 years. Watson was the man to beat, at a time when Jack Nicklaus was still winning championships, from the mid-1970s to the mid-1980s, and he was the winner of what may go down as the greatest championship of all time: the 1977 Open at Turnberry. Watson went into that championship as Masters champion, after beating Nicklaus in another wonderful duel at Augusta.

A westerly wind was blowing on the final day of the Turnberry Open and of the 64 players only seven played to par or better. Nicklaus had 66, Watson 65. The drama centred on three holes. On the tee of the short 15th, Watson was one down in what had become matchplay. Nicklaus found the green; Watson not only missed it but was over 60 feet from the pin. Amazingly, he holed that putt and gave his opponent a long stare. For once, Nicklaus was looking somewhere else. They were all square on the long 17th, which Nicklaus played with a drive and a seven-iron but he appeared to hit it fat – it finished well short of the green – and, although he bunted the ball to six feet, the man who over the years had holed more pressure putts of that length than any golfer who ever lived missed this one.

Watson was ahead for the first time and at the 18th hit a beautiful iron off the tee to the safe part of the fairway. Tellingly, he forced a change of game plan out of Nicklaus, who had used an iron there all week, for fear of running out of fairway. Now he needed to take a chance but, if the seven-iron at the 17th had been bad, this drive was worse and it shot through the fairway and ended at the very foot of a gorse bush. He took a desperate slash at the ball and to a roar of incredulity great swathes of grass were hurled into the air, the ball soared into the heavens – and descended on the green. Okay, it was 30 feet away, but it was on the green.

There was another roar when Watson hit his second, for the ball pitched on the green, ran on and on, and stopped two feet away. Surely that was it, surely the championship was now the pretender's? But Nicklaus has never given in in his life and Watson said later that what happened next was no surprise to him. Nicklaus holed that putt for the most unexpected birdie three that hole is ever likely to see. Now Watson had a two-foot putt for the Open and, in that wonderfully brisk manner of his, he took what little time he needed and holed it.

In 1983 he seemed irresistible. He had been the No. 1 on the US money List for four of the previous six years, been third and fifth in the other two years, and had won an incredible 25 events.

If Turnberry was the greatest head-to-head conflict in a major, then one of the greatest shots played in the closing stages of a major was by Watson in the 1982 US Open at Pebble Beach. The 17th is a fearsome hole and when Watson reached it he was trying to recover from the shock of bogeying the 16th. He faced a shot of just over 200 yards, into a slight breeze, to a pin fiendishly situated close to the left edge of the green. It needed a gentle draw to get it close but overdo it and the left rough would ensure a bogey. Watson took the two-iron – that club again – and overdid the draw, the ball ending in what seemed to be calf-deep rough, only 15 feet or so from the pin. Watson needed a par finish of 3,5 to tie Nicklaus but now the best he could do, it seemed, would be 4,4. However, the ball had not settled deep into the roots and when his caddie said, 'Get it close,' Watson replied, 'Close, damn it. I'm going to hole it.' And he did. And he won the title. 'That shot had more meaning than any other in my career. It was the best shot of my life.'

In July that year, Watson had the Open championship at Troon handed to him by a faltering Nick Price but he was, of course, in a position to take advantage of that collapse, which is the prime requirement. In any case, Watson proved over the years that he could win in all manner of ways. His first major, the 1975 Open at Carnoustie, came in a play-off against Jack Newton; his second was the 1977 Masters, when he beat off Nicklaus and his third was the Turnberry/Nicklaus affair. In the 1980 Open at Muirfield he proved he was a good front runner, beating Lee Trevino by four; and in the 1983 Open at Royal Birkdale he hit that magnificent two-iron at the last hole – 'the best of my life' – to win under the severest of pressure.

In 1983 he seemed irresistible. He had been the No. 1 on the US money List for four of the previous six years, been third and fifth in the other two years, and had won an incredible 25 events. He won three more in 1984, before getting to St Andrews and the trauma of the Road Hole. From 1985 to 1996, he won only twice more on the US Tour: the Nabisco Championship of Golf in 1987 and in 1996, as an amazing afterthought, the Memorial Tournament. The 1998 Mastercard Colonial was an after-afterthought.

What had happened in the interim was that Tom Watson became one of the most celebrated victims of the twitch. He declined from one of the great holers-out to one of the worst. Every time he got into contention, which was quite often because his long game was still strong, he began to putt like a beginner. He even brought a new word into golf's vocabulary – the 'flinches'. This was the bodily equivalent of the twitch. It was an affliction which occurred when an important short putt had to be holed, and it manifested itself in a sharp upraising of the head, and with it the shoulders, as the putter closed in on the ball. It was as if Watson could not bear to see the putter hit the ball and was 'flinching' away from the moment of contact.

'I have always subscribed to the fact that nerves, or desire, in golf only last so long,' he said. 'They are not going to be so good at 40 as at 30. In the days of my great putting I could see the line and I just laid the putter down and hit the ball on that line – and from 20 and 30 and 40 feet they went in. Since then I've started getting no kind of feel at all over the short putts. In the third round of a Players' championship I missed from three feet and I thought afterwards that I'd moved my head, moved it forwards, but in fact I'd moved it back, away from the ball. There are times when I don't know what the hell I'm doing on the short putts.'

Watson was never short of advice, most of it directed at

getting him to try the broomhandle putter, or the Langer Lock, or any variation of it. He always refused. He received hundreds of letters, goofy putting contraptions and putters but no solution. It was a chronic condition.

There may be another reason for Watson's decline after St Andrews, 1984. 'There came a point,' he said, 'when I decided that it was time to take a breather, to stop and smell the flowers. I didn't work as hard at the game as I had, or as I could. Working hard in this game gives you the edge, and I wasn't. I suppose making too much money has a softening effect and I'd made as much as I felt I was ever going to need. Family commitments dull the edge too and as you get older it becomes harder to hone it. Then, as my golf game got worse there was self-doubt, frustration and disappointment. But I had to recognize that I'd brought a lot of it on myself.'

Before the first of the 'afterthoughts', the win in the Memorial, Watson had played in, and not won, 141 tournaments in nearly nine years and in a practice round found himself almost at the end of his tether. He hit a truly awful, duck-hooking drive at the 18th of the Muirfield Village club and said despairingly, 'You know, I hate this game.'

He could hardly have expected, or been prepared for, the rebuke he got from Bruce Edwards, a friend as well as long-serving caddie. 'Don't ever say that,' he said. 'Remember what this game means to you and think about your Dad as well. Dedicate this week to him.' Watson's father, who had started his son in the game at the age of six, had suffered a stroke the previous week and Edwards' words stung. Watson realized that self-pity definitely was not the answer.

That week he played inspired golf through the green and putted just about adequately, which for him meant wonderfully. For the most part he had mid- to long putts, which he got close enough to tap in, rather than the four-foot variety and he also had a new putting attitude. Edwards said, 'He had forgotten the essence of the game, just get it in the hole. He had become totally stroke-conscious, thinking about that rather than the line.'

When Watson won, the first man on to the 18th green to congratulate him was the tournament's founder and a man who had played such a huge part in his life – Jack Nicklaus. Surveying the scene, Edwards smiled and said, 'Feels like the good ol' days.'

NANCY LOPEZ

Nancy Lopez illuminated the LPGA Tour from the first moment she sashayed smiling down its fairways. She became known and loved all over the world, perhaps the most universally recognized woman golfer of all time. She was – is – a fierce competitor but what really makes her stand out is a rare warmth and a confident humility, a charismatic combination that brings to mind Bobby Jones and Arnold Palmer. The player who did much to catapult the women's game into the modern, moneyed, country club era of widespread television coverage and corporate sponsorship started at the age of eight on the local municipal, trailing after her parents Domingo and Marina. She gave notice of an exceptional talent early on, winning the New Mexico Women's Amateur championship at the age of 12. At 18, still an amateur, she shared second place in the 1975 US Women's Open, behind Sandra Palmer and in 1977, a fledgling professional, she was second again, two shots behind Hollis Stacy.

Dark-haired, bright-eyed, with a swoon-inducing smile, Lopez made the transition from attractive asset to superstar sensation in the course of 1978, her official rookie season. She won nine times, including an unprecedented five in succession.

She was a tour dream, appealing to fans, sponsors and the media. She was the right person at the right time. David Foster, Colgate's chief executive and the man responsible for the Dinah Shore tournament, had started putting money into the LPGA in the early 1970s and using players to advertize his products. Ray Volpe, a marketing whiz from New York, was appointed commissioner of the LPGA in 1975 and then this

Nancy Lopez.

talented girl-next-door appeared and broke all records. She was rookie of the year, player of the year, leading money-winner and winner of the Vare Trophy (for the lowest scoring average) in the same season – a unique combination, unmatched even by the likes of Beth Daniel, Laura Davies, Annika Sorenstam and Karrie Webb, whose subsequent exploits were to be stunning enough.

In 1979, there was more of the same as she won eight times and scooped the money title, player of the year and the Vare Trophy. 'I hope my winning so often isn't bad for the tour,' Lopez said. The tour managed to cope with more television coverage and more prize money but some people resented the fact that Lopez got all the attention and others sniped that her swing had so many faults that it would not last. There was – still is – an idiosyncratic little hitch of the hands at the start of the backswing but her rhythm and timing compensated for any unorthodoxy and through the hitting area she was dead solid perfect. She kept on winning tournaments – and hearts.

Like Palmer, she was the superstar with the common touch, accommodating people if she could, posing for photographs, signing autographs and exchanging friendly greetings. Partly it was in her nature and partly it was because she remembered the boorish behaviour of a professional (male) at one tournament she'd attended as a spectator. 'He thought he was better than the gallery,' Lopez said, 'and I promised myself that I'd never be that way.' She handled the attention admirably but she couldn't understand the adulation. 'You kinda look at people and wonder what they see. I felt like they were just worshipping me for the way I was playing and to me I was just playing golf.'

She was No. 1 again in 1985 when doubters thought motherhood – Ashley, the first of her three daughters, was born in 1983 – would blunt her edge but husband Ray Knight, who won baseball's World Series with the New York Mets, encouraged her to exploit her talent to the full. He set goals and Lopez became a member of the Hall of Fame in 1987, the year after Erinn, her second daughter was born. The wins no longer came in bunches but neither did the tournaments she played in and the victories did not dry up until 1994.

In January 1996, on her 39th birthday, Lopez seriously considered quitting. Her clothes didn't fit her and her golf was not up to standard. She was feeling fat, frustrated and fearful of 40. 'I wasn't happy,' she admitted. 'It wasn't my family. It wasn't my husband. It was just me. It's embarrassing being humiliated by your golf game and, as competitive as I've always been, playing that kind of golf and being away from my family, I felt like I was wasting my time. I love being inside the ropes and competing and I wasn't able to do that.'

Lopez set to work. She hired a personal trainer, spilling sweat and tears on a Churchillian scale. A few months later, she was more supple and full of energy than she had been for years. Her mood improved, so did her golf and her shape, always inclined to the cuddly. By this time she had dropped from a size 14 (tight) to a size 10 (loose) and the ball was whizzing off the clubface. At last, in April 1997, she won again, at the Chick-fil A Charity championship in Georgia. It was her 48th victory and the first that her third daughter, Torri, could appreciate. The tournament was only 36 holes because of bad weather but no one cared. There was just delight that Lopez was back and in July, at Pumpkin Ridge in Oregon, it looked as though she might win her first US Women's Open to complete the fairytale. She became the first woman to break 70 in all four rounds, but at the end of an enthralling contest Alison Nicholas, the mighty mite from England, had pipped her by a shot. Through her tears, Lopez was graciousness itself and, in January 1998, the USGA presented her with its highest honour: the Bob Jones Award for sportsmanship. He'd have recognized a soulmate in Lopez.

SEVERIANO BALLESTEROS

Severiano Ballesteros is unquestionably the finest, the greatest thing ever to happen to European golf. No golfer has ever made more impact on a whole Continent than the dashing, crashing Spaniard: Seve of silken swing; Seve slash-and-burn; Seve of the Spanish Main, sword in teeth, carrying off the crinolined crumpet.

Ballesteros is the man all male golfers want to be. His is a remarkable marriage of style and substance; he is a man who has dominated his sport not just through his achievements but also by the manner of them. Perhaps no one, not even Arnold Palmer, has hit more bad shots in top tournaments but no one has hit so many breathtaking ones to recover, for this was for the whole of his career a man who rejected the entire concept of losing.

There is never any danger of not knowing his mood. He is an emotional man who is not only unafraid of crying but also cannot imagine why he should not. He cries in joy and sadness, in victory and defeat, the sign of a man totally sure of himself. This absolute belief in himself is inherent in anything he does. On the course, no shot is too difficult, no situation beyond

Perhaps no one, not even Arnold Palmer, has hit more bad shots in top tournaments but no one has hit so many breathtaking ones to recover, for this was for the whole of his career a man who rejected the entire concept of losing.

redemption. Off the course, it is the same. When he fell in love, for example, it was with Carmen Botin, daughter of the owner of the Bank of Santander and one of the wealthiest men in Spain. The family, with the haughtiness of Spain's ruling class, immediately put up the shutters. Who was this peasant who had had some success at a game almost unknown in Spain? Ballesteros is now married to Carmen, they have three children and Seve plays golf with a father-in-law who can hardly believe his great good luck.

On the course, Ballesteros has sometimes stretched the boundaries of belief. He has hit shots that were clearly impossible but which have illuminated the ages. They are shots hit with club and ball but which are something other than just golf shots. The first example of its audacious kind, in the 1976 Open, announced his career in dramatic fashion. He began as he meant to go.

He was 19 and, on the 18th hole at Royal Birkdale, was faced with a chip shot which apparently needed to be lofted over some intervening bunkers and which would result – if it was a good shot – in a putt of about 20 feet. But Ballesteros spotted another route. He elected to chip and run the ball along a narrow isthmus of grass between the bunkers. It had to pitch on a sixpence, take a kindly bounce and above all be perfectly weighted. It had about a 10 per cent chance of success and, to an enormous roar, it succeeded. As it rolled to a halt, two feet from the hole, the applause was tumultuous. A new genius had been sighted and accepted. It meant he tied for second with Jack Nicklaus, behind Johnny Miller.

Ballesteros won the 1988 Open at Lytham with a similar shot, when he needed a par at the 18th to close out Nick Price. In tangled, twisted rough to the left of the green, the Spaniard produced a shot of such delicacy it seemed like sorcery. It finished dead and the roars were of acclamation, not surprise, for no golfer has had a softer, more educated pair of hands than this man.

It is tempting to describe a man who hits impossible shots as lucky but that has never been true of Ballesteros, a fact recognized by Raymond Floyd for one. At the Masters one year, Ballesteros found himself short and right of the green at the fourth, with the pin short and left. There was a bunker intervening and the green, lightning fast and sloping away from the Spaniard, was only 30 feet wide at the point the ball needed to land. Ballesteros hit a shot that flew almost vertically in the air, pitched by the pin and screwed to a halt two feet away. It was as near miraculous as makes no matter but Floyd had no illusions. 'He does that sort of thing all the time,' he said afterwards. 'Don't make the mistake of thinking that it's luck.'

Such shots were particularly suitable to matchplay and Ballesteros broke hearts on a regular basis in the World Matchplay championship. One year, he was playing Arnold Palmer, then 54 and having one last hurrah at Wentworth, who was one up at the 18th and certain of a birdie four. How could Ballesteros, 30 yards from the hole, get out of this one? He chipped in, of course – and won on the 21st.

Not all the Ballesteros miracles were short shots. He was capable, too, of delivering huge hits. In his youth and before a chronic bad back was to afflict and affect him, no one was longer off the tee than Ballesteros. In 1980 he overwhelmed Augusta, hitting the ball to places only Jack Nicklaus before him, and Tiger Woods after him, had been. He led by 10 shots with nine holes to go before subconsciously easing up and winning by four. In 1983 he hit one of the greatest bunker shots of all time at the PGA National course in West Palm Beach, Florida, in the Ryder Cup. Ballesteros had driven into deep clinging rough on the 18th in his match against Fuzzy Zoeller. His recovery only succeeded in finding the bunker that was meant to penalize the drive and the Spaniard, all square, was in trouble. To the astonishment of everyone, Ballesteros then took a three-wood from his bag. There seemed no conceivable reason for so doing, for the ball was lodged in the face of a fairly steep bunker, some 245 yards from the green. A really, really good player might have got a six-iron at it. Seconds later, the ball was on the edge of the green and there was an awed silence all around. No one could believe what they had just seen, least of all Zoeller who was in shock.

Very few people knew then about the Ballesteros upbringing: how he had learned the game with only a three-iron, how he had to use that club for everything, including shots that ordinarily demanded a wedge. That three-wood shot was like the conjuror's last trick – not just difficult but actually impossible. And, like the conjuror, Ballesteros pulled it off.

In 1983 he won the Masters again, the Westchester Classic, the British PGA championship, the Carrolls Irish Open and the Lancôme Trophy. 'When I was playing good,' he says now of that period, 'I knew I was in control. I was in control of the galleries, of the golf courses, even the other players. I *knew* I would win and the winning was enough. I did not celebrate when I won and I never have. The winning was always enough and the celebration was the feeling of controlling everything around me. There was never any big meal. There was no wine. I had to be ready for the next week. I have only been drunk twice in my life and that was at Christmas. I hated it. I was out of control.'

In those days everyone else expected Ballesteros to win, as well as Seve himself. But it didn't happen by accident; victories were not gifted to him because of his outrageous talent. This genius realized the need for perspiration to create the inspiration. He worked like a man possessed: in golfing parlance, he made the hands bleed. 'If I didn't play well I would say to myself, "You dummy, you don't deserve to eat," and I would miss dinner. Definitely I miss a few dinners, so' – and he smiles a big smile – 'I used to eat some big breakfasts.'

Seve has had two great stages on which to perform: Augusta National and the Ryder Cup. He won the 1980 Masters, at the age of 23, with a performance of such magnitude that at the time it seemed he might win the Masters for ever more. The official account agreed, noting, 'Ballesteros was the tournament as he roamed the Augusta National golf course with a brilliant display of boldness, recovery, charisma and class. His instinct with a golf club has gained for him at a tender golfing age the respect and admiration of competitors and those who follow the game.'

He won by four shots that year but with fewer pars than any champion ever. Seve was – and is – a birdie, bogey, eagle man. He also won by four in 1983, starting the last round birdie, eagle, par, birdie. At the second he hit a four-wood 245 yards to within 15 feet and Tom Kite was incredulous. 'Man,' he said, 'I can't even stop a wedge that close on that green.' Ben Crenshaw expanded, 'Seve's got shots people don't even know about. He can hit sand shots with a two-iron and make them stop next to the pin. There may be times when he seems to be in trouble but actually he's never in trouble. He's the most talented, inventive shotmaker we have in golf today.'

At the second he hit a four-wood 245 yards to within 15 feet and Tom Kite was incredulous. 'Man,' he said, 'I can't even stop a wedge that close on that green.' Ben Crenshaw expanded, 'Seve's got shots people don't even know about.

It's a matter of some incredulity that he has not won another Masters. Ballesteros believes he should have done, not least in 1986, the memorable Nicklaus year, but the Spaniard is philosophical about it. 'Destino,' he said, 'plays a big part in everyone's life. You play good, you hit a good drive at the last hole and it is in a divot hole in the middle of the fairway. That has to be destiny ... What is the difference between a great putt and a perfect putt? Of course, the perfect one goes in, but why? Destino decided I would not win the Masters in 1986. Everything possible happened for Nicklaus to win there.'

The other great stage has been the Ryder Cup although perversely for such an individualist the best Ballesterian moments have been in partnership with someone else. In 1983 he was called on to partner Paul Way, aged 20 and in 1987, when he had to partner the emergent Jose Maria Olazabal, he knew what he had to do. They became a legendary partnership, winning 12 points from 15 matches, and after their first outing no one was ever able to work out who was holding whose hand.

Throughout the late 1970s, all through the 1980s and into the 1990s, he has been a majestic figure to Europeans of all nationalities. He wears his emotions for all to see and, when Costantino Rocca took three putts from 15 feet and lost a match he should have won, Ballesteros was sent to console him. 'It was okay,' said Rocca later, 'I managed to stop him crying after a while.' When Bernhard Langer three-putted to lose the match at Kiawah, Ballesteros was adamant that no one, and certainly not himself, could have holed that last putt and went to tell the German so, tears streaming down his face. Langer, who'd been coping all right, burst into tears too.

Ballesteros's major tally is five – two Masters and three Opens – all won in compelling style. At Lytham in 1979, he hit the ball as hard as he could, whiplashing ferociously through the ball and some Americans, blind to all but the wild shots, claimed he was a lucky winner. They could not believe he could play like that all the time but others, while stunned, were thrilled. In *The Guardian*, Peter Dobereiner wrote, 'He kicked down the doors, elbowed the mighty Jack Nicklaus, Tom Watson, Hale Irwin aside and plonked himself down on the seat of honour. The dust of that brutal assault has not yet settled. Debris continues to fall. It will take a while for the spectators of the violence to recover; we are dazed like witnesses to a nearby explosion ... not a scratch on us but the medics know that we are candidates for a cup of sweet strong tea and a quiet lie down.'

Nine years later he won again at Lytham, with one of the great rounds of championship golf, a 65. It flummoxed Nick Price, who had started out leading by two, shot 69 and lost by two. Ballesteros was brilliant, in the way that word is used of diamonds – the finest cut, of many facets. There was an eight-hole spell, starting at the sixth, which Price played in five under par – and found himself a further stroke behind. Not that the Zimbabwean had much chance anyway, for Seve had enlisted the fates. 'I was wearing the same trousers and the same sweater that I wore here in 1979,' he said, 'and I was carrying the same driver, three-wood, sand-wedge and putter.' He was also carrying, unbeknown to most, a small heated pad sewn into his shirt in the area of the small of his back, in an attempt to remain fluid. That whiplash swing which had won him his first Open was having its effect.

Severiano Ballesteros.

From then until the end of 1999 there were to be 18 tournament victories but no more major championships. In that time Seve's star shone in the Ryder Cup and never more brightly than when he captained Europe to victory at Valderrama in September 1997. He had wanted to play, but his game by now had deserted him and at the time the Cup came around he was 293rd in the world rankings.

But still the eyes flashed, the teeth were bared and Ballesteros, by showing his soul to his team, inspired them. He was everywhere that week, materializing whenever he was needed, and often when he was not. Typically, having made a raging success of the job, having been acclaimed the length and breadth of Golf Europe, having received a congratulatory call from his King, Ballesteros resigned. 'I want to play in the Ryder Cup again,' he said simply.

He finds it hard to keep a caddie, too. Like most players, he is apt to blame the only person around – the caddie – when things go wrong. But Ballesteros keeps on and on about it, giving out grief long after the time has come to forget it. He is not, in caddie parlance, a good bag and it is an unattractive side to a compellingly attractive man.

As with every obsessive, there is another side to Ballesteros. He is no paragon and there is no doubt that he is capable of trying to intimidate rules officials into giving him a better option than the one first suggested, although he does not always succeed. Once, at the 10th at Augusta, he was about to get an advantageous drop when playing-partner Ken Green asked for another opinion. Michael Bonallack, secretary of the R&A ambled over, took one look and said, 'Play it.' Seve played it, without a murmur. Again, at the 18th at Valderrama in a Volvo Masters, he pleaded with John Paramor, one of the finest and fairest rules officials in the world, for a free drop away from what he claimed was a hole made by a burrowing animal. Paramor could see no signs of an animal nor any droppings and refused, incensing the Spaniard. 'The Tour are out to get me,' he claimed, stupidly. The last thing the PGA European Tour want to 'get' is Ballesteros but just occasionally he becomes paranoid about these things.

It is the same when he is penalized for slow play. He used to be quick but he has become slow and refuses to acknowledge it. Instead he rants against those who warn him or penalize him and often seems to be demanding special treatment because of who he is.

He finds it hard to keep a caddie, too. Like most players, he is apt to blame the only person around – the caddie – when things go wrong. But Ballesteros keeps on and on about it, giving out grief long after the time has come to forget it. He is not, in caddie parlance, a good bag and it is an unattractive side to a compellingly attractive man.

Given the intensity Ballesteros brought to the game in his early years, it was always likely that it would fade relatively suddenly and quickly. In 1995 he was saying, 'I admit that my desire is not as much as before. My mind is not as positive as it used to be and playing golf is really hard for me. I try and try and it is like there is a wall in front of me. It is hard to leave home, too. You know, there has always been a lot of pressure on my shoulders. For many years in Europe everything was focused on me and that demands a lot of strength, physically and mentally.

For all the Ballesteros flair and romanticism, there is a strong streak of realism. 'There is only one bad thing in this life,' he said. 'There is no mulligan. If I had a chance to go back 20 years I would not do it all the same. I would make many changes.' He was unwilling to elucidate – 'It is important to be a little bit mysterious' – but he conceded that he would have taken greater care of himself physically, particularly his back and that at times he tried *too* hard. 'No one has the strength to do what I have done for a long time. It is very hard to be a champion.'

Ballesteros still rages against the dying of the light, not for him a quiet acceptance of the ageing process but we should be grateful that this meteor of a man, who has burned so brightly in our golfing skies, has already burned for so long.

GREG NORMAN

Take a look inside Greg Norman's garage: over there a Bentley, in the other corner a Mercedes, and scattered all around there are six or seven – he isn't sure which – Ferraris. Fancy air through your hair? A couple of Harley Davidsons await your be-leathered pleasure. Move outside and go to the lakeside dock at the end of the Normans' garden. Five boats, including a US$5 million ocean-going yacht. At the nearby airfield, in the hanger, are not just two helicopters at US$4 million apiece but also a private jet, coming in at a few million more.

These are the executive tools and toys of the highest earner and the biggest spender the game of golf has known. This is a man who, wanting to build his ideal home on a particular spot of the Florida coastline, bought the house that stood there for over US$2 million, pulled it down, and built one he preferred. This is a man, too, who invested a couple of million dollars in the Cobra golf company and, when it was bought out, took away US$40 million.

It is an extraordinary, almost inexplicable fact that the man who has won the money to pay for all this is the same man who, at the end of 1999, was so good at golf that he was in a 33-way tie for 39th place in the all-time list of winner of major championships. Norman was still top of the career money list on the US Tour with over $12 million – although with Tiger Woods and David Duval earning many millions in 1999 alone, the Australian's lead was being rapidly eroded. Yet, in the matter of major championships, no fewer than 38 golfers had won more than Norman, including Densmore Shute, Ralph Guldahl, Cary Middlecoff, Larry Nelson, Hale Irwin, Nick Price and Payne Stewart – and 32 had won the same number. Some 25 golfers had won two majors in one year and Jack Nicklaus had managed that particular trick no fewer than five times.

So what is he, this blond-haired, icy-blue-eyed man with broad shoulders, flat belly, slim hips and long legs and who is likely to be wearing a big hat, a garish shirt and tight trousers? Is he a great golfer or a charismatic clotheshorse? Is he the most imposing player in modern professional golf or a total poser? The questions follow him around the world.

First, a personal disclaimer: I have absolutely no problem with Greg Norman being extremely rich. Nor do I envy him his toys, although one of the Ferraris would be nice. I am delighted for him and his success and for as long as I have known him, which is over 20 years, he has been totally upfront and honest. Were he not a star and were he British, he would be 'a good bloke'. As he is actually Australian he epitomizes 'mateship', that concept which places loyalty to your mates above anything else except family. For me and many others, these are the highest values of all.

But the mega-amounts he has been able to earn from the game, while failing to do what traditionally has to be done – win majors – does pose one question. What is the point, the purpose, of professional golf? Depending on what you consider to be the correct answer to that question, Norman's career has either been the most astounding success or the most catastrophic failure.

The dictionary definition of professional sport tells us that it is activity conducted in return for sums of money and there is no doubt as to Norman's success on that score. Because his presence in a tournament enhances the publicity value of that event, people are willing to pay him, in the late 1990s, up to US$300,000 to play. Various manufacturers, because of his high profile, are willing to pay him millions of endorsement dollars per year to use his image, words or presence to promote their goods. There is also his course design work, which he loves, at which he is extremely good and which brings in millions of dollars per go.

He makes plenty of prize money too: he has eight times finished in the top 10 of the US money list, topping it three times. Norman has won 74 tournaments and had 53 second places around the world. He finishes in the top 10 of a tournament 40 per cent of the time, an amazing percentage and one topped only by Nicklaus who runs at 53 per cent. Nick Faldo is a mere 21 per cent.

'I'm a winner. I just didn't win today. I'm not a loser. I'm not a loser in life, I'm not a loser in golf tournaments. I win golf tournaments and I've won more than my share.' Norman after the 1996 Masters.

By the end of 1999, a season truncated by a shoulder injury that required surgery, Norman had been officially ranked No. 1 in the world for 305 out of the 574 weeks that the rankings have existed, including a record 96 weeks in succession, and he has set course records everywhere his feet have touched the ground. These on-course achievements have kept the off-course earnings running like the production line at the Mint, so if the purpose of professional golf is purely to make money then perhaps no one has had greater success than Norman.

But there are a great many people who would argue that the criteria for being regarded as a successful professional golfer have almost nothing to do with money and everything to do with winning major championships. These are the imperishables of the sport. Money means nothing when considering the great players of the game, with journeymen now making more in one ordinary event than Ben Hogan and Sam Snead in their entire careers.

Majors are what matter – and Greg Norman only has two of them. What is almost worse, he has eight second places including losing all four major championships in play-offs. Only two players in the history of the game have been runner-up more often: Nicklaus, 19, and Arnold Palmer, 10, but they also won 18 and seven majors respectively. By these criteria, imposed by the game and accepted by the vast majority within it, Norman fails.

Strangely, while the man himself would never agree that he had failed at anything, he would probably accept that majors are the yardstick by which careers are and should be measured. He has never had any time for the world rankings, despite the fact that he has dominated them for so long and he has always freely admitted that the one thing in the world he wants above all else is a 44-inch jacket, colour green, courtesy of the Augusta National Golf Club. He would not hesitate to trade his latest jet for one.

The way that he failed in his attempt to add that jacket to his wardrobe in April 1996 provides a telling commentary not just on the Masters championship for that year but also as a paradigm of the Norman career.

Majors are what matter – and Greg Norman only has two of them. What is almost worse, he has eight second places including losing all four major championships in play–offs.

There are days such as the opening day of Augusta 1996 when Norman is just irresistible. 'It was like holding the reins of a horse,' he was to say later. 'It wanted to run and I just let it go. I felt my swing was getting on to a good plane on the range and when I carried the bunker on the first, that was it – I knew I was going to score in the 60s.' The only danger to that prediction was that he might actually score in the 50s, for he eventually signed for a course record-equalling 63, nine under par. 'On a scale of 1 to 10, that was a 9,' he said. Neither the second nor third rounds was of that standard but they were quite good enough. With 18 holes to play Norman had a six-stroke lead over his nearest rival, Nick Faldo, and back in Australia they were already celebrating. As far as their newspapers were concerned, Norman had already won the Masters. One headline ran, 'Is Greg Australia's Greatest Sportsman Ever?' It proved premature.

In what the *Sydney Morning Herald* was to call 'one of the greatest chokes in sporting history', Norman lost that six-shot lead and went on to lose to Faldo by five. Perhaps worst of all, from an Australian point of view, was that his conqueror was a Pom, an Englishman who, as the final ignominy, took pity on the man he had just demolished, embraced him and said, 'I don't know what to say. I just wanted to give you a hug.'

One awful, almost unthinkable statistic says it all. Losing a six-shot lead after three rounds was the worst collapse by anyone, ever, in a major championship. At Amen Corner, usually buzzing, there was a sepulchral silence and at the 18th, with Faldo leading by four, the silence was profound: surely no golf tournament was ever won and lost in such an eerie atmosphere. In the clubhouse, Nick Price, Norman's Florida neighbour and close friend, was watching on television. He had to stop. 'This is upsetting,' he said. 'It hurts to watch. It's making me feel sick.' That feeling was echoed everywhere. The huge media centre at Augusta is normally an almost raucous place on that final afternoon. That Sunday even the cynics were speaking in whispers as they watched what one newspaper called 'a giant tested to destruction'.

When it was all over, Norman was fantastic. With the possible exception of Nicklaus, he is the best loser the game has known and his words after the event reflected that. 'I screwed up today,' he said. 'Of course I did. I really screwed up. But it's not the end of the world for me, it's really not. God, I'd love to be putting on a green jacket but I'm not going to fall off the face of the earth. You know, I'm secure for the rest of my life, my kids will be secure and so will my kids' kids. I think that's the most important thing, that I've been able to do something for my family, to set up something that will endure for hundreds of years.'

He went on, 'I'm a winner. I just didn't win today. I'm not a loser. I'm not a loser in life, I'm not a loser in golf tournaments. I win golf tournaments and I've won more than my share. I feel confident and my approach to whatever I do is that I can do it. If I wanted to be a brain surgeon and took the time to study it, I could do that. I want to win the Masters. I didn't win the Masters, Nick Faldo won the Masters, so he's got something I haven't got – yet.'

If ever anyone has made his own misfortune, Norman is that man. It is possible to argue that he has thrown away at least 10 championships, starting with the Masters in 1981 when, in the final round, he snap-hooked into the trees at the 10th when leading and took a double-bogey six. His other failures include the 1986 Masters when, needing a par at the last for a play-off, he hit a four-iron miles right into the crowd, and the 1989 Masters when, again needing par for a play-off, he hit a five-iron so far short it did not even stay on the green. Only in the 1987 Masters, when Larry Mize hit a chip that would not go in again in another thousand years, could Norman feel aggrieved.

In the 1984 US Open he played the last three holes unbelievably badly and then lost a play-off to Fuzzy Zoeller, 67 to 75, while in 1986 he led after three rounds at Shinnecock Hills only to take 75. He was co-leader at the same venue in 1995 after three rounds but this time took 73 and lost by two to Corey Pavin.

Norman really should have won the Open at Royal Troon in 1989. Having produced a 64 to get into a three-way play-off with Wayne Grady and the eventual winner, Mark Calcavecchia, Norman birdied the first two holes of the four-hole aggregate decider. Then he bogeyed the short 17th and never did finish the 18th where, after driving into a bunker he did not think he could reach, he exploded into another one and thence out-of-bounds.

Twice he should have won the US PGA. In 1986, the year of his Saturday Slam when he led all four majors after three rounds and won only one, he led the PGA at Inverness by four shots with 18 holes to go. Bob Tway holed a bunker shot at the last hole to win but Norman was in the process of taking 76 – after opening rounds of 65,68,69. Finally, in 1993, again at Inverness, after leading overnight by one, he was caught by Paul Azinger and, at the second hole of a sudden-death play-off, three-putted from maybe 14 feet.

This catalogue of catastrophe is not only sad but is also almost impossible to understand when viewed in the light of Royal St George's 1993. After his wonderful win at Turnberry in 1986, Norman had said that now 'the monkey is off my back ... I can go on and win 10, 15, maybe 20' major championships. The night before he won, Nicklaus, the man whose books Norman had used to learn the game, told him, 'There is no one in the world who wants you to win a major more than I do. You really deserve it.' Norman said he was 'choked' but he did not choke the next day, slowed down by caddie Pete Bender's haul on his sweater when he took off after a bad drive at the seventh. 'Greg, I want you to walk at my pace,' he insisted and they slow marched to victory – and a champagne celebration on the 18th green at midnight.

By the time Norman got to St George's there had been no more celebrations despite 24 attempts on majors, which resulted in a couple of seconds. Furthermore, having missed the cut in the US Open a month earlier, he was not among the favourites to win the 1993 Open.

However at St George's he was as near invincible as makes no matter. He played some of the most powerful and perfect golf witnessed in an Open championship. On the final day he got round in 64, six under, for a championship-record total of 267, 13 under. That day, he despatched the field from his presence with a regal wave of whichever club he had in his hand. This was not a round that owed everything to a putting stroke, as 64s commonly do; it was a round complete with an array of shots that dazzled hardened watchers of the game. Little wonder that Gene Sarazen, invited to be present on the 60th anniversary of his win at

Prince's, said, 'This must be the greatest championship ever played. I've never seen such shots.' Norman himself remarked, 'I never mishit a single shot. I hit every drive perfectly, I hit every iron perfectly. I'm in awe of just how well I hit the golf ball today.' So was Bernhard Langer, his playing partner, a man not given to hyperbole, 'That was an unbelievable round of golf.'

Norman's Royal St George's will rank with Watson's Turnberry in 1977, Faldo's Muirfield in 1987 and Severiano Ballesteros' Lytham in 1988 and, in dismissing the world's finest golfers that sunny Sunday afternoon, Norman also dismissed some of the doubters. It had taken a long time, it seemed, to come to maturity but finally, surely, he had achieved it. One of the finest ball-striking talents the world had known – certainly the longest, straightest driver of a ball – had come into his kingdom.

But why? Why was he able to do it then when he had not been able to do it so many times before and, as it turned out, was not able to do it in the future? Jack Nicklaus, after first saying that he had no complete answer to the dilemma, did express half a theory in *My Story*. 'There are times,' said Nicklaus, 'when aggressiveness will achieve wonders on the golf course, and other times when it will kill you stone dead.' Norman's first instinct was to put it down to technical improvements but later he talked about the value of being positive. 'I've always been a believer in that,' he said. 'Never have anything that is negative. That's true of life and also on the golf course. When Tway and Mize beat me, I had no control over them, only over myself. If I screw up, I can get mad at myself. When somebody does it to you, forget it.'

But Norman did not forget those incidents for several years, as he admitted. 'To forget them, you have to talk about them, and I didn't until 1992.' In that year, former Australian Prime Minister Bob Hawke interviewed him for television, and it all came bursting out. After that, Norman stood in front of a mirror for a very long time and had a very long talk with himself. He knew he could, at that point, walk away from golf and never have to face a four-footer again. 'But I knew that I wanted not just to come back but to be the best in the world. I'm a very competitive person, so I went out and I worked harder than I ever have before.'

There have been times when he had to re-dedicate himself to what he always calls 'the gamergolf', times when his business interests and high-powered friends like President Bill Clinton held more attractions but Norman will keep trying because he has a regard for the process that provides him with his affluence and influence: playing golf. 'I love my trophies,' he said. 'They're in the hallway at home and sometimes, after putting the kids to bed, I stop by them and recall and reflect and reminisce' – particularly about Turnberry 1986 and Royal St George's 1993, when he was as good as any golfer can be. Meanwhile the rest of us can wonder if it is fair to say, as Peter Thomson did, that Norman 'has not reached the great heights we hoped for and dreamed of.'

NICK FALDO

Nick Faldo is without doubt the most successful British golfer there ever has been: not statistically, for that honour at the end of 1999 still lay in

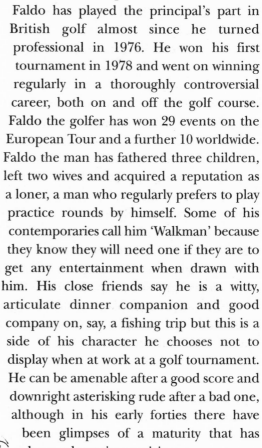

Nick Faldo.

Harry Vardon's lap, with six Open championships and one US Open; yet Faldo may be said to have surpassed Vardon by winning three Opens and three Masters, in the infinitely larger cauldron that is international golf in the late 1990s.

Faldo has played the principal's part in British golf almost since he turned professional in 1976. He won his first tournament in 1978 and went on winning regularly in a thoroughly controversial career, both on and off the golf course. Faldo the golfer has won 29 events on the European Tour and a further 10 worldwide. Faldo the man has fathered three children, left two wives and acquired a reputation as a loner, a man who regularly prefers to play practice rounds by himself. Some of his contemporaries call him 'Walkman' because they know they will need one if they are to get any entertainment when drawn with him. His close friends say he is a witty, articulate dinner companion and good company on, say, a fishing trip but this is a side of his character he chooses not to display when at work at a golf tournament. He can be amenable after a good score and downright asterisking rude after a bad one, although in his early forties there have been glimpses of a maturity that has been a long time arriving.

Faldo appears to hate large sections of the British press and strongly dislikes the remainder. Some of this is understandable, for his divorce from his first wife, Melanie, got the full tabloid treatment, as did his separation from his second wife, Gill. He claimed that reporters had gone through his rubbish bins in search of information, that one reporter had made 27 consecutive telephone calls, leaving the same message each time and that even his children had been harassed.

He can be amenable after a good score and downright asterisking rude after a bad one, although in his early forties there have been glimpses of a maturity that has been a long time arriving.

Excesses like that are reprehensible, but Faldo's relationships with the sports media over the years have also been prickly. In large part, this is because of the tendency of sportsmen the world over to react only to criticism. They accept praise as their due but believe all adverse comment to be totally without foundation or, at the very least, without any understanding.

One of the defining moments of Faldo's relationship with the press was the 1983 World Matchplay championship at Wentworth. He had already won five European Tour events and was plainly going to become a big international star. Hard though it may be for Faldo to believe, the golfing press are desperate to have big international stars and to write nice things about them but his behaviour then made that extremely difficult.

In his match against Graham Marsh, Faldo's second shot at the 16th careered through the green but was kicked or thrown back and ended on the putting surface. Faldo won a hole he would undoubtedly have lost and eventually won the match. He was completely blameless, not having seen what happened but television replays *ad nauseam* made it clear that Marsh had suffered an injustice. The next day, however, Faldo eschewed any sportsmanship-in-retrospect. There was no hint of remorse and he spectacularly missed the point when he said, 'I had to do what I did. This was the World Matchplay, not the Wentworth Christmas Alliance.' All he had to do was apologize to Marsh, say that he would have preferred not to win like that and he would have received a terrific press. Instead, to the satisfaction of no one, he was slated and a tone had been set. It became not so much an arms-length relationship as barge pole. The press wanted a *Boys' Own Paper* person, who routinely did three good deeds before breakfast. What they got was a seriously good golfer, with tunnel vision, able only to see his own way forward. It was never likely to work and it didn't.

However, none of this made any difference to Faldo the golfer. He went on winning, apart from the period when he underwent the David Leadbetter conversion – a decision that showed yet again the steely side to his character. He sacrificed at least two years of his career in order to play the way Leadbetter wanted him to and so, Faldo has always believed, he could produce his best at times of the severest stress. He has done that but whether that is due to the constant care he got from Leadbetter or is a consequence of natural talent allied to immense hard work is another matter. John Jacobs was one who maintained that the swing had not changed that much while others believed that anyone who had worked as hard as Faldo would find a repeating swing anyway. Eventually Leadbetter, too, was to find himself not wanted on vogage, and was dismissed – by letter.

Unlike so many professional golfers Faldo has always realized that money is transitory. He always wanted to win Cups – that is championships and trophies, something permanent. Just before turning professional, at the end of a hugely arduous season, he playing in an inconsequential tournament called the Champion of Champions, an event that meant nothing much. 'It's a great title to have,' he said and he won it, following one Sandy Lyle, who had won the year before.

Another recurrent theme in the early days of Faldo's career was rivalry with Lyle, a man who could hardly be more different in almost every aspect of life. Lyle as an amateur and in his early professional days was effortlessly good. He had huge advantages, the principal one being that he had hit his first golf ball aged three, Faldo at 13. Lyle, the son of a professional, was a prodigy; Faldo knew nothing but arduous hours on the practice ground. Lyle dominated as if by right at every level he experienced right up to the very heights of the game; Faldo had to grind away, experimenting, adapting, adopting, learning the things that Lyle had absorbed as a child. Lyle was long, Faldo was not. Lyle ambled amiably round the course, chatting about this and that; Faldo, needing to concentrate all his efforts and energies on golf, was dour and uncommunicative. For a man with an ambition that burned as brightly as did Faldo's it was galling in the extreme to be beaten so often by such a seemingly casual talent. There was a real rivalry, certainly as far as Faldo was concerned, and on one occasion it spilled over into an incident.

The two were playing together in a Safari Tour event in Africa and after a while Lyle placed some sticking plaster on his putter head to stop the sun glinting off it. Faldo said nothing but when they finished he reported Lyle for altering the playing characteristics of the club. The report was upheld but it was the manner of it rather than the fact of it that won Faldo no friends.

It is probably true that overall the desire to see off Lyle benefitted Faldo. He simply had to learn to beat this infuriating figure who hardly ever seemed to practice, who was hugely popular with press and public and who was beating him to all sorts of goals. It was Lyle who first won an Open championship, at Royal St George's in 1985, and in 1989 when Faldo won the 1989 Masters it was Lyle, the first Briton to win the title, helping him into his green jacket.

Of course, nobody can sustain a career on a rivalry with one other person, and Faldo did not have to. In 1987 he produced a magnificent performance at Muirfield to win the Open and, quite apart from achieving a life's ambition, he stepped aside from the shadow cast by Lyle. Once done, he went on to win a total of six majors in 10 years, easily the best among his peers worldwide.

The 1987 championship was notable for Faldo's feat in recording 18 successive pars in his final round, to beat Paul Azinger. It led to him being labelled 'machine-like' and 'boring', yet nothing could have been further from the truth. Some of Faldo's pars were as exciting as any eagle, given the strain of the occasion. At the eighth, he was in a bunker some 30 yards from the green and hit it to four feet, to save his four. His huge sigh of relief was echoed later when he described that moment as crucial. At the 18th, a terror of a finishing hole, he had 190 yards to the green, normally a four-iron but he reckoned on the adrenalin factor and took the five.

'You can't imagine what it's like to try and play in those conditions,' he said. 'It's like those heart-stopping moments when you think you're going to be involved in a car crash. You go all hot and cold. It's such an important moment and yet it's over in seconds. I had to hit the shot and I didn't know if I could – but I knew it had to be done. Then, suddenly, there it was flying straight at the green and all I could think was "Cor, look at that"'.

Over the next few years, there was to be a lot of looking at Faldo, now established as one of the game's finest players, as he added consistency to his burning ambition. By 1990 he was the best player in the world – a position Lyle had occupied two years before. Not only did he retain his Masters title but he also came within a 10-foot putt of making a play-off for the US Open and at St Andrews he won the Open with a record-setting total of 18 under par, posting rounds of 67,65,67,71.

At Muirfield in 1992, he won his third Open and his fifth major and his performance on the golf course was of a degree of character not often witnessed even at the rarified levels at which he was operating. He led by four from John Cook after rounds of 66,64,69 but, with four holes to play, he was two behind the American and rescued a seemingly desperate situation with a display that took the breath away. At the 15th, he hit his second shot to two feet and, after a birdie four at the 17th, he hit a 'fantastic' – his word – three-iron to the 18th.

It was magnificent but off the course Nicholas Alexander Faldo lived up to his initials, turning in a performance that was socially awkward, worthless and rubbishy. It was also naive and to witness it was to be embarrassed – for him.

At the closing ceremony, he took the opportunity to settle, as he saw, some old scores. Some television commentators were ridiculed, but it was the press who caught the sharp edge of what was obviously a prepared speech. 'I would like to thank them,' he said, 'from the bottom of my … er, well … from the heart of my bottom.' Then he decided to sing, producing a brief rendition of Frank Sinatra's 'I did it my way.' Unlike the golf he had played, it was hopelessly flat.

That capacity for excruciating behaviour and sublime golf is part of the Faldo mix and does not make him an easy team man but, in every Ryder Cup side from 1977 to 1997, he was the man that Europe looked to for solidity and certain points and he was usually able to oblige. There were blips – Kiawah in 1991 was not great for him – but the more matches he played the more he appreciated the nuances of teamwork and by 1995 he was thoroughly involved and, in the pivotal match against Curtis Strange, produced the shot of the year under unbelievable pressure. Two years later, he became the player to amass the most points in the Ryder Cup – on either side – to confirm his status statistically.

In a career that is not yet over, nothing can be the absolutely definitive performance but it is safe to say that anything that beats the final day of the 1996 Masters will be something the like of which has not yet been seen on a golf course. On that day Faldo did superlatively the thing that he does best. He set himself to play fault-free golf, play to the absolute limits of his concentration, bear down relentlessly on his opponent and give him not a glimmer of encouragment.

He knew that if he did all these things, and that if a few putts were to drop as well, he might have a very distant chance of catching and maybe even forcing a play-off with the world No. 1, Greg Norman, who led the championship after three rounds by six shots. Norman had been brilliant all week; Faldo by his standards merely humdrum. Norman confessed he wanted nothing more in the whole world than a green jacket; Faldo already had two of them. Norman's game might have been made for Augusta; Faldo has won there in spite of not being, ideally, long enough.

On that Augustan Sunday, Norman disintegrated but Faldo stayed steadfast and ignored the burning building, the crashing car, the sinking ship that was alongside him and simply played his own game. No one in world golf was better suited to that task and without hitting any scintillating shots, but without making a mistake, Faldo got round in 67 and won by five shots. It was a stunning upset, achieved mostly in silence, not because people did not appreciate what Faldo was doing but because they were distressed at what Norman was doing to himself.

Afterwards Faldo said, a little sadly, that he would like his win to be recognized for some of the great golf he had played but realized that it was more likely to be remembered for Norman's collapse. That indeed is what happened immediately but as time goes by the credit that is due to Faldo's monumental determination on that day is paid more and more readily. The Masters is after all played over 72 holes and at the end the man who had won was Nick Faldo.

LAURA DAVIES

The essence of Laura Davies is captured in one short story. The night before a tournament in France, Davies was opening a tin of caviar and sliced a bit off her left index finger. Did she withdraw from the tournament? Did she heck. The next day, suitably bandaged, she used an interlocking grip for the first time, went round in 66 and had the first hole-in-one of her career. That's typical Laura: brimming with style and talent.

In March 1997, her 12th year as a professional, she reached the landmark of 50 career victories worldwide – 'I remember every one' – with a suitably historic flourish, winning the Standard Register Ping tournament at Moon Valley in Phoenix, Arizona, for the fourth consecutive season. No woman had done that before – Louise Suggs, Kathy Whitworth and Sandra Haynie had won an event three years in succession – and only two men: Gene Sarazen and Walter Hagen. She acknowledged that it was particularly appropriate that it was happening at Moon Valley, home for Karsten and Louise Solheim. 'They've been such great supporters of women's golf,' Davies said.

Davies, kind-hearted, generous and clannish, thinks of herself as one of the gang, playing football, cricket, tennis, ice hockey, whatever is on the agenda, with her mates, an assortment of caddies and fellow professionals. She is never happier than when kicking a ball – she supports Liverpool and is on the roster of the American soccer side, the Myrtle Beach Sea Dawgs; or placing a bet – Las Vegas is a favourite venue; or attempting an outrageous shot at goal, at the basket or at the hole. However, this dedicated player of games is a woman apart, for she has been blessed with a talent so immense that she has the ability to do things that are beyond even the most gifted of her contemporaries. The most obvious is the length she hits the ball, sending it on its way in such a high arc that it is often still rising when it passes the point where an opponent's ball has come to a stop. She reckons that her average belt with the driver is 275–280 yards. In favourable conditions, blows of over 300 yards are not uncommon. Playing in a skins game with John Daly in Australia, she was outdriven by 60 yards, but Tom Watson, no slouch off the tee, had to work hard to keep up with her.

People who are seeing Davies play for the first time look on with the expression of amused bemusement that Daly and Tiger Woods induce and Jack Nicklaus used to. Davies, not a great one for technicalities, used to say she hadn't a clue when asked how she hit it so far. Now she thinks it's a combination of broad shoulders, strong legs, brute force and timing. Whatever the reason, when it all comes together it is awesome.

It took Davies a while to impose herself on the LPGA Tour, although she had no such problems in Europe. After an amateur career that was ordinary rather than extraordinary, bar a Curtis Cup appearance in 1984, she turned professional in 1985, with £1,000 borrowed from her mother Rita. It was repaid within a couple of weeks and Davies was rookie of the year and No. 1 in Europe. She was No. 1 again in 1986 and won the British Women's Open

Laura Davies.

at Royal Birkdale. That victory earned her a place in the US Women's Open the following year and it was at Plainfield, New Jersey, that the tall, big-hitting blonde from Surrey launched herself into the big time. She won the title, defeating JoAnne Carner and Ayako Okamoto in a play-off over 18 holes. Carner, 48, twice Open champion was the sentimental favourite and Okamoto was the best player in the world at the time but the young Englishwoman with the swashbuckling style overcame – and impressed – them both.

Davies was a member of the 'never had a lesson in life' tendency, developing her touch and feel by watching people like Faldo and Ballesteros on television, or in the flesh, and then experimenting on the course. She hates being told what to do but has a sharp eye, an absorbent mind and wonderful hands. She is possessed of a Seve-like flair for seeing things that others don't. At Woburn once, narrow, tree-lined and congenitally anti-Davies, she

She reckons that her average belt with the driver is 275–280 yards. In favourable conditions, blows of over 300 yards are not uncommon.

drove miles right on to the wrong fairway and had a flourishing forest plus a large chasm between her and the green. She blasted an iron through and over everything to the front edge. 'How wide was the gap?' asked a stunned spectator. 'There was no gap,' came the reply.

Davies became peripatetic as well as prodigious when she joined the LPGA Tour in 1988, dividing her time between America, Europe, Japan, Australia, Asia and anywhere else that golf was on the agenda. She missed her first two cuts as an LPGA member but won twice and finished a respectable 15th on the money list. The US Open win had raised expectations to Himalayan heights but it took her until 1994 to be leading money-winner, at which time she started winning tournaments by the handful all over the world. She won eight times that season on five different Tours – in America, Europe, Japan, Asia and Australia. The following year, she won seven times but had to settle for being No. 2 in the US and Europe, pipped on both Tours by Annika Sorenstam, a metronomically consistent Swede. In 1996, the best season of her career, Davies won nine times worldwide including two major championships, was world No. 1, leading money-winner in Europe and player of the year on the LPGA Tour for the first time.

She always wanted to be a millionaire – with the revealing proviso that she'd like to earn it not win it on the pools – and she has earned millions already. She knows how to spend them, too: on presents for family and friends; a house with several acres that are being turned into a sporting complex so varied that rumour had it that Laura was considering putting in a bid to host the Olympics in 2000 and something; clothes; slot machines; gadgets; gambling; cars. A red Ferrari was one of her toys but scarcely counted as an extravagance since its owner won US$340,000 in a skins game, a world record, in 1996. Davies enjoys the money and some of the fame – not the speeches – but above all she loves the game and the competition. And the presence of Karrie Webb, Se Ri Pak and Sorenstam should ensure that the best of Laura Davies, providing she rationalizes her punishing schedule, is yet to come.

TIGER WOODS

There were, perhaps, many moments when Tiger Woods might have been said to have 'arrived'. It might have been when he won his first US Boys championship, or indeed when he won his second or his third. Or it might have been when he won his first US Amateur title, to confirm that he could translate that boyish talent into youthful accomplishment; or again it might have been when he won his second such title, or his third. Or maybe his first win as a professional might be nominated as 'the moment,' coming as it did in only his fifth tournament as a professional, or, again, his second such win, or his third.

Or it may be none of those moments. It may be that the moment that Tiger Woods actually arrived was halfway through the US Masters of 1997, in the press centre of the Augusta National golf club. Jack Nicklaus had just compiled a second round 70, had made the cut at the age of 57 and, a happy man, was answering questions from the world's press.

Over the years Jack Nicklaus has heard every question there is to ask of him, but the one in particular of which he has wearied is about each and every new hot-shot. 'Is he,' Jack is asked 'the new Nicklaus? Is this the Bear-Apparent?' It has been asked of many candidates; there have been many noviciates, but none has gone on to become the High Priest. There have been Hal Sutton and Sandy Lyle; Scott Verplank and Robert Gamez; Phil Mickelson and Ernie Els, to name but a few. All of them were staggeringly good very early in life and Nicklaus was unfailingly courteous not just to the questioner but about the abilities of the golfer concerned.

Two days after Nicklaus had spoken, Woods won the Masters. It was the first time Tiger had played in a major championship as a professional and the totality of his victory was shocking.

He would find something good to say about him, without ever quite answering the question itself. 'Hal/Phil/Ernie,' the reply would go, 'is a wonderful prospect. He has a great long/short game and is a wonderful driver/putter of the ball. He has a chance at the top.'

But Nicklaus always stopped short of the full blessing, the total endorsement, until that day in April 1997. It was then that Nicklaus spoke these words, as recorded by a stenographer. They came after Woods had scored a 66 in the second round of the Masters, to be the halfway leader by three shots.

'Well,' said Nicklaus, 'I'm going to tell you one thing. It's a shame Bob Jones isn't here. He could have saved the words for me in 1963 for this young man, because he's playing a game we're certainly not familiar with.' Nicklaus, in paraphrasing the tribute by Jones from all those years

Woods and caddie,
1997 Masters.

ago, when Jones said, 'Mr Nicklaus plays a game with which I am not familiar,' could not have made his meaning clearer if he'd been wearing cassock and surplice and wearing a Bishop's mitre. It was the moment of Annointment, the passing of the torch, the bestowing of a mantle to a young man, the only young man who in all the years possessed the same gift that made Nicklaus himself so exceptional. Not since the 20-year-old Nicklaus was destroying both the competition and the golf courses of the day has there been a man who routinely hit the ball with such raw power and, in the main, straight.

Nicklaus went on: 'Tiger had a 30 on the back nine in the first round and that's pretty phenomenal.' But he made the point that Woods had hit a wedge into the green at most of the par fours. Nicklaus recalled the day he shot a 64, to set what used to be the Augusta course record. 'That round of golf,' he said, 'was like walking down Main Street. It was nothing. That day I hit something like 10 wedges for my second shot and the par fives were only middle irons. 'Tiger has the ability to do that and that's why he is so special. He makes the golf course into nothing.'

And that, verily, was the Blessing. There was an almost religious awe with which Nicklaus had been regarded all those years and there was a definite sense of succession present in that interview room.

Two days after Nicklaus had spoken, Woods won the Masters. It was the first time Tiger had played in a major championship as a professional and the totality of his victory was shocking. He simply obliterated the field. He won with a total of 270, 18 under par, a record. He averaged 67.5 strokes per round, which – and it hardly bears thinking about – was exactly seven strokes per round better than the average of the field. He won by 12 strokes, also a record and one which beat, by three strokes the previous best, established, fittingly, by Jack Nicklaus.

Woods won his first major in his first championship attempt as a professional, and only eight months after relinquishing his amateur status. In that time he had won three US Tour events, announcing himself in a more spectacular fashion than anyone since Nicklaus. The latter had taken only seven months, from November 1961 to June 1962, to win his first major as a professional, but it was also his first win as a professional, whereas it was Woods' fourth.

It could also be said that Woods had, in many ways, more success as an amateur than did Nicklaus. The Bear won two US Amateurs, the Tiger three, and the Tiger also won those three Boys championships, too, and the six were in consecutive years. Only Bobby Jones, who won a United States Golf Association championship in eight consecutive years, has ever done better than Woods in that regard, although Woods is the only player in history to have won both the Boys and the full Amateur championships, let alone complete a hat-trick in both.

There was, though, a strange hiatus in the Woods amateur career – the Walker Cup of 1995 at Royal Porthcawl. Not only were the United States beaten by Great Britain and Ireland, Woods was beaten by Gary Wolstenholme in a vital singles match that was to have a great bearing on the overall result. He had been placed in the anchorman role at the end of the first series of singles matches and, in drawing Wolstenholme, found himself playing one of the shortest hitters in amateur golf.

Whether Woods felt that the challenge from Wolstenholme was not worthy of his consideration, or not, the fact was that he could not get away from him and they arrived at the last tee all square. It is indicative of the relative strengths of the two players that Wolstenholme required a wood for his second shot, and found the green, while Woods needed only a nine iron – and hit it out of bounds.

He lost both hole and match, and it meant that his team, who would have been level had he won, trailed by two points going into the last day. On the second day Woods and John Harris lost their foursomes match in the morning and although he was to win his final singles, revenging himself by 4&3 over Wolstenholme, the match overall had already been lost.

Woods was oddly quiescent all week. The American team naturally looked to him for leadership, but instead he missed a practice session with stomach trouble and never imposed himself on the occasion. It was claimed, on his behalf, that he could not get used to the 'foreign' food and was denied his beloved hamburgers and fries; a strange excuse on a big international occasion.

There was another blip relating to his amateur days when, after he had turned professional, he refused to go to the Fred Haskins Award Dinner for the leading college golfer of the year, because he was 'tired.' He subsequently apologized, the dinner was re-arranged, and he attended.

If those controversies were inadvertent, Woods has embraced the idea of deliberately creating turbulence in what were the relatively calm waters of WASP golf in America. When he turned professional he received, instantly, by courtesy of Nike and Titleist what the Americans call 'screw you' money: money which enabled him to say whatsoever he liked to whomsoever he liked. He and Nike then chose to aim his first televised advertisements at the community that inhabits America's golf and country clubs, places that embrace the white tribe of the United States, places that are temples of conservatism, capitalism and complacency. The

Woods script read, in part: 'There are still golf courses in the United States that I cannot play because of the colour of my skin.'

The outrage that followed this exceedingly moderate statement of the truth was impressive. He was accused of capitalizing on his colour, of sensationalism for the sake of profit and, horror of horrors, accused of 'playing the race card'. That the people accusing him of this had themselves been playing the race card ever since slavery was imported did not seem to occur to them. There are still places where Tiger could not play because of his colour and there are still a great many more places where a black man who does not hit the ball 360 yards off the tee and has not the right to a green jacket, could not play. Woods remained untroubled by the furore, as he did by the further incident to arise from his third Amateur championship success, which he so nearly didn't win.

Woods had been five down to Steve Scott after the first 18 of a 36-hole final and had been a long time in making up the difference. In fact he

Surveying a putt.

was still two down playing the 34th but had a six-foot birdie putt to make it only one. He moved his ball out of Scott's line and then, when it was his turn to putt, forgot to replace his marker at the original spot. Scott could have kept quiet, and had he done so and Woods had putted from a wrong place, Scott could have claimed not just the hole but, as it happened, the match and the title. Sportingly, though, Scott pointed out Woods's error, the birdie putt was holed, so was a 30-footer at the next and Tiger won at the second extra hole.

The fact of that win, and his reaction to it, created yet another furore. When the winning putt dropped Woods began punching the air extravagantly, dancing around the green while so doing, while his mother and father raced across the green, vying to be first to embrace him. All the time the beaten Scott was waiting to shake the hand of his conqueror – in vain. After it was all over, both contestants were interviewed by television and Scott paid generous tribute to Woods. He said: 'That was probably the greatest amateur match ever played and I'm proud to be a part of it. I feel like a complete winner – I was trying to stop history.' Woods, in his interview, did not mention Scott at all. Later the USGA magazine chose to use, on its cover, a jubilant picture of Woods in full celebratory mode and there were strong reactions from readers criticizing the unsportsman-like behaviour of Woods.

The odd controversy not withstanding, Woods' incredible talent and prodigious length off the tee have never been in doubt. Because, as Nicklaus puts it, he 'reduces courses to nothing' he has a massive advantage over his fellows, although no one is very clear how that advantage arises. Most people who hit the ball extreme distances do so for obvious reasons, like John Daly's massive overswing, or Jarmo Sandelin's 54-inch driver which produces the same effect of a hugely long arc.

But Woods makes a point of never taking the club head past the parallel and is consistently 50 yards or more past everyone. The effect Woods' hitting has on most of his partners is to make them look away. In 1995 Jose Maria Olazabal, the defending champion at Augusta, was drawn with Tiger, then the US Amateur champion. Olazabal had heard about the distance Woods drove the ball, of course, but was still surprised when, on the first tee, with the hole playing into the wind, Tiger took aim on the right-hand fairway bunker. 'I thought that he could not carry that bunker,' said Olazabal afterwards, 'I thought that no one that day could carry that bunker. But he did and had half a wedge to the green.

'At the second, he aimed at the fairway bunker again and I knew that it was 276 yards to carry it. He couldn't do it – but he did. After that, whenever he teed up I was looking at my shoes, or I was fixing my hair, or brushing my trousers or cleaning my spikes, anything not to look.'

What that extreme length does for Woods at Augusta is relieve the necessity for strategy. The conventional thinking has always been that in order to play Augusta National successfully the player has to be in the right position on the fairway in order to be able to reach the best position on the green. This is absolutely true when the shot to the green is being played with a mid or long iron: when it is being played with a wedge it hardly matters where you are so long as you can actually see the pin.

Extreme length always excites and draws crowds and wherever Woods goes, spectator numbers are up – often hugely so. A 1996 trip to Sydney, for instance, was a perfect example of 'Tigermania', for the first day of the Australian Open attracted 28,000 spectators, a 65 per cent increase on the first day of the previous year. As Greg Norman had played both years, the only difference was Woods, and it meant increased takings of A$270,000 for the first day alone.

It is, of course, marvellous that more people are watching golf, but better than that is the ethnic mix that Tiger attracts to tournaments. Watch Tiger, but watch also who is watching Tiger. Not only is every racial hue represented, so too is every age group from five to 75. It has long been said, in America, that it was Arnold Palmer who put golf on the map and it could be said that the late Sir Henry Cotton did the same in the United Kingdom and that Severiano Ballesteros did the same for the Continent of Europe.

It was the affluent middle-classes who seized on the message being passed by these great golfers but what Tiger has done is to take it into the ghettoes of America and into the kampongs (villages) and sprawling cities of Asia. He is a role model to whom the world's huddled masses can relate for not only is he Afro-American-Asian and not only is he young and charismatic but he is also capable of smashing the white man out of sight, the ultimate attraction.

What Woods has brought to golf is indeed a revolution. He is helping to drag the game out of the country clubs and introduce it to the tenements and the streets. He has added black to the white without making grey and removed the game from the cosy, traditional thinking patterns of playing safe. He substituted aggression for patience but was nearly upstaged by the precocious talent of Sergio Garcia at the US PGA Championship at Medinah.

Woods prevailed, to end the millennium on the highest of notes and with Garcia, and others, responding to the challenge, the Tiger's tale was only beginning.

A FINAL THOUGHT

The very nature of a golf course creates drama. It presents a physical challenge – can you actually hit the ball 220 yards on to this green? – and a mental challenge at the same time – can you hit the ball 220 yards on to this green, over that water? That drama has expressed itself in many ways over the century and, towards its close, Mastercard decided to try to adjudicate on what they called 'The Best of the Best'. What they wanted to identify, they said, was the single greatest moment in golfing history.

This, of course, is impossible as their eventual choice was to prove, but a list of 25 possibilities provided some ruminative material. They did it chronologically, as follows:

1. 1744 – Rules code is adopted by the Honourable Company of Edinburgh Golfers.
2. 1860 – Open championship is played for the first time.
3. 1870 – Young Tom Morris wins his third consecutive Open, at Prestwick, breaking his own scoring record by five strokes.
4. 1911 – USGA adopts national handicap system.
5. 1913 – Francis Ouimet, a local amateur, defeats Harry Vardon and Ted Ray in the US Open.
6. 1914 – Harry Vardon wins sixth and last Open championship.
7. 1929 – Joyce Wethered wins British Ladies' championship, four years after retirement.
8. 1930 – Bobby Jones completes the Grand Slam, winning the Open and Amateur championships of the US and the UK in the same year.
9. 1935 – Gene Sarazen's albatross at the 15th at Augusta gets him into a play-off, which he wins, for the Masters.
10. 1945 – Byron Nelson wins 11 consecutive tournaments, and 18 altogether.
11. 1950 – Ben Hogan wins US Open after near-fatal car accident.
12. 1951 – Joint Rules Conference of R&A and USGA adopt uniform rules worldwide.
13. 1953 – Ben Hogan wins Triple Crown – Masters, US Open and The Open championships.
14. 1954 – Babe Zaharias wins US Women's Open just months after her first cancer operation.
15. 1958 – Peter Thomson wins the Open championship for the fourth time in five years.

16. 1960 – Arnold Palmer drives the first hole in the final round of US Open at Cherry Hills and wins.

17. 1961-Present – Jack Nicklaus' career accomplishments.

18. 1968 – Lee Trevino wins US Open and becomes first player to score in the 60s in all four rounds of that championship.

19. 1973 – Johnny Miller's record 63 in the final round at Oakmont wins him the US Open.

20. 1977 – Tom Watson wins the Open championship at Turnberry by one stroke over Jack Nicklaus, 268,269.

21. 1978 – Nancy Lopez wins five tournaments in a row and nine overall at the age of 21.

22. 1982 – Tom Watson chips in at 17th at Pebble Beach to win US Open.

23. 1986 – Jack Nicklaus wins sixth US Masters at the age of 46, 18th professional major.

24. 1987 – European team wins the Ryder Cup on US soil for the first time.

25. 1995 – Ben Crenshaw wins Masters just days after being pallbearer for friend and mentor, Harvey Penick.

Of these 25 worthy, if a little dull and predictable, selections, some were clearly included just to make up the numbers. Only numbers 8, 11, 13 and 17 ever had a realistic chance of 'winning', in my view and the actual order was, in fact, 8, 17 and 10. That Bobby Jones (No. 8) was selected ahead of Jack Nicklaus is a wonderful tribute to the man's achievements, his Grand Slam and to the memories of the selectors involved. Jones is certainly the only man that Nicklaus could bear to come second to.

Of course, lists like the above can be great fun, provided they are not taken too seriously. And here, offered for debate, and in no sort of order at all, are an Alternative 25 reasons for the appeal of golf and why it has developed as it has.

1. Invention of the lawnmower.

2 Discovery of fine turf grasses – one type in a Korean graveyard.

3. The relatively cheap, readily available golf ball.

4. The use of persimmon for clubheads, giving that fantastic feel, that fantastic crack off the clubhead.

5. The use of steel for shafts – hickory would have run out by now.

6. The invention, by Frank Stableford, of his points system, thereby creating user-friendly golf.

7. The chance to wear colourful clothes or, as film star Robin Williams once said, 'The opportunity for middle-class white men to dress up like black pimps.'

8. The creation of that fount of all wisdom, the father confessor, the teacher, the stockbroker, DIY expert and general all-round good ol' boy, – the club professional.
9. The chance to see lots of lovely places, either personally or on TV.
10. The opportunity to play a game played by those pillars of society, the Masons.
11. The opportunity to follow royalty – Mary Queen of Scots, the Duke of Windsor, the Sultan of Brunei, Prince Bertil of Sweden, King Leopold of Belgium – on to the course.
12. The opportunity to play the same game Presidents play.
13. The chance to hear the crunch of your spikes on a path and know that it is precisely the same sound as that made by Nicklaus.
14. The invention of waterproofs to enable you to play when you shouldn't.
15. The realization that there is lots more land out there that is useless for anything but golf.
16. The chance to appreciate Walter Hagen's lifestyle.
17. The chance to appreciate Bobby Jones' incredible charisma.
18. The chance to appreciate Arnold Palmer's sex appeal.
19. The chance to appreciate Donald Ross' genius.
20. Caddies mean that everyone, just for a few hours in their lives, can have a butler.
21. The game provides an outlet for every conceivable condition of man- and womankind.
22. It is the only sport where genuine competition is provided by an absent opponent. Old Man Par wins most of the time.
23. Hot tea and toast afterwards.
24. The game appeals to the honest and the honourable, to the best not the base instincts of all.
25. Someone has to drink all the Kummel, so why not the golfers.

There are other matters to talk about, of course, and there should be some lively discussions as we enter the year 2000 as people make comparisons, however invidious or odious they are supposed to be, between this player and that, this championship and the other. Was Bobby Jones, for example, really a greater golfer than Jack Nicklaus and were either or both of them greater than Ben Hogan? Was Hogan better than Snead, or Arnold Palmer or Severiano Ballesteros and what can 'better' mean in this context anyway? Were the fabulous five championships of Ballesteros better than the less-than-scintillating six of Nick Faldo and was Gary Player, with nine championships to his name, really the third best professional, jointly with Hogan, the game has known?

Was Gene Sarazen's shot which gave him the albatross and helped him eventually to win the 1935 Masters better than Sandy Lyle's bunker shot at the 18th, which gave him the birdie that won the 1988 edition? And was Hogan's one-iron second to the 18th at Merion, which eventually so emotionally won the 1950 US Open, better than Tom Watson's little chip that he holed at the 17th at Pebble Beach to win the 1982 US Open?

Could the 1977 Open championship at Turnberry be regarded as greater than the 1986 Masters, or the 1975 Masters greater than the 1993 Open at Royal St George's? And was the American Ryder Cup team of 1981 better than the European version in 1987?

These are all magnificent imponderables, but all the better for the pondering.

INDEX